television and

Channels

contemporary criticism

of

second edition

Discourse,

edited by robert c. allen

Reassembled

the university of north carolina press   chapel hill & london

© 1987, 1992 The University
of North Carolina Press
All rights reserved
Manufactured in the
United States of America

The paper in this book meets the guidelines
for permanence and durability of the
Committee on Production Guidelines for
Book Longevity of the Council on Library
Resources.

01   00   99   98   97

7   6   5   4   3

Library of Congress Cataloging-in-
Publication Data
Channels of discourse, reassembled :
television and contemporary criticism /
edited by Robert C. Allen. — 2d ed.
    p.   cm.
Rev. ed. of: Channels of discourse. c1987.
Includes bibliographical references and
index.
ISBN 0-8078-2036-9 (cloth : alk. paper). —
ISBN 0-8078-4374-1 (pbk. : alk. paper)
    1. Television criticism.   2. Criticism.
I. Allen, Robert Clyde, 1950– .
II. Channels of discourse.
PN1992.8.C7C48   1992
791.45′015 — dc20   91-50784
                                    CIP

CONTENTS

CHANNELS

OF

DISCOURSE,

REASSEMBLED

INTRODUCTION
TO THE SECOND
EDITION

MORE TALK ABOUT TV

r o b e r t   c.   a l l e n

Why Study Television at All?

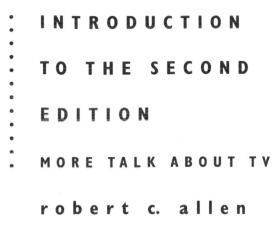

hy study television? For starters, because it's undeniably, unavoidably "there." And, it seems, everywhere. What people do with television is a topic worth thinking about and studying because television enters into the everyday lives of so many different people in so many different places in so many different ways. Today, around the world, 3.5 billion hours will be devoted to watching television.[1] But nowhere is television such an integral part of everyday life as in the United States. Ninety-two million homes in the U.S. have at least one TV set (98 percent of the total population). Nearly 70 percent of those homes have more than one set. More American homes are equipped with television sets than with telephones. Those sets are on in the average household for more than seven hours every day. Between seven and eleven P.M., Americans of every demographic, social, and economic group are spending most of their time in a place where a television set is playing. Nearly 60 percent of U.S. households now have cable television, and nearly three in four U.S. households with TV sets also own videocassette recorders. The family with a VCR rents an average of eighty-seven tapes each year from one of more than 30,000 tape rental outlets. The total value of these tape rentals already surpasses the total U.S. movie box office receipts. One in ten American families owns a video camera. Most Americans cannot remember a time in their lives when television was not a part of it. Babies as young as ten months have been observed to stop whatever they are doing when they hear the *Sesame Street* theme and to clap, bounce, and gurgle in anticipation of seeing their favorite puppet characters.

But fascination with television and its attendant technologies is by no means a uniquely American phenomenon. At least 90 percent of families in Venezuela have access to television, and by nine o'clock in the evening, 71 percent of those sets are switched on. Worldwide, more than one hundred million households own videocassette recorders, and several countries surpass the U.S. in the proportion of the population that owns or rents VCRs—Japan, Great Britain, Saudi Arabia, and Norway among them. On the streets of Taipei, you can buy a videotape of the previous night's output of Japanese television, recorded off the air in Tokyo and delivered to Taiwan by early morning flight. In India there are 12,000 licensed long-distance "video buses." The introduction of television to the largest cities of the People's Republic of China in the early 1980s has been called the most important cultural event since the Cultural Revolution; nearly every urban Chinese family now has access to television.[2]

The goal of this collection of essays is to provide you with some ways to think about and to begin to account for the processes by which people make sense of and take pleasure from their encounters with television. I introduced the first edition of this book in 1987 with a paradox: despite the fact that television structures everyday life for many people in unprecedented ways, the nature of our relationships with television is poorly understood and, for the most part, not very well studied. The principal reason for revising and expanding *Channels of Discourse* is to reflect the growth in television studies over the past five years. As the heft of the updated bibliography at the end of this collection attests, during these years many more scholars, from a variety of disciplines, have produced analyses of television programs and of the strategies by which those programs and other discourses of television attempt to sell us to advertisers, sell us things, tell us stories, represent the world outside our living rooms, stir our passions, amuse us, and, above all, keep us watching. But the scope, complexity, and dynamism of life with television always outrun our attempts to capture them adequately in words and theories. Regardless of how frequently or conscientiously we might update this collection, it will always remain a starting point and never the last word on TV.

Making Television "Strange"

It is the very ubiquity of television and the intricate ways it is woven into the everyday lives of so many people that make it so difficult to analyze. In order to study anything systematically, we must first constitute it as an object of study: as something separable and distinct from its surroundings and foregrounded in our consciousness. In the case of some phenomena, this objectification is not hard to achieve: we can move amoebas from their natural settings to the laboratory and place them under the lens of the microscope. But for many people (myself included), television has the same status in their lives as the food they eat for breakfast or the way their faces look in the mirror in the morning: it is something so close, so much a part of day-to-day existence, that it remains invisible as something to be analyzed or consciously considered.

Pioneer ethnographer Alfred Schutz suggested that, in order to understand the implicit assumptions that underlie his or her own culture, the investigator has to make that culture "anthropologically strange." That is to say, the anthropologist has to make visible and "objectified" those aspects of everyday life that ordinarily remain unnoticed, unspoken, and taken for granted.[3] In a sense, one of the goals of this collection is to make the sounds and images of television that accompany so much of our everyday lives "critically strange." These essays attempt to call to our attention some of the ways in which television in its various forms entertains, tells stories, engages the viewer, and constructs fictional and nonfictional worlds.

I've said that one reason it is so difficult to make the structures of television visible is that—for many people, most of the time—TV is simply part of the unnoticed domestic environment. But there's another reason. For most people around the world, television is primarily a source of entertainment. To be sure, television is other things as well and can be used in many other ways. But television's reach into the homes of hundreds of millions of families worldwide has not been accomplished chiefly because those families wanted to acquire an educational tool or an audiovisual newspaper. As studies of television viewing consistently show, for the most part people turn on the television set hoping to be entertained—by sitcoms, soap operas, dramas, music videos, movies, sporting events, quiz shows, or any of the dozens of other genres of television programming that have been developed to provide what we variously (and vaguely) call relaxation, escape, enjoyment, pleasure, diversion, or whatever. In other words, one barrier to taking television seriously as an object of study is that we don't regard many of the programs we watch as serious, consequential, or important. They're not "supposed" to be taken seriously, and they certainly don't seem to require close analysis to be comprehended or made enjoyable. Indeed, some of my students fear that studying television will somehow forever diminish their pleasure in watching. (Obviously, I don't think it does.) Furthermore, the institutional status of television —at least in the United States—as a form of commercial popular entertainment encourages the belief that it does not deserve "serious" analysis and that its programs are so simple (and, some would say, simple-minded) that there is nothing in them to analyze.

Although there are many aspects of television that can and should be studied and taken seriously, the essays in this collection foreground entertainment programming and our relationships with that very large and diverse category of television. In doing so, the authors make several points. The ways in which we make sense of and take pleasure from even the most inconsequential moments of television are worth thinking about because— if for no other reason—the aggregate of those moments constitute a good portion of millions and millions of people's waking hours. It is estimated that during his or her lifetime, the "average" American will spend more than seven full years watching television.[4] Also, we hope to show that neither entertainment programs nor our relationships with them are simply or self-evidently structured. There is, in fact, a great deal to be studied if we are to understand how a soap opera can draw us back into its world day after day, year after year, or how a sitcom makes us laugh every week. Moreover, examining the pleasures and meanings of the television we watch "for fun" might shed some light on other aspects of our everyday lives: how narratives work, how our notions of masculinity and femininity are constructed, how and why different cultural products appeal to different groups of people, and, most generally and most importantly, how we make meaningful and pleasurable the numerous and enormously diverse symbol systems we encounter every day.

One way to organize a collection of critical essays on television would be to devote individual chapters to particular programs or types of programs: an essay on TV drama, one on comedy, one on news, and so forth. For several reasons, though, the essays that follow in this book are organized by approach rather than program type. Program types and individual programs vary from country to country and change over time. The growth of cable TV in the United States and elsewhere, the explosion in the availability of videotaped programming for rental and sale throughout the world, and the expansion of satellite systems in Europe and other places have combined to produce geometric increases in the amount and variety of programming coming through many people's television sets. Accounts of how individual programs "work" are important, but what is more important, especially for the person just beginning the study of television, is that he or she develop ways of thinking about television that cut across different types of programming and that could be applied to whatever new programs might appear next week or next year.

Television Study and Contemporary Criticism

The genesis of this book lies in a dilemma I faced several years ago while teaching an introductory graduate-level course in television criticism. For reasons I will go into shortly, the field of mass communication research had not provided me with a great wealth of material for use in suggesting to students how television programming was structured and how we might begin to account for our curious relationships with television in general. And yet I was aware of the recent and very exciting approaches to the study of literature, film, and other aspects of culture that had been developed since the 1960s—some of which were beginning to be applied quite fruitfully to television. I saw the need for a book that would bring together some of these approaches, lay out their principal tenets, discuss how each might address television as an object of study, and provide examples of the kind of analyses each approach might produce as a result. I contacted colleagues with backgrounds in the various strands of what I will call contemporary criticism who also taught and wrote about television. Our efforts constituted the first edition of *Channels*, and our revisions fill the pages that follow.

As you'll discover as you read, the approaches we discuss are not nearly as distinct and separate as the chapter divisions and titles suggest, despite the fact that I asked each contributor to emphasize the particularities of the approach he or she describes. The theories we outline are connected by the fact that all of them grew out of, were strongly influenced by, or were developed in reaction to the insights into language and culture provided by structuralist linguistics and the "science of signs" (semiotics) spawned by structuralism. Hence my use of the term *contemporary criticism* as a shorthand designation for this diverse (and frequently contentious) family of critical approaches: semiotics, narrative theory, genre theory, reader- or audience-oriented criticism, ideological analysis, psychoanalytic criticism, feminist criticism, and British cultural studies.

The general orientation of contemporary criticism toward the critical enterprise and the object of critical analysis set it apart from traditional literary criticism on the one hand and, because the object of study here is television, from traditional mass communication research on the other. Other strands might also have been included and other ways of carving up contemporary criticism into chapters might easily have been devised. Yet I felt in 1985—and four years of using the first edition in the classroom have largely confirmed—that each of these approaches is sufficiently coherent and its influence sufficiently important to justify separate treatment. Furthermore, each grows out of somewhat (and, in some cases considerably) different theoretical ground, so that each constructs television as object in a different way and emphasizes some aspects of television over others. One important addition to this second edition is James Hay's concluding essay on the relationships among the approaches this collection takes up. Hay addresses the points of convergence, dispute, and divergence among those approaches. The second major addition is Jim Collins's new chapter on the relationship between postmodernism and television. As Collins makes clear, postmodernism is less a critical approach than a description of a cultural condition. Yet because so many scholarly and journalistic critics have begun talking about certain forms of television in terms of postmodernism, I felt it important that this relationship be addressed.

Ellen Seiter's chapter considers in some detail the major tenets of semiotics, its elaboration and revision by critics in what has been called the post-structuralist reaction to semiotics, and the implications of semiotics and post-structuralism for the study of television. It might be useful here at least to suggest some of the common ground shared, to a greater or lesser extent, by the specific critical approaches discussed in each chapter. All of the approaches regard television as one of a number of complex sign systems through which we experience and by which we know the world. Given the capacity of television to "carry" so many other symbol systems (verbal language, gesture, music, graphics, photography, cinema, etcetera), perhaps it would be more precise to say that television represents multiple and ever-changing points of intersection for those systems. The great contribution of semiotics has been to focus attention upon and develop a vocabulary to describe the operation of symbol systems, their interrelationships, and their effects on the way we understand the physical and social worlds we inhabit.

As I have hinted, the implicit organizing question that runs through this collection and through each chapter is: How are meanings and pleasures produced in our engagements with television? The apparent natu-

ralness with which we understand the sounds and images on television might seem to render this question unnecessary. After all, no one had to teach us how to "read" television programs. But, as semiotics has shown us, the naturalness of our relationship with television is illusory. Television, like cinema, painting, or photography, does not simply reflect the world in some direct, automatic way. Rather, it constructs representations of the world based on complex sets of conventions—conventions whose operations are largely hidden by their transparency. Like television itself most of the time, these conventions are so familiar in their effects that we don't notice them. It is only when the conventions are violated, or when a technical glitch renders them visible, or when we watch another culture's television operating from a different set of conventions that we become aware of just how constructed and unnatural the world of television really is.

Furthermore, despite the seemingly self-evident manner in which we are able to make sense of television, that ability is, in fact, a result of our having learned the conventions of television reading—even though we are usually not conscious of their operation nor can we remember having been taught them. For example, somewhere along the line we learned that it is "normal" for several disembodied heads to occupy portions of a single television image and to converse with each other as if they were in the

same room rather than thousands of miles apart, or that a giant network logo hurtling through space is not to be taken as evidence of an extraterrestrial invasion. But we can no more recall when or under what circumstances we learned to read these curious conventions of television than we can remember how we first acquired the ability to understand spoken speech. In light of the evidence that many of us began to interact in significant ways with television sounds and images before the age of one, it appears that our ability to use television is acquired at about the same time we learn to use language.[5]

Following another insight of structuralism, the strands of contemporary criticism employed in the following essays emphasize relations rather than objects. Contemporary criticism's foregrounding of the codes and conventions at work across individual works (or texts, as they will be commonly referred to in the following essays) and of the inevitable circuit of reference set up between texts is particularly appropriate in the case of television. Our experience of television is usually not of isolated works but of chunks of time filled with multiple texts. Networks attempt to structure the flow of texts so that one moment of television seems to lead naturally to the next. With the remote control, viewers can order their own flow, "zipping" from one text to the next and creating textual interruptions and juxtapositions that broadcasters never anticipated.

Contemporary criticism has also led to a reconsideration of the role of the author in the production and reception of art—a reconsideration particularly germane to the production and reception of commercial entertainment television. The traditional notion of the author or artist as the ultimate and single source of meaning within a work is difficult to maintain once we acknowledge the complex network of codes, conventions, precedence, and expectations in which every work inevitably participates and over which the author has little, if any, control. Nevertheless, if this were a collection of essays on contemporary painting, or the contemporary novel, or even contemporary cinema, there would be the temptation to organize it according to artist, author, or director. However, because of the technological complexity of the medium and as a result of the application to most commercial television production of the principles of modern industrial organization (including mass production and detailed division of labor), it is very difficult to locate the "author" of a television program—if by that we mean the single individual who provides the unifying vision behind the program.

To be sure, in some cases writers and producers (occasionally even directors) leave recognizable "marks" that distinguish their work. In Great Britain and elsewhere, the survival of the "one-off" teleplay, a tradition of "serious" television drama, and the more important institutional role of the television scriptwriter make it easier and probably more rewarding to locate these marks of authorial difference. Even in American commercial television, a particular style or set of narrative concerns can sometimes be discerned in the work of one producer or production company.[6] Even so, for the most part the production practices of television hide marks of authorship and limit any one person's ability to make his or her work stand out in identifiable ways. In American commercial television, producers might come up with the basic idea and characters for a television series, but they rarely are involved in the writing of individual episodes.

Television writers frequently work in teams, and their jobs are finished with the completion of a script that conforms to limitations already laid down by the producers. A given series might well employ a number of directors, who are unlikely to have had any part in the scriptwriting process and whose directorial styles necessarily must be indistinguishable from one another. Furthermore, American commercial television programs are usually not attributed to a particular author, nor do we as viewers usually think in terms of authorship as we watch a sitcom or soap opera.

Contemporary criticism has also dealt with the question of the artwork's ability to represent the "real" world. The capacity of television technology to show us seemingly unmediated pictures of events around the world at the moment of their occurrence would appear to endow television with a unique power to show us the world "as it really is." The "realseemingness" of television influences fictional entertainment programming as well. Hardly has a news event passed out of the newspaper headlines and television newscasts before it becomes the subject of a docudrama; the social issue you read about in a magazine today forms the basis for a soap opera plot line next week. Thus it might seem reasonable to expect a collection of essays on television criticism to assess television in terms of its success or failure in portraying the "real" world on the screen. However, one of the most important insights of structuralist linguistics is that no symbol system directly reflects the real world. Contemporary criticism assumes that we experience the world through systems of representation that, at the very least, condition our knowledge of the world and, some would argue, construct that world. Even when the following essays take up television news and documentaries, those discussions will not revolve around notions of bias and objectivity. Framing a discussion with these terms obscures the fact that there is no totally unbiased manner in which television or any other system of representation can show us the world. For the contributors to this volume, the question is, How do television programs construct their representations of the world? rather than, Does television give us the "truth" about the world?

Contemporary versus Traditional Criticism

The general thrust of contemporary criticism outlined above represents a fundamental departure from what we might call traditional criticism. Traditional criticism is the set of assumptions about literature and the critical act that governed literary criticism in the West for most of the last

fifty years and continues to condition what many people (including literature professors) commonsensibly accept "literature" and "criticism" to be.
Because dramatic television programs share some of the characteristics of
literary and theatrical works and because television increasingly has become an object of study for literary scholars and in literature classes, it is
important to make clear the differences between contemporary and traditional critical approaches.

Whereas traditional criticism emphasizes the autonomy of the artwork,
contemporary criticism foregrounds the relationships between texts and
the conventions underlying specific textual practices. Traditional criticism
is artist centered; contemporary criticism stresses the contexts within
which the production of cultural products occurs and the forces that act
upon and channel that production. Traditional criticism conceives of meaning as the property of an artwork; contemporary criticism views meaning
as the product of the engagement of a text by a reader or groups of readers. Traditional criticism frequently sees as its function not only the establishment of what a work means but also the separation of "literature"
from "nonliterature" and the erection of a hierarchy of greatness among
works. Contemporary criticism examines the criteria by which those in a
position to define literature make such determinations and would expand
the scope of literary studies to include both "nonliterature" and critical
discourse about texts.

It is also important that we understand the degree to which everyday
commercial television challenges the assumptions of traditional criticism.
To begin with, traditional criticism assumes that, generally speaking, there
is little difficulty deciding what the text to be studied *is*. That is to say,
except for works with problematic publication histories or old works of
which multiple versions survive, little thought need be given to whether,
when we talk about *The Sound and the Fury* or *Great Expectations*, we're
all talking about the same thing. The assumption is that the text begins
and ends in the same way and in the same place regardless of where or
when one reads it—everyone is assumed to be dealing with the same
"work." But what are the television "texts" to be studied? If I want to
conduct a critical analysis of *Dallas* or *EastEnders*, do I constitute the
"text" as one episode? A year's worth of episodes? All the episodes ever
broadcast? How do I deal with the fact that the text is still being produced? That any analysis I make of an ongoing program necessarily remains contingent upon episodes yet to be produced and "read"?

Traditional criticism further assumes that, however it is defined, the
individual, autonomous text is the basic object of analysis. Those autono-

mous texts are separable from everything else; that is, we identify the text to be studied in part by excluding from our consideration everything that is not the text. Some years ago, literary and cultural critic Raymond Williams suggested that, unlike literature or even feature films, television constitutes a sort of oceanic "flow" of textual material constantly streaming into our homes. This metaphor of flow suggests not a series of isolated texts but a river of images and sounds—channeled and dammed in places, but no part of which is ever completely isolated from all the rest. In the years since Williams's description of television as a textual flow, it has become even more difficult to conceive of the medium as anything like a line of novels on a shelf or even like a succession of moviegoing experiences. New U.S. cable television services—CNN, the Home Shopping Network, the Weather Channel, MTV—have further "detextualized" television. They contain fewer and less definable demarcations between one "program" and the next, being based upon the constant repetition and updating of textual material. The remote control device encourages the sampling of programs and makes it easier to alternate among programs available at the same time. And digital television quite literally makes it possible to view two programs simultaneously.

It is also clear that it is difficult to regard our modes of engagement with television in the same way as we do our engagement with literature or even film. Traditional criticism assumes that reading is an act that by its very nature separates our engagement with the world in the text from the rest of our experiential world. Indeed, reading would seem necessarily to require disengagement from all that is not the text. Movie theaters are designed to limit sensory input to only the sounds and images coming from the screen. We are enveloped by larger-than-life images that fill our perceptual field. Television, by contrast, is part of a larger environment with which we remain connected even while we watch. As a domestic appliance, television must fit into the social world of the family; its sounds and images compete or coexist with whatever else is going on in that world and with other activities in which we might be engaged. Television viewing appears to be social rather than self-absorbing. Even if its programs pull us into a level of engagement approaching that of cinema or literature, its commercials push us back into the social world with their admonitions to leave the television set and go somewhere else: to the grocery store, the shopping center, the kitchen, and so on. Furthermore, it is difficult to separate the television world from the non-TV world because television occupies such a prominent place in so many of our lives. In Britain more than one-third of the average person's waking hours each week are spent in contact with television; in the average U.S. household, the proportion is twice that.

The uneasy fit between commercial television and assumptions of traditional criticism partially explains the relative lack of a tradition of television criticism in the United States. It also helps to account for the fact that, in the United States at least, the "golden age" of traditional television criticism corresponds with the "golden age" of television: that brief period of live, original television drama in the 1950s. Such self-contained, "serious" television dramas as *Marty*, *Requiem for a Heavyweight*, *Visit to a Small Planet*, and *The Rack* most closely resembled the model of dramatic and narrative art with which traditional critics felt most comfortable.

Contemporary Criticism and Traditional Mass Communication Research

Whereas traditional literary or dramatic critics have had relatively little to say about television in the United States—except to bemoan the fact that it bears little resemblance to works of traditional high culture—American social scientists have been occupied with the study of commercial broadcasting for more than a half-century. Perhaps because broadcasting in the U.S. (at least since the late 1920s) has been thought of more as an advertising and journalistic vehicle than an art form, research into broadcast programming and the relationship between programs and audiences has been primarily sociological and psychological rather than aesthetic in orientation. There is not enough space here to examine in detail the philosophical and methodological bases of traditional social science research into broadcasting. However, it is important to note that the project of television analysis that has grown out of contemporary criticism represents a radical departure from the traditional sociological study of television. This difference is particularly evident in the kinds of questions each asks about television.

From the earliest days of broadcasting as an advertising medium to the present, a great deal of the sociological research on broadcasting has been done in direct or indirect response to the needs of broadcasters. In all television systems based on the sale of advertising time by broadcasters and the "sale" of audiences to advertisers, it is vital that broadcasters know the size and constitution of the audiences that watch particular programs in particular locations at particular times. Most of what we "know" about television audiences takes the form of this kind of measurement. It is also helpful for broadcasters to learn how various groups of people decide what to watch on television, what prompts them to change channels, how much they remember of what they watch (particularly of commercial messages), and what kinds of programming seems to appeal to what kinds of viewers.

Broadcasters are also obviously interested in what behavioral or attitudinal effects the watching of particular broadcast messages might have on various groups of viewers. If television commercials do not in some way affect the decision to purchase a particular product, then billions of advertising dollars, pounds, pesos, and yen are being wasted each year. The effects of watching television have also been studied by social scientists with a very different agenda—those concerned about the potential deleterious consequences of television viewing. For nearly forty years, scholars have attempted to discern the effects of TV on children's attitudes, beliefs, and behaviors. Others have attempted to assess the impact of television viewing on the viewer's perception of the outside world. Scholars in the Third World have studied the effects of the newly introduced television on the organization of daily life and on expectations of living standards.

Early mass communication scholars were impressed by broadcasting's apparent potential to produce direct, immediate, and drastic effects on behavior and attitudes. The second phase of traditional mass communication research attempted to account for the fact that few of these dramatic consequences could be verified. Scholars turned instead to an examination of how the potential power of broadcasting to change people's minds and actions was mediated and diffused. For example, it was suggested that the media did not tell people what to think so much as they told people what to think *about*; the media, in other words, set the agenda for public discourse. Another line of research, the "uses and gratifications" or functionalist approach, grew out of the observation that people use television and radio to fulfill certain psychological and social needs and to gratify certain desires.

This very schematic account of traditional mass communication research is laughably inadequate in capturing the scope and diversity of this line of inquiry. It is presented merely to suggest the kinds of questions mass communication researchers have, in the past, tended to ask and the areas that have not received very much attention within this tradition. For example, quite a lot of attention has been focused on the ability (or inability) of discrete television "messages" to produce observable changes in the viewer's behavior or explicitly reported changes in his or her attitudes and beliefs. Broadcasting audiences have been measured in various ways almost constantly for the last forty years. The impact of television on social institutions, particularly politics, has been assessed from a number of different perspectives. Much less attention has been devoted within traditional mass communication research to the study of the texts of television, or what we in this collection will call the *discourses* of television: the complex of all the ways television addresses us, appeals to us, tells us stories, entertains us, and represents itself and the world. Neither has traditional mass communication research addressed the seemingly self-evident but, as it turns out, enormously multiform and complex question: What is going on as people interact with television? Or, in other words, how do people make sense of and take pleasure from television?

Traditional mass communication research has had a difficult time dealing with the discourses of television and the place of TV in everyday life in large measure because, since the 1930s, it has turned to the natural and physical sciences for its model of how knowledge about media-audience relationships might be generated. The application of the scientific method to media research is, in part, a result of the need felt by some scholars to legitimize the field of mass communication research and to carve out a place for it among other and better-established social science disciplines in the university. Thus media research methods have been made to resemble those of the physical science laboratory wherever possible. Safeguards have been established to minimize the possible effects of the investigator's own expectations on the results of studies, and investigatory procedures have attempted to reduce the phenomenon being studied to a limited set of variables. The data collected by traditional mass communication research methods have been expressed for the most part in quantitative terms, and elaborate statistical procedures have been applied to mass communication research.

The usefulness of approaches designed for the study of chemistry and physics in helping us understand the complex and dynamic nature of our relationships with television has increasingly been called into question over the past decade. Procedures that work well enough in the study of algae or inorganic chemicals don't work nearly so well when the object of study is human, social, ever changing, enormously variable, cognitive as well as affective, conscious and unconscious, and thoroughly embedded in the "invisible" assumptions and contexts of everyday life—that is to say, when what we are trying to account for is how people derive sense and pleasure from television.

The field of mass communication research is changing rapidly, and, as one researcher has put it, the challenge represented by alternative approaches to the study of television has been "met with trepidation and skepticism in some quarters, but also with a healthy curiosity."[7] Certainly the influence of the approaches represented in this collection (as well as other "qualitative" approaches) on the field of mass communication research as a whole is much greater today than when this volume was first conceived seven years ago. But because the scientific, "quantitative" approach to television research remains dominant at a significant number of universities around the world, it is important to distinguish that method from what we are doing in this book.

The approaches represented here begin with the belief that relationships between viewer and television are so complex and multidimensional that they resist all attempts to reduce them to phenomena that can be explained by the same procedures that work for the chemist. What scientific law explains our curious relationship with fictional television programs, for example? We know that the characters and situations presented to us are not "real," that a character who dies in a TV drama is played by an actor who will go home at the end of the day and have dinner just as always. And yet we sometimes endow those characters and situations with sufficient "realseemingness" that they can move us to anger or to tears. How can reducing the world of that drama to a set of content categories account for this paradox? How much can the quantified responses to a survey questionnaire reveal about our willingness to "suspend our disbelief" every time we enter the narrative world of our favorite soap opera? This is not to say that there is something inherently wrongheaded about the use of quantitative methods or statistical procedures in mass communication research. Nor is it to argue that the alternative to quantitative research is a flight into impressionistic opinions about television to which no standards of rigor or validity can be applied. Rather, it is to point out that there are theories and approaches developed largely in other disciplines (literature, film, cultural studies) and informed by a different set of philosophical assumptions from those that underlie traditional American media research that might provide fresh insights into our relationships with television.

The Political Economy of Commercial Television

In light of the fact that the following essays emphasize entertainment programming, particularly that provided by advertiser-based commercial broadcasting, we need to keep in mind that such programs serve very different functions for broadcasters and advertisers than they do for viewers. Within the context of American commercial television, at least, the principal aim of broadcasting is not to entertain, enlighten, or provide a public service; it is to make a profit. The ways in which that profit is gained (or rather those profits, because there are several profit-seeking players in the game of commercial television) are by no means evident to the viewer, who probably sees television programming merely as a source of "free" entertainment for which the only price paid is the annoyance of having programs interrupted by a series of advertising messages. In fact, on the other side of the screen from the viewer is an economic system of commercial broadcasting that, in the United States, involves nearly 1,100 television stations, four principal programming networks, dozens of program suppliers, tens of thousands of companies with products or services to sell, and hundreds of advertising agencies. The sounds and images we see on the screen represent the intersection between that system and its other crucial component: more than 200 million potential television viewers. The economic value of this system, measured strictly in terms of revenues generated by broadcasters, is more than $25 billion per year in the United States alone.

The system rests upon policy established by the U.S. government more than half a century ago—and subsequently "exported" to countries around the world—regarding how the nation's radio airwaves would be utilized, by whom, and for what purposes. Television signals travel through the air as electromagnetic signals riding on naturally occurring waves. They share the electromagnetic spectrum with other forms of electronic communication—FM and AM radio, shortwave radio, and microwave transmissions, among others. By the 1920s, it had become clear in the United States that, as a public utility belonging to the nation as a whole, the finite spectrum space had to be regulated if this natural resource was to be utilized beneficially and if broadcasting chaos was not to ensue. The Federal Radio Commission later the Federal Communications Commission (FCC)—was formed to allocate spectrum space to various services, assign stations in each service by issuing operating licenses, and regulate existing stations by establishing guidelines and acting on requests for license renewals. Unlike Great Britain and most other European countries, the U.S. government decided not to become involved in broadcasting itself, but Congress did charge the FCC with the task of assuring that the airwaves were used "in the public interest."

In the early 1920s, radio set manufacturers themselves invested heavily in broadcasting; it was difficult to persuade anyone to buy a radio if there was nothing to listen to on it. By the mid-1920s, broadcasters were searching for ways to cover the costs of programming. One way was to persuade a product manufacturer or retailer to finance a program's production in exchange for promoting that product or store on the air. With the advent of the radio network in 1926 (in which an affiliated group of individual stations across the country broadcast the same programming, which originated at one central station and was carried by telephone lines), the possibility of a national advertising vehicle to rival newspapers and magazines became a reality.

By the end of the 1920s, although neither the Congress nor the FCC had ever established the system as policy, broadcasting in the United States had become synonymous with commercial, advertiser-based broadcasting. It was firmly entrenched as a large, profit-making industry despite the fact that, in order to receive an operating license, each broadcaster had to convince the FCC not that he or she could make a profit, but that the station would serve "the public interest, convenience, and necessity." Moreover, the license itself—without which the broadcaster could not operate but with which the broadcaster was granted exclusive use of a piece of a natural resource as a vehicle for potentially making millions of dollars —this license cost the broadcaster not one penny. By the early 1930s, writes pioneer broadcast historian Eric Barnouw, "the industry had developed what was already known as the American system of broadcasting, which made the salesman the trustee of the public interest, with minimal supervision by a commission."[8] By the time television emerged as a mass entertainment form in the U.S. in the late 1940s, there was very little debate over its use: it also would be primarily a vehicle for broadcasters to sell people to advertisers.

It may sound cynical to say that television is in the business of selling people to advertisers, but that is, crudely speaking, the way commercial broadcasters make their money. Brandon Tartikoff, former head of the NBC network, says the same thing but uses different terminology: "My basic job is to provide a certain level of profits for my division, and my division includes virtually all programming the network turns out. . . . NBC guarantees RCA, its parent corporation, certain profits every year, and I'm obliged to deliver those profits. The higher the ratings of my shows, the greater the profits NBC enjoys." A Hollywood studio executive (the old film studios—Universal, Columbia, MGM/UA, Paramount, Warner Bros.—are now the major suppliers of programming to the networks) puts it a bit more bluntly: "The primary purpose of American television, as it's presently constituted, is to deliver an audience to an advertiser at the lowest cost per thousand. Quality, style, content—these are all matters of subjective taste, and they are important only as they relate to the rise and fall of ratings, which are the yardstick by which television time is sold."[9]

The ratings spoken of here in such reverential tones are indeed the mechanism by which people watching television are made into a commodity to be sold in lots of one thousand. Television is not in the business of selling goods and services to people; following a particularly convincing ad for a laundry detergent, you cannot reach through your TV screen to buy a package from the broadcaster who ran the ad. Indeed, it is only with the advent of specialized cable channels like the Home Shopping Network that television has been used on a large scale as a direct-sale medium. Instead, broadcasters make their money by selling a portion of their broadcast air time—which they control by virtue of having been allotted a portion of spectrum space by the FCC and which they are allowed to "sell"—to an individual or a company for its own purposes. Theoretically an individual or company might purchase thirty seconds of air time to read a poem or display an experimental film, but with the cost of a thirty-second network slot in prime time costing several hundred thousand dollars, the only companies likely to purchase this time are those that expect to realize more than the cost of that time as a consequence of broadcasting their message. In other words, broadcast air time is purchased by companies in order to promote the sale of their goods or services.

The price that thirty seconds of air time will command is determined by the statistical probability that a certain number of people fitting certain demographic descriptions are tuned to the station selling the air time at the moment the advertising message is to be broadcast. In practice, this means that a relatively small sample of television households (around five thousand) are selected to represent more than ninety million U.S. families with television sets, and their viewing behavior is extrapolated to the total TV-viewing population. The advertiser must judge whether the rate charged for thirty seconds during that time period represents a good buy in relation to the number of people likely to see that company's message—in other words, whether that company can reach a hypothetical one thousand people at a low cost compared with other means of reaching the same thousand—including magazines, newspapers, billboards, and direct mail.

For the advertiser, television programs—which are the television texts viewers turn on the set to see and which they think of *as* television—are merely the bait that is likely to lure a particular audience to the TV set. For the broadcaster, programming represents a cost, not a product; it is whatever the station or the network must offer in order to get viewers to tune in. Stephen Dandel, one of television's most prolific writers who has written for network shows from *Mannix* to *Mission: Impossible*, once said in an interview that he owed his success to his ability early in his career to discern the "essential quality" of television: "simply, that it's a method for selling toilet paper, and writing is a very minor adjunct."[10]

The commercial broadcast networks (ABC, NBC, CBS, and FOX) do not produce their own prime-time (evenings between eight and eleven o'clock) entertainment programming. Rather, they buy network broadcast rights for particular shows from programming suppliers: Hollywood studios or some of the independent production companies that have grown up since the 1970s (Lorimar, Embassy, MTM, Spelling, and others). The license fee paid by the networks for two broadcasts of an episode of a prime-time sitcom or dramatic series usually covers only 75–85 percent of production costs. Thus production companies generally realize a profit not from the original sale of a program to the networks, but only when their programs remain on the network broadcast schedule long enough to qualify them for the next level of program distribution: syndication.

Of the 1,100 commercial television stations in the United States, approximately 600 are affiliated with ABC, CBS, or NBC, another 140 with the newer FOX network, and the remaining stations are not affiliated with any network. Even network affiliates receive only a portion of each day's programming from the network. FOX affiliates receive only a few evenings of prime-time network programming each week. The rest of the broadcast day must be filled either by locally produced programming or by programming purchased from distributors called syndicators. With the exception of local news programs and a few public affairs programs produced to satisfy the vestigial remains of the FCC's "public interest" mandate, the vast majority of commercial stations produce little if any local programming. The cost of such programs cannot be justified in relation to the ratings those shows are likely to produce and, as a consequence, the local advertising revenues likely to be realized.[11] Instead, local stations buy from syndicators the rights to show movies, game shows, and reruns of network hits at times when network programming is not available. In the case of independent (non–network affiliated) stations, the entire broadcasting output may be made up of syndicated programming.

Because a production company retains the syndication rights to its programs, it stands to make enormous profits by selling broadcast rights for a successful network-broadcast program in each of the approximately two hundred local television markets in the United States. The initial domestic syndication of *Magnum, P.I.* brought its producers in excess of $100 million, and the subsequent syndication of early episodes of *The Cosby Show*, which is still running on NBC, set syndication sales records well above this figure.

Dynasty in Norway: The International Television Economy

The enormous profits to be realized in the high-stakes game of commercial entertainment television production in the United States helps to explain several features of American broadcasting—indeed, of broadcasting systems around the world. Local stations in the U.S. usually "strip" reruns of network programs: a weekly series is run daily, Monday through Friday. In order to be marketable in syndication, a series must contain a minimum of approximately one hundred episodes, which works out to about four years of network broadcasts. Therefore, there is tremendous incentive for producers to keep a show on the network as long as possible. Because a given show will be kept on the network schedule only so long as it garners acceptable ratings, producers are not likely to introduce changes in the show that might cause a ratings decline. As far as the networks are concerned, once a show has demonstrated its ability to produce high ratings, they are more likely to stick with it for as long as those ratings are consistent rather than taking a gamble on a new, untried program. It is easy to see, then, why it is possible to watch daily local reruns of *The Cosby Show* or *Cheers* in virtually every city and town in America, despite the fact that there are 1,100 separately programmed television stations serving those communities and despite the fact that every single one of those stations has the production facilities to make its own programming. Those shows deliver higher ratings at a lower cost to the local broadcaster than would programs that station produced itself.

One of the thorniest broadcasting policy issues in many countries is the degree to which foreign programming should be allowed to dominate television schedules. Although television programming circulates from country to country around the world, much of the controversy in foreign countries centers around the importation of American shows. The debate over foreign programming involves both cultural and economic concerns. To what degree does a nation want its airwaves to be filled with programming made in a different country, using a different cultural context, aimed at different audiences, and speaking in a foreign language? The image of American television as a giant threatening to dominate the airwaves of other countries is based not only upon fears (whether grounded or not) of cultural imperialism but also, and more concretely, on the position of American television within the world television market.

The American domestic television market is the richest and largest in the world. Because U.S. advertisers are willing to pay more than $300,000 for thirty seconds of air time during a top-rated show, American networks can afford to pay producers as much as $2 million per episode for a half-hour sitcom like *The Cosby Show*. *Cheers*, NBC's top-rated show in 1990, cost the network $1.25 million per episode but earned the network an estimated $2.6 million in advertising revenue. From the twenty-five-week season of new episodes and summer reruns, NBC realizes annual revenues of $115 million from *Cheers* alone.[12] For established network hits, producers may be able to negotiate a network license fee that exceeds the cost of production (*Cheers* producers demanded a 284 percent increase in license fees for the 1991–92 season, to $4.8 million per episode), but other shows can be sold to the networks for less than it costs to make them because they potentially can realize hundreds of millions of dollars in syndication sales.

Having already covered their costs and made a profit from the licensing of a successful program to the network and its subsequent syndication, American producers can afford to offer broadcast rights for that program in another country at a fraction of what it would cost that country's television system or a local producer to make a program that would appeal to as many viewers. The price at which the program is offered need bear little relationship to the cost of making it, because production costs have already been recovered in the American domestic market. For example, in 1983 the Norwegian Broadcasting Corporation paid only $1,500 per episode for *Dynasty*, which at that time was at the height of its international fame. Episodes of popular half-hour American programs have been offered to countries like Zambia and Syria for as little as $50.[13] In Great Britain, it costs an average of roughly £60,000 ($100,000) to produce an hour of television programming for national broadcast, and some dramatic productions cost much more. Even at £10,000 per episode, it is still much cheaper to import a dramatic series produced in the United States than to produce an hour of domestic programming.

Making it even more difficult for local broadcasting systems and independent producers to compete against American programming is the fact that audiences frequently associate the "look" of American television with high quality. With average budgets of $1 million per hour, American programs can afford what are called high production values. Alternative "looks" can be achieved on smaller budgets by local producers, but they might be regarded by viewers not merely as different but as technically inferior to the American product. At least commercial broadcasters outside the United States can recoup part or all of the costs of local production from the sale of advertising. For "public service" broadcasting systems that operate from TV license fees or government appropriations, the temptation to buy imported programming rather than making their own is even greater, because for them programming is an absolute and unrecoverable cost, not an investment.

Ironically, or predictably, the economics of present-day American broadcast television and its impact on the world market make it very difficult for foreign broadcasters to get a foothold in the world's largest and potentially most lucrative television market. There is simply very little incentive for the American networks to import foreign programming. Network programming executives assume that the great mass of American television viewers will not watch foreign programming—even if it is in English. No other country is in the position of being able to make large quantities of very expensively produced programs with the expectation of being able to cover production costs in the domestic market and thus being able to sell foreign rights for a pittance per episode to foreign countries. Indeed, few if any foreign-produced series have ever made it into the prime-time network schedule in the United States.

The essays in this collection use as their principal illustrations examples of American television. In part this is because the contributors are based in the United States and have access primarily to American television. As we've seen, access to non-U.S. programming is much more limited —both for us and for other American television viewers. It is also the case, however, that because of the economic structure of the world television market described above, people around the world are more likely to be familiar with examples of American television programming than they are with programming from any other country aside from their own. *Dal-*

las, for example, has been viewed by people in more than ninety countries. We use these examples of American television despite our recognition of the fact that the meanings and pleasures of *Twin Peaks* or *The Simpsons* inevitably change as those texts circulate around the world and as people from different cultures encounter them. For better or worse, American television provides us with the closest thing we currently have to a common set of television texts.

The Dual Economies of Television

This very brief overview of what is called the political economy of television hardly does justice to the complexity of either the political or the economic issues it has raised. At the very least, I hope it has made the point that there is nothing innocent or inconsequential about the commercial television system that provides us with such seemingly inconsequential programming—programming upon which the following essays will concentrate. Obviously, there is a great deal at stake for U.S. broadcasters as they attempt to secure their share of a $25 billion domestic market. *Cheers* might be a half-hour of mindless entertainment to us, but to NBC there's nothing funny about the hundreds of millions of dollars in advertising revenues that half-hour generates.

The system of commercial broadcasting in the United States also has important consequences for viewers as well. Commercial broadcasters have taken to calling their output "free television" to distinguish it from pay-per-month cable services like HBO, the Disney Channel, or Showtime. But commercial broadcasting is *not* free, at least for the viewing public. In being granted a broadcast license, station owners are given—at no cost to them—the right to exclusive use of a part of a natural resource (the electromagnetic spectrum) upon which a value can and is placed whenever a television station and its accompanying license is sold. Certainly commercial broadcast time is not "free," and yet its only value results from large numbers of viewers being successfully recruited to serve as commodities that can be sold to advertisers. Canadian media scholar Dallas Smythe has gone so far as to argue that, by watching television, we function in the economic system of commercial television not only as commodities but as laborers. As he puts it: "The work which audience members perform for the advertiser to whom they have been sold is to learn to buy particular 'brands' of consumer goods, and to spend their income accordingly."[14] The low cost at which American programming is offered in foreign markets carries the hidden price of undercutting a country's domestic program production and cultivating production standards against which that country's domestic programs will find it difficult to compete.

John Fiske has suggested that there are two "economies" of commercial television: a political economy and a cultural economy. The first produces an audience that can be sold to advertisers as a commodity. But, Fiske argues, the viewer's relationship with television cannot be reduced to that process of commodification because there is another economy at work on the other side of the screen. In the cultural economy of television, traditional economic distinctions rapidly blur. Viewers might well be commodities to broadcasters and advertisers, but they are sentient, thinking commodities. Their willingness to "consume" programming provides a basis for commercial television, but through their consumption viewers simultaneously produce meanings and pleasures.[15] As we shall see, those meanings and pleasures almost certainly differ among audience groups and might well be quite different from the meanings and pleasures anticipated by program producers.

Understanding how both economies work is obviously important, but each starts from a different place. Political economists begin their studies in the boardrooms of a handful of giant corporations; in this collection of essays we start from the living rooms and bedrooms in which hundreds of millions of people experience the results of the decisions made in those boardrooms. Exploring how people make moments of television meaningful and pleasurable seems to us a sensible way of beginning the critical study of television. Having gained a better grasp of the complexities of television's discourses and our everyday experiences of them, we should be in a better position to begin to relate those discourses and experiences to other aspects of our lives and to other aspects of television.

Some Final Introductory Thoughts and a "TV Guide" to the Rest of the Book

The essays you are about to read are certainly not arranged in order of perceived significance (either ascending or descending) or in the belief that the final chapters provide the ultimate answers to the problems left unsolved in earlier essays. Indeed, the two concluding essays are designed to open up new questions about television and the ways we might study it. For this second edition, each of the collection's central chapters has been revised to take into account recent scholarship and to respond to the feedback we have received from some of the thousands of teachers, students, and other readers who have used the first edition.

We have also updated the examples we use to illustrate critical points in each chapter. There is no way a book on television can be "current." The television schedule in place at the time we write is certain to be different by the time this edition is published, and it will be different still at the time you read this. For this reason, choosing examples from programs likely to be familiar to the reader is a tricky business. Some examples are drawn from the "current" prime-time schedule; others are from programs in their second lives in U.S. syndication or in worldwide release; still others are from programs, last seen on U.S. network television decades ago, that have found third, fourth, or subsequent "lives" through new delivery systems—cable, satellite, or videocassette. In his essay on postmodernism, Jim Collins discusses how these "old" programs become new texts when framed by different discourses.

The poor quality of television images in the book is not the fault of the production process but is rather the result, in most cases, of their having been shot directly from the television screen. Because film is a photograph-based medium, frame enlargements of film shots reproduced in books sometimes look better than the moving images from which they are taken. Conversely, because the television image is in constant motion, freezing it always results in a loss of quality. Nevertheless, we felt that some analyses needed to be anchored by visual reference points—however blurry —taken from the text under discussion.

Our discussion of television begins with Ellen Seiter's essay on the influence of semiotics and post-structuralism on television studies. Seiter lays out the basic terminology of structuralism and semiotics, which has become the standard for describing the ways in which various symbol systems, including television, represent the world. She also takes up the challenges and emendations to early structuralist work that evolved as that work came to be applied to everything from verbal languages to strip-tease shows.

With Sarah Kozloff's essay, we move from a general theory of the nature of relationships among all types of signs to a consideration of a special kind of semiotic organization: the narrative. Understanding the way in which narratives work is crucial to understanding our relationships with television; except for oral storytelling, television is the most prolific and important narrative medium in the world today. In addition to fictional stories, television also structures "real" events in narrative terms. Thus narrative theory attempts to account for patterns of organization that run through all narrative as well as for differences among types of narrative.

My own essay takes up the flip side of narrative theory. Narrative theory begins with the recognition that every narrative is not just a story, but a story told by someone in a particular way. What I call reader-oriented criticism begins with an equally commonsensical insight: every story is told with someone else in mind and is made sense of by the "listener" in particular ways. In its ways of addressing its viewers, television draws upon both cinema and face-to-face communication, making the role of the spectator particularly complex. My essay discusses critical approaches to television drawn from reader-oriented theories of literature as well as strategies borrowed from anthropology and cultural studies for understanding the role of television in everyday life.

In her essay on genre theory and television, Jane Feuer argues that part of the process of making sense and deriving pleasure from any given text involves relating that text to others. Genre theory helps to provide us with ways of relating industrial practice in television (the need to turn out, on a regular schedule, huge numbers of texts that must appeal to millions of different viewers) to the texts that are produced as a result of this process and both to the expectations of audiences.

Mimi White's essay on ideological analysis again reminds us that by agreeing to be viewers we implicitly become parties to a contract between ourselves and an enormous institution. Ideological analysis concerns itself with the nature and functioning of television as institution, the assumptions and values that underlie the texts it produces, and the manner in which we are positioned relative to both institution and text. As White demonstrates, even the act of watching a rather unremarkable commercial carries with it an enormous range of assumptions about television in general and the cultural contract we make with it.

Sandy Flitterman-Lewis reconceptualizes the relationship between viewer and text in terms of contemporary psychoanalytic theory, particularly that developed to account for our relationship with movies. She takes as her starting point the suggestive analogy between the act of dreaming and that of watching a film. Although acknowledging the relevance of that analogy in connecting the desires of the spectator with the fantasies enacted in visual narratives, Flitterman-Lewis goes on to demonstrate the important differences between film and television and the resultant modifications that must be made if cine-psychoanalysis is to help us understand television texts and "tele-spectators."

Throughout the history of American commercial broadcasting, the industry has regarded women as the prime audience for many types of programming. Indeed, around the world, programs are made that attempt to appeal especially to women. In her essay on feminist criticism and television, E. Ann Kaplan considers both how women are represented on television and how women as television spectators are addressed and engaged by the medium.

John Fiske examines the strand of television analysis that has emerged from the cluster of approaches commonly called British cultural studies. British cultural studies has conceived of culture as an arena of struggle between those with power and those without it. Watching television, Fiske argues, is not a process by which messages are implanted in the consciousness of a uniform mass audience, but rather a process of negotiation between groups of viewers in different social situations and television texts that are themselves open to a variety of interpretations.

In the first of two essays added for the revised edition, Jim Collins asks whether the term *postmodernism* might be applied to some of the distinctive features of television. Because the label *postmodernist* has been used in a variety of ways to describe everything from architecture, furniture, and fashion to literature, cinema, and *Twin Peaks*, it is important to examine what "condition" postmodernism attempts to account for and whether or not this account tells us anything useful about television.

The afterword arose from the reaction of a reader and teacher of television studies to the first edition. James Hay felt that too much emphasis had been placed on the connections among approaches. Readers needed to know, he argued, that the approaches also differed from each other in significant ways. His essay places the approaches up against one another, points out their differences, and discusses how each constitutes television as an object of study in a unique way.

Each chapter concludes with suggestions for further reading on the critical approach dealt with and includes key works of television criticism produced from that perspective. A more general bibliography of television criticism can be found at the end of the book. Citations for general theoretical works are given at the end of each chapter. Full citations for works of television criticism are included in the bibliography.

You should keep in mind that these essays in no way do justice to the complexities of the individual approaches they discuss. We have not attempted to substitute a *Reader's Digest* account for the need to grapple with the central works in each of these areas. Instead, we lay out in a provisional and necessarily schematic fashion some of the ways these approaches might aid in an understanding of television. We leave it to you to explore these critical frameworks further and to test and challenge the relationships between them and television that we have proposed.

NOTES

1. Robert Kubey and Mihaly Csikszentmihalyi, *Television and the Quality of Life: How Viewing Shapes Everyday Experience* (Hillsdale, N.J.: Lawrence Erlbaum Associates, 1990), p. 1.

2. This overview of the television environment was compiled from the following: *Broadcasting Yearbook, 1990* (Washington, D.C.: Broadcasting Publishing Co., 1990); *Statistical Abstract of the United States, 1990* (Washington, D.C.: Government Printing Office, 1990); James Lull, ed., *World Families Watch Television* (Newbury Park, Calif.: Sage, 1988), Douglas Boyd, Joseph Straubhaar, and John Lent, *Videocassette Recorders in the Third World* (New York: Longman, 1989); Keith G. Fleer, Gregory M. Paul, and Michael H. Lauer, eds., *Following the Dollars from Retail to Net Profits: An Examination of the Businesses of Creating and Using Revenues from Motion Pictures and Television Programs* (Los Angeles: University of California, 1986); Thomas Lindlof, ed., *Natural Audiences: Qualitative Research of Media Uses and Effects* (Norwood, N.J.: Ablex, 1987); and Robert T. Bower, *The Changing Television Audience in America* (New York: Columbia University Press, 1985).

3. Alfred Schutz, "The Stranger: An Essay in Social Psychology," in *Collected Papers* (The Hague: Martinus Nijhoff, 1964), 2:91–105.

4. Kubey and Csikszentmihalyi, *Television and the Quality of Life*, p. xi.

5. See Dafna Lemish, "Viewers in Diapers: The Early Development of Television Viewing," in Lindlof, *Natural Audiences*, pp. 33–57.

6. See, for example, John Tulloch's examination of writer Trevor Griffith's work in the context of British television (*Television Drama: Agency, Audience, and Myth* [London: Routledge, 1990]); and Jane Feuer, Paul Kerr, and Tise Vahimagi's consideration of the MTM Company in relation to issues of authorship (*MTM: "Quality Television"* [London: British Film Institute, 1984]).

7. Lindlof, *Natural Audiences*, p. x.

8. Eric Barnouw, *A Tower in Babel* (New York: Oxford University Press, 1966), p. 281. By the time you read this, it is very likely that the fifteen or so commercial television licenses in Great Britain will for the first time be awarded to the highest bidders. License holders (the ITV companies) also pay a tax on their profits, which helps to support the alternative commercial channel, Channel 4. American commercial broadcasters pay no special tax.

9. Richard Levinson and William Link, *Off Camera: Conversations with*

the Makers of Prime-Time Television (New York: New American Library, 1986), pp. 247–48, 267.

10. Ibid., p. 37. Dandel goes on to illustrate his point with an incident from his early days as a writer in Hollywood. While working on a western series called *Tucson Trail*, he wrote a moving story about a Catholic priest who discovers he has strong homosexual feelings; to test his sexual orientation, the priest initiates a love affair with a woman. Much to Dandel's surprise, the production company agreed to shoot his script. However, two days before production was to commence, the producer called to say that he had just secured the free use of a trained collie for a few days and instructed him to rewrite the script, dropping the female lead and adding a part for the collie. Dandel remarks: "That's when I realized what television was. A love affair between a homosexual and a straight collie."

11. The one major exception to this generalization is local news, which in the last twenty years has emerged as a profit center.

12. John Lippman, "Paramount, NBC Battle over New *Cheers* Price," *Raleigh News and Observer* (N.C.), 11 February 1991.

13. Jostein Gripsrud, "Toward a Flexible Methodology in Studying Media Meaning: *Dynasty* in Norway," *Critical Studies in Mass Communication* 7 (1990): 117–28.

14. Dallas Smythe, "Communications: Blindspot of Western Marxism," *Canadian Journal of Political and Social Theory* 1 (1977): 3.

15. John Fiske, "Popular Television and Commercial Culture: Beyond Political Economy," in *Television Studies: Textual Analysis*, ed. Gary Burns and Robert J. Thompson (New York: Praeger, 1989), pp. 21–40.

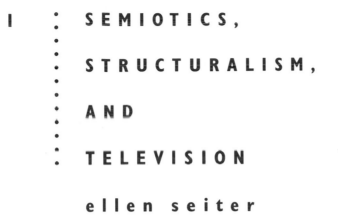

1 : SEMIOTICS, STRUCTURALISM, AND TELEVISION

ellen seiter

ontemporary television criticism derives much of its vocabulary from semiotics and structuralism. This chapter will introduce the basic terminology of these methods, offer a case study of structuralist methods applied to children's television, and introduce some of the concepts the so-called post-structuralists have used to critique and expand upon semiotics and structuralism. The late Paddy Whannel used to joke, "Semiotics tells us things we already know in a language we will never understand." Learning the vocabulary of semiotics is certainly one of its most trying aspects. This vocabulary makes it possible, however, to identify and describe what makes TV distinctive as a communication medium, as well as how it relies on other sign systems to communicate. Both questions are vital to the practice of television criticism, and these terms will be encountered in a broad range of critical methods from psychoanalysis to cultural studies.

Semiotics is the study of everything that can be used for communication: words, images, traffic signs, flowers, music, medical symptoms, and much more. Semiotics studies the way such "signs" communicate and the rules that govern their use. As a tool for the study of culture, semiotics represents a radical break from traditional criticism, in which the first order of business is the interpretation of an aesthetic object or text in terms of its immanent meaning. Semiotics first asks *how* meaning is created, rather than *what* the meaning is. In order to do this, semiotics uses a specialized vocabulary to describe signs and how they function. Often this vocabulary smacks of scientism to the newcomer and clashes with our assumptions about what criticism and the humanities are. But the special terminology of semiotics and its attempt to compare the production of meaning in a diverse set of mediums—aesthetic signs being only one of many objects of study—have allowed us to describe the workings of cultural communication with greater accuracy and enlarged our recognition of the conventions that characterize our culture.

The term *semiotics* was coined by Charles S. Peirce (1839–1914), an American philosopher, although his work on semiotics did not become widely known until the 1930s. The field was also "invented" by Swiss linguist Ferdinand de Saussure. The term he used to describe the new science he advocated in *Course in General Linguistics*, published posthumously in 1959, was *semiology*. Structuralism is most closely associated with anthropologist Claude Lévi-Strauss, whose studies of the logic and worldview of "primitive" cultures were first published in the 1950s. Although it relies on many of the principles of semiotics, structuralism engages larger questions of cultural meaning and ideology and thus has been widely used in literary and media criticism. Semiotics and structuralism are so closely related they may be said to overlap—semiotics being a field of study in itself, whereas structuralism is a method of analysis often used in semiotics.[1]

Structuralism stresses that each element within a cultural system derives its meaning from its relationship to every other element in the system: there are no independent meanings, but rather many meanings produced by their difference from other elements in the system. Beginning in the 1960s, some leading European intellectuals applied semiotics and structuralism to many different sign systems. Roland Barthes carefully analyzed fashion, French popular culture from wrestling to wine drinking, and a novella by Balzac. Umberto Eco turned his attention to Superman comic strips and James Bond novels. Christian Metz set out to describe the style of Hollywood cinema as a semiotic system. By addressing the symbolic and communicative capacity of humans in general, semiotics and structuralism help us see connections between fields of study that are normally divided among different academic departments in the university. Thus they are specially suited to the study of television.

The Sign

The smallest unit of meaning in semiotics is called the *sign*. Semiotics begins with this smallest unit and builds rules for the combination of signs. Fredric Jameson has pointed out that this concern with discerning the smallest unit of meaning is something that semiotics shares with other major intellectual movements of the twentieth century, including linguistics and nuclear physics, but it is an unusual starting point for criticism, which has tended to discuss works as organic wholes. Taking the definition of the smallest unit as a starting point indicates a shift in the sciences from perception to models: "where the first task of a science henceforth seems the establishment of a method, or a model, such that the basic conceptual units are given from the outset and organize the data (the atom, the phoneme)."[2] Saussure conceptualized the sign as composed of two distinct parts, although these parts are separable only in theory, not in actual communication. Every sign is composed of a *signifier*, that is, the image, object, or sound itself—the part of the sign that has a material form—and the *signified*, the concept it represents.

In written language, the sign *rain* is composed of the grouping of four letters on this page (the signifier) and the idea or concept of rain (the signified)—that is, the category of phenomena we reserve for water falling from the sky. Saussure stressed that the relationship between the signifier and the signified in verbal language was entirely conventional, completely arbitrary. There is no natural or necessary connection between *rain* and the concept for which it stands. Furthermore, words have no positive value. A word's meaning derives entirely from its difference from other words in the sign system of language. On the level of signifier, we recognize *rain* through its distinguishability from *brain* or *sprain* or *rail* or *Braille* or *roan* or *reign*. The signified is meaningful because of its difference from *sprinkle, drizzle, downpour, monsoon*, or from *hail, sleet*, or *snow*. Other words could be invented, such as *raim* or *sain*, that use the same alphabet and are pronounceable, but because these "words" do not enter into relationships with other signs in the system in a meaningful way, they remain at the level of nonsense.

Each language marks off its own set of meaningful differences: we can imagine an infinite number of possibilities for signifiers and signifieds, but each language makes only some differences important and detectable. Learning a second language is difficult because each language consists of a set of signs whose meanings derive from differences to which we might not be sensitive—phonetic distinctions we can't "hear," grammar rules that make distinctions unfamiliar to us, and words that are untranslatable into our first language. However, studying a second language does make us aware of Saussure's point about the arbitrary nature of verbal languages. The signifier for rain changes to *pluie* in French and *Regen* in German. Neither has any more natural connection to the notion of water falling from the sky than does *rain*. Even onomatopoeia—words that seem to imitate the sounds they signify—turn out to be partly conventional. For English speakers, a rooster goes "cock-a-doodle-doo." For Germans he goes "Kikeriki."

Saussure was interested in studying the structure of language as a system, and he bracketed off the real objects to which language refers: its *referents*. Semiotics does not concern itself with the referent of the sign rain, that is, actual water falling from the sky on a particular day at a particular place. The concept of rain is independent of any given occurrence of the actual event. Moreover, both Saussure and Peirce recognized that some signs have no "real" object to which they refer: abstractions (truth, freedom) or products of the imagination (mermaids, unicorns). More important, they wished to argue that all signs are cultural constructs that have taken on meaning through repeated, learned, collective use. Peirce emphasized that even when we try to define a sign, we are always forced to use another sign to translate it; he labeled the sign that we use to describe another sign the *interpretant*.

In this book, for example, we will be describing television's audiovisual sign systems using linguistic signs (words on these pages) and black-and-white still photographs that are in many ways quite distant and different from the original object. To take another example, when an image on the television news is identified as "Corazon Aquino," a sign produced by an electronic image is translated into another sign system—that of proper nouns. Proper names are a special class of signs that seem to have a real, easily agreed-upon referent. But our understanding of persons (especially those represented frequently on television) is filtered through sign systems: we don't "know" anything or anyone (even ourselves) except through language.

Images do not have an unmediated relationship with their referents. The image of Aquino could be understood in terms of general categories ranging from "world leaders" to Filipino women. The referent of Aquino's image will vary greatly depending on the cultural context—for example from the United States to Japan. The proper name could refer to another interpretant, such as "president of the Philippines." Even if we were in the same room with Aquino and used our index fingers to point to her and say, "*There* is Corazon Aquino," we would have used another set of signs, gestural and verbal ones. Charles S. Peirce saw the process of communication as an unending chain of sign production, which he dubbed "unlimited semiosis." Peirce's concept of the sign forces the realization that no communication takes place outside of sign systems — we are always translating signs into other signs. The conventions of the sign system control the ways we are able to communicate (that is, produce signifiers) and limit the range of meanings available (that is, what signifieds can be produced).

Umberto Eco defines a sign as "everything that, on the grounds of a previously established social convention, can be taken as something standing for something else."[3] Surprisingly, Eco means to include in this definition even those signs that at first glance seem to be more "natural" than linguistic ones. It is through social convention and cultural appropriation that a dark, cloudy sky becomes a sign for "impending storm." Those same dark clouds could be used to signify bad luck, or nature responding in kind to one's own gloomy mood (as in the literary convention of pathetic fallacy). The meaning of rain can vary greatly from one culture to another: in some Polynesian societies, a rainstorm is taken to mean that the sky is crying for the death of a child.

Eco's conception of the sign is adapted from the work of Peirce, who did not limit himself to symbolic signs (language), as Saussure did, but attempted to account for all types of signs, including pictorial ones. To do so, he introduced specific definitions of the terms *icon* and *index*. The categories *symbolic*, *iconic*, and *indexical* are not mutually exclusive. Television constantly uses all three types of signs simultaneously. Television images are both iconic and indexical, and programs often use words (symbolic signs) on the screen and the soundtrack.

In the iconic sign, the signifier structurally resembles its signified. We must "learn" to recognize this resemblance just as we learn to read maps or to draw. The correspondence between a drawing of a dog, for example, and the signified "dog" (which might be a particular specimen of dog or the concept of dog in general) could take many different forms. The drawing could be skeletal or anatomical, in which case it might take a trained veterinarian or zoologist to recognize any structural similarity between the drawing and the signified "dog." The iconic sign could be a child's drawing, in which case another kind of expert decoder, for instance the child's parent or teacher, might be required to detect the structural resemblance. Most drawings rely on rules that dictate point of view and scale; an "aerial view" of a dog, a head-on angle, or a drawing done twenty times larger than scale would be much harder for most of us to recognize than the conventional side-angle view in which two legs, a tail, a pointed ear, and whiskers will do the job, even if no attempt is made at coloration and the drawing appears only as an outline in black. Most of these admonitions about the conventionality of drawings hold true for video images as well, even though we think of television as more lifelike.

Indexical signs involve an existential link between the signifier and the referent: the sign relies on their joint presence at some point in time. Drawings do not qualify as indexical signs because we can make a drawing of something we have never seen. Maps are iconic rather than indexical because a cartographer can create a map solely on the basis of other iconic signs, such as diagrams and geological surveys; she may never have been to the place the map will signify.

Indexical signs are different from iconic ones because they rely on a material connection between signifier and signified: smoke means fire, pawprints mean the presence of a cat; a particular set of fingerprints signifies "Richard Nixon"; red spots signify "measles." Most images produced by cameras belong to Peirce's class of "indexical signs" because they require the physical presence of the referent before the camera lens at some point in time for their production. This fact about an image is, however, virtually impossible to verify without being present at the time the image was made. Stand-ins and look-alikes, trick photographs, special effects, computer-generated graphics, multiple exposures, and animated images can all be used to lie to the camera. Even images that we treat as particularly unique because they have as their signified an individual living creature may be dictated by convention. Throughout Lassie's career as a television character, many different dogs (most of them male) have been used in the part, often within the same episode. Although many individual Lassies have now died, the iconic sign "Lassie" lives on, thanks to the skills of the various production crews and the animal trainers who find new dogs whenever a new version of the Lassie series is produced. It may be a blow to our faith in physiognomy, but we can be fooled by pictures of persons almost as easily.

Indexical signs are also established through social convention. Animals have left pawprints for as long as they have roamed the earth, but their pawprints became a sign only when people began to use them for tracking. As Umberto Eco explains: "The first doctor who discovered a sort of constant relationship between an array of red spots on a patient's face and a given disease (measles) made an inference: but insofar as this relationship has been made conventional and has been registered as such in medical treatises a *semiotic convention* has been established. There is a sign every time a human group decides to use and recognize something as the vehicle for something else."[4] Indexical signs are no less tainted by human intervention than symbolic or iconic ones; they require the same accumulation of use and the same reinforcement and perpetuation by a social group to be understood as signs in the first place.

To understand television images, we must learn to recognize many conventions of representation. One of the characteristics of such representational codes is that we become so accustomed to them that we may not recognize their use; they become as "natural" to us as the symbolic signs of language, and we think of iconic signs as the most logical—sometimes as the only possible—way to signify aspects of our world. We can watch this learning taking place when infants and toddlers begin to watch television. Toddlers, for example, like to touch the screen frequently as they struggle to understand the two-dimensional nature of television's iconic signs. Conventional expectations of scale, perspective, camera angle, color, lighting, lens focal length, and subject-to-camera distance (that is, nonrepresentational aspects of the image) are acquired through exposure to television; if a camera operator violates too many of these conventions, we may not be able to "recognize" the image at all.

In its strict sense, Peirce's model does not require the "intention" to communicate: signs may be produced by nonhuman agencies (such as when a TV set's technical breakdown produces "snow" on the screen), for example, or by unconscious senders. Peirce's model does not necessarily require a human receiver of the sign, or any receiver at all, although, because signs are social and conventional, there must be the possibility that a given sign would be understood by a potential receiver. Signification cannot take place outside of human communication, but semiotics does not require the existence of empirically verifiable receivers of its signs, and it cannot promise that all receivers will agree on the relationship of signifier to signified. Thus authorial intention is not included in the study of signs and neither is the interpretation or reception of the message by empirical audiences.

"The camera never lies" is a statement that tells us a lot about the way we accept many photographic or electronic images as real when they involve indexical signs, even if, from a semiotic point of view, the statement is a falsehood. Many television images are produced in such a way that we are encouraged to understand them only as indexical signs. Stand-up shots of reporters on location are one example of this: we may not be able to decipher from the image itself whether Andrea Mitchell is really standing on the White House lawn, but TV places an enormous stress on the connection between the image and this location as it exists in real time and space.[5] Since its invention, so much has been made of the objectivity of the camera as a recording instrument that we often fail to recognize the extent to which camera images are produced according to rules just as drawings are. Semiotics reminds us that the signifiers produced by TV are related to their signifieds by convention, even if, when we watch something like the news, we tend not to think of the active production of signs involved in TV but simply receive the news as pure information, as an unmediated signified.

To engage in fantasy for a moment, consider producing a newsbreak about a completely fictional event for broadcast on network TV. If we gave some careful thought to the way newsbreaks are written and the topics usually covered in them, we could script and storyboard a newsbreak that exactly conformed to the mode or presentation typical of U.S. network newscasting. If we had access to the facilities, technicians, equipment, supplies, and personnel of one of the networks, and if we could coerce an anchor to violate professional ethics (or find a convincing impostor) and read our script, we could produce a newsbreak, complete with "live action" reports, that would be indistinguishable from the authentic item. Semiotics reminds us that with nonfictional television, no less than with its fictional counterpart, we are dealing not with referents but with signs. In the end, it is impossible to verify the referent from television's sounds and images. Perhaps this is why, as Margaret Morse argues, the person of the news anchor, in his or her "ceremonial role," has become increasingly important in securing our belief in the news and our sense of its authenticity.[6] In this and many other ways, television relies heavily on the figure of the unique individual, the television personality. Most of television's signs are easily copied because they are based in convention, but the on-camera talking head of a known television personality is still one of the more difficult aspects of the image to fake.

Umberto Eco has criticized Peirce's distinction among symbolic, iconic, and indexical on the grounds that it tends to overlook the historical and social production of all signs. Instead, Eco offers a definition that casts all signs in terms of this context: "Semiotics is in principle the discipline studying everything which can be used in order to lie. If something cannot be used to tell a lie, conversely it cannot be used to tell the truth: it cannot in fact be used 'to tell' at all."[7] Television communication is no more mediated or contaminated than other forms of communication—spoken language, written language, still photography—in its relationship to reality. The important insight that can be gained from the study of semiotics and structuralism is that all communication is partial, motivated, conventional, and "biased," even those forms such as print journalism that are founded on a reputation for truth-seeking and attempt to convey the impression of reliability. The study of semiotics insists that we should discern the distinctive ways of producing and combining signs practiced by particular kinds of television, in particular places, and at a particular point in time, because these codes are inseparable from the "reality" of media communication.

Denotation and Connotation

So far we have been discussing the sign in terms of denotative meaning. Connotative meanings land us squarely in the domain of ideology: the worldview (including the model of social relations and their causes) portrayed from a particular position and set of interests in society. Roland Barthes devoted much of his work to the distinction between *denotation* and *connotation* in aesthetic texts. In images, denotation is the first order of signification: the signifier is the image itself and the signified is the idea or concept—what it is a picture of. Connotation is a second-order signifying system that uses the first sign, (signifier and signified), as its signifier and attaches an additional meaning, another signified, to it. Barthes thought of connotation as fixing or freezing the meaning of the denotation; it impoverishes the first sign by ascribing a single and usually ideological signified to it.[8] This is why it takes many words to describe the signifier at the first level—we must include camera angle, color, size, lighting, composition, and so on. But connotations can often be described in just one word (noble, romantic, gritty, patriotic, humorous). Sometimes the difference between connotation and denotation seems rather mechanical in television criticism because television's signs are nearly already complex messages or *texts*, making it difficult to isolate the difference between the two levels of signification. Perhaps it is best to think of connotation as a parasite attaching itself to a prior signification.

To begin with a simple denotation, the fade to black has as its signifier the gradual disappearance of the picture on the screen and, as its signified, simply "black." This sign has been strongly conventionalized in motion pictures and television so that it exists as the following connotative sign: the signifier is "fade to black" and the signified is "ending" of a scene or a program. Television production texts insist that students must always use the fade to black at the end of every program and before any commercial breaks.[9] The fade to black has become part of a very stable signification. But connotations may eventually change through repetition. On *Knots Landing*, a CBS prime-time soap opera that has cultivated an image as a "quality program," each segment ends with a fade to black that lasts several beats longer than in most programs. This "fade to black" is part of the tone of *Knots Landing*; it is used for the connotation "serious drama" or "high-class show" (suggesting that the audience needs a moment to collect itself emotionally, to think over the scene before going on to the commercial). The longer fade to black now appears on many shows that aspire to such a connotation, including *thirtysomething* and *L.A. Law*. Connotations fix the meaning of a sign, but in other kinds of texts—those not of broadcast television—the denotation "fade to black" could take on other meanings as well. In a student production, frequent use of the fade to black could connote "rank amateur direction"; in an art video, it could connote "experimental, modernist style."

To give another example, hair color can be singled out in a television image as a denotation. Many TV actors are women whose hair is light blond. On a connotative level, shades of hair color (the first level of signification) are used to produce signifieds such as "glamorous," "beautiful," "youthful," "dumb," or "sexy" on the second level of signification. These connotations, widely known through their repeated use in film and television, are ones that have a specific history in the United States, one that stems from glorifying the physical appearance of Anglo women (based on their difference from and presumed superiority to other races and ethnicities). But they are also subject to change or revision over time. Compare, for example, the changing connotations of blondness in the television images of Farrah Fawcett on *Charlie's Angels* (youthful, pure), Linda Evans on *Dynasty* (virtuous, rich), and Madonna in her music videos and public appearances such as the 1991 Academy Awards ceremony (in which she deliberately "quoted" Marilyn Monroe's hairstyle and what *it* connotes: sexiness as a costume).

Some aspects of the image and soundtrack that we think of as nonrepresentational actually function as symbolic signs and often carry connotative meanings; examples may include the color of light (pink for femaleness, white for goodness); music (minor chords and slow tempos signifying melancholy, solo instrumentals signifying loneliness); or photographic technique (soft focus signifying romance, hand-held cameras signifying on-the-spot documentary). Television is not completely different from written language in this respect. Printed words are inseparable from their nonrepresentational form in terms of typeface, size of type, boldness, color of paper, and so forth. These signs are all established through convention and repeated use. Such nonrepresentational signs have not been studied as thoroughly by semioticians as have representational ones.[10] One of the goals of semiotic analysis of television is to make us conscious of the use of connotation on television, so that we realize how much of what appears naturally meaningful on TV is actually historical, changeable, and culturally specific.

Barthes argued that connotation is the primary way in which the mass media communicate ideological meanings. A dramatic example of the operation of "myth," as Barthes called such connotations, and of television's rapid elaboration of new meanings is explosion of the space shuttle *Challenger*. The sign consisted of a signifier—the TV image itself—that was coded in certain ways (symmetrical composition, long shot of shuttle on launching pad, daylight, blue sky background) and the denoted meaning or signified "space shuttle." On the connotative level, the space shuttle was used as a signifier for a set of ideological signifieds including "scientific progress," "manifest destiny in space," and "U.S. superiority over the Soviet Union in the cold war."

On 28 January 1986, these connotations were radically displaced. On that day, all three commercial networks repeatedly broadcast videotape of the space shuttle exploding. This footage was accompanied first by a stunned silence, then by an abundance of speech by newscasters, by expert interviewees, by press agents, and by President Reagan (who canceled his State of the Union address to speak about the explosion), much of which primarily expressed shock. The connotation of the sign "space shuttle" was destabilized; it became once again subject—as denotation—to an unpredictable number of individual meanings or competing ideological interpretations. It was as if the explosion restored the sign's original signified, which could then lead to a series of questions and interpretations of the space shuttle relating to its status as a material object, its design, what it was made out of, who owned it, who had paid for it, who had built it, what it was actually going to do on the mission, how much control the crew or others at NASA had over it. At such a moment, the potential exists for the production of counterideological connotations. Rather than scientific progress, the connotation "fallibility of scientific bureaucracy" might have been attached to the space shuttle; "manifest destiny in space" might have been replaced by "waste of human life"; and "U.S. superiority over the U.S.S.R." by "basic human needs sacrificed to technocracy."

Television played a powerful role in stabilizing the meaning of the space shuttle. The networks, following the lead of the White House, almost immediately fixed on a connotation compatible with the state ideology. This connotative meaning is readable in the graphic, devised by television production staffs, that appeared in the frame with newscasters when they introduced further reports on the *Challenger*: an image of the space shuttle with a U.S. flag at half mast in the left foreground. This image helped to fix the connotation "tragic loss for a noble and patriotic cause" to the sign "space shuttle." Television produced this new connotation within hours of the event. Some of its force comes from its association with cultural and ideological codes that already enjoy wide circulation: the genre of war films, the TV news formula for reporting military casualties, the history of national heroes and martyrs. Later interpretations of the *Challenger* explosion or the space shuttle program had to compete with this one.

The study of connotation indicates the importance of understanding television signs as a historical system—one that is subject to change. Semiotics allows us to describe the process of connotation, the relationship of signs within a system, and the nature of signs themselves. But the study of connotation also directs us outside the television text and beyond the field of semiotics. We might want to study the producers of television messages (television networks, NASA, the White House press corps), the receivers of messages (the U.S. public), and the context in which signification takes place (the object of study of economics, sociology, political science, philosophy). Semiotics often leads us to questions about these things, but it cannot help us answer the questions because the study of the referent is outside its domain.

Combinations and Codes

A semiotics of television provides us with a set of problems different from those we encounter when we study written or spoken language. What is television's smallest unit of meaning? Does the set of rules governing combinations of sounds and images on U.S. television constitute a grammar? To answer these questions, it will be necessary to introduce several more terms from the special vocabulary of semiotics: *channel*, *code*, *syntagm*, *paradigm*, *langue*, and *parole*.

In language a small set of distinctive units—letters and sounds (phonemes)—are used to create more complex significations: words, sentences, paragraphs. Unlike language, television does not conveniently break down into discrete elements or building blocks of meaning; it has no equivalent of an alphabet. The closest we can come to a smallest unit is the technological definition of the frame from Herbert Zettl's widely used textbook: "A complete scanning cycle of the electron beam, which occurs every ⅟₃₀ second. It represents the smallest complete television picture unit." But images already are combinations of several different signs at once and involve a complex set of denotations and connotations. Furthermore, if we use the frame as the smallest unit of meaning, we ignore the soundtrack, where ⅟₃₀ second would not necessarily capture a meaningful sound and where speech, sound effects, and music may be occurring simultaneously. Christian Metz has given painstaking attention to this problem as it exists for the cinema. When he wrote his semiotics of the cinema, he identified five channels of communication: image, written language, voice, music, and sound effects. (In borrowing these categories, I substitute the term *graphics* for *written materials*) so as to include the logos, borders, frames, diagrams, and computer-animated images that appear so often on our television screens. In *Cinema and Language*, Metz concluded that television and cinema were "two neighboring language systems" characterized by an unusual degree of closeness. Unfortunately, he never analyzed television in the same meticulous way he did the cinema.

Before returning to the question of TV's smallest unit of meaning, it will be useful to review some recent theoretical work on how TV uses these five channels and how this usage compares to that of the cinema. It is a commonplace remark that TV is nothing but talking heads—which tells us that facial close-ups and speech are singularly important to it. Television production textbooks warn students of the need for simplicity in the image and explain how to achieve this through visual codes like symmetrical composition, color compatibility, and high key lighting. These conventions of TV production represent an *interpretation* of video technology and its limitations but are not a necessary consequence of it. Most college textbooks on television production offer us a kind of grammar of television with a conservative orientation; their aim is to educate students to observe the rules of the system of U.S. broadcast television as it is currently practiced. John Ellis has explained the logic of these visual codes thus: "Being small, low definition, subject to attention that will not be sustained, the TV image becomes jealous of its meaning. It is unwilling to waste it on details and inessentials."[11] In part, these codes dictate both how the images are produced and what is represented: on commercial U.S. television we see more shots of actors, emcees, newscasters, politicians, and commodities than of anything else. But television varies greatly under different cultural and economic systems. Public television in Europe, for example, often employs more aesthetically prestigious "cinematic" codes: long shots, less talk on the soundtrack, longer takes, an image originally shot on film.

Broadcast TV in the United States uses graphics to clarify the meaning of its images, and it does so to a much greater extent than the feature film, where graphics appear only in the beginning and ending titles sequences. Diagrams are superimposed over news or sports images to invite a quasi-scientific scrutiny of the image. Borders and frames mask out the background of already pared-down images. Words constantly appear on the screen to identify the program, the sponsoring corporation, the network or cable station, the product name, the person portrayed. Words and graphics are especially important in certain television genres such as commercials, sporting events, news programs, and game shows. Often the words on screen echo speech on the soundtrack.

In his analysis of other forms of mass communication, Roland Barthes described verbal language as always providing the definitive meaning for the image: "It is not very accurate to talk of a civilization of the image—we are still, and more than ever, a civilization of writing, writing and speech continuing to be the full terms of the informational structure."[12] In Barthes' view, verbal language is used to close down the number of possible meanings the image might have. This "anchoring" of the image by the verbal text frequently supplies a bourgeois worldview: "The anchorage may be ideological and indeed this is its principal function; the text directs the reader through the signifieds of the image, causing him to avoid some and receive others; by means of an often subtle *dispatching* it remote-controls him towards a meaning chosen in advance."[13]

John Ellis and Rick Altman have argued that the television soundtrack—speech, music, sound effects—entirely dominates the image by determining when we actually look at the screen. The soundtrack is so full, so unambiguous that we can understand television just by listening to it. Because television is a domestic appliance that we tend to have on while we are doing other things—cooking, eating, talking, caring for children, cleaning—our relationship to the television set is often that of auditor rather than viewer. Altman argues that sounds such as applause, program theme music, and the speech of announcers tend to precede the image to which they refer and serve primarily to call the viewer back to the screen: "The sound serves a value-laden editing function, identifying better than the image itself the parts of the image that are sufficiently spectacular to merit closer attention by the intermittent viewer."[14] Altman asserts that the television soundtrack acts as a lure, continually calling to us: "Hey, you, come out of the kitchen and watch this!"

From a semiotic viewpoint, one of the most important characteristics of television in general (and one that is shared by many genres) might be its tendency to use all five channels simultaneously, as television commercials typically do. This might also explain television's low status as an aesthetic text; on TV too much goes on at once and there is too much redundancy among sound and image elements for it to be "artistic." The primacy of the soundtrack violates conventional notions in cinema aesthetics about the necessity of subordinating soundtrack to image.

The high degree of repetition that exists between soundtrack and image track and between segments is mirrored at the generic level of the series, which is television's definitive form. As Umberto Eco explains the debased aesthetic status of TV: "This excess of pleasurability, repetition, lack of innovation was felt as a commercial trick (the product had to meet the expectations of its audience), not as the provocative proposal of a new (and difficult to accept) world vision. The products of mass media were equated with the products of industry insofar as they were produced *in series*, and the 'serial' production was considered as alien to the artistic invention."[15]

Because semiotics recognizes the role of combination in all verbal and visual sign production—including aesthetic production—it tends to take a less condemning view of television and therefore may have more to say about TV as a communication system than have more traditional approaches in the humanities, which tend to dismiss TV as a vulgarity. Other kinds of performances that rely on just one channel at a time (music only, or images only, or printed words only) enjoy a higher and more serious aesthetic status. In comparison to novels or silent films or oil paintings, television is a messy thing. But this is precisely why it has been of interest to semioticians: simply describing its signs presents a formidable challenge. Indeed, semiotics and structuralism have played a polemical role in universities by presenting television as a complex experience worthy of serious analysis.

Christian Metz concluded that the cinema is so different from language that we must be wary in applying linguistic theory to it. Metz discerned no smallest units in the cinema. Instead, he felt, it must be analyzed at the level of the shot, which he called its "largest minimum segment." This resembles Eco's conclusion that iconic signs such as images are not reducible to smaller units; they are already "texts"—that is, combinations of signs—and they are governed by a code that is weak compared with the grammar rules that govern language. Weak codes are flexible, change-able, and can produce an unforeseeable number of individual signs.[16]

Metz was able to explain a great deal about editing as a code of the classical Hollywood cinema, using the shot as his "minimum segment" and applying the semiotic concepts *paradigmatic* and *syntagmatic*.[17] A *syntagm* is an ordering of signs, a rule-governed combination of signs in a determined sequence. Syntagms are normally linear and must follow a strict order. A *paradigm* is a group of signs so similar that they may be substituted for one another in a syntagm. A simple sentence provides an example of a syntagm: "Rosa throws the ball." This sentence follows the grammatical rules of order (or the syntagmatic code) for English: subject/verb/direct object. We cannot change the order of the words in the sentence without making it nonsensical or unidiomatic ("Ball the Rosa throws"). The sentence can be thought of as drawing on some paradigms defined grammatically (nouns, verbs, and articles). Another paradigm could be verbs synonymous with *throw* that might be substitutable here: *pitch, hurl,* or *toss.* Of course, we change the meaning of the syntagm every time we make a substitution from a paradigm.

To take another example, a meal can be thought of as a syntagm: glass of Chianti, tossed salad, spaghetti with meat sauce, chocolate cake, coffee. This syntagm follows American dietary customs that designate the order in which dinner items will be served. This syntagmatic code is: beverage, salad, main course, dessert, coffee. Different cultures or even different families might eat these things in a different order, using a different code and producing a different syntagm—for example, coffee, spaghetti, wine, green salad, chocolate cake. Or we can imagine an idiosyncratic, unconventional code in which someone always started with dessert. A paradigm would consist of all foods that could fall under the same category, such as dessert or main course. In a restaurant, we would have many choices within each category—among types of wine (red, rosé, or white, or more elaborate listings of the year, winery, and place of origin), among different kinds of pastas (spaghetti, linguine, fettucine) and sauces (alfredo, meatless, etc.), or among an assortment of items on the dessert tray. The menu's alternatives in each category constitute the paradigmatic sets for that particular menu; the individual meal ordered is the syntagm.

Paradigms are classifications of signs; Barthes wrote that in a given syntagm the individual signs are "united in absentia" with others of the paradigm that were *not* selected.[18] The meaning of a given syntagm derives in part from the absence of other possible paradigmatic choices. By some, the meal syntagm used as an example here might be deemed unhealthy, a judgment based on the *presence* of certain ingredients (an alcoholic drink, red meat in the sauce, sugar and chocolate in the dessert, caffeine in the coffee) in our syntagm as well as the *absence* of some others (more vegetables and fruit, whole grain pasta, fruit for dessert, decaffeinated coffee, and water to drink).

For television we could argue that one paradigmatic category, based on subject-to-camera distance, consists of the class of signs we identify as close-ups; others would be head-and-shoulders shots, medium shots, long shots, and extreme long shots. Another paradigmatic category might be "all shots of Bill Cosby." Many television programs are produced inside a studio, with three cameras filming the action at once. The director calls the shots, speaking to the camera operators through headsets and asking for specific shots that may be used next: a close-up, a two-shot, a long shot. Thus the paradigm during taping consists of the shots available from cameras one, two, and three; the syntagm consists of the sequence of shots actually selected, "switched" in the control room in a definite order (only one at a time) and lasting for a specific period of time. In short, every television program consists of a set of paradigmatic and syntagmatic choices.

The concepts *paradigmatic* and *syntagmatic* may be applied to a level of organization higher than the edited sequence. They are also useful in describing the diverse types of materials one encounters in the "flow" of U.S. broadcast television. We could define as different paradigmatic sets TV commercials, trailers for upcoming programming, station identifications, program end credits, opening sequences, and the programs themselves. On a given evening on a given channel, a syntagmatic chain that selects from this paradigm might follow this order: closing credits of *The Cosby Show*; cereal commercial; Armed Forces commercial; continued closing credits of *The Cosby Show*; trailer for upcoming special; trailer for the next evening's programs; commercial for local automobile dealer. On a larger scale, we might think of an individual episode as one element in the syntagmatic chain of the chronological airing of an entire series over a period of weeks and years.

Because television in the United States is often broadcast twenty-four hours a day and because it is so discontinuous, combining many different segments of short duration, determining the beginning and end of these "syntagmatic chains" presents special problems for the TV critic. Does it make sense to analyze an individual episode apart from its place in the entire series? Can we ignore the commercial breaks when writing about the experience of watching a television program? One of the biggest differences in television programming among different countries has to do with the organization of its syntagmatic relations. Europeans often express shock when they see U.S. television for the first time; they are bewildered by the continual interruptions, the brevity of the program proper, and the plethora of various advertisements. Raymond Williams coined the term "television flow" after such an experience. On the other hand, Americans watching German public television for the first time often find the pace slow because the units that compose the daily schedule are longer in duration and fewer in number. On the evening newsbreak, for example, news readers may read copy for fifteen minutes, uninterrupted by on-the-scene accounts from other reporters, commercials, or previews. When soap operas produced in the United States, such as *Dallas*, are shown on such a noncommercial station, the precommercial "mini-climaxes" (zoom-ins for facial close-ups, music building to a crescendo) appear strange when they are followed not by a commercial but by the next scene of the program. Such an example could be described as a change in the syntagmatic chain—and a decrease in the number of paradigmatic sets used to construct it.

Syntagms and paradigms can be found in relationships between texts as well as within a single text. A generic paradigm of "TV game show" might include *Wheel of Fortune, Let's Make a Deal, The $64,000 Question, Queen for a Day, What's My Line?, Jeopardy!, Double Dare*, and *Remote Control*. A television genre critic would need to provide a rationale for this grouping and analyze similarities among the programs. A syntagmatic arrangement of game shows might be based on their sequence in programming—their place on the TV schedule, with morning shows first and evening shows later. Another kind of syntagm might be based on their chronological appearance in the course of TV broadcast history, with an older show like *Queen for a Day* preceding a more recent one like *Remote Control*. Paradigmatic associations are *synchronic*: we group signs together as though they had no history or temporal order. Syntagmatic relationships tend to be *diachronic*: they unfold in time, whether it be a matter of seconds or of years.

The meaning of every television program is influenced by syntagmatic and paradigmatic relationships. *America's Funniest Home Videos* acquires some of its meaning by its differences from (as a comedy competition using home videos) and similarities to (presence of studio audience, prize money, host) other TV game shows and contests. It also derives meaning from its position on the weekly TV schedule (some viewers may not consider it a game show because it is broadcast on Sunday evenings during prime time

—thus violating recent expectations as to when a game show will be encountered) and its place on the time line of broadcast history (it offers
itself as a new kind of programming, and television publicity is notoriously amnesiac about its own past).

Saussurean linguistics is a synchronic model for the study of language;
that is, it insists that sign systems are to be studied as they exist at one
point in time. This is partly a consequence of its working methods: one of
the principles of semiotics is that the _langue_ (the total sign system) can be
inferred from studying _parole_ (individual utterances or signs). Saussure
argued that one can learn the whole system from an individual case. And it
is true that verbal language—as a system of paradigmatic and syntagmatic
rules—changes very slowly. Although the vocabulary might be somewhat
different, a Shakespeare play written four hundred years ago is still "readable" today as an English-language _parole_. Semiotics was founded, then, on
a static model of the sign. Some of the gravest shortcomings of semiotics as
a theory are a consequence of this: it inherits the tendency to ignore change,
to divorce the sign from its referent, and to exclude the sender and receiver.

These characteristics limit the usefulness of semiotics in the study of
television. Because television is based on weaker codes than those that
govern verbal language, it is, as a system of communication, unstable; it is
constantly undergoing modification and operates by conventions rather
than by hard-and-fast rules. In semiotic terms, communication involves
encoding and _decoding_. Each _parole_ (instance of communication) is _encoded_
in a particular communication system (written Spanish, Braille, Morse
code). The message is _decoded_ by someone who is competent in that particular code. Unlike verbal language, with which any user of the system
can produce meaningful utterances, television is a communication system
to which most of us have access only as viewers and listeners, not as
producers/encoders. Historically, television production has been for the
most part restricted to a specialized, professional elite, those with access
to costly technologies and large and highly specialized division of labor.
Public-access television and home videos employ different conventions of
sign production and require different decoding skills from their audiences.

Structuralism

Structuralism has proven a very useful tool in studying television because, as a method, it characteristically sets aside questions of aesthetic
worth or value to concentrate on the internal rules for the production of tele-

vision meaning. As developed in linguistics and anthropology, structuralism sought to understand a language or a culture on its own terms and urged the analyst to put aside judgment and evaluation. Journalistic television criticism has often been so interested in critical dismissal that careless generalizations and faulty descriptions have been the rule rather than the exception. The application of structuralist methods has made television criticism more rigorous, more accurate in describing its object, and less evaluative. As do semioticians, structuralists study things synchronically and are interested in the system as a whole more than in particular manifestations of it. Rather than studying forms of language, as semioticians normally do, structuralists study the way that a cultural system produces a set of texts or signs, which could be anything from folktales to kinship relations to dietary rules. Characteristically, a structuralist analysis proposes binary oppositions such as individual/community, male/female, nature/culture, or mind/matter and argues that every element within the system derives its meaning from its relationship to these categories. A structuralist analysis often leads to a description of the worldview of a culture—its organizing principles for making sense of relationships among people who live in the same society and between people and their material environments.

The work of Robert Hodge and David Tripp on children's animated series provides a good example of the usefulness of semiotics and structuralism in the analysis of television, as well as the problems and further questions raised by such methods. Hodge and Tripp argue that cartoons— widely considered one of the lowest forms of television—are surprisingly complex. The reason children are fascinated by cartoons is not because they have been turned into television zombies but because they are understandably engaged by the complex blend of aesthetic, narrative, visual, verbal, and ideological codes at work in them. Though cartoons are characterized by a great deal of repetition and redundancy, Hodge and Tripp argue that their subject matter and their way of conveying it is complicated stuff. Children use cartoons to decipher the most important structures in their culture. To make this point, Hodge and Tripp analyze the titles sequence of the unexceptional 1978 cartoon *Fangface*, an animated series about the adventures of werewolf Sherman Fangsworth and his teenage companions Kim, Biff, and Pugsie. Generically, the series was based primarily on a comedy-mystery type of story (sometimes called the "Let's get out of here" adventure formula) found in many examples of cartoons from *Scooby Doo* (1969–80) to *Slimer and the Real Ghostbusters* (1986–).

Hodge and Tripp base their analysis on a single twenty-minute cartoon. This starting point is significant in that it is the typical founding gesture of the semiotician to gather a small, manageable, and synchronic (contemporaneous) text or set of texts for analysis and, using the text as a basis, try to establish the conventions governing the larger system (in this case the series *Fangface* and the larger system of children's animated television). Compared with other studies of children's television, Hodge and Tripp's work seems startling new. For, in fact, cartoons have only occasionally been subjected to any kind of literary analysis, and never to the painstaking detail Hodge and Tripp expend on *Fangface*. Instead, child psychologists and media sociologists have tended to use the methods of quantitative content analysis to "measure" the children's cartoon during a fixed block of hours in the broadcasting schedule.

Content analysts count how many acts of violence occur, how many male and female characters there are, how many minority characters appear, how often villains speak with a foreign accent, and so on. The virtue of a structuralist/semiotic analysis in this case, then, is that it focuses on both syntagmatic and paradigmatic relations. These combinations and structures are usually lost in content analysis, in which the meanings of discrete units of information within a television program are not thought to depend on the context in which they appear. This is another important principle of structuralism: the meaning of each sign within a text derives from its relationship to other signs in the same system. As Terry Eagleton puts it: "Structuralism proper contains a distinctive doctrine . . . the belief that the individual units of any system have meaning only by virtue of their relations to one another. . . . [Y]ou become a card-carrying structuralist only when you claim that the meaning of each image is wholly a matter of its relation to the other[s]."[19]

In this essay, I will limit myself to recounting Hodge and Tripp's discussion of the fifty-second opening of *Fangface*, which they describe as "highly compressed, using rapid, small-scale syntagms." In most cases, these openings will be "the most salient memory children will have" of a program and its characters. In the first image, Fangface appears wearing a red hat. He licks his lips and smiles. Hodge and Tripp analyze the image this way:

> The picture itself is a syntagm, consisting of a face of an animal with a hat. How do we categorize the two elements, to make up a meaning? Or what categories are implied by meanings that we assign it? The hat looks odd, on Fangface's head. To express the oddness, we can point to the animal nature of Fangface, and the human, cultural quality of the hat. . . . In the paradigmatic dimension the options are a pair of categories *nature/culture* (or *animal/human*, which is a more specific instance of the broader pair), which is the source of the im-

age's meaning. We can translate this meaning into words—Fangface is both animal and human, both nature and culture. This meaning, of course, also underlies the concept of a werewolf. Fangface's hat is odd in another way: it faces backwards. Here one set of paradigmatic categories concerns the position of a hat. This pair backwards/forwards constitutes a single structure. Forwards signals, among other things, conformity, normality; backwards, therefore, signals the opposite: abnormality, non-conformity.[20]

In this passage, Hodge and Tripp have introduced the binary opposition (nature/culture) and proceeded to organize the elements of the television image into paradigmatic sets. Even at this early point, they acknowledge that their description of this one image is partial and incomplete. They have not discussed Fangface's tooth (single like a baby tooth, but big and powerful like adult permanent teeth), or the color of his hat (red, contrasting with other primary colors and with brown, a secondary color).

Hodge and Tripp continue with a description of the next three shots, which follow a bolt of lightning and the title "Fangface":

The sequence is clearly organized by a movement from outside to inside, from nature (as a dangerous threatening force) to culture, the house and the bassinet and the baby protected within by both, . . . starting with a shot of the moon (outside, nature) then showing the

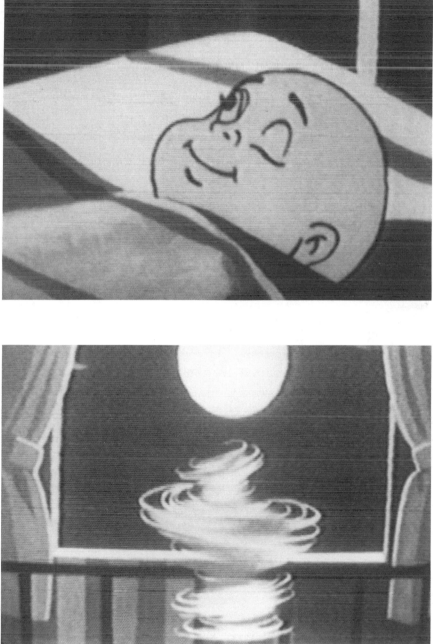

baby at the window (not threatened by nature). The baby spins rapidly, like a whirlwind (nature) or like a machine (culture), and turns
into a baby werewolf (nature). However, this werewolf is not a threatening figure. It has a cute expression, and wears a nappy (human
culture). Then, with the soundtrack saying "only the sun (nature) can
change him back to normal," we see a picture of the sun with alongside it the words "Sunshine Laundry."[21]

A zoom-out reveals that the sun that changes Fangface back into Sherman Fangsworth is not the real sun but a picture of the sun on a box of
laundry detergent in the kitchen. To Hodge and Tripp, this signals another ambiguous rendering of the nature/culture split, in this case between the sun belonging to nature—one of the stars—and the sun used
for the purposes of a commercial trademark and located in the domestic
sphere (culture). So far, Hodge and Tripp have covered only the first nine
shots of the titles sequence. This is one of the perennial problems plagu-
ing the semiotician, especially the semiotician of television, in which each
segment, each image, can produce an enormous (some would say prepos-
terous) amount of analytical text.

Hodge and Tripp's analysis of the verbal track is more concise. The
voice-over in this opening sequence explains: "Every 400 years a baby
werewolf is born into the Fangsworth family, and so when the moon shined

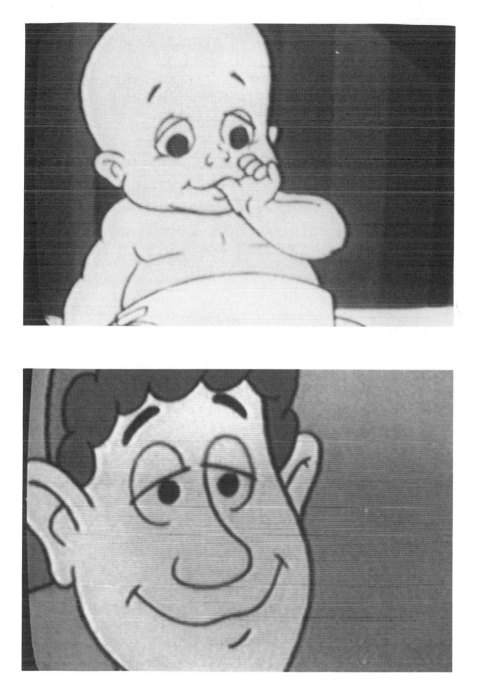

on little Sherman Fangsworth he changed into Fangface. A werewolf! Only the sun can change him back to normal. And so little Fangs grew up and teamed with three daring teenagers, Kim, Biff, and Pugsie, and together they find danger, excitement and adventure." The verbal track is used for conveying time, causal relationships, and exposition—for example, the tale of Fangface's origins. Following Barthes, Hodge and Tripp find that the verbal channel anchors the meaning of the visual. But Hodge and Tripp note that even the verbal track offers some "interesting illogicalities." They focus on the use of "so" to suggest a causality where none logically exists between being a werewolf and growing up and teaming up with "three daring teenagers." However, most viewers would never notice this contradiction unless the words of the *Fangface* opening were printed out for them to read. The words alone do not reveal the strong parodic connotation of the "voice of God" style in which the opening is read and the announcer's voice—deep, booming, masculine, and middle-aged.

Despite the length and detail of many structuralist analyses, critics of the method have accused structuralists of ignoring stray meanings in the text and of closing off potential interpretations. The organization of all the various elements here into one class or the other, nature or culture, is an example of this flaw. But Hodge and Tripp do not impose a singular, unifying meaning in the television opening: "The pattern throughout this sequence is built up of different arrangements of primary opposition: nature-culture; human-animal. The result is not a single consistent message about the relations between the two. Sometimes nature is seen as threatening, sometimes as compatible with culture. Fangface is the focus of both ambiguity and ambivalence."[22]

Is Hodge and Tripp's analysis relevant to other cartoon examples? Does it have a usefulness beyond the specific example of *Fangface*? It may be helpful to attempt to extend this kind of analysis to a more recent example of the television animated series, *Teenage Mutant Ninja Turtles*. In the series opening sequence, the main characters are revealed to be a group of four teenagers, as in *Fangface*. The turtles do not undergo any physical transformations (from human to werewolf); rather, they personify the combination of nature and culture. The turtles are green amphibians "in a half-shell" (nature), but they are also mutants who speak, walk on two feet, bear the names of Renaissance painters, and wear clothing (culture). Each of them wears a masklike scarf over his eyes (in blue, red, orange, and purple) and matching sweatbands around his knees, wrists, and ankles. Each also wears a belt around the waist that secures different martial arts weapons (threatening), and the theme song informs us that they are a "fear-

some fighting team" against the evil Shredder. Yet they have big cute eyes and are not yet grown up (safe). The theme song repeatedly offers the combination of *Ninja* and *teenager* (as in the line, "Splinter taught them to be Ninja teens"), a paradox that emphasizes the oppositions of old/young, discipline/rebellion. *Teenage Mutant Ninja Turtles* seems to reinterpret the nature/culture split as freewheeling, nonconformist American adolescence (nature) versus strict, conformist Japanese adulthood (culture).

Hodge and Tripp find that the nature/culture axis is a highly significant one in the world of *Fangface*, and our brief analysis suggests that it might be applied to *Teenage Mutant Ninja Turtles* as well. Lévi-Strauss found that the same binary opposition underlay the mythological systems of South American tribal cultures. Is nature/culture a binary opposition so basic to narrative that it will always figure in the structuralist's findings? Are structuralism's categories predetermined for the critic by the body of work that has gone before? Or are they so general that the same categories will be found everywhere, in all kinds of texts, thus becoming too general to be valuable as a critical tool? The answers to these questions seem to be both yes and no.

There is a suspicious resemblance between Lévi-Strauss's findings and those of Hodge and Tripp, despite a great divergence in historical and cultural settings. But one can also look at the larger field of children's literature, animated television, and commercial culture and find that the nature/culture division, or the blurring of the two, is a central characteristic of children's media. Animal characters who dress in clothes, talk, and walk on two feet have appeared with ever greater frequency in children's literature throughout the twentieth century: all of them can be seen as negotiating in some ways the nature/culture, animal/human oppositions. Television animation is especially fond of such characters, and they are often treated by journalists and experts on childhood as a new, bizarre, and grossly commercialized example of collusion between toy manufacturers and the television industry. Teenage Mutant Ninja Turtles are just the most recent example.

Many of the licensed characters that proliferated in children's television in the 1980s lend themselves to a structuralist analysis using the nature/culture pair: My Little Ponies (horses in pastel colors and makeup); Thundercats (tigers, lions, and cheetahs operating high-tech spacecraft); Ghostbusters (the spirit world tamed by the technical gadgetry of ecto-blasters and proton packs). But how do we explain specific manifestations of the binary opposition? The figures of the werewolf in *Fangface* and Splinter (who is simultaneously a Japanese Ninja master and a rat) in

Teenage Mutant Ninja Turtles are products of different historical moments and different racial ideologies. Does the use of the binary opposition nature/culture to analyze these cartoons obscure important differences by being too universalist?

Terry Eagleton has remarked that one of the primary drawbacks to structuralist research is that it is "hair-raisingly unhistorical." To take just one example, the history of children's television and animation lend some important information for an understanding of *Fangface*, although Hodge and Tripp, like most structuralists, do not concern themselves with this context. The animated television series found on Saturday morning television and throughout syndication today are very different from "cartoons" in the sense of animated motion picture shorts by Disney and Hanna Barbera —Donald Duck, Bugs Bunny, or Tom and Jerry. A historical approach could trace these important changes: "limited" animation techniques (fixed backdrops and restricted character movement) were developed in the 1950s for animated television series like *Fangface* in an effort to cut time and costs; these new series then adapted storytelling conventions from the television series and the comic book. Interviews with children suggest how important it is to understand television in such "intertextual" frames. Many children, on seeing *Fangface* for the first time, whispered "Scooby Doo" and "Incredible Hulk" to one another during the opening sequence—

they immediately recognized the show's similarity to other television texts.

A historical approach to the animated television series would also allow us to contextualize and explain the kinds of changes that can be observed in different series from the 1970s to the 1990s, between series like *Fangface* and *Scooby Doo* and contemporary examples like *Teenage Mutant Ninja Turtles*. In the 1970s, the groups of four adventurers were usually made up primarily of human beings, with a token female making one of the four. By the 1990s, many programs had few humans and no females among the group. The settings changed from the small town and the countryside to Manhattan and Tokyo. The villains have been transformed from the cold war's mad scientists, complete with Russian or German accents, into Japanese technocrats; the generic references are no longer to the mystery story and horror film but to the martial arts movie, although both the series discussed here retain many of the conventions of science fiction. All of these comparisons need to be pursued by someone studying the cartoon from the perspective of genre criticism or narrative or ideological analysis. If we pursue a structuralist analysis alone, we might simply arrange the different elements in *Fangface* and *Teenage Mutant Ninja Turtles* into nature/culture oppositions and conclude that they are very similar, whereas a critic better versed in the history of the animated series and the different cultural and political contexts in which they were made might see the differences between the types of series and be better able to explain these differences.

Post-structuralism

The classical structuralist does not look beyond the text to "real" readers, viewers, and listeners to verify whether others find the same kinds of meanings that s/he does. Television studies, over the past fifteen years, has become increasingly preoccupied with this omission and with other limitations of semiotics and structuralism. Although they continue to use the concepts of text, signification, and code, TV scholars have also sought to address the problem in various other ways. Hodge and Tripp's larger study, which includes many different kinds of audience studies in addition to textual analysis, reveals the influence of *post-structuralism*. For example, they showed the *Fangface* episode to groups of children, held discussions with them about the episode, and compared the children's verbal and nonverbal responses to their own semiotic analysis. In another study, they asked teachers to keep a diary recording the (rather infrequent) instances when children mentioned television at school. In the first study, Hodge and Tripp acknowledge the role of the unconscious in shaping the children's and their own interpretations of the text. In the second, they recognize that meanings are influenced by the social institutions—in this case, school—that control and censor children in certain ways.

Throughout their work, Hodge and Tripp recognize that their own analysis is partial and is formed by their own position as adults, academics, and men and by their own subjectivities. In this, they part company with the neutral and objective voice of the semiotician and insist on the necessity of being self-critical about their research. Hodge and Tripp freely admit that they are imposing a logical, rational organization of meanings on the text and, in doing so, are likely to exclude other possible meanings. The meanings they find in Fangface may not be thought of as "residing" in the text at all but are, rather, a product of their own interaction with the text. They allow for the options of chaotic or idiosyncratic meanings in the children's decoding of *Fangface*, as well as for the possibility that children will ignore many elements in the cartoon simply because they are irrelevant to them.[23]

Semiotic analysis tends to "neaten up" the texts it studies: some elements are picked out for significance and others are excluded, repressed. Post-structuralism emphasizes the slippage between signifier and signified —between one sign and the next, between one context and the next —while emphasizing that meaning is always situated, specific to a given context. What gets excluded in a structuralist analysis, and why, has been the subject of such post-structuralists as Jacques Derrida and Julia Kristeva. Theories of psychoanalysis and of ideology, under the influence of post-structuralism, focus on the gaps and fissures, the structuring absences and the incoherencies, in a text like *Fangface*.

Hodge and Tripp are not ready to discard signification altogether or to argue that "anything goes" in interpreting cartoons. They go on to study *Fangface* through empirical tests in which they screen the cartoon opening for children and discuss their understanding of it. They are well aware of the limited and partial nature of the responses that children (and adults) will make about television: how these will be created by the context—the classroom, the home, the laboratory—in which the children are speaking; how gender, race, and age differences within the group will influence the discussion. This brings us to another important insight that Hodge and Tripp adapt from the post-structural critique. We know television through talking and writing about it, through *discourse*. Emile Benveniste used the term discourse to refer to "every utterance assuming a speaker and a hearer, and in the speaker, the intention of influencing the other in some way."[24]

In its current usage, discourse carries the stronger implication of speech governed by social, material, and historical forces, which disallow certain things from being said or even thought while forcing us to say certain other things. The term has been used by scholars frequently throughout the 1980s, often in a rather vague way. Many scholars use it in Michel Foucault's sense to refer to a set of complex, multilayered texts that determine and limit what can be said or known about certain subjects and therefore serve particular interests in the power structure of society. Foucault focused on questions of power and knowledge in various discourses—many of them scientific ones—about sexuality, mental illness, and criminality.

In society various discourses about television compete with one another; each is informed by and represents a specific set of interests. For example, in writing about children's television, competing and contradictory discourses are produced by industry producers, such consumer protection groups as Action for Children's Television, and academic "childhood professionals" such as educators, pediatricians, psychologists, and social workers. Each of these groups contributes to a discourse that allows certain things to be said and rules out other things—or makes them unimaginable. The discourse of child experts usually assumes a certain normative view of what children are like (naive, impressionable, uncritical), of what television should do (help children learn to read and to understand math and science), of what is an appropriate way to spend leisure time (being physically and mentally active, *doing* things), and of what television viewing is (passive and mindless). These ideas derive from larger medical, religious, and social science bodies of thought.[25]

Discourse is not "free speech." It is not a perfect expression of the speaker's intentions. Indeed, we cannot think of communicative intentions as predating the constraints of language at all. When Hodge and Tripp interviewed children about *Fangface* and other television shows, they found, in analyzing videotapes and transcripts of the discussion, that in many instances boys silenced girls, adults silenced children, and interviewers silenced subjects—through nonverbal censure of some remarks (glances, laughter, grimacing), by wording questions and responses in certain ways, or by failures to comprehend each other's terms. We can never think about the meaning of television outside of these contexts. As Hodge and Tripp put it, "Verbal language is also the main mediator of meaning. It is the form in which meanings gain public and social form, and through discussion are affected by the meanings of others."[26] They remind us that the entire topic of children and television is circumscribed by spoken and written discourse. No matter how complete the textual analysis of television, no matter how well designed the audience study, it "would still be partial because it would still be located in particular social and historical circumstances."[27]

Perhaps the best way to think of semiotics and structuralism is as a kind of useful exercise for making sure that we know our object before venturing out into other models of study. As a descriptive method, it makes sure we have spent sufficient time with a text before moving on to a series of questions regarding audience activity and the play of television as discourse.

Semiotics frequently speaks of a text as though its meanings were pre-given and would be understood in precisely the same way by everyone. At worst, it operates as though all meanings are translatable and predictable through the work of a gifted, scientifically minded semiotician, whose own unconscious and subjectivity have no effect on the analysis produced. Structuralism challenges traditions in Western philosophy that are based on the notion of the individual as a transcendent, self-present, free agent who exists apart from any social or ideological constraints. Contrary to this position, structuralism is based on a model in which individuals are at birth subjected to the structures of culture and society. However, the flaw in the structuralist model, as post-structuralists have been quick to point out, is that it is inevitably idealist in the philosophical sense that ideas are seen as relatively independent, primary forces that determine reality, rather than as the products of human beings in particular material circumstances. In semiotics and structuralism, signification becomes a kind of pure mental activity divorced from the material world. The post-structuralists have emphasized the contingency of meanings as derived from cultural texts such as those of television, the instability of the signifieds linked to signs, and the importance of the unconscious "structured like a language" in the formation of the subject.

Semiotics is extremely useful in its attempt to describe precisely how television produces meaning and its insistence on the conventionality of the signs. For if signs are conventional, they are also changeable. But semiotics remains silent on the question of how to change a sign system. Stubbornly restricting itself to the text, it cannot explain television economics, production, history, or the audience. Still, semiotics and structuralism, even with their liabilities, have raised questions about theories of gender, of the subject, of psychoanalysis, of ideology—and about the practice of all cultural criticism—that have been usefully applied to television in a wide range of critical practices discussed in the chapters that follow.

NOTES

1. Terry Eagleton, *Literary Theory: An Introduction* (Minneapolis: University of Minnesota Press, 1983), p. 100.

2. Fredric Jameson, *The Prison House of Language: A Critical Account of Structuralism and Russian Formalism* (Princeton, N.J.: Princeton University Press, 1972), p. 105. In a similar vein, Raymond Williams discusses the borrowing of the term *structural* from the sciences and the problems this created (*Keywords* [New York: Oxford University Press, 1976], pp. 254–55).

3. Umberto Eco, *A Theory of Semiotics* (Bloomington: Indiana University Press, 1976), p. 16.

4. Ibid., p. 17 (Eco's italics).

5. See the description of television coverage at the White House in Thomas Whiteside, "Standups," *The New Yorker*, 2 December 1985, pp. 81–113.

6. Margaret Morse, "The Television News Personality and Credibility," in *Studies in Entertainment: Critical Approaches to Mass Culture*, ed. Tania Modleski (Bloomington: Indiana University Press, 1986), pp. 55–79.

7. Eco, *Theory*, p. 7.

8. Roland Barthes, "Myth Today," in *The Barthes Reader*, ed. Susan Sontag (New York: Hill and Wang, 1982), pp. 93–149.

9. Herbert Zettl, *Television Production Handbook* (Belmont, Calif.: Wadsworth Publishing Company, 1984), p. 596.

10. Richard Dyer makes this point in "Entertainment and Utopia," in *Movies and Methods II*, ed. Bill Nichols (Berkeley: University of California Press, 1987), pp. 226–27.

11. John Ellis, *Visible Fictions: Cinema, Television, Video* (London: Routledge and Kegan Paul, 1982), p. 130.

12. Roland Barthes, "Rhetoric of the Image," in *Image/Music/Text*, trans. Stephen Heath (New York: Hill and Wang, 1977), p. 38.

13. Ibid., p. 40.

14. Rick Altman, "Television/Sound," in Modleski, *Studies in Entertainment*, pp. 39–54.

15. Umberto Eco, "Innovation and Repetition: Between Modern and Post-Modern Aesthetics," *Daedalus* 114 (Fall 1985): 162.

16. Eco, *Theory*, p. 214.

17. Christian Metz, *Film Language: A Semiotics of the Cinema*, trans. Michael Taylor (New York: Oxford University Press, 1974), p. 106.

18. See Roland Barthes, *Elements of Semiology*, trans. Annette Lavers and Colin Smith (New York: Hill and Wang, 1968), pp. 58–59.

19. Eagleton, *Literary Theory*, p. 94.

20. Robert Hodge and David Tripp, *Children and Television: A Semiotic*

Approach, pp. 26–27.

21. Ibid., pp. 26–27.

22. Ibid., p. 28.

23. Morley makes this point, which has been increasingly taken up by cultural studies, in *Family Television: Cultural Power and Domestic Leisure* (London: Comedia, 1986), p. 30.

24. Emile Benveniste, *Problems in General Linguistics* (Coral Gables, Fla.: University of Miami, 1971), p. 209.

25. See Ellen Seiter, "Sold Separately: Aspects of Children's Consumer Culture" (tentative title), publication forthcoming.

26. Hodge and Tripp, *Children and Television*, p. 71.

27. Ibid., p. 27.

FOR FURTHER READING

The secondary literature is a good place to start in this difficult field. See Terence Hawkes, *Structuralism and Semiotics* (Berkeley: University of California Press, 1977); Terry Eagleton, *Literary Theory: An Introduction* (Minneapolis: University of Minnesota Press, 1983); or Rosalind Coward and John Ellis, *Language and Materialism* (London: Routledge and Kegan Paul, 1977). After that one might tackle some of the primary texts: Roland Barthes, *Elements of Semiology*, trans. Annette Lavers and Colin Smith (New York: Hill and Wang, 1968); Umberto Eco, *A Theory of Semiotics* (Bloomington: Indiana University Press, 1976); and Ferdinand de Saussure, *Course in General Linguistics*, trans. Wade Baskin (New York: McGraw-Hill, 1966.) A useful introduction and a couple of brief, primary texts by Claude Lévi-Strauss and Jacques Lacan may be found in Jacques Ehrmann, ed., *Structuralism* (New York: Anchor Books, 1970).

The problem of verbal and visual codes in media is taken up by Roland Barthes in *Image/Music/Text*, trans. Stephen Heath (New York: Hill and Wang, 1977). Barthes' entertaining observations about popular culture are collected in *Mythologies*, trans. Annette Lavers (New York: Hill and Wang, 1972). Umberto Eco has written specifically about television in "Interpreting Serials," in *The Limits of Interpretation* (Bloomington: Indiana University Press, 1990), pp. 83–100, and in a number of essays entitled "Reports from the Global Village," in *Faith in Fakes* (London: Secker and Warburg, 1986), pp. 133–80. E. H. Gombrich supplies invaluable background on the importance of nonrepresentational codes in images in *Art and Illusion* (Princeton, N.J.: Princeton University Press, 1972).

A good introduction to semiotics as applied to television criticism may be found in John Fiske and John Hartley, *Reading Television* (London: Methuen, 1978); the differences between broadcast television and film are provocatively described in John Ellis, *Visible Fictions: Cinema, Television, Video* (London: Routledge and Kegan Paul, 1982). An exhaustive application of semiotics to television that also offers an excellent discussion of its limitations is Robert Hodge and David Tripp, *Children and Television: A Semiotic Approach* (Stanford, Calif.: Stanford University Press, 1986); Hodge and Tripp's work is highly recommended reading for everyone, even those uninterested in the specific topic of children's television. Another useful book is Roger Silverstone, *The Message of Television: Myth and Narrative in Contemporary Culture* (London: Heinemann, 1981).

Television scholars John Fiske, Margaret Morse, and David Morley consistently have used semiotics and structuralism in their work. Fiske's "Moments of Television: Neither the Text nor the Audience," in *Remote Control: Television, Audiences and Cultural Power*, ed. Ellen Seiter, Hans Borchers, Gabriele Kreutzner, and Eva-Maria Warth (London: Routledge, 1989), pp. 56–78, discusses the difficulties in defining television as a text as well as the opportunities for "unlimited semiosis." Margaret Morse offers detailed formalist analyses of various nonfiction television genres in "Talk, Talk, Talk—the Space of Discourse in Television," *Screen* 26, no. 2 (1985): 2–15. David Morley links semiotics and structuralist analysis of television news to the audience members in *The "Nationwide" Audience: Structure and Decoding* (London: British Film Institute, 1980); "Texts, Readers, Subjects," in *Culture, Media, Language*, ed. Stuart Hall, Dorothy Hobson, Andrew Lowe, and Paul Willis (London: Hutchinson, 1980); and *"The 'Nationwide' Audience*: A Critical Postscript," *Screen Education* 39 (Summer 1981): 3–15.

To date, film has been analyzed more carefully by semioticians than has television; some central works that may prove useful are Christian Metz, *Film Language: A Semiotics of the Cinema*, trans. Michael Taylor (New York: Oxford University Press, 1974); and *Language and Cinema*, trans. Donna Umiker-Sebeok (The Hague: Mouton, 1974); Jurij Lotman, *Semiotics of Cinema*, Michigan Slavic Contributions no. 5 (Ann Arbor: University of Michigan Press, 1976). Bill Nichols relates semiotic issues to ideological analysis in *Ideology and the Image* (Bloomington: Indiana University Press, 1981). A lucid case study of a film that uses structuralist methods and attempts to combine these with a historical, Marxist, and psychoanalytic interpretation is Charles Eckert, "Anatomy of a Proletarian Film: Warner's *Marked Woman*," in *Movies and Methods II*, ed. Bill Nichols (Berkeley: University of California Press, 1987). Reading Eckert's response to the critics of this article and his own second thoughts about the method can give us a sense of the reception of structuralism by U.S. film scholars in the 1970s (see "Shall We Deport Lévi-Strauss?," *Film Quarterly* 17, no. 3 [Spring 1974]: 63–65).

2 : NARRATIVE THEORY AND TELEVISION

sarah kozloff

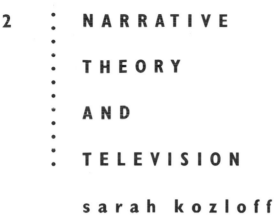hereas our ancestors used to listen to tall-tale spinners, read penny dreadfuls, tune in to radio dramas, or rush to the local bijou each Saturday, now we primarily satisfy our ever-constant yearning for stories by gathering around the flickering box in the living room. Television is the principal storyteller in contemporary American society.

But what kind of storyteller is it? In what ways are stories presented on television similar to those transmitted through other media? How can approaching television as a narrative art deepen our understanding of individual shows or of the medium as a whole? How can looking at television help us with our research on narrative itself?

The same decades that have brought the invention, birth, and increasing maturity of broadcast television have also played host to the development of a new critical field, *narratology*, or more simply, *narrative theory*. This theory has its roots in the Soviet Union of the late 1920s, specifically in the work of the Russian Formalists and Vladimir Propp; it has since been fed by the studies of a diverse, international group of linguists, semiologists, anthropologists, folklorists, literary critics, and film theorists. Although several people have made outstanding contributions, the field does not rest on the work or the authority of any founding figure(s). Moreover, although the practitioners come from different disciplines and study various questions in a diverse selection of texts, the field has been (comparatively) free of heated dispute. Topics have been raised, sifted, argued, and tested until a general outline of narrative structure and process has emerged and won widespread—if not absolute—consensus.

Many of the major studies of narrative were published during the 1960s and 1970s; by the early 1980s the field could be synthesized and disseminated to a wider audience. The most recent work in narrative theory is more in the nature of refinement and extension than of discovery or creation.[1] Although many questions remain to be settled (and some once-settled issues are now being rethought) narrative theory is well established as a field of academic study.

There are several books (to which I am deeply indebted) that summarize the fundamentals of the theory.[2] I hope that the interested reader will consult such texts for more detailed explanations of the key concepts and more accurate discussion of the ambiguities than is possible here. My task is to use the fruits of this theory to focus on the nature of television narratives.

First, however, we must understand the limitations of narrative theory as a tool. Because this field is concerned with general mappings of narrative structure, it is inescapably and unapologetically "formalist" (that is, it concentrates on describing or analyzing the text's intrinsic formal parameters), and it is up to the individual practitioner to use the insights gained about narrative structure to analyze a text's content or ideology. Similarly, because narrative theory concentrates on the text itself, it leaves to other critical methods questions about where the story comes from (for instance, the history, organization, and regulation of the broadcast industry, the influence of the networks, or the contributions of individual professionals) and the myriad effects (psychological or sociological) that the text has upon its audience. Later chapters will demonstrate critical approaches that fill in these large voids.

Yet, at the same time, we must not underestimate the importance of narrative theory as a critical vantage point, because American television is as saturated in narrative as a sponge in a swimming pool. Most television shows—the sitcom, the action series, the cartoon, the soap opera, the miniseries, the made-for-TV movie—are narrative texts.[3] Moreover, programs that are not ostensibly fictional entertainments, but rather have other goals such as description, education, or argumentation, tend to use narrative as a means to their ends.[4] On the evening news, an unembellished recital of the latest economic figures is merely informative, but the story of the Congressional battle over passage of a hotly debated bill is just that: *a story*.[5] A commercial for pain relievers may rely on comparison and argument, or an ad for a car may be abstract and descriptive, but a vast number of advertisements offer a compressed narrative exemplifying the products' beneficial effects. Music videos often enact the storyline of the song's lyrics. Nature documentaries tend to follow the story of the animal's life cycle or of the seasonal progression in a geographic area.

The only television formats that consistently eschew narrative are those that are highly structured according to their own alternate rules: game shows, exercise shows, news conferences, talk shows, musical performances, sports contests. Yet even in such cases, narrative may infiltrate: football games, for instance, can be seen as stories of one team's triumph and the other's defeat, narrated by the sports announcers.

Thus, narratives are not only the dominant type of text on television, but narrative structure is, to a large extent, the portal or grid through which even nonnarrative television must pass. The world that we see on television is a world that has been shaped by the rules of this discourse. It well behooves us, then, to examine its rules carefully.

To this end, we learn from narrative theory that every narrative can be split into two parts: the *story*, that is, "what happens to whom," and the *discourse*, that is, "how the story is told." (Please keep in mind that this is an artificial or "theoretical" distinction.)[6] To recognize television's specificity, I believe we need to add a third layer, *schedule*, that is, "how the story and discourse are affected by the text's placement within the larger discourse of the station's schedule." Let us begin with the innermost layer.

Story

Shlomith Rimmon-Kenan defines a story as "a series of events arranged in chronological order." She correspondingly defines an event as "a change from one state of affair to another."[7] Tzvetan Todorov uses different terms, but he is talking about the same phenomenon when he defines a minimal narrative as a move from equilibrium through disequilibrium to a new equilibrium.[8] For example, a United Airlines commercial presents a mother and young daughter in loving embrace (equilibrium). The mother leaves the girl at a day care center and flies off to New York for a business meeting (disequilibrium). The mother flies back in time to pick up the daughter at the end of the day (new equilibrium). Rimmon-Kenan's and Todorov's definitions do not quite make explicit the fact that events cannot occur in a vacuum—they must be enacted by a given set of characters or *actants* in a certain setting. Seymour Chatman groups characters and setting under the label *existents*. Together, events and existents are the basic components out of which stories are made.

Out in the "real world," things may happen totally at random, but in stories they are linked by temporal succession (X occurred, then Y occurred) and/or causality (because Y occurred, Z occurred). Television, like all other narrative forms, takes advantage of the viewer's almost unquenchable habit of inferring causality from succession. For example, a simple commercial for NyQuil (a patent cold remedy) first shows a man and a woman together in a double bed, both snuffling and sneezing. We understand them to be husband and wife, afflicted with horrible colds. Without dialogue, the woman takes some NyQuil from her bedside table and offers it to the man; he declines and takes another medication. A title reads LATER; then we see the woman fast asleep while the husband is still miserably awake. Note that the commercial links these two scenes merely by an indicator of temporal succession, but the advertisers know full well that the viewer will make a causal connection: the wife is sleeping peacefully *because* she took NyQuil.

Not all story events are of equal importance. As Roland Barthes was the first to point out,[9] one can determine a hierarchy between the events that actively contribute to the story's progression and/or open up options (Chatman labels these *kernels*) and those events that are more routine or minor (Chatman's *satellites*). In the NyQuil commercial, the important, kernel event is the decision to take the medication: "sitting up in bed," "reaching for the bottle," and "unscrewing the cap" may be events, but they are minor satellites.

In stories, events do not progress randomly. For millennia, one of the tasks of critics has been the discovery and description of stories' underlying structures. It was Aristotle who first pointed out the seemingly banal but actually vital fact that the plots of tragedies have a beginning, a middle, and an end.[10] Over a century ago, German playwright and novelist Gustav Freytag elaborated on this insight by describing the typical "dramatic triangle": well-made plays begin with an expository sequence setting out the state of affairs, rise through various twists and turns of complicating actions to a climax, and then fall off in intensity to a coda that delineates the resolution of the crises and the new state of affairs.[11] With the exception of serials (to be discussed later), Freytag might have been describing American television.

Noting that stories often share an overall arc of development is one thing, but arguing that story events fall into predictable, specific patterns is another. In his pathbreaking study, *Morphology of the Folktale*, first published in 1928, Vladimir Propp studied a group of Russian fairy tales. He invites the reader to compare such events as "1. A tsar gives an eagle to a hero. The eagle carries the hero away to another kingdom. . . . 2. An old man gives Súčenko a horse. The horse carries Súčenko away to another kingdom."[12] Obviously, something uncannily similar is going on here.

Propp concludes that although different tales may feature different characters, these characters fall into one of seven types of dramatic personae: hero, villain, donor, dispatcher, false hero, helper, and princess and her father. Moreover, despite surface variability, the actions of these personae serve identifiable purposes in terms of their "function" in moving the story along. Propp thus was able to formulate the following "laws":

1. Functions of characters serve as stable, constant elements in a tale, independent of how and by whom they are fulfilled;
2. The number of functions known to the fairy tale is limited;
3. The sequence of functions is always identical; and
4. All fairy tales are of one type in regard to their structure.[13]

Propp compiled a list of thirty-one functions occurring in his tales. These tales trace a hero's quest and/or contest with a villain; thus, typical functions include such activities as "#6: The villain attempts to deceive his victim in order to take possession of him or of his belongings" and "#12: The hero is tested, interrogated, attacked, etc., which prepares the way for his receiving either a magical agent or helper." Propp's list of functions specifies all the different categories of events found in these tales and the sequence in which they transpire.

Consider the following:

1. Housewife X's sink is clogged. Josephine the plumber suggests Liquid Plumr. The drain cleaner cuts through the clog and the problem is solved.
2. Customer Y has dry, chapped hands from washing dishes. Madge the manicurist suggests Palmolive dishwashing detergent. Customer Y gratefully returns to the beauty parlor with restored hands.
3. Housewife Z makes bad coffee and husband complains. Mrs. Olson recommends Folger's coffee. Housewife Z tries Folger's and wins husband's praise and affection.

In each of the above stories, the heroine has a lack or misfortune (Propp's function #8a), which is noticed (#9). She comes into contact with a donor

(#13), who suggests the use of the magical agent (#14). The initial misfortune or lack is liquidated (#19). Often the heroine is then praised and thanked by family members (figuratively, #31: "The hero is married and ascends the throne").

Obviously, it is sorely tempting to try to fit television narratives into Propp's schema of functions and his categories of personae. Indeed, Roger Silverstone has worked out a detailed analysis of a British series, *Intimate Strangers*; David Giles has worked on police shows; Arthur Asa Berger has studied *The Prisoner*.[14] (In other contexts, Propp has been applied to films, novels, and even to the Bible.)[15] Yet there have always been questions as to the validity of Propp's particular schema, and David Bordwell has recently argued that: (a) there are legitimate questions about the accuracy of Propp's original scholarship; and (b) followers of Propp are overly casual in their application of his schema, using it piecemeal, constantly stretching points, making exceptions, and forcing things to fit.[16]

If we must accordingly be wary of relying too heavily on Propp's specific schema, we might still be open to, and perhaps excited by, the possibility of determining general rules of story construction. Taking off from Propp's lead, several structuralist narrative theorists have argued that stories are governed by a set of unwritten rules, acquired by all storytellers and receivers in somewhat the way we all acquire the basic rules of grammar. This conclusion explains both stories' variability and consistency: a sentence can be composed from an almost infinite choice of subjects, verbs, and objects, but to be comprehended, these choices must be arranged according to certain shared conventions. One major strand of narrative theory has concentrated on further specifying these rules; the theories expounded by Tzvetan Todorov, Claude Bremond, Thomas Pavel, A. J. Greimas, and others are generally more "abstract" than Propp's and are bent on working out, via the methodology of linguistics and semiology, patterns of relations that apply to all stories.[17] None of these competing theories has won complete acceptance, and to my knowledge, only Greimas's schema has ever been applied to television.[18]

The search for underlying structure may be particularly relevant to television, which, as critics have so often complained, is highly formulaic. Some formulas are unique to particular shows: one can practically guarantee that each week on the original *Star Trek* the USS *Enterprise* will encounter some alien life form, members of the crew will be separated from the ship (which will itself be place in jeopardy), one crew member will have a romantic interest, and all will be resolved through the crew's resourcefulness or high-mindedness. Other formulas may apply across genres (see Jane Feuer's chapter): harmony must be restored at the end of each sitcom; detectives will solve the crime; investigative reporters will uncover a scandal, and so on.

Such predictability has led scholars to remark on television's deficiencies in terms of one of the major engines driving narrative suspense. As Roland Barthes argues in *S/Z*, each significant event opens up a number of possibilities; the reader or viewer is constantly in a state of suspense and anticipation, wondering "what next? what next?"[19] Because episodic series on television are so formulaic, and because we know that, except in special cases, the hero or heroine will be back next week, critics have argued that we rarely feel the same anxiety with TV, as we do with a film or novel, about whether the hero and his love interest will triumph—or even survive.[20]

Although this "low suspense" generalization has validity, there are exceptions. In addition to their moral and political significance, the Watergate scandal and the Persian Gulf War were compelling *as stories*; each evening news broadcast revealed complicated and unpredictable twists and turns, and it was by no means certain that the good guys were going to win out, or at what cost.

Moreover, certain regularly scheduled television shows can be excruciatingly suspenseful. Consider *Rescue 911*. This program blends reenactments and documentary footage, actors and "real people," to recreate the "true stories" of victims of life-threatening situations, victims who were saved by the assistance of emergency personnel. (Hence the title, which refers to the phone number that Americans dial to reach emergency assistance.) Let us look in greater detail at an episode that aired during the 1990–91 season. The story can be summarized as follows:

The Kopsticks are ending their vacation in a resort condominium. Christine is in the kitchen washing dishes while her husband, Terry, loads the car with luggage. The two children are watching television. Unseen by Christine, two-and-a-half-year-old Ross goes into the bedroom and looks out the window at ducks in a pond below. Ross leans on the screen—it gives way, and the boy falls three stories into the pond. His parents notice that he is missing, and, initially without anxiety, start to look for him. Meanwhile the boy's body, floating in the water, is seen by the Smith family; Lindell Smith dives in and pulls him—apparently lifeless—to shore. An ambulance is called for. The parents realize what is going on and are distraught. Terry attempts CPR on his son, he is soon replaced by the resort's landscapers, who are more effective. Ross starts to breathe and moan. The ambulance arrives; the paramedics are concerned that Ross may have suffered spinal injuries in the fall. He is carefully loaded in the ambulance and taken to the hospital. Doctors examine him for six hours and conclude that he has escaped all injury; the parents are overjoyed. Drawn together by the accident, the Kopsticks and the Smiths become friends.

This story proceeds by prompting a series of questions. When will the parents realize that the boy has fallen out the window? Will the Smiths realize that the object they see in the water is a child? Has Lindell Smith pulled him out of the pond in time? Will the artificial respiration work? When will more help arrive? How bad are the boy's internal injuries? Did he suffer brain damage? As soon as one question is answered, another, seemingly equally critical, takes its place. The viewer doesn't quite believe that the boy will die; we feel certain that the producers would never offer up such a tragedy. (To my knowledge, although *Rescue 911* has offered stories that end with the victim suffering amputation or paralysis, it has never presented a story in which the victim died.) And yet the show manages to build up a great deal of suspense and tension. I can think of three reasons for this unusually high level of suspense: (1) This story is a self-contained episode. The Kopstick family are not "regulars" on *Rescue 911* and the viewer has no expectations of seeing them again next week. Thus, their future is not predetermined by the demands of the "series" format; (2) The story itself has the unpredictability, the unforeseeable "messiness," of "real life" (these twists and turns are not likely to occur to television scriptwriters); and (3) The show capitalizes on a certain "reality effect"—knowing that the action really transpired along these lines makes the peril and the stakes much higher than they would be in an overtly fictional text.

Ongoing, scripted, fictional television narratives have learned to compensate for their lack of suspense by proliferating storylines. Often a show will use the same protagonist for separate storylines, as when detective shows involve their heroes in both a case and a romance. Other series will use different family members as the leading players in separate storylines; soap operas keep as many as five or six storylines hopping simultaneously. Each given storyline may be formulaic, but the ways in which it combines with, parallels, contrasts, or comments upon another storyline may add interest and complexity.

Let us look, for illustration, at an episode of *Roseanne* broadcast during the 1990–91 season. Roseanne and Dan are planning to take a long weekend vacation together alone in Las Vegas, a vacation that they have been looking forward to and scrimping for. They encounter complications: Roseanne's new boss at the diner tells her that he was never told of her intention to take the weekend off and that if she doesn't show up for work he will fire her; Darlene and Becky are planning to give a party in their parents' absence, and Dan must set down rules and arrange for his sister-in-law, Jackie, to supervise; and a terrible snowstorm grounds the plane on the runway. The dominant storyline, which centers on Roseanne and Dan's marital needs and desire for pleasure, is intersected by the ongoing story of Roseanne's relationship with her boss and her job and by the continuing saga of their teenage daughters' attempts at independence and romantic involvements. Thus, Roseanne's bristling at her boss's authority is echoed by the girls' attempted defiance of their parents, and the parents' sexuality is mirrored by the girls' interest in their boyfriends.

The strategy of proliferating storylines diffuses the viewer's interest in any one line of action and spreads that interest over a larger field. In general, I would extend Robert Allen's insight about soap operas to cover the lion's share of narrative television: television stories generally displace audience interest from the syntagmatic axis to the paradigmatic—that is, from the flow of events per se to the revelation and development of existents.[21]

"Existents" includes both characters and setting, but television narratives commonly underutilize setting. Theatrical films will lavish money and time on capturing details of the setting with infinite care, making the Western prairie, the futuristic cityscape, or the urban ghetto a major component of the tale, a character in its own right. But the average prime-time series has a relatively undistinguished setting; opening montage sequences may situate the show in a particular locale, but once the action begins, the living room, bedroom, office, restaurant, or hospital studio sets are not particularly evocative or individualized. (Commercials, with higher budgets, make more use of scenery.)

In fact, as others have noted, it is characters and their interrelationships that dominate television stories.[22] The way the medium presents characters contrasts markedly with the situation in literature; despite the apparent individuality and vibrancy of an Emma Bovary or Huckleberry Finn, theorists argue over whether, or in what way, literary characters can truly be said to exist. Some claim that it is nonsense to think of them as people—they are merely phantasms, nothing but a concatenation of the actions they perform or the traits ascribed to them. Ultimately each dissolves into nothing but words on a printed page. However, television narratives, like films, indisputably offer more than words on a page. Television performers and their character roles are hardly equivalent: television characters "die," whereas the actors who portrayed them blithely move on to other projects; by the same token, performers may be involved in scandal or controversy that doesn't affect their characters. Yet because of the indexical nature of the television sign (see Ellen Seiter's chapter), whenever we are watching *Roseanne* and we see the image of a rotund female, we know that a living, breathing woman once stood in front of a camera and uttered those lines.

Predictable as their events may be, television stories offer us a wide gallery of vibrant characters. Many of these characters can be slotted into certain categories of narrative personae. One could use Propp's original model (hero, helper, dispatcher, donor, villain, princess and her father, false hero) or Greimas's recasting of Propp (subject, object, sender, helper, receiver, opponent). Or perhaps, with less theoretical ambition but more practical efficacy, one could categorize characters by their genre "role": "father" in domestic comedy, "detective" in a cop show, "co-worker" in a situation comedy, "evil woman" in a soap opera, and so on. The point is that, although character roles are quite formulaic in American television, the viewer's interest is continually engaged by the personalities who fulfill these roles. Cliff Huxtable is the "father figure" in *The Cosby Show*, and as such he fulfills certain set expectations (dispenser of wisdom, disciplinarian, breadwinner, devoted husband), but he fulfills these functions in quite a different way than Ward Cleaver in *Leave It to Beaver*.

Moreover, as David Marc argues, each episode of a series contributes to the series' "broader cosmology."[23] Television series often create in their initial premise a tension or enigma that centers on character development or relationships. Will Mary Richards (*The Mary Tyler Moore Show)* be able to make it on her own? Will Alex Keaton (*Family Ties*) renounce greed and ambition and embrace more human values? Will the *thirtysomething* group figure out how to be happy and "have it all"? Numerous shows (such as *Gunsmoke, The Avengers, Cheers, Moonlighting*) thrive by exploiting the tension of covert or undeclared passion: will Matt and Kitty, John and Emma, Sam and Diane, David and Maddie ever declare, or consummate, their love?

To take an example, the central question of *Roseanne*, as I see it, is "How are Roseanne and Dan to cope with the limitations of their life?" They are explicitly drawn as working class and as such are subject to problems not faced by the characters on *thirtysomething*. Roseanne and

Dan will never "have it all"; the question is, "How to be happy with what you've got?" Whereas *The Waltons* (poor but proud) answered, "Through family togetherness and personal integrity," *Roseanne* is much more cynical. Love is all right, but one must also adopt an attitude of defiance and self-deprecating humor as armor and compensation against life's troubles. The last scene of the episode referred to above shows Dan and Roseanne dancing to Wayne Newton records in their own candlelit living room, wiping out their disappointment over the canceled trip by jokingly pretending that Las Vegas has been sucked underground by a terrible earthquake and removing the sting of Roseanne's humiliation in front of her boss by fantasizing that he begged her to come back and has given her a $100 an hour raise.

Television stories may be formulaic, but the ways in which they are told can vary considerably. Thus, let us move on to look at narrative discourse.

Discourse

PARTICIPANTS

On your way to the store you may witness a series of events enacted by various personages in a given setting—say a purse-snatching and the apprehension of the thief—but what you have witnessed is not a narrative; it only becomes a narrative when you relate what you have seen to your friends. Narration is a communicative act: to have a narrative, one must have not only a tale, but also a teller and a listener.

A substantial portion of narrative theory has focused on studying the participants in this special exchange. As Robert Scholes and Robert Kellogg noted some years ago, our model of narrative transmission comes from the days when one sat and listened to a physically present storyteller spin his or her fantasies.[24] With the move to literary narratives, the situation became more complicated, because instead of actually listening to a storyteller, we read a printed text in which an author has deliberately inscribed an imitation storyteller, that is, the narrator. In fact, on a theoretical level, literary narratives always involve the following six participants:[25]

TEXT

Real	Implied			Implied	Real
Author →	Author →	Narrator →	Narratee →	Reader	→ Reader

To (briefly) describe these six participants, let us pretend that the text under consideration is *Huckleberry Finn*. The "real author" is Samuel Clemens. The "implied author" is the imaginary conception of "Mark Twain" that a reader constructs from the text.[26] (Because each reader formulates his or her own image of Twain from weighing subtle hints in the text, readers may not always agree on his characteristics; some argue that the person behind this work is terribly racist, others that he is a fierce critic of racism.) The "narrator" is Huck; he is explicitly set forth in the opening lines as the voice telling the tale: "You don't know about me without you have read a book by the name of *The Adventures of Tom Sawyer*; but that ain't no matter." The "narratee" is the unspecified person, the "you" above to whom Huck is supposedly speaking. The "implied reader" is the imaginary person for whom the implied author seems to be writing—someone, in this case, who is willing to criticize the foibles of civilization. The "real reader" is the flesh-and-blood person reading the book in his or her armchair.

Because the above chart grew out of theorists' analyses of literature, complications arise in applying it to film and television. As Robert Allen notes in the introduction to this book, assigning individual authorship to a TV series is, for a variety of historical, economic, and technical reasons, nearly impossible. Who, for instance, is the real author of the *Star Trek* series? With rosters of individuals working on a program over its lifetime, it is difficult to assign to a single individual the title and status of authorship.[27]

The "implied author" of a television show, like that of a novel, is not a flesh-and-blood person but rather a textual construct, the viewer's sense of the organizing force behind the world of the show. Many shows are so conventional that it is hard to get a definite sense of such a figure, but one can sometimes make broad contrasts. Behind *Hill Street Blues*, one senses someone fatalistic and irreverent; behind *The FBI* stands someone who believes in law and order and humorless professionalism; behind *Murder, She Wrote* flits a lighthearted yet conservative imp.

The question of the existence of a cinematic or television narrator has sparked much discussion in narrative theory. Our prototypical model of a narrator is a person speaking aloud. Films and television proceed instead through the unrolling of a series of moving images and recorded sounds. Yet we sense that someone, or some agency, is presenting these images in just this way—someone/something has chosen just these camera setups and arranged them in just this fashion with just this lighting, these sound effects, and this musical score. As Christian Metz leads us to see, because it is narrative, someone must be narrating. This intangible narrating presence need not be thought of as a person, but rather as an agency, that which chooses, orders, presents, and thus *tells* the narrative before us.[28]

Alerted, one can see marks of the television narrating agency at work. The last scene of the *Roseanne* episode starts with a close-up showing a phonograph turning, a Wayne Newton record album, and two burning candles; the camera then pans up to reveal Dan and Roseanne waltzing. This composition and this movement *tell* us that the couple has made up for missing the Las Vegas show by creating their own special evening. The music is romantic but jaunty, a perfectly apt commentary on the couple's attitude toward their troubles. (Music, in film and in television, is a key channel through which the voiceless narrating agency "speaks" to the viewer. The Gershwin score underlying the United Airlines commercial described earlier grows ineffably tender during quiet moments and rises to a resounding climax at the end.)

Partly because the narrating presence behind most television shows is impersonal and nebulous, time after time television naturalizes this strangeness by offering a substitute human face and/or voice. In the fifties the dramatic anthology series had "hosts" who would appear before the story itself and act as introducers and emcees. This practice continued through the sixties in Rod Serling's and Alfred Hitchcock's introductions to *Twilight Zone* and *Alfred Hitchcock Presents* and figures to the present day in Adam Walsh's role on *America's Most Wanted* and William Shatner's on *Rescue 911*. On-camera hosts lend their charms and credibility, and their mere humanness, to the amorphous television narrating agency; they serve to personalize the impersonal. Shatner, indeed, is a good choice as figurehead of *Rescue 911* because he carries viewer associations with his roles as the captain of technology (James T. Kirk on *Star Trek*) and a policeman (on *T. J. Hooker*).

In other cases, the narrator is humanized not by means of a substitute body but merely through a disembodied voice, through voice-over narration. Commercials, of course, use voice-overs incessantly, as do documentaries, newscasts, and sports events. The voice works in tandem with the visual track, telling us what we are seeing or what to think about what we are seeing, providing the commentary or exposition we are accustomed to from narrators in novels.

Fictional television programs use voice-over more frequently than one might at first realize. Some utilize such voices at the beginning to set up the premise of the series (remember the song that introduces *The Beverly*

Hillbillies?); others, like *The Wonder Years*, make oral narration an integral, ongoing facet of the text. Narrative theory helps us break down such voice-over narrators into two types: those who are situated outside of the story they relate, and those who also double as characters within that story. We will look at voice-over narrators more in the next section.[29]

Robert Allen will develop the concept of television's narratee more fully in his chapter. As he notes, the concept of the "narratee" is particularly helpful for the study of television because, inasmuch as the shows are broadcast so widely to vast, impersonal audiences, producers have frequently resorted to using stand-ins. How many times have we heard, "Show X was filmed live before a studio audience"? Consciously or not, the producers invite these audiences to make the communicative act concrete —the story is now being told for real listeners (as opposed to video lenses), and the actors and director can get immediate feedback from the audience's reactions. Furthermore, the viewer isolated at home can now get the sense that he or she is experiencing the narrative communally, and his or her reactions are likely to be augmented by the example of the studio audiences. Alternatively, producers may skip the trouble of inviting a live audience and instead substitute canned narratees in the form of a laughtrack.

Another type of television narratee is the "perfect listener." The visiting star on the *Tonight Show* or a Barbara Walters special recounts the story of his or her career/drug/personal crises and recovery to Johnny Carson or Walters. Similarly, reporters in the field address their stories not straight to the audience at home but rather to the network anchor. The talk show hosts and the news anchor fulfill identical functions—they listen eagerly and sympathetically and ask intelligent questions. Their interest and attention serves as a model for the viewer eavesdropping in on this conversation at home.

The "implied viewer" of television narratives is again a fictional construct, the person who communes perfectly with the implied author. Thus, the implied viewer of *Gabriel's Fire* believes in women serving as attorneys and in interracial friendships; the implied viewer of *Twin Peaks* appreciates a macabre sense of humor. Though it may seem self-evident, it is worth noting here that Schlitz beer commercials are addressed to people who drink, not to abstainers. In short, each commercial creates an implied viewer who is interested in its message. Even if you don't own a dishwasher, when you watch a Cascade commercial you must pretend that you do in order to meet the narrative on its own terms.

Finally, however difficult audience demographics may seem to the Nielsen Company, to narrative theorists the "real viewer" is an unproblematic entity, that flesh-and-blood person sitting in front of the television set. However, as both Robert Allen and John Fiske discuss, there is nothing simple or unproblematic about the ways those "real" viewers engage with television's narratives or about the processes by which those stories are woven into the everyday lives of millions of people. (The social dimensions of our relationships with television narratives are clearly important; however, their investigation lies beyond the reach of narrative theory.)

This model of narrative participants can help us understand a facet of television so often commented upon: the medium's propensity for "direct address," an aspect of what Robert Allen refers to as television's "rhetorical mode."[30] Direct address refers to the situation that occurs when someone on TV—a news anchor, a talk show host, a series host, a reporter —faces the camera lens and appears to speak directly to the audience at home. When this happens, we have an apparent precipitous collapse of the six narrative participants into merely two, the speaker and the viewer. When Dan Rather faces the camera and relates the evening news, he simultaneously figures as real author, implied author, and on-screen narrator, while I, sitting at home, am simultaneously narratee, implied viewer, and real viewer. Although theoretically there is always a distinction between these roles, the distinction in such cases is nearly indiscernible. Such a strong impression is given of direct, interpersonal exchange that when Rather says, "Good night," I, for one, am likely to answer back to the screen, "Good night, Dan."

Whenever we get down to two participants, we are back to the original model of the prototypical narrative exchange—the oral storyteller and the physically contiguous listener. In *Reading Television*, John Fiske and John Hartley refer to television's "bardic" function. They argue that television serves the same function in a community as a traditional tribal poet like Homer, who sang of epic heroes and their exploits, in that, like a bard, television conveys the culture's dominant values and self-image.[31] I suggest that the medium is also "bardic" in that, despite its technological sophistication, it frequently seeks to imitate the most traditional and simplest of storytelling situations.

TYPOLOGY OF NARRATORS

Narrative theory can provide crucial help in analyzing television narrators because the field has isolated a host of issues concerning the relationship of a narrator to his or her tale and to the world constructed by that tale—what in narrative theory is called the *diegesis*. In the following discussion, we will look at six of the most important of these variables.

First, is the narrator a character in the story he or she tells, or is the narrator outside of the story-world?

I referred to this distinction briefly above. Thomas Magnum and John-boy Walton are character-narrators (in Gérard Genette's terminology, they are *homodiegetic*—that is, situated within the world they tell us about), whereas the anonymous narrators of PBS documentaries come from another realm (they are *heterodiegetic*). The distinction between these two types of narrators can be important because, by convention, character-narrators are considered less objective and less authoritative than heterodiegetic narrators. The former are personally involved in the stories they relate; the latter merely observe from some more or less Olympian vantage point.

Second, does the narrator tell the whole tale, or is his or her story embedded within a larger "frame" story? (Narrative theorists always explain embedding by reference to nested Russian dolls.)

Whenever a character within a program tells another character a story, that narration is embedded with the overarching discourse of the narrating agency. Because the embedded narrators are themselves enfolded within the discourse of the whole text, they are assumed to be less knowledgeable and powerful. Such discriminations help us understand the dynamics of *Rescue 911*. William Shatner acts as the personification of the heterodiegetic narrator of the entire show: he introduces each episode, provides information and commentary, and draws conclusions. The various participants in the accidents also narrate—they recount their own memories of the events—but their storytelling is enfolded within Shatner's. Thus, the stories that Christine Kopstick, Terry Kopstick, Lindell Smith, Connie Smith, and Kendell Smith offer are inferred to be partial, even colored by their involvement and distress. Like Shatner, the participant-narrators speak both in voice-over and on camera; however, on screen their gaze is slanted to the side, presumably toward an interviewer who is eliciting their accounts. Only Shatner, the personification of the frame narrator, looks straight ahead, meeting the gaze of the camera. Through the editing back and forth amongst the participants' stories, through the reenactments, through the choices of camera placement, through the musical score, and through Shatner's spoken commentary, the television narrator ties together all the threads of the story to provide the viewer with the complete overview.

Third, what degree of distance, in terms of space and time, exists

William Shatner as frame narrator

between the story events and the time and place of the narrator's narrating?

John boy Walton narrates from the vantage point of a grown man; his tone is nostalgic and reflective. (John-boy is portrayed on screen by Richard Thomas, but an older actor provides John-man's voice-over). On the other hand, Thomas Magnum narrates as his story unfolds. He is more wrapped up in the action; his narration is more anxious and immediate.

Fourth, what degree of distance in terms of transparency, irony, or self-consciousness does the narrator exhibit?

The vast majority of television narrators strive for neutrality and self-effacement, as if viewers are supposed to overlook the fact that the story is coming through a mediator and instead believe that they are looking in on reality. Other styles are possible, however. Some shows—I'm thinking of *Moonlighting*—convey an "arch" tonality and an assertive self-consciousness, deliberately flouting conventions of realism. Hand-held camera movement, so typical on contemporary commercials, conveys an artlessness so studied that it is paradoxically quite self-conscious. And the decision to use an actor as a narrating figurehead (either on screen or in voice-over) is always a move toward foregrounding the discourse. In fact, many hosts/voice-overs are not at all shy about acting like the talkative narrator of a Victorian novel. At the end of each episode of *Rescue 911*, Shatner always draws a moral: parents should teach their children how to call for assistance, everyone should learn CPR, and so on.[32]

Fifth, is the narrator reliable? If unreliable, does the narrator withhold the truth through his or her own limitations (that is, is the narrator fallible), or in order to mislead us?

The way to tell whether a narrator is unreliable or not is to look for discrepancies between what the narrator tells us and what we intuit the implied author believes. Heterodiegetic voices generally strive for perfect sincerity, and every other facet of the text is designed to bolster their credibility. Character voice-over narrators are more likely to be fallible. On an episode of *Magnum, P.I.* entitled "Old Acquaintance," Magnum is to meet a woman he has not seen since they were high school friends. His voice-over states: "I had to admit I was a little nervous about seeing Goldie again after all these years. But one thing I wasn't worried about was whether I'd recognize her or not. There was a bond between us, a history, a camaraderie that went beyond the physical. It was a spiritual sort of thing." Meanwhile, the shot shows Thomas craning around a hotel lobby and overlooking a lovely redhead—Goldie—who is blatantly trying to attract his attention. This dichotomy shows us that Thomas has been spouting garbage; his "spiritual bond" is not strong enough to overcome his memory of Goldie's unattractiveness in high school.

Finally, one might look at the narrator's degree of omniscience. Omniscience may involve one or more of the following traits: knowing the story's outcome, having the ability to penetrate into characters' hearts and minds, and/or having the ability to move at will in time and space. One common way to judge the narrator's omniscience is to see whether or not the narration is "restricted," that is, whether or not we follow only the actions and knowledge of a leading character, or whether the narrator moves at will between characters and thus is "unrestricted." In some crime shows, such as *Hawaii Five-O* or *Columbo*, the camera shows the viewer the guilty party at the outset; we side with the narrator in a position of knowledge and wait for McGarrett or Columbo to catch the crook. In other cases, the television narrator Knows All but resists Telling All; it shows the murder being committed but coyly keeps the murderer's face off screen. (In *Dallas*, the narrator knew full well who shot J. R. Ewing; it just wouldn't tell us until the following season.) Most television narrators display a large degree of omniscience.

To summarize, narratologists look carefully at a cluster of markers indicating the narrator's position vis-à-vis the tale and the consequences of this position to the discourse as a whole. Identical story events can seem radically different depending upon the narrator's slant and on the degree of the narrator's power, remoteness, objectivity, or reliability. As Walter Benjamin once put it, "Traces of the storyteller cling to the story the way the handprints of the potter cling to the clay vessel."[33] Analyzing television narrators, then, involves putting a magnifying glass to these individualized handprints.

TIME

Christian Metz has written, "There is the time of the thing told and the time of the telling. . . . One of the functions of narrative is to invent one time scheme in terms of another time scheme."[34] The binary nature of time in narrative is considered one of its distinguishing characteristics and has been much studied.

Story events, by definition, proceed chronologically. But when the teller tells the tale, that teller is not bound to follow chronological order; events can be presented in any order the teller finds most effective. A television narrator frequently teases the viewer with flashforwards of the action to come; on *Rescue 911*, for instance, Shatner intones, "When we continue . . ." and presents us with a clip showing Christine Kopstick's hysteria when she realizes what has happened to Ross. Alternatively, a narrator might employ a flashback to orient the viewer and bring him or her up to date; news stories often intercut file footage from previous events, and serials often begin with a montage of scenes from earlier shows.

Television narrators often must convey simultaneity. As mentioned above, television texts frequently present more than one storyline; in the story-world these events may be happening at the same moment, but a narrator can only tell one thing at a time. Before television was invented, film developed several techniques for indicating simultaneity: titles such as "meanwhile, back at the ranch"; large clocks placed in every location; verbal indicators; and parallel montage (cutting back and forth between separate locations).

Television has taken parallel montage to a high art. The United commercial mentioned earlier lasts a mere sixty seconds but is composed of twenty-six shots. The narrator cuts back and forth between mother and daughter, paralleling their activities throughout their respective days. This linkage is a key component of the text's message. Designed as it is to appeal to businesswomen, the commercial offers a reassuring fantasy that one can travel out of town and still be back in time to pick up the kids—in

1. Mother and daughter together

6. Daughter painting

2. The parting

7. Mother relaxes on plane home

3. Daughter builds tower

8. Daughter naps

4. Chrysler Building (another tower). Mother is in New York

9. Re-UNITED

5. Mother at easel

The commercial has no dialogue, only music, until the ending moments, when a male voice-over states, "For a half century and more, business travelers have depended on United Airlines to get them to their most important meetings. United. Rededicated to getting you the service you deserve. Come fly the Friendly Skies."

other words, that one can combine family and career (with the help of United Airlines). The day care center is presented as a warm, wonderful place, and the little girl—who, like her mother, will obviously grow up to have a career—is presented as a tomboy in patched jeans, playing with blocks instead of dolls. The parallel montage both implies the similarities between them—"like mother, like daughter"—and also suggests that even though the mother is separated by distance from her child, their lives are indissolubly linked.

Not only can discourse reorder the *sequence* of story events, it can also alter those events' *duration*. Building on Gérard Genette's work in *Narrative Discourse*, Seymour Chatman details the following five possible matches between story and discourse duration:[35]

1. *Summary: Discourse-time is shorter than story-time.*

Verbal narratives rely heavily on summary. In visual media, summary is less common and proves slightly awkward because time condensation is more difficult without verbal tenses. Perhaps the closest that television comes to summary is in montage sequences (particularly those used in tandem with voice-over narration). Thus the title sequence of *Gilligan's Island* condenses events that must have taken some hours or days into a few moments.

2. *Ellipsis: Discourse time is zero.*

Television narratives depend on ellipsis. Every time the camera cuts from a man leaving a building to that same man getting out of his car, it has cut out all the story-time in between. This habit of eliding routine events or nonpertinent stretches of time allows television to present a story that supposedly has a duration of several hours, days, weeks, or months within the confines of a half-hour or hourlong text.

3. *Scene: Story-time and discourse-time are equal.*

Whenever a television show allows the camera to present story events in full, without temporal cuts (the camera may change its spatial position at will so long as no time is lost), we have congruence between story and discourse-time. The scene is the basic building block of television narratives. *Roseanne*, for instance, unrolls through a series of scenes. Visual variety is accomplished by means of cutting back and forth between cameras, but the conversations unroll without a temporal break.

4. *Stretch: Discourse-time is longer than story-time.*

The best example of stretch is slow motion. In slow motion the narrator takes longer to relate the events than the events originally lasted in the story. (Fast motion, which is less common, qualifies as a form of summary.)

5. *Pause: The same as stretch except that story-time is zero.*

One example of a pause would be a complete freezing of the frame while the narrator—perhaps a sports announcer—analyzes that action. Commercials also use pauses, particularly in product shots. At the end of the NyQuil commercial mentioned above, we get a freeze frame of the couple in bed and a superimposed picture of the product, while print and voice-over simultaneously proclaim: "Vicks NyQuil, the nighttime sniffling, sneezing, coughing, aching, stuffy head, fever, so you can rest medicine, from Vicks, of course." The action has paused, but the narrator continues to speak and to drive home the moral of the story.

As Genette also pointed out, narratives have several options in terms of their correspondence between story and discourse frequency. Each narrator has a choice between the *singulative*, the *repetitive*, and the *iterative*. That is to say, a narrator can: tell once what happened once (one shot of the quarterback's brilliant pass); tell *n* times what happened once (replaying the shot of the pass *n* times); or tell once what happened *n* times (using one shot of one brilliant pass to stand for all the brilliant passing the quarterback did in that game.)

What is the point of identifying these time distortions? For one thing, it can be intriguing to consider what lies behind the temporal choices. Interestingly enough, commercials often strategically elide story-time; they cut from the "before" situation to the "after"—we see the dirty shirt and then the clean one, but all the work of doing the laundry is hidden. Similarly, a show may begin with some exiting action to grab the viewer's interest and only flash back to provide less eye-catching background information once its hold on the viewer is firmly established. The United commercial uses both stretch and ellipsis: it uses slow motion during the moments of parting and reunion, lingering over the time the mother and child are together, whereas it proceeds quickly through the time they are apart.

Moreover, examining the temporal distortions can help us characterize television narrators. The closer the discourse approaches to congruence with story-time through presenting singulative scenes in chronological order, the less interventionist and the more invisible is the narrator; the more the discourse distorts story-time through achronological order, unusual pacing, or repetition, the more the narrator's hand is revealed. Sitcoms tend to have self-effacing narrators and to proceed chronologically from scene to scene, whereas music videos make time distortions part of their style.

Narrative theory also provides us with a framework for understanding one of the unique qualities of television—the ability to broadcast "live." "Liveness" may be defined as the apparent congruence between discourse-time and reception-time—that is, no time gap exists between the narrative's production and its consumption. We have become accustomed to films' and novels' "having been spoken" many years before we happen upon them. In the case of film, this "past-tense" quality is a function of technology: the moment of recording the film always precedes the moment of our watching that recording. Television, on the other hand, is both a recording medium (videotape) and a medium for simultaneous transmission. Other chapters will take up the question of "liveness" as a defining quality of television. Here let me just point out that "live" broadcasts offer a simulation of traditional oral storytelling, in which the audience hears the tale at the moment that the storyteller speaks it.

But on television, what was once live can be taped and rebroadcast later (and the quality of videotape recording makes it literally impossible for the viewer—without other clues—to know the difference). In other words, there are really three time schemes operating: the time of the told, the time of the telling, and the time of the broadcasting. Let us turn now to look at this third, outermost layer.

Schedule

Compared with television, novels and films are comparatively "freestanding" in terms of their exhibition or consumption, and the reader or viewer has relatively unfettered access to such texts. Television narratives are unique in the fact that all texts are embedded within the metadiscourse of the station's schedule. A viewer can circumvent some of the extrinsic consequences of this embedding by using a videocassette recorder; one can, for example, watch a show at a more convenient time, or watch it again, or fastforward through commercials. But this embedding has also led television narratives to make certain intrinsic adjustments.

American television schedules are like jigsaw puzzles. They are composed of scores of separate pieces that must fit together in set patterns and thus must conform to standardized rules. For instance, each piece of the puzzle must fit into a specific time frame controlled to the last second. Accordingly—unlike oral, literary, or cinematic narratives, which are much more likely to last as long as their story requires—television narratives have to fit into an assigned Procrustean bed. This frequently means that long television movies and miniseries are "padded" with insignificant events, whereas many commercials and news stories don't have enough time to develop their stories before they must conclude.

Another principle of most television schedules is that each text must accommodate interruption. The most common form of interruption, of course, is the commercial break, but one should not overlook the "pledge breaks" on public television stations or "the kitchen and bathroom" intermissions that cable networks insert into long feature films. Television narratives have learned to compensate for and even take advantage of the inevitable interruptions in various ways. First, they typically tailor their discourse to fit "naturally" around the commercial breaks, so that, for instance, the exposition fits before the first break and the coda after the last. Second, shows build their stories to a high point of interest before each break to ensure that the audience will stay tuned. (Or actually, as Kenneth Hey notes of the classic television drama *Marty*, crescendos are so structured as to deliver "emotionally sensitive viewers straight into a commercial message.")[36] Finally, programs frequently time the placement of commercials to coincide with a temporal ellipsis so that while the viewer's attention has been diverted, the story can gracefully leap ahead several hours or days.

In recent years, advertisers have actually begun to use interruption as part of their own texts: one now sees commercials that break themselves into two parts. In the first "act," someone pours milk onto a bowl of cereal. The commercial is "interrupted" by one or two other nonrelated advertisements, then we return for the second part of the story—lo and behold, the cereal has not gotten soggy!! Such commercials use interruption as part of their sales pitch.

Because most television stations broadcast around the clock or nearly so, they have a voracious demand for material. To maximize investments in time and money, it is cheaper to continue using the same cast and set than to create all new shows. Moreover, as writers of comic strips, popular novels, and radio shows had already discovered, using the same existents has the advantage of building audience familiarity and loyalty.[37] Thus, as we all know, few television narratives are self-contained, single broadcasts; thus the development of series and serials.

Series refers to those shows whose characters and setting are recycled, but the story concludes in each individual episode. By contrast, in a *serial* the story and discourse do not come to a conclusion during an episode, and the threads are picked up again after a given hiatus. A series is thus similar to an anthology of short stories, while a serial is like a serialized Victorian novel. Serials can be further divided into those that do eventually end (despite the misnomer, miniseries belong in this category) and those, such as soap operas, that may be canceled but never reach a conclusion, a new equilibrium.

The series format has several consequences for television narratives, some of which have been mentioned above. For one thing, because the characters must continue from week to week, suspense is diluted; the viewer knows that the hero is never in mortal danger. For another, because each show repeats without progression, the viewer finds surface variability on top of a rigid formula—a "new" mystery (which will be solved), a "new" villain (to be vanquished), a "new" love interest (to flirt with, but separate from), a "new" embarrassment or misunderstanding (to forgive or unravel). One truism of television criticism is that series characters have no memory and no history: amazingly, they don't notice that they said and did exactly the same things the previous week. (However, although past events disappear into a black void, characters' interrelationships do grow from week to week.) Moreover, as long as the series continues, the viewer can bank on the fact that the central tension or premise will not be resolved; for instance, on a given *Star Trek* we do not expect that the *Enterprise* will complete its mission and return to earth. As John Ellis has noted, "The TV series repeats a problematic. It therefore provides no resolution of the problematic at the end of the run of the series. . . . Fundamentally, the series implies the form of the dilemma rather than that of resolution and closure. This perhaps is the central contribution that broadcast TV has made to the long history of narrative forms and narrativised perception of the world."[38] Only on red-letter occasions will a series reach an Aristotelian *end*. The last episode of *M*A*S*H* attracted national attention because the show actually created a new state of affairs: the Korean War ended and everyone got to go home.

Because serials progress from week to week, they face special dilemmas. First, they must bring up to date viewers who do not usually watch the show or who have missed an episode. To this end, many begin by offering a flashback recap of ongoing storylines ("Previously, on *L.A. Law* . . ."). Another option, characteristic of daytime soap operas, is to have the characters redundantly discuss the most significant past events. Second, serials must generate enough viewer interest and involvement to survive their hiatus. Some offer flashforwards to tease the viewer with bits of upcoming action; frequently, they also turn to the technique made famous by movie serials—the cliffhanger. The general rule seems to be, "the longer the hiatus, the higher the cliff"—witness the spectacular cliffhangers whipped up on *Dallas* and *Dynasty* for the last show of each season.

I am tempted to claim that one of the distinguishing characteristics of American television over the last five years has been its blurring of the distinction between series and serials, or, to be more precise, its increased tendency toward serialization. (Surely it is significant that even commercials have recently adopted a serial format—for example, the Nissan Pathfinder's ongoing expedition to Rio de Janeiro, or the unstoppable Energizer bunny, or the burgeoning romance between neighbors who borrow Taster's Choice instant coffee.) But the line between series and serial may have been blurry to begin with. Even in a "classic" series like *I Love Lucy*, some storylines—such as Lucy's pregnancy—necessarily carried over week to week. And many series have always evinced nonreversible changes over the years: within a given season, each episode of *M*A*S*H* may be freestanding and all episodes may be watched in any order, but the shows dating from the years after Colonel Blake's departure necessarily represent narrative development over those made before he left. On the episode of *Roseanne* mentioned above, the central storyline about vacation plans reaches resolution, but Darlene and Becky's party introduces events involving the girls' boyfriends that link up with earlier and later programs. *St. Elsewhere*, *L.A. Law*, and similar shows have merely developed a distinctive, stable amalgam of series and serialization; on such shows, one or more of the half-dozen storylines featured on a given night may conclude, but others will develop over a number of weeks.[39] Perhaps the distinction between serial and series should be seen more as a continuum than as an either/or situation.

Series may spill over into serialization because, as Jane Feuer has noted, the boundaries of television dieseses are strangely, uniquely permeable. With novels and films, the reader/viewer believes that the action takes place within a discreet, enclosed time and place, a fictional world, a diegesis. Yet with TV, one notes a constant "bleed over" of characters and themes from one text to another: characters from one series make appearances on another series; the news at eleven will offer more information about the social problem (child abuse, gambling addiction) just featured in the made-for-TV movie. Texts even physically overlap one another, as when voice-over advertisements for a later program are placed on top of the closing credits of the present text. Jane Feuer goes so far as to claim that, because there are so many interruptions of television narratives, "the very concept 'diegesis' is unthinkable on television."[40] Certainly the boundaries are shakier and more permeable than is the case with other narrative mediums.

One of the questions asked at the beginning of this chapter was, "What qualities are specific to television narrative?" I'd like to avoid answering, partly because narrative codes on television, as in all mediums, are in flux and change through time. Partly also because television offers so many disparate types of texts (commercials are obviously quite different from soap operas or TV movies) that generalizations are of limited value. Similarly, some of the qualities I perceive as characteristic of television can also be found on radio dramas or in serialized novels. Nevertheless, in order not to shirk my responsibilities, and to summarize the preceding discussion, I will hazard the following list of American television narrative's most common traits in the early 1990s:

- predictable, formulaic storylines;
- multiple storylines intertwined in complex patterns and frequently interconnecting;
- individualized, appealing characters fitting into standardized roles;
- setting and scenery either very evocative (commercials) or merely functional (series);
- substitute narratees, voice-over narration, and direct address often employed to "naturalize" the discourse;
- complex interweaving of narrative level and voices;
- tendency toward omniscient, reliable narration;
- reliance on ellipsis and scene;
- achronological order to entice (previews) or inform (flashbacks);
- series, serial, and "hybrid" formats;
- accommodation of interruptions;
- lengths cut to fit standardized time slots; and
- permeable diegesis.

This concatenation of traits adds up to a manifestation of narrative rather distinct from that found in other mediums. And it would be a grave mistake, I think, to underestimate the efficacy and sophistication of television's narrative structures; certainly many of the texts I have studied closely offer evidence of great refinement and complexity.

I have been treating the television schedule as a kind of discourse. In a sense I believe that we can also look behind each station's schedule to see a *supernarrator*. These supernarrators are personified and individualized by three primary means: logos (the NBC peacock, the CBS eye); signature music; and voice-over narrators who speak for the station or network as a whole. The voice-over narrators are perhaps most significant—each station routinely uses certain voice-over narrators who speak to the viewer, providing flashforwards of coming attractions, justifying schedule changes, or pleading technical difficulties.

Because they are the narrators of the outermost frame, these strange storytellers are in the position of the utmost power and knowledge. They sit outside and above all the embedded narratives, unaffected by them. And it is through their sufferance that all the other texts are brought to us: they can interrupt, delay, or preempt the other texts at will. I am intrigued by the fact that in recent years the American Movie Channel and WNET have sought to personalize their station spokespersons by using on-screen figureheads. AMC offers us silver-haired Bob Dorian, speaking from a traditional study or library, offering gossipy details about the classic films. WNET presents the much more "with it" image of Louis Dodley, younger, black, with fine-chiseled features, seated at a television control panel. They are the mouthpieces for the stations, seeking to form personal, not technological, connections.

Perhaps television is conscious of its role as storyteller. The Bard is dead . . . long live the (TV) Bard.

NOTES

1. I'm thinking of Gérard Genette's *Narrative Discourse Revisited*, trans. Jane E. Lewin (Ithaca, N.Y.: Cornell University Press, 1988), which itself is a gloss on Genette's own pathbreaking *Narrative Discourse: An Essay in Method*, trans. Jane E. Lewin (Ithaca, N.Y.: Cornell University Press, 1980), and of Seymour Chatman's *Coming to Terms: The Rhetoric of Narrative in Fiction and Film* (Ithaca, N.Y.: Cornell University Press, 1990), which takes as its explicit goal the need to standardize the terminology of the field.

2. My largest debts are to Seymour Chatman, *Story and Discourse: Narrative Structure in Fiction and Film* (Ithaca, N.Y.: Cornell University Press, 1978); and to Shlomith Rimmon-Kenan, *Narrative Fiction: Contemporary Poetics* (London: Methuen, 1983). For other sources, see "For Further Reading" below.

3. Scholars disagree over the basic definitions of *narrative* and *drama*, thus

leading to some confusion about to where to slot television and film. Chatman argues persuasively that narrative is the larger field, with *diegesis* (roughly, "telling" or "narrative") and *mimesis* (roughly, "showing" or "dramatic") as subsets (*Coming to Terms*, pp. 109–15). See my discussion below on the existence of the television narrator.

4. Chatman speaks of one text-type being at another's "service" (*Coming to Terms*, p. 10).

5. See Sharon Lynn Sperry, "Television News as Narrative," in *Understanding Television: Essays on Television as a Social and Cultural Force*, ed. Richard P. Adler (New York: Praeger, 1981), pp. 295–312; and Robert Stam, "Television News and Its Spectator," in *Regarding Television—Critical Approaches: An Anthology*, ed. E. Ann Kaplan, American Film Institute Monograph Series, vol. 2 (Frederick, Md.: University Publications of America, 1983), pp. 23–43. For a discussion of narrative strategies in a science documentary, see Roger Silverstone, "Narrative Strategies in Television Science—a Case Study," *Media, Culture, and Society* 6 (1984): 377–410.

6. As Wlad Godzich, following Genette, reminds us, "actions do not exist independently of their representation" (foreword to *The Poetics of Plot*, by Thomas G. Pavel [Minneapolis: University of Minnesota Press, 1985], p. xix).

7. Rimmon-Kenan, *Narrative Fiction*, p. 15.

8. Tzvetan Todorov, "The Grammar of Narratives," in *The Poetics of Prose*, trans. Richard Howard (Ithaca, N.Y.: Cornell University Press, 1977), p. 111.

9. Roland Barthes, "Introduction to the Structural Analysis of Narratives," in *Image/Music/Text*, trans. Stephen Heath (New York: Hill and Wang, 1977), p. 93.

10. Aristotle, "Poetics," in *Critical Theory since Plato*, ed. Hazard Adams (New York: Harcourt Brace Jovanovich, 1971), p. 52.

11. Gustav Freytag, *Technique of the Drama: An Exposition of Dramatic Composition and Art*, trans. Elias MacEwan (New York: Benjamin Blom, 1968), pp. 114–40.

12. Vladimir Propp, *Morphology of the Folktale* (Austin: University of Texas Press, 1970), pp. 19–20.

13. Ibid., pp. 21, 22, 23.

14. Roger Silverstone, *The Message of Television: Myth and Narrative in Contemporary Culture* (London: Heinemann, 1981); Denis Giles, "A Structural Analysis of the Police Story," in *American Television Genres*, ed. Stuart Kaminsky with Jeffery H. Mahn (Chicago: Nelson-Hall, 1986), pp. 67–84; Arthur Asa Berger, "Semiotics and TV," in Adler, *Understanding Television*, pp. 91–114.

15. Roland Barthes, "Struggle with the Angel," in *Image/Music/Text*, pp. 125–41.

16. David Bordwell, "ApProppriations and ImPropprieties: Problems in the Morphology of Film Narrative," *Cinema Journal* 27, no. 3 (Spring 1988): 5–20.

17. For descriptions of other "narrative grammars," see Rimmon-Kenan, *Narrative Fiction*, pp. 22–28, 34–35.

18. Silverstone, *Message of Television*.

19. Roland Barthes, *S/Z*, trans. Richard Miller (New York: Hill and Wang, 1974).

20. David Bordwell helps us see how differently classical Hollywood films handle suspense. In particular, such films crank up the tension by creating and emphasizing deadlines (*Narration in the Fiction Film* [Madison: University of Wisconsin Press, 1985], pp. 157–66).

21. Robert C. Allen, "On Reading Soaps: A Semiotic Primer," in Kaplan, *Regarding Television*, p. 103.

22. "Over and over again, when I asked executives which factors weighed most heavily in putting shows on the air, keeping them there, shaping their content, I heard a standardized list. At the top, the appeal of actors and characters" (Todd Gitlin, *Inside Prime Time* [New York: Pantheon, 1985], pp. 25–26).

23. David Marc, *Demographic Vistas: Television in American Culture* (Philadelphia: University of Pennsylvania Press, 1984), p. 12.

24. Robert Scholes and Robert Kellogg, *The Nature of Narrative* (New York: Oxford University Press, 1966), pp. 240–82.

25. Chatman, *Story and Discourse*, p. 151.

26. Actually, the question of the existence of the "implied author" is one of the more contested topics in narrative theory. The term originated with Wayne C. Booth in *The Rhetoric of Fiction* (Chicago: University of Chicago Press, 1961); it was adopted by Chatman (*Story and Discourse*), attacked by Genette (*Narrative Discourse Revisited*), and then defended again by Chatman (*Coming to Terms*).

27. See Randall Rothenberg, "Yesterday's Boob Tube Is Today's High Art," *New York Times*, 7 October 1990.

28. For more on the question of the cinematic narrator, see Robert Burgoyne, "The Cinematic Narrator: The Logic and Pragmatics of Impersonal Narration," *Journal of Film and Video* 42, no. 1 (Spring 1990): 3–16. For an opposing view, see Bordwell, *Narration in the Fiction Film*, p. 62.

29. For more about the voice-over, see Sarah Kozloff, *Invisible Storytellers: Voice-Over Narration in American Fiction Film* (Berkeley: University of California Press, 1988).

30. See Michele Hilmes, "The Television Apparatus: Direct Address," *Journal of Film and Video* 37, no. 4 (Fall 1985): 27–36.

31. John Fiske and John Hartley, *Reading Television* (London: Methuen, 1978), pp. 85–100.

32. Linguist William Labov, in researching "natural narratives" (oral, unrehearsed stories of personal experiences), has found that they break down into six parts: abstract, orientation, complicating action, evaluation, resolution, and coda. *Rescue 911* follows his schema exactly. See Labov, "Transformation of Experience in Narrative Syntax," in *Language in the Inner City: Studies in Black English Vernacular* (Philadelphia: University of Pennsylvania Press, 1972), pp. 354–96.

33. Walter Benjamin, "The Storyteller," in *Illuminations*, ed. Hannah Arendt, trans. Harry Zohn (New York: Schocken Books, 1968), p. 92.

34. Christian Metz, "Notes toward a Phenomenology of the Narrative," in *Film Language: A Semiotics of the Cinema*, trans. Michael Taylor (New York: Oxford University Press, 1974), p. 21.

35. Chatman, *Story and Discourse*, pp. 68–78. See also Genette, *Narrative Discourse*, pp. 33–160.

36. Kenneth Hey, "*Marty*: Aesthetics vs. Medium," in *American History/ American Television: Interpreting the Video Past*, ed. John E. O'Connor (New York: Frederick Ungar, 1983), p. 115.

37. See Roger Hagedorn, "Technology and Economic Exploitation: The Serial as a Form of Narrative Presentation," *Wide Angle* 10, no. 4 (1988): 4–12.

38. John Ellis, *Visible Fictions: Cinema, Television, Video* (London: Routledge and Kegan Paul, 1982), p. 154.

39. See Caren J. Deming, "*Hill Street Blues* as Narrative," *Critical Studies in Mass Communication* 2 (March 1985): 1–22.

40. Jane Feuer, "Narrative Form in American Network Television," in *High Theory/Low Culture: Analyzing Popular Television and Film*, ed. Colin MacCabe (Manchester, Eng.: Manchester University Press, 1986), p. 104.

FOR FURTHER READING

Anyone interested in pursuing this subject should begin with a general overview of narrative theory. I recommend: Seymour Chatman, *Story and Discourse: Narrative Structure in Fiction and Film* (Ithaca, N.Y.: Cornell University Press, 1978), which is highly readable; Wallace Martin, *Recent Theories of Narrative* (Ithaca, N.Y.: Cornell University Press, 1986), which compares competing theories, includes useful diagrams and examples, and offers a thorough bibliography; and Shlomith Rimmon-Kenan, *Narrative Fiction: Contemporary Poetics* (London: Methuen, 1983), which is both concise and thorough and also offers an excellent annotated bibliography. A useful addition to one of the above general handbooks is Gerald Prince, *A Dictio-*

nary of Narratology (Lincoln: University of Nebraska Press, 1987), which discusses concepts of narrative theory in a handy dictionary format.

Having mastered the basic tenets of narrative theory, one can proceed further into the field along any number of byways. I have noted below only a handful of the many paths one might follow.

Those interested in storyline or plot would do well to start with Vladimir Propp, *Morphology of the Folktale* (Austin: University of Texas Press, 1970), which is a pathbreaking study of story structure that is short, readable, and intriguing; another seminal study of story events is found in Roland Barthes, "Introduction to the Structural Analysis of Narratives," in *Image/Music/Text*, trans. Stephen Heath (New York: Hill and Wang, 1977). Jonathan Culler's *Structuralist Poetics* (Ithaca, N.Y.: Cornell University Press, 1975) traces narrative theory's debt to structuralism and offers insights on naturalization and convention.

Those interested in narrators, discourse, and studies of what used to be called "point of view" should start with Wayne C. Booth, *The Rhetoric of Fiction* (Chicago: University of Chicago Press, 1961), which helped define the field, and then move on to Gérard Genette, *Narrative Discourse: An Essay in Method*, trans. Jane E. Lewin (Ithaca, N.Y.: Cornell University Press, 1980), which is a sustained analysis of Marcel Proust's *A la recherche du temps perdu* mixed with rigorous theory. Genette has provided his own corrections and additions to his previous text in *Narrative Discourse Revisited*, trans. J. E. Lewin (Ithaca, N.Y.: Cornell University Press, 1988). Both of Genette's studies should be consulted by anyone interested in time.

Different, valuable approaches to narrative theory are offered by William Labov, "Transformation of Experience in Narrative Syntax," in *Language in the Inner City: Studies in Black English Vernacular* (Philadelphia: University of Pennsylvania Press, 1972), pp. 354–96, which offers an alternate model of narrative structure, and by Robert Scholes and Robert Kellogg, *The Nature of Narrative* (New York: Oxford University Press, 1966), which provides an overview of the development of narrative form from the time of the ancient Greeks to the twentieth century.

Whereas the works cited above couch themselves as studies of general narratology (and primarily restrict their examples to literature), many texts explicitly apply narrative theory to film. One might begin with Christian Metz, "Notes toward a Phenomenology of the Narrative," in *Film Language: A Semiotics of the Cinema*, trans. Michael Taylor (New York: Oxford University Press, 1974), a rich, though brief, essay. Next one might turn to David Bordwell, *Narration in the Fiction Film* (Madison: University of Wisconsin Press, 1985), which is a lengthy and scholarly discussion drawing on the work of the Russian Formalists and later narrative theorists. Seymour Chatman's *Coming To Terms: The Rhetoric Of Narrative in Fiction and Film* (Ithaca, N.Y.: Cornell University Press, 1990) offers the latest thinking on many thorny issues. My own *Invisible Storytellers: Voice-Over Narration in American Fiction Film* (Berkeley: University of California Press, 1988) may be useful.

The number of journal articles dealing with film and narrative is large and growing. Students would do well to consult such journals as *Film Quarterly*, *Screen*, *Journal of Film and Video*, *Cinema Journal*, and *Wide Angle*. Let me specifically draw attention to: Robert Burgoyne, "The Cinematic Narrator: The Logic and Pragmatics of Impersonal Narration," *Journal of Film and Video* 42, no. 1 (Spring 1990): 3–16; Francesco Casetti, "Antonioni and Hitchcock: Two Strategies of Narrative Investment," *Sub-Stance* 51 (1986): 69–86; André Gaudreault, "Narration and Monstration in the Cinema," *Journal of Film and Video* 39, no. 2 (Spring 1987): 29–36; Brian Henderson, "Tense, Mood, and Voice in Film," *Film Quarterly* 36, no. 4 (Fall 1983): 4–17; and Marsha Kinder, "The Subversive Potential of the Pseudo-Iterative," *Film Quarterly* 43, no. 2 (Winter 1989/1990): 3–16.

The body of literature dealing with television narratives is also growing. Some of these studies offer valuable descriptions without resorting to narrative theory per se; for example, see John Ellis, *Visible Fictions: Cinema, Television, Video* (London: Routledge and Kegan Paul, 1982); and David Marc, *Demographic Vistas: Television in American Culture* (Philadelphia: University of Pennsylvania Press, 1984).

Other texts apply various aspects of narratology to television. For a sampling, see Roger Silverstone, *The Message of Television: Myth and Narrative in Contemporary Culture* (London: Heinemann, 1981); Robert C. Allen, *Speaking of Soap Operas* (Chapel Hill: University of North Carolina Press, 1985); John Fiske, *Television Culture* (London: Methuen, 1987). In anthologies, see Sharon Lynn Sperry, "Television News as Narrative," in *Understanding Television: Essays on Television as a Social and Cultural Force*, ed. Richard P. Adler (New York: Praeger, 1981), pp. 295–312; Jane Feuer, "Narrative Form in American Network Television," in *High Theory/Low Culture: Analyzing Popular Television and Film*, ed. Colin MacCabe (Manchester, Eng.: Manchester University Press, 1986), pp. 101–14; and several useful essays by Robert Allen, Sandy Flitterman, Maureen Turim, and Robert Stam in *Regarding Television—Critical Approaches: An Anthology*, ed. E. Ann Kaplan, American Film Institute Monograph Series, vol. 2 (Frederick, Md.: University Publications of America, 1983).

Among the many journal articles dealing with television and narrative, see especially Caren J. Deming, *"Hill Street Blues* as Narrative," *Critical Studies in Mass Communication* 2 (March 1985): 1–22; Phillip Drummond, "Structural and Narrative Constraints and Strategies in *The Sweeney,"* *Screen* 20, no. 1 (1976): 15–35; and Mimi White, "Crossing Wavelengths: The Diegetic and Referential Imaginary of American Commercial Television," *Cinema Journal* 25, no. 2 (Winter 1986): 51–64.

3 : AUDIENCE-
ORIENTED
CRITICISM
AND
TELEVISION

robert c. allen

This chapter focuses on the experience of watching television—an experience that, as I suggested in the introduction, is a pervasive and almost universal feature of modern life. And yet, precisely because it is so much a part of the fabric of everyday life, it is not very well understood. All of the essays in this book address the general question: How do we make sense of and derive pleasure from watching television? This chapter zeros in on the meeting place between television's discourses and television viewers. We will approach this intersection between the world inside the set and the viewer in front of it from three directions. First, I assess the general strand of contemporary literary theory called reader-oriented criticism to see what light it might shed on how we understand television narratives. Sarah Kozloff's chapter on television narratives has examined the relationship between the tellers of "tele-tales" and the tales themselves. In part, this chapter takes up the relationship between television's tales and the viewers of those tales. If every story presumes a teller, it also presumes someone to whom the story is told.

But television is not just a series of tales; it is a performance medium, and in some ways it resembles the I/you relationship of face-to-face communication more than the removed and mediated writer/reader relationship of literary communication. With most novels, the reader's role in the exchange process between writer and reader is hidden; the reader is seldom addressed or appealed to. Commercial television, on the other hand, constantly addresses, appeals, implores, demands, wheedles, urges, and attempts to seduce the viewer. If literature and cinema attempt to draw us out of our everyday worlds and into their make-believe universes, commercial television projects itself, its stories, its products into the everyday world of the viewer. In short, we need to consider ways in which television's discourses and modes of address engage the viewer differently than either both literature or film.

The ways in which viewers make sense and pleasure from their engagements with television depend in part on the particularities of the act of television viewing. The expression *watching television* subsumes a wide variety of modes of engagement with the television set, from rapt attention to occasional glances in the direction of the screen while you are doing something else. But whatever mode of television viewing you're in, it is not the same kind of experience as reading a book or even watching a movie in a theater. Therefore, we consider what we might learn about the general processes of television viewing from the results of what might be called ethnographic audience research—direct observation of television viewing behavior.

Reader-Oriented Criticism

Reader-response criticism, reception theory, and *reader-oriented criticism* are all names given to the variety of recent works in literary studies that examine the role of the reader in understanding and deriving pleasure from literary texts. Reader-oriented criticism starts from the belief that the meaning of a literary text does not reside in any absolute sense within the text itself. Rather, texts are made to have meaning by readers as they read. Reader-response criticism places this process of meaning and pleasure production—the act of reading—at the center of the critical enterprise. In doing so, it attempts to make explicit what has long been a hidden and largely unacknowledged phenomenon: the confrontation between the reading act and textual structure.

The commonsense observation that meaning does not occur except through the reading act has given rise not so much to a single approach to literature (or film, or television) as to a large and frequently contentious field of inquiry. Perhaps because they come so close to the heart of criticism itself and to our relationship with those curious other worlds we call literature, film, or television, questions regarding the reading act have not been answered in a single voice or asked from within a single theoretical framework. Questions about reading and readers have been raised within phenomenology, structuralism, semiotics, feminism, Marxism, and psychoanalysis—not to mention cognitive psychology, information theory, and several branches of sociology. As Elizabeth Freund puts it in her survey of reader-response criticism: "The trend to liberate the reader from his enforced anonymity and silence, to enable him to recover an identity or the authority of a force, is bedevilled by all the concomitant hazards, schisms, anxieties, and jargons of liberation movements." Reader-response criticism is, she concludes, a "labyrinth of converging and sometimes contradictory approaches."[1]

Rather than try to follow all the paths in this critical labyrinth, I will organize my discussion of this approach around what I see as a set of key questions—key both to the project of reader-oriented approaches in general and to their possible application to television narratives. In doing so, I will necessarily gloss over many of the philosophical and methodological differences between the various schools of reader-response criticism that stand out so sharply to literary theorists. What is most important to the student of television is the question that reader-oriented criticism thrusts into the critical foreground: What happens when we read a fictional narrative? But we must also ask, What issues and complications arise when the narrative text being "read" is televisual rather than literary?

One branch of reader-response criticism has concerned itself particularly with the ways in which the reader is implicated in the text and in which he or she constructs a rich imaginary world out of the stark black words of the fictional text. The literary theories of Roman Ingarden, Wolfgang Iser, and Hans Robert Jauss grow out of the more general philosophical position known as *phenomenology*. Given its name by philosopher Edmund Husserl in the 1930s, phenomenology concerns itself with the relationship between the perceiving individual and the world of things, people, and actions that might be perceived. These are not two separate realms connected only by the passive sensory mechanisms of the individual, declared Husserl, but rather they are inextricably linked aspects of the process by which we know anything. All thought and perception involve mutually dependent subjects and objects. I cannot think but that I think *of something*. Thus to study any *thing* is to study that thing as it is experienced or conceptualized within the consciousness of a particular individual. Reality, in other words, has no meaning for us except as individually experienced phenomena.

Phenomenology views reading fiction as a special and fascinating instance of the more general process by which meaning is imposed upon the world by the individual consciousness. The act of reading is not merely a mechanical process of sense making, but rather a curious and paradoxical process by which lifeless and pitifully inadequate marks on a page are brought to life in the reader's imagination. This process occurs in reading the simplest fictional narrative (a joke or folktale) as well as the most complicated and extended literary exercise. It occurs so quickly and seemingly so automatically that it would appear to short-circuit conscious thought and logic.

What happens when reader meets text, when consciousness encounters the printed page, can be, and has been, conceptualized in any number of ways: as a sort of mutually sustaining collaboration; as a surrender of the reader to the thoughts of an absent other; and even as a struggle for power between the text and the reader. All such conceptualizations of reader-text interaction recognize that the world constructed as a result of the reading act has existence only in the mind of the reader, and yet its construction is initiated and guided by the words the reader encounters in the text. Furthermore, those words were selected and organized by someone else, and yet that person (the author) is always absent from the reading process. To Roman Ingarden, a student of Husserl, the literary work is like a musical composition. As a piece of sheet music, the musical text is still only a set of possibilities. This musical *text* becomes a musical *work* only when a performer "concretizes" the text in performance. The musical composition certainly exists apart from any particular performance of it, but it has meaning for us only as a performance. Similarly, the literary text for Ingarden is but a "schemata," a skeletal structure of meaning possibilities awaiting realization by the reader.

[As an arrangement of words on the page, the literary text is but half of the perceptual dynamic; it is an object, yet without a perceiving subject. In the reading act, the fictional world represented by the words on the page is constructed and given life within the consciousness of the reader. That world is created as the reader follows the cues provided by the text, but also—even more important, according to Ingarden—as the reader fills in the places the text leaves vacant. Gap filling is the process by which the imaginary world suggested by words in the text is constructed in the mind of the reader. The notion of gap filling recognizes that reading a novel involves not merely following a mental recipe using ingredients supplied by the text, but a much more complex process in which the reader brings to bear upon the words of the text previous experiences with liter-

Ingarden-
gap-filling by
reader

ary texts, knowledge of other texts of the same type, and an array of mostly unconscious assumptions drawn from his or her own experiential world. Because those experiences and knowledge vary from culture to culture, group to group, and individual to individual, there will be different fictional worlds constructed by different readers on the basis of the same textual instructions. Furthermore, gap filling accounts for one of the most fascinating qualities of imaginative literature: The worlds we construct in reading literature appear to us to be fully formed and complete from the time we get our first descriptions of them on page one until after we have finished reading the final paragraph of the book. Reading a novel is not like playing "connect the dots." We don't start with an apparently random arrangement of words that take on meaning and life only at the end of the reading process. Even on the basis of the tiniest fragment of narrative information, we will provide whatever is missing until we have organized those scraps into a complete imaginary world.

Gap filling is also affected by our movement through the text. The confrontation between our initial expectations and the text forms a sort of provisional fictional world, on the basis of which we develop further expectations of what is likely to happen next as well as assumptions about the relationship between any one part of this fictional world and any other. As we read further, those expectations are modified so that we can keep a coherent world before our mind's eye at all times. In short, Ingarden reminds us that reading is a dynamic tension between the reader's expectations and the text's schematic instructions for meaning production. The result is a constantly changing fictional world, but one that appears to us as whole and complete at any moment during the reading act.

Ingarden's description of the reading act is the starting point for Wolfgang Iser's *The Act of Reading*.[2] Iser points out that our relationship with narrative artworks is fundamentally different from that with painting or photography. A painting can be taken in all at once. The only time we experience a novel as a whole, however, is when we have finished experiencing it—that is, only after we have read it all. Instead of being outside the work contemplating it as a whole, the reader of a narrative takes on what Iser calls a "wandering viewpoint," a constantly changing position within the text itself.

Although Iser seems to exclude visual narratives (film and, by extension, television) from his account of the wandering viewpoint, it is clear that any narrative form involves the reader's—or viewer's—movement through the text, from one sentence, shot, or scene to the next. Because narratives unfold in time (reading time or screen time), as viewers or

Iser - maintains reader wandering viewpoint → any narrative form involves the readers movement through the text

Iser: protension (expectation) & retension (Knowledge to that pt.)

Iser - gap filling paradigmatic assoc- (concept) syntagmatic (ends of chapters)

readers we are always poised between the textual geography we have already wandered across and that we have yet to cover. This tension between what we have learned from the text and what we anticipate finding out occurs throughout the text and at every level of its organization. Each sentence of a literary narrative or each shot of a television narrative both answers questions and asks new ones. Iser describes this process as an alternation between *protension* (expectation or anticipation) and *retention* (our knowledge of the text to that point). To continue the geographic metaphor, each new "block" of text we cover provides us with a new vantage point from which to regard the landscape of the text thus far, while at the same time it causes us to speculate as to what lies around the next textual corner. Hence our viewpoint constantly "wanders" backward and forward across the text.

According to Iser, although the text can stimulate and attempt to channel protension and retention, it cannot control those processes, because both occur in the places where the text is silent—in the inevitable gaps between sentences, paragraphs, and chapters. And, I would add, in the gaps between shots, scenes, segments, and episodes. It is in these holes in the textual structure that we as readers and viewers "work" on that structure. We make the connections that the text cannot make for us.

Iser's theory of reading activity as gap filling relies on a basic semiotic distinction (discussed in Ellen Seiter's essay) between *paradigmatic* (associative) and *syntagmatic* (sequential) organization. The gaps in the text to which Iser refers involve the syntagmatic arrangement of textual segments—the space between one chapter and the next, for example. These gaps provide us with an opportunity to consider possible paradigmatic relationships between the segments as well. In other words, how might they be related associatively or conceptually?

As I have noted, Iser limits his theory of the reading act to literature. As a scholar whose examples are drawn predominantly from the realm of "high art" literature, Iser might be horrified at the prospect of someone applying his theory of reading not just to television, but to one of the most popular and least "artsy" of television narrative forms: the soap opera. Yet this is precisely what I propose to do. The phenomenological theory of reading activity developed by Ingarden and elaborated by Iser helps to account for the curiously structured and quite complex fictional soap opera worlds that viewers encounter daily. Furthermore, given that some aspects of "reading" soap operas overlap with the processes involved in reading any narrative broadcast on commercial television, a reader- or viewer-oriented account of the relationship between soap operas and their viewers might help us to understand our relationship with television narratives more generally.

Serial narrative—what we usually call soap opera—is the most popular form of television programming in the world. Telenovelas dominate the evening television schedule in many parts of Latin America. Brazil's largest commercial television company, TV Globo, not only produces that country's most popular soap operas, which are in turn the country's most popular programs, but it exports its *telenovelas* to dozens of countries around the world. One soap opera or another is usually the most-watched program in Australia in any given week, and for the past thirty years a soap opera has been the most popular program in Great Britain. In the winter of 1991, a new serial in the People's Republic of China took that country by storm. Since the early 1930s, American daytime television schedules have been dominated by serial drama, and the success of *Dallas* in the 1970s led to a proliferation of serials in the evening schedules as well.

The most striking narrative feature of soap operas—as the term *serial narrative* implies—is their openness. Closed narratives (found in most feature films and novels) resolve all the major narrative questions raised in the plot by its end. The pleasure derived from reading or watching closed narratives is closely connected to that moment of ultimate closure —when secrets are revealed, riddles solved, obstacles overcome, and desires fulfilled. Open narratives, on the other hand, do not tie up all their narrative loose ends. Questions, problems, mysteries might remain unsettled or their resolutions might provoke still further questions, problems, and complications.

Some serial forms are more open than others. Latin American soap operas, for example, tend to last only a few months. At the end of their runs, there is some attempt to close off some of the major plot lines. Here we need to make a distinction between American prime-time serials, which are shown in weekly, one-hour episodes (*Dallas, L.A. Law, thirtysomething, Twin Peaks*), and daytime soap operas, which are either a half-hour or an hour long and are shown five days a week (*Santa Barbara, General Hospital, As the World Turns*). An episode of a prime-time American serial usually contains at least one plot line that is closed off by the end of the episode, along with a few others that might be stretched over several episodes or an entire season. American daytime serials and British and Australian soap operas (*EastEnders, Coronation Street, Neighbors, Home and Away*) implicitly assume they will never end, and they very seldom produce narrative closure within a given episode. Every plot line continues across a number of episodes.

In applying some of the insights of reader-oriented criticism to the soap opera, I want to concentrate on the American daytime soap opera because it demonstrates most clearly the peculiar narrative qualities of the serial form in general. However, most of the points I make about American daytime soaps are applicable to British and Australian soaps as well. The openness, longevity, and frequency of American daytime soap operas (which I will henceforth simply call soap operas) result in a staggeringly large amount of text devoted, ostensibly at least, to the relating of the same overall story. Each year an hour-long soap opera offers its viewers 260 hours of text. Most of the soaps currently being run on American commercial television have been on the air for at least ten years. In cinematic terms, this represents the equivalent of 1,300 feature-length films! One soap opera, *Guiding Light,* has enjoyed a continuous television run since the early 1950s, giving it a text that would require more than a year of nonstop viewing to "read."

Another distinctive feature of the soap opera text is its presumption of its own immortality. Closed narrative forms are conceived backward, with the ending of the story dictating what leads up to it. Soap operas have no point toward which all movement in the plot is directed. Rather than being based around a single resolving plot line, soap operas disperse their narrative energy among a constantly changing set of interrelated plots, which may merge, overlap, diverge, fragment, close off, and open up again over a viewing period of several years. Individual episodes advance the plots incrementally, but no one watches a soap opera with the expectation that one day all of the conflicts and narrative entanglements will be resolved so that the entire population of the soap opera universe can fade into happily-ever-after oblivion.

A final resolution to a soap opera's narrative seems so unlikely in part because we follow the activities of an entire community of characters rather than observing the fate of a few protagonists. It is not at all unusual for a soap opera to feature more than forty regularly appearing characters at any given time—not including those characters who have been consigned to the netherworld between full citizenship in the community and death: characters who long ago moved to another town, or characters whose fate is uncertain (dozens of soap opera characters have been presumed dead, only to be resurrected years later). These large communities represent elaborate networks of character relationships, in which *who* someone is is a matter of *to whom* he or she is related by marriage, kinship, friendship, or antagonism. These complex character networks in American daytime soap operas distinguish them even from their prime-time counterparts such as *Dallas* or *L.A. Law*, whose "permanent" residents are fewer (a dozen as opposed to thirty or forty) and whose narratives depend much more upon a few central characters.

In an attempt to account for the soap opera viewing process, we might begin by recalling Iser's point that we can never experience a narrative text in its totality while we are reading it; we are always someplace "inside" its structure rather than outside of it contemplating it as a whole. However, unlike closed narrative forms (the novel, the short story, the feature film, the made-for-TV movie or teleplay), the soap opera does not give us a position after "The End" from which to look back on the entire text. The final page of a soap opera never comes, nor is it ever anticipated by the viewer. As soap opera viewers, we cannot help but be inside the narrative flow of the soap opera text. Furthermore, our "wandering" through the soap opera text as viewers is a process that can occur quite literally over the course of decades.

Even if we wished to view the entire text of *All My Children* or *Coronation Street* to this point in its history, we would be unable to do so; a soap opera is like a novel whose chapters we rip up immediately after reading them. Our viewing of soap operas is regulated by their being parceled out in daily installments. Unlike our reading of a literary text, the rate at which we "read" films or television programs is a function of the text itself rather than our reading activity. The exception—and it is becoming a rather important one—occurs when we watch programs on videotape and thus can zip, zap, and freeze the flow of images; otherwise those images flash by at a predetermined and unalterable rate. With soap operas, and to a lesser degree with other series and serial forms of television narrative, this reading regulation is not just technological but institutional as well—a measured portion of text is allocated for each episode and for each scene within each episode. Unlike the series form of television narrative, wherein a complete story is told in each episode and only the setting and characters carry through from week to week, the soap opera simply suspends the telling of its stories at the end of each episode without any pretext of narrative resolution. In the 1930s and 1940s, radio soap operas ended each episode with the announcer asking, for example, "Will Mary forgive John's thoughtlessness and agree to marry him? Join us tomorrow." The announcer's role was eliminated as soap operas shifted from radio to television, but the calculated suspension of the text at the end of each episode of a television soap opera implicitly encourages the viewer to ask the same sort of question and provides the same answer: You'll have to tune in to the *next* episode to find out.

Viewed in terms of reader-oriented criticism, the time between the end of one soap opera episode and the beginning of the next constitutes an enforced gap between syntagmatic segments of the text. Iser comments on a parallel pattern of textual organization in the novels of Charles Dickens, which were first published in weekly installments in magazines. Thus, during his lifetime, many of Dickens's readers read his novels over a period of months, one chapter each week. Iser claims that they frequently reported enjoying the serialized form of a given novel more than they did the same work when it was eventually published in book form. Their heightened enjoyment Iser explains in terms of the protensive tension provoked by the strategic interruption of the narrative at crucial moments. Every chapter ended with a major unanswered question, but the reader had to wait until the next issue of the magazine before it would be answered. By structuring the text around the gaps between installments and by making those gaps literally days in length, the serial novel supercharged the reader's imagination and made him or her a more active reader.[3]

The relationship Iser sees between "strategic interruption" and heightened enjoyment would seem to apply with particular force to the experience of watching soap operas. It might also be responsible, in part at least, for the frequently mentioned loyalty of many soap opera viewers and for the pleasure many viewers take in talking about their "stories" (my mother's generic term for soap operas) with other viewers. The regular suspension of the telling of those stories increases the desire to once again join the lives of characters the viewer has come to know over the course of years of viewing. And because the viewer cannot induce the text to start up again, some of the energy generated by this protensive tension might well be channeled into discourse about the text among fellow viewers.

When Dorothy Hobson interviewed women office workers in Birmingham, England, to determine how talk about soap operas fit into the everyday work environment, she discovered that the opportunity to talk about soaps in the "gap" between episodes was just as important to these viewers as watching the soap. Their lunchtime and work-break conversations frequently revolved around soap operas, as they anticipated what might happen next, debated the significance of recent plot events, analyzed the motives and behaviors of particular characters, and related the fictional world of the soap opera to their own experiences. Indeed, several women decided to begin watching a particular soap opera because they found lunchtime discussion about it so important to their colleagues.[4] The range of protensive possibilities these and other viewers of soap operas might discuss is considerably wider than in many other types of narrative. Unlike texts that have a single protagonist with whom the reader identifies almost exclusively, the soap opera distributes interest among an entire community of characters, thus making any one character narratively dispensable. Even characters the viewer has known for decades may suddenly die in plane crashes, lapse into comas, or move to Cleveland.

Textual gaps exist not only between soap opera episodes but within each episode as well. Each episode is planned around the placement of commercial messages, so that the scene immediately preceding a commercial raises a narrative question. For the sponsor, the soap opera narrative text is but a pretext for the commercial—the bait that arouses the viewer's interest and prepares him or her for the delivery of the sales pitch. For the viewer, however, the commercial is an interruption of the narrative—another gap between textual segments, providing an excellent opportunity to reassess previous textual information and reformulate expectations regarding future developments. We might even argue that the repetition and predictability of commercial messages encourage this retentive and protensive activity. A given commercial might be novel enough to warrant our attention the first time we see it, but is unlikely to sustain our interest on subsequent viewings.

Iser theorizes that textual gaps can also be created by "cutting" between plot lines in a story. Just when the reader's interest has been secured by the characters and situation of one plot line, the text shifts perspective suddenly to another set of characters and another plot strand. Because of this, says Iser, "the reader is forced to try to find connections between the hitherto familiar story and the new, unforeseeable situations. He is faced with a whole network of possibilities, and thus begins himself to formulate missing links."[5] As regular soap opera viewers know, in any given episode there are likely to be several major plot lines unfolding. The text "cuts" among them constantly. The action in one scene might simply be suspended for a time while we look in on another plot line. Later in the episode we might rejoin the action in scene one as if no time had elapsed in the interval, or we might join that plot line at a later moment in time.

The gaps that structure the soap opera viewing experience—between episodes and between one scene and the next, as well as those created by commercial interruptions—become all the more important when one considers the complex network of character relationships formed by the soap opera community. In a sense, the soap opera trades narrative closure for paradigmatic complexity. Anything might happen to an individual character, but in the long run it will not affect the community of characters as a whole. By the same token, everything that happens to an individual character affects other characters to whom he or she is related.

When I first began to watch soap operas regularly, I was struck by the amount of narrative redundancy within each episode. One episode of *Guiding Light*, I remember well, consisted basically of scenes in which different members of the community learned that two couples were about to be married. I could understand why this information might be repeated in subsequent episodes—not every viewer is able to watch soap operas every day—but why was it necessary to repeat it over and over again within the *same* episode? This is a puzzle only for the inexperienced soap opera viewer. The regular viewer, familiar with the paradigmatic structure of that particular soap (that is, its network of character relationships) will know that *who* tells *whom* is just as important as *what* is being related. Having been conditioned to think of a narrative primarily in syntagmatic terms (what happens when), I did not realize that in soap operas, what happens is important only as it affects the soap's network of character relationships. Each retelling of the information "Skip and Carol are to be wed" is viewed against the background formed by all the characters' interrelationships. Thus the second and third retellings within the same episode are far from being *paradigmatically* redundant.

How is this paradigmatic complexity related to the structuring of gaps in the soap opera text? The size of the soap opera community, the complexity of its character relationships, and the fact that soap opera characters possess both histories and memories all combine to create an almost infinite set of potential connections between one plot event and another. The syntagmatic juxtaposition of two plot lines (a scene from one following or preceding a scene from the other) arouses in the viewer the possibility of a paradigmatic connection between them. But because the connection the text makes is only a syntagmatic one, the viewer is left to imagine what other connection, if any, they might have. The range of latent relationships evoked by the gaps between scenes is dependent upon the viewer's familiarity with the current community of characters and his or her historical knowledge of previous character relationships. For example, one episode of a soap opera might be structured around the wedding of two young characters. Following a scene showing the exchange of vows, we might see the bride's divorced parents arguing at the reception, while in the next scene two young friends of the bridal couple exchange amorous glances across a crowded dance floor. The text itself does not indicate what paradigmatic relationship the viewer is to construct among these three syntagmatically linked scenes. But the viewer may well see connections among the ritual union of two characters, the effects of the dissolution of the union between the parents of one of them, and the possible beginning of a romantic union between two other characters. In a very real sense, then, the better one knows a soap opera and its characters, the greater reason one has for wanting to watch every day. Conversely, the less involved one is in a given soap opera's textual network, the more that soap opera appears to be merely an unending series of plot lines that unfold so slowly that virtually nothing "happens" in any given episode, and the more tiresomely redundant each episode seems.

Television's Modes of Address

As we have seen, narrative theory begins with the observation that every story is told *by someone* and in particular ways. Reader-oriented criticism takes up the corollary to this observation: every story entails someone to whom and for whose benefit the story is being told. In attempting to specify "to whom" a story is told and the role this hypothetical listener/reader ought/might play in the reading process, reader-oriented theorists have proposed a bewildering array of readers—fictive reader, model reader, intended reader, ideal reader, implied reader, and super-reader, to name but a few. Although each of these readers is somewhat different, they all refer to the fact that—as anyone who has ever tried to tell an anecdote or a joke knows—every story is constructed around a set of assumptions the teller makes about his or her audience: what they know or don't know; what their attitudes are toward certain groups of people; why they are willing to listen to the story to begin with; how it is likely to fit in with other stories or jokes they might have heard; and so forth. *Model, ideal, super, implied*—these words all refer to the composite of these assumptions as they are manifested within the narrative itself.

For example, the university where I teach (the University of North Carolina at Chapel Hill) has an intense sports rivalry with another campus of the state university system that is located just twenty miles away (North Carolina State University). The rivalry has prompted a number of jokes told by students and alumni (all right, yes, sometimes by faculty, too) of one school about the other. At a UNC alumni reception a few years ago, someone asked me if I knew how one could identify a funeral procession for a State alumnus? "The lead tractor," he said, "has its lights on." The fact of his telling me this joke assumes a number of things about me as a listener: (1) that I am aware of the rivalry between the two schools;

(2) that I know that N.C. State is the campus in the state system that specializes in agriculture; (3) that I know that a tractor is an inappropriate vehicle in a funeral procession; and (4) that I side with UNC in this rivalry and thus am likely to find the joke both relevant and funny rather than pointless and insulting.

One of the most obvious ways the reader can be acknowledged and assumptions about him or her manifested is by referring directly to the reader: addressing the reader directly, confiding in the reader, appealing to the reader, describing what the reader knows or might feel, even questioning or challenging the reader's interpretation of the text thus far. In other words, the text might create a *characterized fictional reader*. Such a strategy was common in the eighteenth-century British novel (Henry Fielding's *Tom Jones*, for example), reaching its most elaborate (and funniest) use in Laurence Sterne's *Tristram Shandy*. But the fashion for characterized fictional readers waned in the nineteenth century (compare Dickens with Fielding), and by the twentieth century the reader was largely ignored in mainstream fiction. Even when the author employed first-person narration to personify the voice of the storyteller, there was seldom a corresponding personified reader to whom the first-person narrator told his or her tale. Adopting the narrational style of the nineteenth-century novel and drama, Hollywood cinema also pretends the viewer isn't there and tells its stories, for the most part, through the inhuman objectivity of the "third-person" camera.

Thus, despite reader-oriented criticism's usefulness in foregrounding the role of the reader, the relationship between addresser and addressee in television needs to be distinguished from that in literature as well as from that in cinema and theater. In all these modes of storytelling, says Marie Maclean, we have a type of performance. A novel, film, play, or television program is a presentation, a display text arranged in a particular way for a particular audience in the hopes of eliciting a particular set of responses. Each of these forms carries within it traces of the face-to-face communication situation from which each ultimately derived. "Through a narrative text," she writes,

> *I* meet *you* in a struggle which may be cooperative or may be combative, a struggle for knowledge, for power, for pleasure, for possession. The meeting is manifest in the course of the narrative performance in which the performer whether human or textual, undertakes to control the audience by words or signs alone, while they, the partners in the act, use their power as hearers to dictate the terms of the control.

If you tell me a story, I can refuse to listen, but if I become a listener, I can also always remind you that words, in the last resort, can only mean what my mind allows them to mean. I, too, am constantly performing.[6]

All performances, she continues, involve a set of expectations and conventions that form a contractual relationship between performer and audience. This contract might be violated, transgressed, subverted, or amended, but it cannot be ignored because it frames the performance act itself.

Each form of performance (novel, cinema, drama, television) implies a different set of conventions and expectations and hence a different contract between performer and audience. For example, in live performance, performers can regulate their "acts" according to the immediate feedback audience members provide them. A stand-up comic can address an audience member directly, allow him or her to "perform" in answer to a question, exchange barbs with a heckler, or decide to change material in midact if audience response seems to dictate that. By the same token, the audience of the live performance has the power to respond while the performance is occurring, in the same space as the performer, and in such a way that its response can affect the nature of the performance. Literary performance, on the other hand, is but a representation of an enacted performance. The actual "performer" (the author) is always absent from the text and at the moment of the text's "performance" in the mind of the reader. Nor can the author, at the time of his or her "performance" (the writing of the book), see or hear the person by whom the text is meant to be read. In written texts, both performer and audience have become literary conventions; the author may be represented in the text as a narrator and the reader may be characterized by the text, but both have been reduced to linguistic signs. The reader's power to attempt to control the performance contract is similarly limited—at least in relation to the face-to-face performance situation. "Feedback" becomes the reader's interpretation of the text.

Cinema combines features of both live and literary performance. It provides us with an iconic (Peirce might say "indexical") rather than a linguistic representation of the performance act. In other words, cinema is at one level at least a record or simulation of what was, at the moment of recording on film, a "live" performance. Despite the fact that it rarely occurs in Hollywood films, a film performer can appear to address the audience in the movie theater by looking and speaking into the camera. (Woody Allen's *Purple Rose of Cairo* is a fantasy about overcoming the simulated nature of cinema's direct address.) But direct address in the cinema is still only a representation of a face-to-face exchange, because the performer is literally absent both from the film itself and from the time and place of its showing, just as the audience was absent at the moment the performer spoke to the camera. Similarly, although there can be immediate response to the film in the movie theater (laughter, applause, hissing, even verbal retorts), nothing the audience does short of stopping the projector will affect the film's "performance." At one level each showing of the film will be the same as the last, regardless of how demonstrative the audience's response might have been.

Television has a greater capacity to emulate live performance than either cinema or literature. Unlike literature and like cinema, television represents its performers iconically—we see their images on the screen. But unlike cinema, television can serve not only as a recording device but also as a simultaneous transmission device. Direct address in cinema can only allude to a face-to-face communication situation because the address is always frozen in the past. Television can and does simulate face-to-face communication in that a performer's address to the camera can be seen and heard by the viewer at the moment of its articulation. The word *simulation* is very important here. Television creates the appearance of a face-to-face encounter between performer and viewer, but it is an encounter in which the viewer is severely limited in his or her ability to turn the tables and become the addresser. Where that does occur (as with viewer call-in shows or on home shopping cable channels), it is usually via another communication technology, the telephone, which reduces the viewer-as-performer to a disembodied voice. Furthermore, the television performer can control which viewer is allowed to be heard by other viewers and for how long. In short, the issue is not how close television can come to imitating an actual face-to-face communication event, but how, why, and with what effects upon the act of TV viewing television uses its unique capacity to simulate person-to-person encounters.

In terms of the way television addresses and attempts to engage the viewer, we need to keep in mind that television has the ability to "represent" a wide variety of other narrative, dramatic, and performance forms. Television can transmit a "live" theatrical performance or sporting event. It can also broadcast a film made decades ago. In the broadcasting of news conferences, it can show a face-to-face encounter as it happens. In the near half-century of its use as a commercial entertainment medium, television has developed two primary modes of address—what we might call the *cinematic* mode and the *rhetorical* mode.

Drawn from the conventions of Hollywood-style cinema, what I am calling the cinematic mode of address and viewer engagement expends tremendous effort to hide its operation. It engages its viewers covertly, making them unseen observers of a world that always appears fully formed and autonomous. As has been noted, with very few exceptions (most of them in comedies), the viewer of a Hollywood-style film is neither addressed nor acknowledged. One of the cardinal sins of film acting is looking into the lens of the camera, because doing so threatens to break the illusion of reality by reminding viewers of the apparatus that intervenes between them and the world on the screen. This is certainly not to say that there is no "implied" viewer constructed by Hollywood films. Given that the viewer's knowledge of the world of the film comes through the camera, the viewer is quite literally positioned in some place relative to the action in every shot.

We see the cinematic mode of viewer engagement on television not only in televised Hollywood films or made-for-TV movies, but also in television dramas of all sorts as well as in some situation comedies. Indeed, the preponderance of television drama on prime-time American television is shot using the same conventions as "big-screen" filmmaking—especially as those conventions affect address. We would find it astonishing if, during an episode of *Dallas*, J. R. Ewing turned to the camera and said, "What do you think about that?" And even in *Twin Peaks*, a show acclaimed for its narrative and stylistic innovation, the viewer was still ignored, and the narrative unfolded as if no one were watching.

Daytime soap operas and some situation comedies have modified the Hollywood style of shooting to accommodate what is called "three-camera, live-tape" shooting, whereby an entire scene is enacted while being shot and recorded on videotape simultaneously by three (or more) television cameras. The director electronically cuts between one camera's shot and another as the scene is enacted in real time. Live-tape production obviously makes subjective point-of-view shots much more difficult to achieve than in Hollywood-style filmmaking, because repositioning the camera so that it sees what a particular character sees would require penetrating the space of the scene. Hence subjectivity (showing what a character sees or thinks) is usually rendered aurally rather than visually by showing a close-up of a character while his or her thoughts are heard on the sound track. Despite some degree of deviation from Hollywood cinema style, however, live-tape television dramas seldom, if ever, address the viewer.

The rhetorical mode of viewer engagement on television is in some ways the opposite of the cinematic mode. Rather than pretending the viewer

rhetorical mode. simulates face-to-face → direct address

isn't there, the rhetorical mode simulates the face-to-face encounter by directly addressing the viewer and, what is more important, acknowledging both the performer's role as addresser and the viewer's role as addressee. Among the types of programs that rely on the rhetorical mode are news programs, variety shows, talk shows, religious programs, "self-help" and educational programs (cooking, exercise, home study, and gardening shows, for example), MTV (the video-jocks), home shopping channels, sports, game shows, and, of course, many advertisements. The addressers—those whom Sarah Kozloff discusses as the narrator—in these types of television shows play a number of distinct roles: they may be "characterized" as the reporter, anchorperson, announcer, host, sportscaster, moderator, or quiz master. Each characterization, obviously, involves different conventions of address: how the addresser presents himself or herself and how he or she relates to and acknowledges the viewer. But in each case there is an attempt to engage the viewer directly. Furthermore, each involves an attempt, implicitly or explicitly, to recruit people as viewers—that is, to persuade the actual person watching at home that he or she is the "you" to whom the addresser is speaking.

In other words, the television addresser attempts to solicit the viewer's participation in a communication transaction in which a prospective audience member agrees to play the role of listener/viewer. As Maclean points out, every story implicitly begins with the statement, "Listen, and I will tell you something you will want to hear." That is, the story teller attempts to assert his or her role as storyteller and, at the same time, to convince the addressee to accept that role as well as the addressee's own role as listener to the story. Every story—indeed, every face-to-face communication—involves an exchange on the basis of a presumed contract: the addresser offers to tell us something we haven't already heard. By agreeing to listen, we accept the offer. But the addresser also expects something in return for telling us a story or revealing a piece of information: he or she expects some kind of response. And as listeners we expect to be able to respond. At a minimum, the teller looks for a response indicating that the listener understands the point of the story, that he or she now realizes why it was relevant and thus worth listening to. This signal of relevance might be as simple as a nod of the head or a murmured "hmmm." In the case of a joke, the desired response is, of course, laughter. In all performance situations, says Maclean, the audience "experience an obligation to respond and feel cheated if they cannot do so. The response may be positive or negative, it may confirm or contest the expectations of the teller. . . . [Regardless,] the audience, whether willing or unwilling, feel that they have entered into, or sometimes that they have been forced into, a contractual relationship."[7]

The centrality of the rhetorical mode of address to American television becomes apparent when one considers the performance contract Maclean speaks of in relation to the economic basis of commercial television. As I argued in the introduction, television is in the business of selling people to advertisers. Or, to be more precise, broadcasters are paid by advertisers on the basis of the statistical probability that at a certain time of day x number of a particular category of viewers (men or women, teenagers, children) will be tuned to a particular program and thus will be in a position to watch the advertiser's message. Commercial television's job is not to sell products but to recruit people who are available to watch television as viewers. Whatever else a television program does, whatever response it hopes to elicit (laughter, tears, outrage, or whatever), it must first persuade a person in front of television set to play the role of viewer, to enter into a contractual relationship that simulates what we experience in face-to-face situations. Commercial television constantly reminds you that *you* are the "you" it wishes to speak to.

Becoming a watcher of commercial television also involves the viewer in an implicit economic contract as well. Maclean argues that, although every narrative transaction is also an economic transaction (between the producer and the consumer of a cultural product), at the level of reading the nature of that transaction is the giving/accepting of a gift rather than the selling/purchase of a commodity. "The gift economy," she says, "is more flexible than that of merchandise: you can choose not to enter into it, you may even choose not to reciprocate. . . . The worth of a narrative, like the worth of a gift, has nothing to do with its value."[8]

Programming on commercial television arrives in our home as a gift. We haven't asked for it; we don't pay to receive it; and (unless you are one of the families that make up the television ratings sample) no one asks you whether or in what ways you use it. Commercial interruptions are, in one sense, the string that comes attached to the "free gift" of television programming. But commercials are also implicit reminders that the gift was given by the advertiser. Not too long ago most programs (and a few still today) would be preceded or closed by an announcer's voice saying, "This program has been brought to you by . . ." or "This program has been sponsored by. . . ." The minimal response the advertiser implicitly asks from you, as the viewer to whom the program is offered, is that you also agree to play the role of viewer during the commercial message. But the entire economic system of commercial broadcasting is premised upon the expectation that at least some viewers will reciprocate the gift of programming by purchasing the sponsor's product.

This implicit reciprocity underpinning commercial television's viewing contract can be seen more clearly when we compare it to our contractual relationship with the movies. The Hollywood cinema style has developed to serve a system of economic exchange in which the viewer pays "up front" for the opportunity to enjoy the cinematic experience that follows the purchase of a ticket. Thus, in a movie theater, we have different expectations about the nature of that experience than we do in front of the television set. For example, one reason that the showing of product advertisements before a film has not gone over very well in the United States is that people feel they have *paid* to see the movie and therefore should not be subjected to a message they did not pay for and do not necessarily want to see. But once a moviegoer has paid for a ticket, no further action is asked of him or her after leaving the theater to fulfill the implicit contract between "the movies" and the viewer/consumer. By contrast, commercial television succeeds only by persuading the viewer to respond to the "gift" of programming at another time, in another place, in a prescribed manner. In other words, the implicit bargain between the viewer and television is fulfilled not in front of the set but in the grocery store. Television asks us to act; hence it is inherently rhetorical. If the theatrical movie-viewing situation is centripetal (one bright spot of moving light in a dark room draws us into another world and holds us there for ninety minutes or so), then television is centrifugal. Its texts are not only presented for us but directed out at us. Ironically, television's commercial messages drive us away from the set, out into the "real" world of commodities and services.

The nature of the gift economy of television becomes visible only when the system of exchange breaks down. Occasionally, for example, a television program will deal with issues or take a stance that a particular public pressure group finds offensive. That group might urge its adherents to boycott products made by the sponsors of the show as an expression of their disapproval. The pressure group is in effect urging its members to disavow that sponsor's program gift, to leave it and its surrounding advertising messages "unopened," and to not reciprocate the gift by purchasing the sponsor's product.

One of the hallmarks of the rhetorical mode—and another striking difference between its method of viewer engagement and that offered by Hollywood films—is its use of characterized viewers. Direct address is but the most obvious way in which the viewer is represented on television

—for example, as the "person" Dan Rather says "good evening" to at the beginning of the *CBS Evening News*. Television frequently provides us with on-screen characterized viewers—textual surrogates who do what real viewers cannot: interact with other performers and respond (usually in an ideal fashion) to the appeals, demands, and urgings of the addresser.

These on-screen characterized viewers abound on television commercials. An ad for *Time* magazine that aired several years ago, for example, opens with a shot of a man sitting at his desk at home. An off-screen voice asks him, "How would you like to get *Time* delivered to your home every week for half-off the newsstand price?" The man looks into the camera as the voice speaks, but before he can respond the voice adds, "You'll also receive this pocket calculator with your paid subscription." An arm emerges from off-screen and hands the calculator to the man. He nods his acceptance of the offer, but again, before he can speak the voice piles on still more incentives. Finally, with not the slightest doubt remaining that the man *will* become a *Time* subscriber, the voice orders him to place the toll-free call. The man hesitates. "What are you waiting for?" the voice asks. "You haven't told me the number," the man objects. The voice responds with the number, and it magically appears at the bottom of the screen. The ad ends with the man placing the phone call.

Notice that although the characterized viewer (the man in the ad) is constructed so as to resemble the real viewer *Time* hopes to reach with the ad, the former stands in a different relationship to the text's addresser than does the presumed viewer at home. The man in the ad enjoys a direct, face-to-face (or, in this case at least, face-to-voice) relationship with the performer who addresses him. The technology necessary to bring the commercial message "to us" disappears and is replaced by an unmediated person-to-person communication situation. One function of this strategy is to evoke face-to-face communication interaction and the contract that interaction entails.

In other ads, the characterized addressee is established in a setting suggesting that of the implied audience and within which is enacted a drama of face-to-face communication. The characterized addressee confides a problem to a friend (dull floors, constipation, bad breath, gray clothes, or whatever), who predictably offers the solution to the problem in the form of a particular product—frequently as a gift. The characterized viewer responds appropriately by thanking the friend for the gift, acknowledging the wisdom of his or her advice and the solution to the viewer's problem.

The *Time* ad illustrates another aspect of television's use of the characterized viewer—a blurring of the distinction between characterized addressee, implied viewer, and addresser. When the man responds to the voice, he does so by looking directly into the camera. Thus, he looks at "us" as if we were the source of the message. In a Hollywood film, one of the principal ways of establishing identification between the viewer and a character is the use of a strategy called glance/object editing. We are shown a close-up of a character as that character looks off-screen. The second shot, taken from that character's point of view, shows what he or she sees. A third shot returns us to the close-up of the character. In the rhetorical television mode, however, glance/object editing is short-circuited in that "we" turn out to be the object of the character's glance. In the curious logic of this mode, the voice of the commercial is made into *our* voice, as the man establishes the connection between our gaze and "the voice." At the same time, we are also characterized as the man who responds to that voice. He acts as we *should* act. The superimposition of the telephone number at the end of the ad, however, addresses "us" rather than "him," because he attends to the oral recitation of the number rather than to its appearance on the screen—and even if he did notice the printed number, it would appear backwards to him!

The purposive collapsing of addresser, characterized addressee, and implied viewer in television's rhetorical mode creates what Robert Stam has called, with regard to news programming, "the regime of the fictive We." In the middle of a soap opera, the announcer says, "We'll return to our story in just a moment." A promotion for the local newscast says, "Tonight on *Action News* we'll look at the problem of teenage pregnancy." Other examples are obvious and legion on American commercial television. Who is this "we"? Perhaps it merely stands for the collective "senders" of the message—the news staff, the advertisers, the people who run the broadcasting station. But the signified of television's "we" is usually left vague enough to cover both the addresser and the implied addressee. Stam sees the "misrecognition of mirror-like images" in the fictive We to have serious consequences: "Television news . . . claims to speak for us, and often does, but just as often it deprives us of the right to speak by deluding us into thinking that its discourse is our own."[9]

The characterized addressee plays an equally important role in two other television genres, the game show and the talk show. Whereas the commercial and the news program tend to characterize their addressees individually, game and talk shows represent their addressees as a group—the studio audience. Unlike the example of the commercials mentioned above, in which the impersonal experience of watching television is made into an interpersonal one by situating the action on the viewer's side of the television set, in talk and game shows the characterized viewer is made a part of the performance on the *other* side of the screen. The studio audience is "there," where it really happens, able to experience the show "in person" in the same space and at the same time as the performance unfolds. Again television constructs a simulation of a face-to-face performance.

Game shows and talk shows carefully regulate the responses of their studio audiences so that this "live" audience is represented to the home viewer as an ideal audience. With the prompting of "applause" signs in the studio, the audience unfailingly responds at the appropriate moment: when a new guest is introduced, when a contestant wins the big prize, when it is time for a commercial. Game shows and talk shows also employ devices to individualize the studio audience. In some cooking shows, for example, a member of the studio audience is chosen to sample the meal the chef has prepared. On both *Late Night with David Letterman* and *The Tonight Show*, the host goes into the studio audience to talk with individual audience members. *Donahue, Oprah Winfrey, The Joan Rivers Show, Geraldo*, and other such panel talk shows depend on members of the studio audience to ask the show's guests the same type of questions "we" would ask if "we" were there.

Notice, however, that even when the characterized viewer is allowed to speak as an individual member of the studio audience, his or her discourse is carefully regulated and channeled. It is only the host (Oprah, Phil, or Geraldo) who wields the microphone and determines who is allowed to speak and for how long. The audience member speaks to and looks at either the host or the guests on stage. Only the host looks directly into the camera and addresses us. Sometimes the host will become a spokesman for both the studio audience and the presumed home viewer by reverting to the fictive We. (As in: "I think what we all want to know, Dr. X, is what first prompted you to wear a chicken suit in the operating room?") In this way host, studio audience, and home viewer are collapsed, and the means by which the responses of the characterized viewer are regulated is covered over.

In talk shows, although the studio audience is addressed and individual members are allowed to speak, the roles of host, guests, and characterized audience are demarcated, if on some shows purposefully blurred. The audience stays "in its place" offstage; guests are isolated onstage in front of the audience; the host negotiates and regulates the relationship between them and the home viewer. Except in the unlikely event that a studio audience member is called upon to speak for a few seconds, his or

her role is primarily that of an exemplary viewer—one who listens, looks, and responds appropriately. In game shows, however, the characterized viewer crosses the line that normally separates the characterized "audience" from the "show." This transformation of audience member into performer is perhaps best exemplified by announcer Johnny Olson's invitation to "come on down" on *The Price Is Right*. We might speculate that much of the pleasure we derive from game shows stems from the fact that the contestants seem to be more like "us" than like "them." As characterized viewers, they appear to us as "real" people acting spontaneously, not as performers reading lines. This appearance of a shared identity with the viewer at home is, of course, carefully managed on most game shows. Contestants are screened and coached to make sure that they will perform well. Even if drawn at random from the studio audience, the contestant is no doubt aware of the role he or she is expected to play from having watched the show before.

By splitting off one or more characterized viewers from the rest of the studio audience, the game show sets up a circuit of viewer involvement. When Bob Barker asks the contestant to guess how much the travel trailer costs, we almost automatically slip into the role of contestant, guessing along with him or her. If we guess correctly, we vicariously share in the success. But we can also distance ourselves from the contest and take up the position of members of the studio audience as they encourage the contestants and, on *The Price Is Right*, at least, shout out what they believe to be the correct guess. Thus, as we watch a game show we constantly shift from one viewer position to another, collapsing the distance between contestants and ourselves as we answer along with them, falling back into the role of studio audience as we assess the contestants' prowess and luck, and assuming a position superior to both when we know more than they. The viewer-positioning strategy of the game show encourages us to mimic the responses of the characterized viewer in the text. Indeed, I find it difficult to watch a game show *without* vocally responding —whether or not someone else is in the room with me.

In short, it is not coincidental that commercial television has developed a sophisticated rhetorical mode of viewer engagement within which much energy is expended to give the viewer at home an image of himself or herself on screen and to make sure the viewer knows that he or she is the person to whom the show (and its accompanying commercials) is offered. By conflating addresser and addressee under the regime of the fictive We, commercial television softens the bluntness of its rhetorical thrust. By its positioning of "us" in "their" position, we seem to be talking ourselves into acting. By adopting the style and mode of address of commercials, other genres of television programming rehearse "for fun" what the commercials do in earnest. By simulating face-to-face exchanges, television attempts to "de-mediate" our relationship with it and strengthen the contractual obligations we feel toward it. Every commercial is an implicit unanswered question—"Will you buy?"—that calls for an action the commercial text itself cannot provide, because only real viewers can buy the very real commodities the commercials advertise. By offering characterized viewers within the text, commercials fictively answer their own questions with resounding affirmation. We should not be too surprised, then, when talk shows, game shows, religious programs, and other forms of commercial television programming also "write in" their own viewers and provide them with opportunities to respond and act in an affirming, if carefully regulated, manner.

[handwritten margin note: construction of the characterized viewer. (ideal viewer)]

The ultimate expression of television's rhetorical mode can be found on American cable television in the form of home shopping channels. Home Shopping Club, Cable Value Network, QVC Network, and other such operations sell merchandise directly to viewers who order it over the telephone. The merchandise ranges from inexpensive knick-knacks to jewelry and electronic gear priced over $500. In the main, the "programs" on the home shopping channels consist of a "live" host describing a particular

product, which is shown on-screen. The price and telephone order number also appear, along with a running count of the number of units of the item sold. Frequently the item is "available" only for the amount of time it is featured on-screen, and viewers are encouraged to call in their orders immediately. From time to time, viewers who have just ordered an item talk directly with the host "on the air." The host congratulates the caller for making an excellent purchase, and the caller reciprocates by extolling the virtues of the product just ordered.

Home shopping channels must recruit not just viewers but viewers *as purchasers*. There is no separation of "program" from "advertisement." Unlike the rest of commercial television, home shopping channels sell products to viewers, not viewers to advertisers. The success of these channels need not be measured in terms of ratings but is directly related to the number of units sold. Nevertheless, the task of the host and of the "program" as a whole is still to persuade viewers to watch *and* to persuade them to accept the role of *good* viewers, who not only like what they see but buy it as well.

The Home Shopping Club uses the device of club membership to recruit its viewers. It creates an implicit distinction between *viewers* (anyone who happens to be watching) and *club members*, who achieve this status by purchasing the products they see. The process by which thousands of individual viewers—separated from each other and from the "show" by thousands of miles—purchase products by telephone is reframed as a process of interpersonal affiliation. The products become not just objects of individual and anonymous consumption, but objects around which a simulated social organization is created; the phone call to order the product becomes an initiation rite, the product itself a badge of membership. The viewer whose call is put "on the air" becomes a characterized viewer who is empowered to speak directly to the "club's" officers and to have his or her voice heard by the membership at large. Once again, the characterization of the viewer and the simulation of interpersonal communication turn out to be central to television at its most rhetorical.

The Social Contexts of Television Viewing

Despite the insights that reader-oriented criticism provides into the process by which we engage with narratives, there is a danger in discussing the role of the television viewer in terms of the role of the literary reader—as much of this chapter has done. The danger, rather obviously, is that such a discussion obscures important differences between watching television and reading a book. As we have seen, the formal characteristics of commercial television—its oceanic flow of programming, the textual gaps created by the constant interruption of those programs, television's multiple modes of address, and the simultaneity of performance and response—all make the relationship of viewer to text quite different from our experience with either cinema or literature. But we also need at least to acknowledge differences in the actual viewing situation itself, or what we might call the social contexts of television viewing.

Since the advent of broadcast audience research in the 1930s, the investigation has concentrated on two major areas. Broadcasters themselves and advertisers have been interested primarily in *measuring* the audience —determining how many of what kinds of viewers are watching television at a particular moment during the broadcast day. Because the economic relationship between broadcasters and advertisers is based on the statistical probability of viewership, large-scale audience measurement is essential. Ironically, the very power of commercial advertising to affect consumer purchasing decisions long ago provoked concern among academic researchers and other groups that first radio, then television, might have deleterious consequences for audience members. For this reason, researchers have attempted to discern the *effects* upon various audience groups of watching television and listening to radio. They have hypothesized, for example, that television violence might encourage aggressive behavior among children; that viewing stereotypical portrayals of various social groups might reinforce viewer prejudices; that "heavy" television viewing in general might be associated with perceptions of the world as dangerous. This strong line of effects research has itself prompted other scholars to investigate television viewing not in terms of effects but in terms of the *functions* that particular types of programming might serve for particular viewing groups. Watching soap operas, for example, has been explained in terms of the viewer's need for vicarious social interaction or problem solving.

Neither of these major strands of audience research has adequately addressed the basic question, How do television and television viewing fit into the everyday lives, the "lived experience," if you will, of viewers? Or, put another way, how is the process of making sense of and taking pleasure from television affected by the particular contexts within which people make use of television? These questions beg yet another: What does it mean when we say that someone is "watching television"? Broadcasters would like advertisers to think that "watching television" involves rapt attention to the sounds and images coming from the television set, but is this the case? An Oxford University scholar, Peter Collett, conducted an experiment to find out. He constructed a cabinet containing both a television set and a videotape recorder, which was connected to a video camera positioned to capture whatever went on in front of the set when it was turned on. Collett persuaded a number of British families to have this device installed in their living rooms for a few weeks. When he analyzed the resulting videotapes, he found that focused, attentive viewing was a minority mode of engagement with the television set. Most of the time that the set was on, his subjects were doing something else in addition to or instead of watching television. That "something else" might be talking with other family members, eating a meal, reading the newspaper, studying, making love, or a variety of other activities. On many occasions, the subjects were so involved in doing other things (sometimes in other rooms of the house) that they could not be said to be "watching" television at all.[10] Collett's experiment merely confirms our own experience that television is merely one aspect of our complex domestic environments, which are full of other stimuli. Indeed, it has been argued (although I would not totally agree) that television soap operas are made primarily to be heard rather than seen, so that viewers busy with chores around the house can keep up with the narrative without having to visually attend to the screen.

Recently a number of scholars have examined the role of television in everyday life. They have attempted to describe and to begin to account for the complex ways in which television has become a part of daily life, how it fits into patterns of domestic relations, and how its place in the home varies from culture to culture. It is not possible here to give this work and the debates it has engendered the scrutiny they both deserve. However, it does make sense to me to end a chapter on "reading" television with an overview, at least, of some of the ways in which social context appears to affect that reading process.

Although some scholars would argue that they do not conform to the protocols of ethnography as practiced in sociology or anthropology, recent studies of television and everyday life are certainly informed by what we might call the ethnographic impulse. Ethnography, at its most basic, is concerned with the social meanings of human action as that action occurs in its "natural" context. It is particularly concerned with how people understand and organize the world around them and what meanings they attach to their own behavior and that of others. Thus ethnographically inspired TV-audience research strives for "thick" descriptions of the complex ways in which people interact with television, of the relationship between television and other aspects of domestic life, and of the meanings viewers attach not just to the "content" of television but to the very act of viewing itself.

Even within anthropology, there is no standard ethnographic method, but most ethnographic descriptions are based upon prolonged, direct observation of behavior in its natural setting and upon extensive interviews. It is frequently said that ethnographers become "participant observers" of the situations they hope to describe. Ethnographers studying a culture to which they are outsiders immerse themselves in the everyday life of that culture, striving for knowledge of the commonsensical, the taken-for-granted. If the study is successful, they will have traded their outsider's explicit and distanced knowledge of the alien culture for something approaching the insider's implicit and intimate grasp of how things work and what things mean. For scholars studying the relation of television to everyday life in their own culture, the problem is reversed: they must take a phenomenon already so familiar that it disappears into the background of daily life and make it "strange" so that its particularities and subtleties are objectified and rendered visible.[11] Audience researchers primarily interested in measurement or effects are concerned that the cases or samples they choose to study be representative and that the results of their studies have scientific validity (that is, that they be replicable by other researchers if the same methodology, sampling techniques, and so forth are followed). They aim for knowledge that is universal and thus predictive. Ethnographically oriented researchers stress the concrete and the particular rather than the representative and the universal.

David Morley's *Family Television* investigates, as its title suggests, the relationship between television and family life. On the basis of his participant observation and interviews with eighteen South London families, Morley describes the inextricability of television viewing from patterns of domestic power relations within the family. Building on the findings of other studies, Morley describes the differences in social meaning that television takes on for different members of the family. For "fathers" in the study, television viewing frequently was a nighttime respite and escape. They preferred asocial, uninterrupted, intense involvement with the television text. "Mothers," on the other hand, whose workday extended well into the evening hours, necessarily engaged in a more distracted mode of television viewing. Indeed, some women reported feeling guilty about taking pleasure from the rare occasions when they were able to fully attend to their favorite programs. For women, television was also a means of encouraging rather than stifling family talk. Needless to say, these quite different social meanings attached to television viewing by different members of the family sometimes provoked conflict.

Morley also found that new elaborations of television technology quickly become absorbed into patterns of domestic and gender relations within the household. None of the women in Morley's study used the remote control device regularly, and in many cases its "place" was on the arm of the father's chair. Ann Gray describes a similar "gendering" of television technology in her study of VCR use among families in northern England. The VCR usually came into the household as "daddy's toy." The father mastered its controls and made initial decisions as to its use. Some mothers expressed a reluctance to learn how to operate the VCR, not because it was too complicated but rather because they feared it would become yet another piece of domestic technology (like the clothes washer, vacuum cleaner, and microwave) that they would be expected to use to serve the family's needs.[12]

As I mentioned earlier, Dorothy Hobson has pursued the relationship between gender and television viewing—specifically the relationship of female viewers to British soap operas. She suggests that in some cases the viewing experience is merely the beginning of the road along which television becomes intertwined with other aspects of everyday life. Hobson's interviews with female officeworkers during their lunch hours revealed that soap operas provided a focus for socialization as these women shared, challenged, revised, and continually reformed their understandings of the show's plots and character relationships. Her work reminds us that the process by which people make television relevant, meaningful, and pleasurable might be launched by their viewing of programs in the home, but the trajectory of that process may carry it far beyond the immediate viewing environment.[13] Family dynamics might determine whether or not a particular program is viewed and how that viewing occurs for each family member, but these dynamics cannot fully account for what happens when the audience for soap operas, music television, or sporting events is reconstituted at another place and a later time.

Ethnographic studies have also examined cultural differences in television viewing practices as well as the relationship between the age of the viewer and the ways that viewer makes television a part of daily life. Leonicio Barrios's extensive observation of and interviews with thirteen Caracas families reveals the dynamics of family interaction with Venezuela's most popular form of television drama, the *telenovela*. The physical circumstances of viewing these enormously popular soap operas depend on the arrangement of the living space, the economic position of the family, and family politics. Where space is limited, family size large, and economic resources few, viewing is almost inevitably a family affair, as the family "living room" may also be the dining room, kitchen, bedroom, and pathway to other parts of the house. But when a family has the means to purchase two sets, its members tend to disperse, even while watching the same program. Women, in particular, seem to enjoy watching *telenovelas* alone—so much so that one woman interviewed, who watched her favorite soap opera at night with her children, also videotaped it so that she could watch it again alone the following day. The women in Barrios's study were also eager, where possible, to prevent interruptions in their viewing of *telenovelas*, and family members were urged if not coerced to observe the *tranquilos* (quiet) of what one grandmother called her "sacred" time. Echoing Hobson's study, Barrios found that *telenovelas* provided viewers with subject matter for later discussions with friends. This was particularly the case with teenagers but extended to younger children as well. One preschooler, who was not allowed to watch *telenovelas*, nevertheless knew the principal characters and plot lines from her friends' conversations at play.[14]

It is also clear from ethnographic observations of children at home that television becomes a part of our daily lives at a very early age. Dafna Lemish found that by ten months old, some children were already fascinated by *Sesame Street*, and as early as sixteen months, "babies were turning [the] television on by instruction, or at will, for the purpose of actually viewing television." Lemish also observed children learning to deal with the ambiguous status of television's images and sounds. Although the animals, puppets, and people toddlers get to know on television seem to be like those the child experiences on this side of the screen, they cannot be touched or kissed; their appearances and disappearances cannot be controlled by the child; and once they have gone, no searching strategy can locate them. This and other studies of children's interaction with television remind us that we not only must learn how to interpret television's representational conventions (in which dissolve might mean elapsed time, for example), modes of address, and ways of telling stories, we also learn how to *be* a television viewer and how television viewing might fit into the patterns and rhythms of our everyday lives.[15]

Conclusions

This discussion of the ways we "read" television has necessarily omitted several important sets of issues that have considerable bearing upon that process; these issues are, however, taken up in other chapters. Understanding how the viewer is addressed and characterized by television demands a parallel consideration of television's narrational strategies, which Sarah Kozloff examines in her chapter. I have glossed over the crucial fact that we never come to a particular television program viewing experience as a "naive" viewer. That moment of viewing is always conditioned by our experiences with and knowledge of other television texts and is often preceded by promotions for the show, interviews with the show's actors, advertisements in newspapers, and so on. Indeed, perhaps more than any other form of cultural production, television presents texts that never "stand alone." Instead, they continuously point the viewer in the direction of other texts. It is television's relentless intertextuality that forms the subject matter for Jane Feuer's chapter. We must also recognize that we always come to any viewing experience already positioned and defined as social beings. Beyond a point, there is no useful category of "the reader" or "the viewer" separate from *that* reader or *that* viewer's conglomerate and socially specific identity in terms of race, gender, class, ethnicity, region, and other markers of social position. Ann Kaplan, Mimi White, and John Fiske all discuss the social constructedness of television viewing and television viewers in their chapters.

Despite the fact that they, like any approach to television, leave much unaccounted for, both reader-oriented criticism and ethnographic television studies at least raise a set of questions that traditional literary analysis and traditional mass communication research leave unasked. In doing so, they challenge us to reconsider concepts and assumptions that lie at the heart of the critical endeavor. What is a text? How is it made meaningful, relevant, and pleasurable? What is the relationship between the world in the text and the world brought to the reading/viewing experience? How does the text attempt to construct us as readers/viewers? If we accept that texts don't *contain* meaning but are *made* to mean as readers/viewers encounter them, what are the limits of what readers/viewers can do with texts? What, then, is the role of the critic? Given the fundamental nature of these questions, it should come as no surprise that there is little agreement about the answers.

The relationship between television and its viewers provides an excellent laboratory in which to test the insights of reader-oriented literary theorists—even if, as in the case of Wolfgang Iser, some of them might question the applicability of literary theory to the realm of nonliterary popular culture. Reader-oriented criticism begins by sweeping away the myth of eternal and stable textual meaning and substitutes the notion of readers' "activations" of texts within historically specific conditions of reception. Television provides us with texts that are infinitely less stable and more ephemeral than any literary work. It takes a study of the ontological confusion young children experience with television to remind us of the curious way television's images appear and disappear—here for an hour or so and then gone, perhaps forever. Furthermore, few people in the television industry think in terms of programming as a series of autonomous and isolated texts. Because the goal of commercial television is the stimulation of habitual viewing over long periods, programs are conceived of more as waves in the schedule's neverending flow than as books on a shelf.

Ethnographic television studies respond to the critical problem of television's ubiquity and intimacy. By the seemingly simple acts of observing how people interact with television and listening to what they tell us about the meanings those interactions have for them, we begin to glimpse something of the complexities and subtleties of television's roles in our lives. The studies I have referred to in this chapter have value to me primarily because they identify some of the parameters of our engagements with television. That's a nice way of saying that they point out just how little we really know about TV viewing. But they also call to our attention the social nature of television viewing. The simultaneity of television broadcasts, with millions of sets receiving the same images at the same time, makes watching a television program a social phenomenon even if we are "alone" while we watch. The oceanic nature of television programming, its constant references to other texts, and the close connections between television and other forms of textual production all combine to plug any individual act of television viewing into a network of other viewers and other discourses and to link us as viewers with the larger culture. And television's penetration into the private spaces of our lives, its unnoticed connection with the rituals and routines of daily life, inevitably make television viewing a part of our relations with the other people with whom we share those private spaces.

NOTES

1. Elizabeth Freund, *The Return of the Reader: Reader-Response Criticism* (London: Methuen, 1987), p. 6.

2. Wolfgang Iser, *The Act of Reading: A Theory of Aesthetic Response* (Baltimore, Md.: Johns Hopkins University Press, 1978), pp. 3–5.

3. Iser, *The Act of Reading*, pp. 191–92.

4. Dorothy Hobson, "Soap Operas at Work," in *Remote Control: Television, Audiences and Cultural Power*, ed. Ellen Seiter et al. (London: Routledge, 1989), pp. 150–67.

5. Iser, p. 192.

6. Marie Maclean, *Narrative as Performance: The Baudelairean Experiment* (London: Routledge, 1988), p. xii.

7. Ibid., p. 72.

8. Ibid., p. 77.

9. Robert Stam, "Television News and Its Spectator," in *Regarding Television—Critical Approaches: An Anthology*, ed. E. Ann Kaplan, American Film Institute Monograph Series, vol. 2 (Frederick, Md.: University Publications of America, 1983), p. 39.

10. Peter Collett and Roger Lamb, *Watching Families Watching Television*, Report to the Independent Broadcasting Authority (London: IBA, 1986).

11. Thomas Lindlof, ed., *Natural Audiences: Qualitative Research of Media Uses and Effects* (Norwood, N.J.: Ablex, 1987), pp. 4–5; Martyn Hammersley and Paul Atkinson, *Ethnography: Principles in Practice* (London: Tavistock, 1983), pp. 6–13.

12. Ann Gray, "Behind Closed Doors: Video Recorders in the Home," in

Boxed In: Women and Television, ed. Helen Baehr and Gillian Dyer (London: Pandora Press, 1987).

13. Hobson, "Soap Operas at Work."

14. Leonicio Barrios, "Television, Telenovelas, and Family Life in Venezuela," in *World Families Watch Television*, ed. James Lull (Newbury Park, Calif.: Sage, 1988), pp. 49–79.

15. Dafna Lemish, "Viewers in Diapers: The Early Development of Television Viewing," in Lindlof, *Natural Audiences*, pp. 33–57.

FOR FURTHER READING

There are several good introductions to reader-oriented criticism, including two in Methuen's (now Routledge's) New Accents series. Elizabeth Freund's *The Return of the Reader: Reader-Response Criticism* (London: Methuen, 1987) provides a good discussion of the background against which reception theory emerged and has chapters devoted to major American and German theorists. Robert C. Holub's *Reception Theory: A Critical Introduction* (London: Methuen, 1984) offers a critical overview of the work of the German reception theorists, particularly Wolfgang Iser and Hans Robert Jauss. Two excellent anthologies of reader-oriented literary criticism are Susan Suleiman and Inge Crossman, eds., *The Reader in the Text: Essays on Audience and Interpretation* (Princeton, N.J.: Princeton University Press, 1980); and Jane P. Tompkins, ed., *Reader-Response Criticism: From Formalism to Post-Structuralism* (Baltimore, Md.: Johns Hopkins University Press, 1980). Both have good introductory essays and bibliographies.

Several other works position reader-oriented criticism within a more general context of literary theory, among them: William Ray, *Literary Meaning: From Phenomenology to Deconstruction* (London: Basil Blackwell, 1984); Terry Eagleton, *Literary Theory: An Introduction* (Minneapolis: University of Minnesota Press, 1983); and Jonathan Culler, *The Pursuit of Signs: Semiotics, Literature, and Deconstruction* (London: Routledge and Kegan Paul, 1981).

Much of the analysis of soap opera structure in this chapter is based on work by Iser and Jauss. Iser's approach is best laid out in *The Act of Reading: A Theory of Aesthetic Response* (Baltimore, Md.: Johns Hopkins University Press, 1978), but see also *The Implied Reader: Patterns of Communication in Prose Fiction from Bunyan to Beckett* (Baltimore, Md.: Johns Hopkins University Press, 1974). Jauss's more historical theory of reception is proposed in *Aesthetic Experience and Literary Hermeneutics* (Minneapolis: University of Minnesota Press, 1982) and *Toward an Aesthetic of Reception* (Minneapolis: University of Minnesota Press, 1982).

For examples of reader-oriented criticism written from perspectives other than those of Iser and Jauss, see (among many others) David Bleich, *Subjective Criticism* (Baltimore, Md.: Johns Hopkins University Press, 1978); Harold Bloom, *The Anxiety of Influence: A Theory of Poetry* (Oxford: Oxford University Press, 1973); Umberto Eco, *The Role of the Reader* (Bloomington: Indiana University Press, 1977); Stanley Fish, *Is There a Text in This Class?* (Cambridge, Mass.: Harvard University Press, 1980); Norman Holland, *5 Readers Reading* (New Haven, Conn.: Yale University Press, 1975); and Steven Mailloux, *Rhetorical Power* (Ithaca, N.Y.: Cornell University Press, 1989).

The rise of reader-oriented criticism in literature has provoked considerable debate—among its practitioners and between them and theorists/critics of other stripes. Both Freund and Eagleton contribute to these debates, but the primary arena has been journals of literary theory and criticism. Of these, see especially *Diacritics*, *Critical Inquiry*, and *New Literary History*. Although her approach derives more from speech act theory and performance theory than reception studies, I found Marie Maclean's *Narrative as Performance: The Baudelairean Experiment* (London: Routledge, 1988) to be extremely useful in dealing with the performative nature of literary narrative and, by extension, the rhetorical nature of television. My own *Speaking of Soap Operas* (Chapel Hill: University of North Carolina Press, 1985) attempts to develop a "reader-oriented poetics" of the soap opera form.

Interest in the dynamics of television viewing has increased markedly since the publication of the first edition of *Channels of Discourse* in 1987. Playing key roles in arousing the interest of television critics and cultural studies scholars in television viewing and audiences were the works of David Morley, Dorothy Hobson, and Ien Ang: see Morley's *The "Nationwide" Audience: Structure and Decoding* (London: British Film Institute, 1980) and *Family Television: Cultural Power and Domestic Leisure* (London: Comedia, 1986); Hobson's *"Crossroads": The Drama of a Soap Opera* (London: Methuen, 1982); and Ang's *Watching "Dallas": Soap Opera and the Melodramatic Imagination*, trans. Della Couling (London: Methuen, 1985), and *Desperately Seeking the Audience* (London: Routledge, 1991). John Tulloch's work links the dynamics of television production with those of reception. See his *"A Country Practice": Quality Soap* (Sidney: Currency Press, 1986), with Albert Moran, and *Television Drama: Agency, Audience, and Myth* (London: Routledge, 1990). Two useful anthologies of current work on audiences are: Phillip Drummond and Richard Paterson, eds. *Television and Its Audience: International Research Perspectives* (London: British Film Institute, 1988); and Ellen Seiter, Hans Borchers, Gabriele Kreutzner, and Eva-Maria Warth, eds. *Remote Control: Television, Audiences and Cultural Power* (London: Routledge, 1989). As John Fiske's chapter will discuss, much of the impetus behind the works cited above comes from developments in the field of cultural studies. Graeme Turner examines the relationship between cultural studies and television audience research in *British Cultural Studies: An Introduction* (Boston: Unwin Hyman, 1990).

Arising out of somewhat different theoretical concerns has been recent work in the ethnography of television viewing. Two recent collections are: Thomas Lindlof, ed. *Natural Audiences: Qualitative Research of Media Uses and Effects* (Norwood, N.J.: Ablex, 1987); and James Lull, ed. *World Families Watch Television* (Newbury Park, Calif.: Sage, 1988).

4 : GENRE
: STUDY
: AND
: TELEVISION

jane feuer

The term *genre* is simply the French word for type or kind. When it is used in literary, film, or television studies, however, it takes on a broader set of implications. The very use of the term implies that works of literature, films, and television programs can be categorized; they are not unique. Thus genre theory deals with the ways in which a work may be considered to belong to a class of related works. In many respects the closest analogy to this process would be taxonomy in the biological sciences. Taxonomy dissects the general category of "animal" into a system based on perceived similarity and difference according to certain distinctive features of the various phyla and species. As one literary critic has remarked, "biological classification is itself an explanatory system, which has been devised primarily to make sense of an otherwise disparate group of individuals and which is changed primarily in order to improve that sense. While robins and poems are obviously different, the attempt to make a reasoned sense similarly dominates their study."[1] In a similar way, literature may be divided into comedy, tragedy, and melodrama; Hollywood films into Westerns, musicals, and horror films; television programs into sitcoms, crime shows, and soap operas. Genre theory has the task both of making these divisions and of justifying the classifications once they have been made. Taxonomy has a similar task. However, the two part company when it comes to the question of aesthetic and cultural *value*. The purpose of taxonomy is not to determine which species are the most excellent examples of their type or to illustrate the ways in which a species expresses cultural values or to show how that species manipulates an audience—to mention varying goals of genre classification. But rather than discussing genre analysis as a whole, we should distinguish among the uses of the term for literature, film, and television.

Traditionally, the literary concept of genre has referred to broad categories of literature (such as comedy and tragedy) that tend not to be treated as historically or culturally specific manifestations. For example, Aristotle defined tragedy as an ideal type according to which any particular tragedy must be measured. Even though he drew upon the theater of his own society (classical Greece) for his models, Aristotle spoke of "tragedy" as a kind of overarching structure that informs individual works. Once the ideal structure was achieved, Aristotle implied, tragedy could then have its ideal impact on an audience. (In a similar way, although Hollywood film genres are constructed from actual films, the genre itself is frequently spoken of as an ideal set of traits that inform individual films. Thus, although many individual Westerns do not feature Indians, Indians remain a crucial generic element.)

Drawing on Aristotle, the literary critic Northrop Frye attempted in the 1950s to further develop the idea of classifying literature into types and categories that he called *genres* and *modes*. Frye commented that "the critical theory of genres is stuck precisely where Aristotle left it."[2] Frye attempted to further differentiate among types of literature. He classified fiction into modes according to the hero's power of action—either greater than ours, less than ours, or the same as ours—arriving at such categories as myth, romance, epic and tragedy, comedy, and realistic fiction according to the hero's relationship to the reader. Frye points out that over the last fifteen centuries these modes have shifted, so that, for example, the rise of the middle class introduces the *low mimetic* mode in which the hero is one of us (pp. 33–35). As for genres, Frye distinguishes among drama, epic, and lyric on the basis of their "radical of presentation" (that is, acted out, sung, read), viewing the distinction as a rhetorical one with the genre being determined by the relationship between the poet and his public (pp. 246–47).

We can see that the traditional literary view of genre would have only a limited application to film and television. The literary categories are very broad ones. Such literary types as drama and lyric, tragedy, and comedy span numerous diverse works and numerous cultures and centuries. Film and television, however, are culturally specific and temporally limited. Instead of employing a broad category such as "comedy," we need to activate specific genres such as the "screwball comedy" (film) or the "situation comedy" (television), categories that may not correspond to or necessarily be subspecies of the literary genre of comedy. As we will see, attempts to measure the comic forms of mass media against the norms of drama are doomed to failure. At this point in the development of film genre theory, the concept has been applied most usefully to American film and television. Moreover, literary genres tend to be—to employ a distinction from Todorov—*theoretical* to a greater extent than do film and television genres, which tend to be *historical*.[3] The former are "deduced from a preexisting theory of literature," whereas the latter are "derived from observation of preexisting literary facts."[4] That is to say, some genres are accepted by the culture, while others are defined by critics.

Literary criticism, which has been around much longer than either film or television criticism, has described more genres from the theoretical or deductive perspective. Film and television criticism still tend to take their category names from current historical usage. For example, although Homer did not refer to his own work as an "epic" poem, both industry and critics employ the categories of "Western" and "sitcom." One of the goals of film and television genre criticism is to develop more theoretical models for these historical genres, not necessarily remaining satisfied with industrial or commonsense usage. Thus, in film genre study, the theoretical genre called *film noir* was constructed out of films formerly grouped under the historical labels "detective films," "gangster films" and "thrillers." Indeed, even melodramas such as *Mildred Pierce* were discovered to possess the stylistic traits of this newly created theoretical genre.

Television studies is too new a field to have yet greatly differentiated between historical and theoretical genres; however, we are now attempting to redefine, if not reclassify, some of the received categories such as soap opera. Originally a derisive term used to condemn other forms of drama as being hopelessly melodramatic, the term *soap opera* has been refined in a confrontation between such historical examples as the afternoon serial drama, prime-time serials, and British soap operas. British "soaps," for example, cause us to question the equation of the term *soap opera* with the mode of melodrama, because their own mode might better be described as "social realism"; they possess none of the exaggeration and heightened emotion and elaborate gestures of their American cousins. And the middle-class, slowly unwinding, woman-centered world of afternoon soaps bears little resemblance to the fast-paced plutocratic worlds of *Dallas* and *Dynasty*.

Out of this confrontation emerges a new conceptualization of the genre, in which the continuing serial format is not necessarily equated with the descriptive term soap opera. Thus we can retain the *method* of the literary definition of genres without necessarily retaining their *content*. The literary concept of genre is based upon the idea, also common to biology, that by classifying literature according to some principle of coherence, we can arrive at a greater understanding of the structure and purpose of our object of study. Thus the taxonomist begins with already existing examples of the type. From these, she/he builds a conceptual model of the genre, then goes on to apply the model to other examples, constantly moving back and forth between theory and practice until the conceptual model appears to account for the phenomena under consideration. (Of course, this is a lot easier when the genre is already complete and not, as with television, in a constant state of flux and redefinition.)

As Rick Altman points out, every corpus thus conceived reflects a particular methodology. The constitution of a generic corpus is not independent of, nor does it logically precede, the development of a methodology.[5] According to another literary critic, "What makes a genre 'good,' in other words, is its power to make the literary text 'good'—however that 'good' be presently defined by our audience."[6] We might substitute the word *useful* for the word *good* here. Genres are rhetorical and pragmatic constructions of an analyst, not acts of nature. The biological analogy is useful here also. Although those animals that we label "dogs" and "cats" exist naturally, to label them "mammals" is to construct a category that is not natural but culturally constructed. After all, Spot and Morris have no need to call themselves mammals—biologists do. Similarly, each genre analyst has a reason for constructing the genre categories he or she claims to "discover." For example, *Soap Opera Digest* has always covered prime-time soap operas, even when that means placing *The Young and the Restless* and *Twin Peaks* in the same category. It is useful for the fan magazine to attract both audiences to its pages. On the other hand, as Jim Collins notes in his chapter, highbrow critics are motivated to place *Twin Peaks* in a separate category because they feel called to police the boundaries between "art" and "trash," and they want to claim that *Twin Peaks* is art.

The characteristics that make the popular artifacts of movies and television "good" may not correspond to the generic "good" of literary works. It is due to their nature as artifacts of *popular* culture that films and television programs have been treated in a specific way in genre studies. Genre study in film has had a historically and culturally specific meaning. It has come to refer to the study of a particular kind of film—the mass-produced "formulas" of the Hollywood studio system. This concept of formula has been defined by John Cawelti:

A formula is a conventional system for structuring cultural products. It can be distinguished from invented structures which are new ways of organizing works of art. Like the distinction between convention and invention, the distinction between formula and structure can be envisaged as a continuum between the two poles; one pole is that of a completely conventional structure of conventions—an episode of the Lone Ranger or one of the Tarzan books comes close to this pole; the other end of the continuum is a completely original structure which orders inventions—*Finnegans Wake* is perhaps the ultimate example.[7]

In this view, the concept of genre stems from a conception of film as an industrial product. That is, the particular economic organization of the film industry led to a kind of product standardization antithetical to the literary concept of an authored work. Genre offers a way for the film and TV industries to control the tension between similarity and difference inherent in the production of any cultural product. Whereas we expect each bar of Ivory soap to be exactly like the last one we purchased, we expect each Hollywood film we see to be in some ways unique. But completely unique products don't mesh with the system of production regularity and division of labor upon which Hollywood is built. Thus, the classical Hollywood narrative style and genres help to regulate the production of difference by producing their own differences within very circumscribed structures of similarity. In addition, as Cawelti and others have pointed out, genres provide filmmakers with an easy-to-use creative toolbox. Just one shot of horses on the horizon is necessary to establish that a film is a Western. Thus, film genre study is grounded in the realities of the film industry, even though, in theory, any genre critic is free to construct any genre he or she wishes.

Within the institution of film criticism, however, the concept of genre was initially employed to condemn mass-produced narratives such as Hollywood studio films for their lack of originality. It was assumed that genre films could not have any artistic merit, because they were not original works and because they were not authored works. These standards of evaluation are based upon a romantic theory of art that places the highest value on the concepts of originality, personal creativity, and the idea of the individual artist as genius. Ironically, it was through an attempt to establish a romantic, author-centered model for film that the concept of genre began to take on a more positive meaning in film criticism. The *auteur* policy attempted to reconceptualize the anonymous products of the Hollywood assembly line as the creations of individual artists, assumed to be

the directors of the films. The author was constructed by attributing unity
—whether stylistic or thematic or both—to films that bore the signature
of certain directors. One would think that the *auteur* approach would have
further invalidated genre criticism. However, it was discovered that certain authors expressed themselves most fully within a particular genre
—John Ford in the western or Vincente Minnelli in the musical. In some
sense, then, genre provided a field in which the force of individual creativity could play itself out. Some viewed the genre as a constraint on complete originality and self-expression, but others, following a more classical or mimetic theory of art, felt that these constraints were in fact
productive to the creative expression of the author. Thus genre study
evolved within film studies as a reaction against the romantic bias of *auteur*
criticism.

When film studies turned toward semiotics and ideological criticism,
the idea of the genre as a threshold or horizon for individual expression
gave way to an interest in the genres themselves as systems and structures. Thomas Schatz has referred to the semiotic interest in genre as
"the language analogy." He says that genre can be studied as a formalized
sign system whose rules have been assimilated (often unconsciously)
through cultural consensus. Following Claude Lévi-Strauss, Schatz views
genres as cultural problem-solving operations. He distinguishes between
a deep structure that he calls *film genre* and a surface structure that he
calls the *genre film*. The genre film is the individual instance, the individual utterance or speech act (*parole*). The film genre is more like a grammar (*langue*), that is, a system for conventional usage.

According to Schatz, the film genre represents a tacit contract between
the motion picture industry and the audience, whereas the genre film
represents an event that honors that contract. According to this linguistic view, a film genre is both a static and a dynamic system. However,
unlike language, individual utterances do have the capacity to change the
rules.[8] Over many decades, for example, the film Western changed from a
classic pattern in which a lone hero saved civilization to a professional
pattern in which a group of comrades shared adventures outside the boundaries of any community. The TV sitcom in the 1970s and after also moved
away from the nuclear family as its basic setting and toward "families" of
unrelated adults that formed in the workplace. In both cases, these shifts
in the film genre correlate to changes in the culture outside. The most
difficult task of the genre critic is to adequately account for these correla-
tions. Ultimately, genre criticism is cultural criticism.

The language analogy sees an active but indirect participatory role for the audience in this process of genre construction. For the industrial arts, the concept of genre can bring into play (1) the system of production, (2) structural analysis of the text, and (3) the reception process with the audience conceived as an interpretive community—that is, a social grouping whose similarities cause them to interpret texts the same way, as opposed to completely individual interpretations. Rick Altman relates the concept of genre to that of the interpretive community. In his view, the genre serves to limit the free play of signification and to restrict semiosis. The genre, that is to say, usurps the function of an interpretive community by providing a context for interpreting the films and by naming a specific set of intertexts according to which a new film must be read. The genre limits the field of play of the interpretive community. Altman sees this as an ideological project because it is an attempt to control the audience's reaction by providing an interpretive context. Genres thus are not neutral categories, but rather ideological constructs that provide and enforce a pre-reading.[9]

In a similar way, Steve Neale sees genres as part of the dominant cinema's "mental machinery," not just as properties possessed by texts. Neale defines genres as "systems of orientations, expectations, and conventions that circulate between industry, text, and subject." Any one genre, then, is both a "coherent and systematic body of film texts" and a coherent and systematic set of expectations. Neale agrees with Altman that genres limit the possibilities of meaning by both exploiting and containing the diversity of mainstream cinema.[10] Drawing upon Altman and Neale, we can conclude that each theoretical genre is a construct of an analyst. The methodology that the analyst brings to bear upon the texts determines the way in which that analyst will construct the genre. Genres are made, not born. The coherence is provided in the process of construction, and a genre is ultimately an abstract conception rather than something that exists empirically in the world.

Thus we can distinguish a number of different reasons why the concept of genre has figured in both popular and critical discourses as an "instrument for the regulation of difference."[11] From the television industry's point of view, unlimited originality of programming would be a disaster, because it could not assure the delivery of the weekly audience, as do the episodic series and continuing serial. In this sense, television takes to an extreme the film industry's reliance upon formulas in order to predict audience popularity. For the audience—as members of various interpretive communities for American mass culture—genre assures the interpretability of the text. Through repetition, the cultural "deep structure" of a film genre "seeps to the surface." The audience—without conscious awareness—continually rehearses basic cultural contradictions that cannot be resolved within the existing socioeconomic system outside of the text: law and order versus the idea of individual success (the gangster genre); nature versus culture (the Western); the work ethic versus the pleasure principle (the musical).

The approaches to genre that we have discussed might be summarized under three labels—the *aesthetic*, the *ritual*, and the *ideological* approaches. Although in practice these are not absolutely distinct, in general we can use them to distinguish among different approaches that have been taken toward film and television genres. The *aesthetic approach* includes all attempts to define genre in terms of a system of conventions that permits artistic expression, especially involving individual authorship. The aesthetic approach also includes attempts to assess whether an individual work fulfills or transcends its genre. The *ritual approach* sees genre as an exchange between industry and audience, an exchange through which a culture speaks to itself. Horace Newcomb and Paul Hirsch refer to television as a "cultural forum" that involves the negotiation of shared beliefs and values and helps to maintain and rejuvenate the social order as well as assisting it in adapting to change.[12] Most approaches based on the language analogy take the ritual view. The *ideological approach* views genre as an instrument of control. At the industrial level, genres assure the advertisers of an audience for their messages. At the textual level, genres are ideological insofar as they serve to reproduce the dominant ideology of the capitalist system. The genre positions the interpretive community in such a way as to naturalize the dominant ideologies expressed in the text. Some ideological critics allow for constant conflict and contradiction in the reproduction of ideology, as the ruling ideas attempt to secure dominance. A more reader-oriented ideological model would allow for the production of meanings by the viewer as well. Thus recent approaches to genre have attempted to combine the insights of the ritual approach with those of the ideological approach. According to Rick Altman, "because the public doesn't want to know that it's being manipulated, the successful ritual/ideological 'fit' is almost always one that disguises Hollywood's potential for manipulation while playing up its capacity for entertainment. . . . The successful genre owes its success not alone to its reflection of an audience ideal, nor solely to its status as apology for the Hollywood enterprise, but to its ability to carry out both functions simultaneously."[13]

The Situation Comedy

As an example of the generic approach to television analysis, I have chosen to discuss the most basic program format known to the medium —the situation comedy. In general, television taxonomy has not yet advanced to the point where a clear distinction between historical and theoretical genres has emerged. Thus all TV genres in some sense remain historical genres, those defined by a consensus between the industry, *TV Guide*, and the viewing audience. The sitcom is no exception. We are all capable of identifying its salient features: the half-hour format, the basis in humor, the "problem of the week" that causes the hilarious situation and that will be resolved so that a new episode may take its place the next week.

Nevertheless, different methodologies for defining the genre have produced different notions of the sitcom as genre. I will discuss the ways in which three critics have approached the genre in order to demonstrate that each has constructed a *different* genre called the sitcom. David Grote takes an aesthetic approach to the genre and finds that it lacks dramatic development of any kind, serving merely to reassert the status quo. Horace Newcomb also finds the genre limited in its capacity for ambiguity, development, and the ability to challenge our values; however, because he takes a ritual view, he does see the genre as basic to an understanding of the reassurance the television medium provides for its audience. David Marc appears to believe that certain authors can make the sitcom form into social satire; his would also represent an aesthetic approach. Finally, my own approach will be a synthetic one, viewing the sitcom as a genre that *did* develop, for historical reasons, in the direction of the continuing serial.

The most literary—and consequently the most negative—view of the television sitcom is taken by David Grote.[14] According to Grote, television has completely rejected the type of comic plot that has dominated the comedic tradition from Greek and Roman times, a type that, following Northrop Frye, he calls "new comedy." In the tradition of new comedy, a very basic arrangement of plot and character has predominated. In it, a young man's desire for a young woman meets with resistance, usually by her father, but before the end of the play, a plot reversal enables the boy to get the girl. This is the plot of Greek New Comedy which can be dated back to 317 B.C., but it is also the plot of Shakespearean comedies, Hollywood romantic comedies, and many musical comedies. Although few would dispute the *longevity* of this plot paradigm, many might question Grote's next step, which is to make a sweeping historical generalization about the social meaning of new comedy and then to use that generalization to disparage the sitcom as a new form of comedy that rejects that social meaning. According to Grote, the comic plot is social in nature because the forces that keep the lovers apart always represent social authority. The resistance of the young lovers to the parental figure thus represents a threat to power, authority, and stability, because, according to Grote, in this type of comedy father *never* knows best.

At the end of the traditional ("new") comedy, there is a celebration —usually the wedding of the young people, to which the father is invited back in. The authority figure actually admits that he was wrong and the rebellious children right. The basic comic plot uses the young couple's union to symbolize the promise of the future, guaranteeing the possibility of personal change and, with it, social change. In this way Grote assumes that the basic comedy plot has held the same meaning in different cultures and throughout history, thus conceptualizing the genre as an ideal type with a single, ahistorical, acultural meaning. His next step is even more universalizing: he claims that the TV sitcom completely rejects both the form and the meaning of this traditional comic plot, thus symbolizing the "end of comedy" as a progressive social force.

Grote bases his static conception of the sitcom form on its nature as an episodic series, that is, a program with continuing characters but with a new plot (situation) each week. Thus, no matter what happens, the basic situation can't change. From this, Grote generalizes that the sitcom resists the change of the traditional comic plot and indeed resists change of any kind:

> The situation comedy as it has evolved on American television has rejected more than the traditional comedy plot. Not only does boy not pursue and capture girl, he does not pursue *anything*. The principal fundamental situation of the situation comedy is that things do not change. No new society occurs at the end. The only end is death, for characters as well as for the situation itself, the precise opposite of the rebirth and new life promised in the celebrations of the traditional comedy. The series may come on every week for no more reason than that it is convenient for the network and the sponsors, but the messages that accompany those weekly appearances are the messages of defense, of protection, of the impossibility of progress or any other positive change. . . . That such a change occurred is curious, but that such a change occurred in the largest mass medium known to

man, in the most progressive and changeable society in Western history, and was immensely popular, is almost incredible. Everything the traditional comedy stood for, at every level of art, psychology, philosophy, and myth, has been overthrown in this New Comedy of American television.

I have chosen to discuss Grote's "construction" of the genre not because I think it is the construction that does the most "good" for the texts, but rather because I think it takes to an extreme a very common view that the TV sitcom is by nature a conservative and static form. The goal of the sitcom, according to Grote, is to reaffirm the stability of the family as an institution. Thus Grote moves, as would any genre analyst, from an identification of the formal features of the text (in this case the nature of the episodic series and the fact that each episode returns to the equilibrium with which it began), to a generalization about the meaning of these features (they represent a rejection of change of any kind), to a social, cultural, political, or aesthetic interpretation of the genre (the sitcom represents the end of the progressive potential of the traditional comic plot). If we accept Grote's premises, his conclusions are not illogical. However, his entire argument depends on an acceptance of his belief that after centuries of progressiveness, the meaning of comedy suddenly shifted to a regressive one for no reason other than that the television medium has transformed history. Many would find this difficult to accept as an historical explanation.

Yet even the more complex "ritual" view constructed by Horace Newcomb bases its model for the genre on the formal qualities of the episodic series. To Newcomb, writing in the early 1970s, the sitcom formula provides a paradigm for what occurs in more complex program types and provides a model of a television formula in that "its rigid structure is so apparent."[15] The situation is "the funny thing that will happen this week." Next week there will be a new situation entirely independent of what happened this week. The situation develops through complication and confusion usually involving human error. There is no plot development and no exploration of ideas or conflict: "The only movement is toward the alleviation of the complication and the reduction of confusion" (p. 34). Thus Newcomb sees the sitcom as providing a simple and reassuring problem/solution formula. As the audience we are reassured, not challenged by choice or ambiguity; nor are we forced to reexamine our values. When the sitcom shifts its meaning away from situations and toward persons, we find ourselves in a slightly different formula, that of the "domestic comedy," says Newcomb. Newcomb defines the domestic comedy as one in which the problems are mental and emotional; there is a deep sense of personal love among members of the family and a belief in the family —however that may be defined—as a supportive group. Although, as with the sitcom, the outcome is never in doubt, for the domestic comedy "it is also true that there is more room for ambiguity and complexity, admittedly of a minimal sort. Characters do seem to change because of what happens to them in the problem-solving process. Usually they 'learn' something about human nature" (p. 53). Newcomb goes on to point out that the form of the domestic comedy may expand when problems encountered by the family become socially or politically significant (as in *All in the Family* or *M*A*S*H*.)

Newcomb thus constructs the sitcom as the most "basic" of the television genres in the sense that it is the furthest from "real world" problems encountered in crime shows real world forms and value conflicts encountered in soap operas. It is, in a sense, formula for formula's sake; the very ritualistic simplicity of the problem/solution format gives us a comforting feeling of security as to the cultural status quo. Newcomb thus constructs a ritual view of the genre, but a ritual view based on an essentially static conception of the episodic series such as had informed Grote's more universalized and literary account. Newcomb's major interpretation is his equation of the form with a cultural meaning of stability and reassurance. For it is equally possible to view the static nature of the sitcom form as having the potential to challenge our received norms and values.

This is the move that David Marc appears to make in "The Situation Comedy of Paul Henning."[16] Marc attributes the subversive potential of such sitcoms as *The Beverly Hillbillies* to the presence of an author—in this case, the producer Paul Henning—thus making his an aesthetic conception of genre (that is, an author can work in a banal genre like the sitcom and transform it into an individual statement). Nevertheless, the argument for the subversive potential of the static sitcom form need not depend upon the aesthetic conception but may be seen to lie in the ideology of the genre itself, quite apart from what a particular author may choose to do with it.

For Grote and, to a lesser extent, Newcomb, *The Beverly Hillbillies* would qualify as a basic episodic sitcom that endlessly replays the same theme—the virtue of plain values and the rejection of materialism. Marc sees the show as a brilliant caricature of cultural values and conflicts, in its way as much of a social critique as *All in the Family*. The theme of the backwoodsman versus the city slicker is a common one in American folklore and in other television genres as well (the family dramas *Little House on the Prairie* and *The Waltons* frequently featured this theme). In the sitcom, however, the theme is treated comically, giving it a satiric potential.

Marc would agree with Grote and Newcomb that, on *The Beverly Hillbillies*, the plots never develop very far: the Clampetts never adjust to life in Beverly Hills; the family is never accepted by their neighbors; Elly May never marries; Granny never gives up her mountain ways. But Marc does not evaluate this lack of development in a negative light. Rather, he sees the Henning sitcoms as a departure from the formula of the 1950s sitcom. Unlike Newcomb's domestic comedy, in Henning sitcoms the individual crisis of a family member does not provide us with the weekly situation. We don't identify emotionally with the Clampetts' problems as we might in a program with greater psychological character development, so that instead *The Beverly Hillbillies* provides us with an almost pure cultural conflict. Marc says that we are invited to test our own cultural assumptions because "the antagonists are cultures" and the characters "charged cultural entities." He concludes that Paul Henning's *The Beverly Hillbillies*, although it is not satire per se, is nonetheless a "nihilistic caricature of modern life."

Thus Marc differs from Grote and Newcomb not over their description of the sitcom's lack of plot and character development, but rather over their interpretation of what this essentially static genre means. To Grote, it means that the sitcom is inferior to the dominant literary form of comedy; to Newcomb that it aids in the restoration and maintenance of society. To Marc it would seem to mean something entirely different: he implies that Henning's comic treatment may be more socially satiric than the expansive form of domestic comedy that accommodates social and political issues (the Norman Lear sitcoms of the early to mid-1970s being the epitome of this type). In this way the static sitcom structure *can* explore ideas and challenge dominant cultural values, and it is able to do so precisely because it does not allow our individualistic identification with well-developed characters to get in the way. If we follow out the logic of this point of view, it could lead to the conclusion that *The Beverly Hillbillies* was more of a social satire than *All in the Family*, in which our identification with the more well-rounded Archie Bunker was likely to outweigh the positive liberal benefits of the show's intended satire of his racist beliefs.

Although all three models represent useful individual constructions of a television genre, none seems to me to account for the role of the interpretive community in the construction of a genre or the role of history in generic "evolution." In fact, one of the dangers of a generic approach is a built-in tendency to structuralize the model in such a way that it is impossible to explain changes or to see a genre as a dynamic model. The basis of much genre theory in the language analogy tends to remove it from history as well and to emphasize structure over development. When genre theory is applied to the television medium, this danger is even greater, for we already have cultural preconceptions as to the "sameness" of television programming—that is, "if you've seen one sitcom, you've seen them all." The impression of continuity over difference intensifies when television is evaluated according to literary conceptions of genre, with their centuries of evolution, or even according to the half-century span of such film genres as the Western. I would argue, however, that the sitcom has "evolved" in its brief lifetime, in the sense that it has gone through some structural shifts and has modulated the episodic series in the direction of the continuing serial. This is not to say that the genre has "progressed" or become "better," but rather that it has become different. Unlike Grote, I think the changes need to be explained, but I also think that explaining such changes must be part of a complex construction of the genre.

As an example of how I would construct the genre, let's trace the development of the situation comedy from the late 1960s to the present. In order to do this, we have to take into account developments in the industry and in social and cultural history as well as developments more or less internal to the genre.[17] These internal developments might be described as *intertextual*. That is, the sitcom develops by reacting to and against previous sitcoms. As the genre ages, it becomes richer by virtue of an increased range of intertexts that can be cited in each new sitcom.

Popular TV critics explain the move away from the "rural" sitcoms of the late 1960s and toward the social and political domestic comedy of the early to mid-seventies by claiming that the audience "felt a need" for a more sophisticated conception of the genre. Then, in the mid-seventies, they wanted "mindless" teen-oriented sitcoms. In the 1980s, they desired family warmth, which signifies a return to the wholesome domestic comedies of the 1950s. The explanation of generic evolution/programming trends according to an assumed "need" on the part of the interpretive community is the most common way in which industry observers and participants construct TV genres. As an historical construct, it is worthy of analysis in itself (why this construction and not another?); as a theoretical construct, however, it begs the question. The concept of audience "need" is a substitute for an explanation of shifts in a culture, in an industry, and in a narrative form; in itself it does not explain anything. In at least one instance

—the emergence of the MTM and Lear sitcoms in 1971—it can be demonstrated that what changed was *not* the demands of any empirical audience, but rather the industry's own construction of network television's interpretive community. Whereas in the era of the Paul Henning "hayseed" sitcoms, the industry had conceptualized the audience as an aggregate or mass; it was now reconceptualizing the audience as a differentiated mass possessing identifiable demographic characteristics.

This also caused the industry to redefine the measure of the popularity of a particular genre or program. "Popularity" came to mean high ratings with the eighteen- to forty-nine-year-old urban dweller, rather than popularity with the older, rural audience that had kept the Paul Henning sitcoms on the air throughout the 1960s. Later, the industry refined its model audience once again. During the "Fred Silverman years" of the mid- to late 1970s, the audience for sitcoms was defined as mindless teenagers; the result was shows like *Three's Company*, *Happy Days*, and *Laverne and Shirley*. In the 1980s, the desirable audience—at least for the NBC network—became the high-consuming "yuppie" audience, thus defining the popularity of such shows as *Cheers* and *Family Ties*.

Of course, the audience itself no doubt changed from the late 1960s to the mid-1980s—specifically, the baby boomers matured during this period. And of course, cultural changes no doubt influenced the generic shifts in the sitcom. But they did not directly *cause* the genre to change. It seems clear that the industry acted as an intermediary factor in that it was continually redefining the audience for its own ends. An interesting question would be: What caused the industry to redefine the audience at certain points, and to what extent did this really correspond to material changes in the culture? To further complicate the question of causality, the sitcom itself was responding to changes in other television genres—specifically, to what I would label the serialization of American television—throughout the 1970s.

Thus the sitcom, around 1970, shifted away from the "one dramatic conflict series" model of *The Beverly Hillbillies* and toward an expanded conception of the domestic comedy.[18] This was not necessarily as abrupt a shift as it now seems; earlier programs such as *The Dick van Dyke Show* (1961–66) had prepared the way for a reconceptualization of the domestic comedy in the direction of the home/office blend that would characterize the MTM sitcoms of the 1970s. Specifically, in the early seventies the sitcom was further developed by two independent production companies (themselves responses to industrial changes) : MTM Enterprises, which produced *The Mary Tyler Moore Show*, *The Bob Newhart Show*, *Rhoda*, and others; and Norman Lear's Tandem Productions which produced *All in the Family, Maude, The Jeffersons*, and others. The aesthetic view comes into play here in the sense that these independent production companies encouraged the development of the writer/producer as a crucial creative component in the development of the new form of domestic comedy. (Of course, the emergence of the writer/producer was itself dependent upon cultural and industrial factors.)

We might say that the MTM and Lear sitcoms transformed the situation/ domestic comedy by adapting the problems encountered by family members either in the direction of social and political issues (Lear) or in the direction of "lifestyle" issues (MTM). Thus the Bunker family had to deal with problems caused by blacks moving into the neighborhood; whereas Mary and Rhoda had to deal with problems caused by their being representatives of a new type of woman: working, single, independent, and confused. The basic problem/solution format of the sitcom did not change. Instead, the nature of the problems shifted and the conception of character held by the sitcom genre altered.

The Lear sitcoms were more influential in shifting the terrain of the characters' problems, whereas the MTM sitcoms were more influential in altering the conception of character. We have already seen that the assumed apolitical nature of the pre-1970s sitcom is called into question by new constructions of the genre through readings of such programs as *The Beverly Hillbillies*. Such readings assume that over the years the cultural conflict endlessly repeated in that show must have had some impact on the audience, however unconsciously that impact was assimilated. Nevertheless, the Lear sitcoms introduced an overtly political agenda into the genre. But it was in their conception of character that the "new wave" sitcoms of the 1970s most markedly altered the "grammar" of the formula.

The new domestic comedies introduced a limited but significant concept of character development into the genre. Although all comic characters are of necessity stereotyped (that is, they possess a limited number of traits compared to actual individuals), the new sitcom characters were less stereotyped than their predecessors, especially in the MTM "lifestyle" variety. If the hillbillies never adapted to modern life, the same could not be said for Mary, who began her show by moving from a small town to Minneapolis in order to start a career. If previous characters in domestic comedy learned a little from experience, Mary learned a lot. Over the seven years the program was on the air, she became more assertive, more her own person. Similarly, Rhoda went from single womanhood to marriage to divorcée status within the span of her own series, each change registering on the character and deepening our sense of her life experience. As television characters, the MTM women appeared to possess a complexity previously unknown to the genre. When both the nation and the industry grew more conservative in the mid-1970s, the grammatical innovations of the Lear programs appeared passé as political relevance faded from the sitcom's repertoire. But MTM's "character comedy" survived the transition from the new wave sitcoms of the early 1970s to the Silverman programs of the mid- to late 1970s. Then, under the impetus of an overall serialization and "yuppification" of American television in the 1980s, the MTM sitcom emerged as the dominant form of the genre.

The idea of character development inevitably moves a genre based on the episodic series model toward the continuing serial form. This is what occurred, for example, when Rhoda's wedding and subsequent divorce gave the episodes of that sitcom a continuing plot line and character continuity. But character development is also a quality prized by the upscale audience which tends to have a more literary standard of value. We have already seen that the idea of character depth and development does not necessarily make for "better" or even for more sophisticated programming. To value "character comedy" over other comic techniques is to take up an ideological position, to construct the genre in a particular way and to value it for a kind of depth that some would construe as ideologically conservative. According to certain Marxist analyses of art (in particular, Bertolt Brecht's concept of the epic theater), flat characters are more politically progressive because they take us away from our identification with the characters and force us to think about how the play is constructed. According to this view, character complexity and development is merely a representation of bourgeois values. We have already seen a version of the Brechtian position in the argument that the concept of character in *The Beverly Hillbillies* is more socially critical than the concept of character in *All in the Family* or in *Cheers*. And, finally, character growth and development over time, along with an awareness of its own past, has always characterized the continuing serial, which, due to the growing popularity of daytime serials in the late 1970s and the emergence of the prime-time serial with *Dallas*, finally emerged as a new narrative paradigm for generic television. The evolving sitcom had helped to prepare the way for the growth of serial drama; reciprocally, serialization gave a new grammar to the upscale comedies of the eighties.

The original cast of *Cheers* was a good example of how the eighties sitcom was designed to capture the upscale demographic audience. Sam and Diane developed from season to season. After their torrid affair in the second season and their breakup in the third, an episode in the fourth season harks back to the past. Thinking they are about to perish in an airplane crash, Sam confesses that he should have married Diane. That same season, they almost rekindle their lust for one another. This ongoing romantic tension gives their relationship a sense of development and the series a sense of history. At the same time, another "lifestyle" sitcom, *The Cosby Show*, returns us to the father-knows-best world of the 1950s domestic comedy, a world from which class and racial conflict are once again absent. The element of struggle in the Lear sitcoms would seem to have been put aside. Yet this absence has a different ideological motivation in the 1980s. The implication is that racial and economic equality have already been achieved, whereas in the fifties they were not yet seen as problems worthy of incorporation into the ideology of the domestic comedy. Many believe that the renewed emphasis on the stability of the family —especially the return to the nuclear family in *The Cosby Show* and *Family Ties*—reflected the conservative ideology of the Reagan era.

As we move further into the 1990s, it can be argued that we are seeing a return of the Lear-type social-issue sitcom, although "domestic" and "family of coworkers" shows remain in the majority. It is fascinating that in the summer of 1991, after the show had been in syndication for years, CBS showcased episodes of *All in the Family* during prime time. The same types of programs that throughout the 1980s provided afternoon babysitting are now being touted as priceless classics. Among the top-rated sitcoms for 1990–91 were three that dealt regularly and explicitly with social issues: *Roseanne*, *The Simpsons*, and *A Different World*.

Both *Roseanne* and *The Simpsons* return us to the Lear sitcom structure of the blue-collar nuclear family with loud, vulgar, and—in the case of Homer Simpson—bigoted parental figures. True to the Brechtian tradition, the stars of these shows are flat cartoon figures, in the case of the Simpsons quite literally. Roseanne Barr has been criticized for not knowing how to act, but that kind of criticism is probably more applicable in an MTM type of sitcom that emphasizes fully developed characters. *Roseanne* deals more with the social and familial problems of a "realistic" family whose struggles are primarily, if not totally, economic in nature. Although it does not contain the overt social conflict of the Lear shows, its humor tends more in that direction. *The Simpsons*, although subtle and complex in the situations it presents, also stresses class conflict and familial discontent. To judge from these examples, the development of the sitcom would seem to be cyclical rather than linear, dependent on cultural and industrial changes.

In the realm of the work-family sitcom, *Murphy Brown* reconstructs *The Mary Tyler Moore Show* for the 1990s. Indeed, when CBS did a *Mary Tyler Moore Show* twentieth-anniversary retrospective in February 1991, they scheduled it to immediately follow *Murphy Brown*, billing the evening as "Murphy and Mary." The newer show features the same newsroom setting, the same family of coworkers concept, the same home/office alternation, and the same sophisticated humor. Only the character of Murphy differs significantly from the older model; she is a loudmouthed (but gorgeous), successful, single career woman in her forties, who would have been starting her career about the same time that Mary Richards (then 30) joined the WJM news team in 1971. Mary represented the traditional woman caught in a network of social change; Murphy represents the fruition of the middle-class women's movement: tough, successful, and alone as she approaches middle age. In spite of its brilliance, *Murphy Brown* is arguably a program based almost entirely on intertextuality, much more so than other shows that have tapped into the formula of the original Mary Tyler Moore show. *Kate and Allie*, for example, accessed the comradery between Mary and Rhoda but did not provide the family of coworkers. *Designing Women* cites both the coworker and female bonding aspects but does not satirize TV news operations. "Murphy and Mary" is no casual or artificial linkage. The two shows really represent a continuation of the same cultural theme—the earlier show riding the crest of the feminist movement, the later one detailing its ebbing in the "postfeminist" era.

The arguments just made might lead a genre analyst to conclude that the sitcom does not fit theories of generic evolution developed for Hollywood film genres. According to the most teleological version of the theory of generic evolution, a genre begins with a naive version of its particular cultural mythology, then develops toward an increasingly self-conscious awareness of its own myths and conventions. It is implied that the genre is also progressing toward a higher version of its type. Although it is possible to construct the TV sitcom according to this evolutionary model, one could equally argue that the sitcom has gone through repeated cycles of regression to earlier incarnations, as exemplified by the cycle of mindless teen comedies of the 1970s and by the return to the traditional domestic comedy in the mid-1980s. Another theory of film genre development argues that after a period of experimentation, a film genre settles on a classical "syntax" that later dissolves back into a random collection of traits, now used to deconstruct the genre.[19]

This theory does not attempt to judge the value of any stage of generic development, nor does it see a genre as necessarily progressing toward a more perfect form. Yet it is difficult to see how this theory would apply to the TV sitcom, either. There have been sitcoms that reflect back upon earlier ones (elsewhere I have argued that *Buffalo Bill* represented an inversion of the idea of the family of coworkers epitomized by *The Mary Tyler Moore Show*).[20] Yet even when it is possible to identify a period during which a stable "syntax" prevailed in the genre—such as the MTM/ Lear dominance of the 1970s—it is not as easy to point to a movement toward ever greater self-reflexivity in a genre like the sitcom. Rather, it would seem that the genre has gone through a series of transformations, some of which returned it to earlier versions of its own paradigm. Indeed when U.S. network television took on a greater self-reflexivity in the late 1970s with programs like *Saturday Night Live* and *SCTV Comedy Network*, self-consciousness tended to emerge *across* genres rather than *within* them. Perhaps the most self-reflexive program of the 1980s, *Moonlighting*, was a generic hybrid, invoking old detective movies as well as romantic comedy.

The problems involved in applying the theory of film genre evolution to television should remind us that genre theory as a whole might work better for film than for TV. Film genres really were mechanisms for the regulation of difference. The genre organized large numbers of individual works into a coherent system that could be recognized by the interpretive community. Television has always employed standard program types, but arguably this has not been the main principle of coherence for the medium. Television programs do not operate as discrete texts to the same extent as movies; the property of "flow" blends one program unit into another and programs are regularly "interrupted" by ads and promos. Critics have argued that perhaps the unit of coherence for television is found at a level larger than the program and different from the genre—for example, an evening's viewing on a particular network or all the possible combinations of programs a viewer could sample during one evening.

In addition, developments in technology and consequent changes in viewing habits during the 1980s arguably work against genre as the main organizing principle for viewing. With the advent of remote control and multiple-channel cable systems comes the tendency to "zap" from one channel to another. According to a *TV Guide* survey, "There's no question that the remote control switch revolutionized the way we watched TV in the '80s." The survey found that 75 percent of viewers had remote control, and of those, 30 percent said they try to watch two or more shows at once —either occasionally or most of the time. Thirty-seven percent said they liked to flip around the dial rather than tune in for a specific program.[21]

These new viewing practices could mean the end of genre in the sense this chapter has described it. Yet it could also mean that a rapid flow from one genre to another will come to represent the typical viewing experience. Our ability to distinguish genres would have to become even more intuitive and rapidly accessed, even more operative at a subconscious level.

Theories of the evolution of film genres have argued that genres such as the Western and the musical develop by recombining and commenting on earlier instances of their *own* genre. Of course, it was not uncommon during the Hollywood studio era (and it is even more common in contemporary Hollywood films that no longer exhibit the distinct genre boundaries of yore) for new genres to develop out of the recombination of previous genres. After all, one of the best-known musicals ever—*Oklahoma!*—is really a musical Western. But it is arguable that Hollywood genres had a greater tendency to draw upon their own predecessors, thus keeping generic boundaries relatively distinct and enabling them to serve an ideological function for the interpretive community as they recombined in ever more complex ways. Television genres, on the other hand, appear to have a greater tendency to recombine *across* genre lines. For instance, *Hill Street Blues* might be described as a crime show–soap opera–documentary that resembles its progeny—the medical show *St. Elsewhere* and the legal comic drama *L.A. Law*—far more than it does any previous crime shows or soap operas. None of these programs is generically pure. And there exists an entire TV "genre"—the late-night comedy show —whose raison d'être appears to be to comment on the whole range of television genres. This greater horizontal recombination also points up the limitations inherent in the typically vertical consideration of the development of film genres. The genre approach has its limits in the process of constructing an understanding of the medium. Yet, as this chapter has tried to demonstrate, it also has its virtues.

NOTES

1. Adena Rosmarin, *The Power of Genre* (Minneapolis: University of Minnesota Press, 1985), p. 167.

2. Northrop Frye, *Anatomy of Criticism* (Princeton, N.J.: Princeton University Press, 1957), p. 13. Subsequent references will be cited in the text.

3. Tzvetan Todorov, *The Fantastic: A Structural Approach to a Literary Genre* (Cleveland, Ohio: Case Western Reserve University Press, 1975), pp. 13–14.

4. Rosmarin, *Power of Genre*, p. 26.

5. Rick Altman, *The American Film Musical* (Bloomington: Indiana University Press, 1987), p. 13.

6. Rosmarin, *Power of Genre*, p. 49.

7. John Cawelti, *The Six Gun Mystique* (Bowling Green, Ohio: Bowling Green University Popular Press, 1970), p. 29.

8. Thomas Schatz, *Hollywood Genres: Formula, Filmmaking, and the Studio System* (New York: Random House, 1981), pp. 15–20.

9. Altman, *American Film Musical*, p. 4.

10. Steve Neale, *Genre* (London: British Film Institute, 1980), p. 20.

11. Ibid., p. 19.

12. Horace Newcomb and Paul M. Hirsch, "Television as a Cultural Forum: Implications for Research," *Quarterly Review of Film Studies* 8, no. 3 (1983): 45–55.

13. Rick Altman, "A Semantic/Syntactic Approach to Film Genres," *Cinema Journal* 23, no. 3 (Spring 1984): 14–15.

14. David Grote, *The End of Comedy: The Sit-Com and the Comedic Tradition* (Hamden, Conn.: Shoestring Press, 1983), p. 105.

15. Horace Newcomb, *TV: The Most Popular Art* (New York: Anchor Books, 1974), p. 28. Subsequent references will be cited in the text.

16. David Marc, *Demographic Vistas: Television in American Culture* (Philadelphia: University of Pennsylvania Press, 1984), pp. 39–63.

17. For a more extensive discussion of the sitcom, see Jane Feuer, Paul Kerr, and Tise Vahimagi, *MTM: "Quality Television"* (London: British Film Institute, 1984); and Jane Feuer, "Narrative Form in American Network Television," in *High Theory/Low Culture: Analyzing Popular Television and Film*, ed. Colin MacCabe (Manchester, Eng.: Manchester University Press, 1986), pp. 101–14.

18. The phrase "one dramatic conflict series" is from Marc, *Demographic Vistas*, p. 62.

19. Altman, "Semantic/Syntactic Approach."

20. See "The MTM Style," in Feuer et al., *MTM*, pp. 52–56.

21. David Lachenbruch, "Television in the '90s: The Shape of Things to Come," *TV Guide*, Jan. 20, 1990, p. 13.

FOR FURTHER READING

This chapter has emphasized traditional literary conceptualizations of genre. For a contemporary theoretical view of literary genres (at an advanced level), see Adena Rosmarin, *The Power of Genre* (Minneapolis: University of Minnesota Press, 1985).

A readable work on film genre theory that also contains detailed critical and historical analyses of particular genres is Thomas Schatz, *Hollywood Genres: Formula, Filmmaking, and the Studio System* (New York: Random House, 1981). The most complete treatise to date on film genre theory is Rick Altman, *The American Film Musical* (Bloomington: Indiana University Press, 1987), which also contains a complete examination of the musical genre. Less readable, but more in the tradition of continental theory, is Steve Neale, *Genre* (London: British Film Institute, 1980). Neale's work is updated in "Questions of Genre," *Screen* 31, no. 1 (1990): 45–66. An excellent anthology on film genres is Barry Grant, ed., *Film Genre Reader* (Austin: University of Texas Press, 1986).

A highly accessible study of the basic TV genres up to the early 1970s is Horace Newcomb's *TV: The Most Popular Art* (New York: Anchor Books, 1974). A number of books and articles deal with television genres, although not necessarily from a "genre studies" perspective. One article that does deal specifically with the concept, employing Neale's theory of genre, is Paul Attallah, "The Unworthy Discourse: Situation Comedy in Television," in *Interpreting Television: Current Research Perspectives*, ed. Willard D. Rowland, Jr., and Bruce Watkins (Beverly Hills, Calif.: Sage, 1984), pp. 222–49.

For discussions of the limitations of the genre approach, see Robert C. Allen, "Bursting Bubbles: 'Soap Opera,' Audiences, and the Limits of Genre," in *Remote Control: Television, Audiences and Cultural Power*, ed. Ellen Seiter, Hans Borchers, Gabriele Kreutzner, and Eva-Maria Warth (London: Routledge, 1989), pp. 44–55; and Ralph Cohen, "Do Postmodern Genres Exist?," in *Postmodern Genres*, ed. Marjorie Perloff (Norman: University of Oklahoma Press, 1989), pp. 15–32.

A theory of the evolution of film genres is offered in Jane Feuer, *The Hollywood Musical*, 2d ed. (London: British Film Institute/Macmillan Press, 1992), in which I also discuss the idea of a postmodern genre.

IDEOLOGICAL ANALYSIS AND TELEVISION

mimi white

The Context of Ideological Criticism

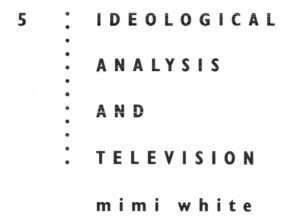"'m not a doctor. But I play one on TV." Thus we are addressed by a male performer on television, in an advertisement for Vicks cough and cold medications. Different versions of the ad subsequently appear, modifying the introductory claims of different spokesmen for the product. Within the flow of television, the advertisement activates a range of assumptions, obvious but usually unspoken, about the medium in general and the normative expectations that inform its functioning. This is at least the case within the context of American commercial broadcasting and perhaps more broadly informs all television viewing in which promotion, even self-promotion, is an issue. Among these assumptions are the following:

1. In the context of American television, advertising is normal. It is recognized by viewers as the source of station/network income and expected within the course of programming, an integral part of television flow. The regular presence of commercials is a given, regulating the rhythm and patterning of programs and viewing. In the process, viewers are addressed as potential consumers, whether or not they actually sit there watching the ads that play on their televisions.

2. The commercial is for a particular brand of cough medicine, one among many other brands that are also promoted on television. They

all claim to offer the best remedy for a particular common ailment. They vary not in what they do—reduce cough and flu symptoms—but in how they structure their appeal to potential consumers. The ad maintains a careful balance between similarity and difference: this product is one version of a range of similar products, differentiated by brand name and by the tactics of a particular campaign.

3. The product is itself divided within the ad. There are different versions of the Vicks formula, each serving as a remedy for a specific combination of flu symptoms. This internal division, wherein an array of products shares a brand and product name, provides an image of bountiful inclusivity. For coughs and flu, one need not look beyond this particular brand name product. However, this division is not exclusive to this product. Other manufacturers of comparable patent medicines offer a similar choice of three or four versions of medicine, each a different color and each designed to alleviate a specific combination of symptoms. The balance of similarity and difference within and among specific brands provides an image of plenitude and free market choice that is extended with the ads for each brand name.

4. The persona of the spokesman is established as authoritative through a structure of discourse—direct address, firm assertion—and his avowal of his status as an actor on television. "I'm not a doctor, *but I play one on TV.*" He is not "really" a medical authority but establishes credibility by acknowledging this from the outset. At the same time, he invokes medical authority in relation to his fictional role elsewhere on television. The appeal of the ad is initiated in the unstable mirroring of references between the commercial text and the discourses beyond it (*extratextual*) and between the commercial text and other discourses of television (*intertextual*): I'm not really a doctor, but I really am an actor; and as an actor in another television text, I really play a doctor. The impact of the commercial as a persuasive consumer message, urging viewers to go out and buy this particular product, is in part anchored in an understanding of the ad as a moment of and within television. It relies as much on reference to other texts within the medium—other ads and other fictional roles—as it does to the world beyond the television screen. This simultaneous referentiality is integral to the comprehensibility of the ad.

As part of this process, the viewer is assumed to be generally familiar with television's modes and genres. Ideally, the viewer will recognize the actor and be able to identify the specific role he plays elsewhere on television. Yet in the absence of this specific knowledge, it is enough to know that there are many places within television where someone could play a doctor and to recognize this particular spokesman as a likely "doctor type." This premise in turn assumes that viewers are also familiar with the practice of using actors in commercials as a basis of celebrity association and appeal. Within this context of intertextual relations, as one moment in television refers to others, the commercial itself may also assume a certain kind of currency and itself become a reference point. This is in fact the case with this particular ad, because the line, "I'm not a doctor . . . ," came to be widely recognized and circulated in other contexts, usually parodic. For example, even five years after the commercial was regularly aired on television, references to that ad campaign were still heard. In a 1991 episode of the situation comedy *Seinfeld*, the main character (played by comedian Jerry Seinfeld) commented in voice-over on another character, a holistic healer: "He's not a doctor, but he plays one on TV."

I have detailed the assumptions and implications of a single advertisement to initiate a consideration of the ideological functioning of television. Ideological criticism has its origins in Marxist theories of culture. It is concerned with the ways in which cultural practices and artifacts—in the present case, television—produce particular knowledges and positions for their users—in the present case, television audiences. These knowledges and positions link viewers with and allow reception of the economic and class interests of the television industry, which is itself part of a broader culture industry (including, for example, book and magazine publishing, radio, the music industry, and the film industry). Ideological analysis is based on the assumption that cultural artifacts—literature, film, television, and so forth—are produced in specific historical contexts, by and for specific social groups. It aims to understand culture as a form of social expression. Because they are created in socially and historically specific contexts, cultural artifacts are seen as expressing and promoting values, beliefs, and ideas in relation to the contexts in which they are produced, distributed, and received. Ideological analysis aims to understand how a cultural text specifically embodies and enacts particular ranges of values, beliefs, and ideas.

Marxist theory conceives of society as a complex interrelationship among different practices and institutions. Within society the ways in which meanings (values, beliefs, and ideas) are expressed through cultural texts, and the ways in which these meanings are received and understood by their audiences, is a dynamic process involving the interaction of multiple influences or determinations. Moreover, within Marxism a range of perspectives on culture and ideology has been developed. The particular approach to ideological criticism that one uses will vary according to one's position within Marxism. Finally, television itself is a mass industrial medium involving a variety of texts, produced by many different groups (and individuals), and aimed at a broad and heterogeneous set of audiences. It thus becomes difficult to talk about a single set of beliefs or ideas that are carried by television in any simple or immediate sense. In the discussion that follows, I offer a cursory overview of some basic Marxist ideas about ideology and culture and draw on these perspectives as an orienting perspective for television analysis.

Within Marxist theories of culture and society, the concept of ideology has been subject to intensive elaboration.[1] Classical or orthodox Marxist theory construes society in terms of a base/superstructure model. According to this model, the primary and crucial organizing factor of a human society is its material or economic *base* (some theorists call this the *infrastructure*)—its mode of production. Fundamental class identities, alliances, and material interests are established at this level of social organization according to who owns, controls, and profits from the basic mode of production. Class divisions are established based on who owns and controls the means of production and who labors within it. The dominant mode of production in turn determines the *superstructure*, which includes the arrangement of political and legal systems, culture, and ideology (including belief systems such as philosophy, religion, and morals). Dominant interests are defined by material interests—the control of economic and productive practices—which are then expressed and manifested in the organization of the superstructure. Within this model, the superstructure is not only organized in line with the interests of the ruling class (which owns/controls the means of production) but thereby functions to sustain and perpetuate the current dominant mode of production.

The cultural artifacts produced within a given mode of production are seen as primarily reflecting dominant class interests. Television—a heavily capitalized and industrialized branch of the entertainment industry—would necessarily reflect the belief system, the ideology, of the dominant class, the bourgeoisie. Viewers, then, are seen as buying into the beliefs and meanings expounded on television, no matter what their positions within the economic system. This occurs for a number of reasons. In the first place, because the dominant class owns and operates the television industry—including production and programming—it is assumed that other sets of meanings and beliefs are rarely, if ever, given a full public airing. Alternative meanings simply are not available in the same way that dominant ideology is. Second, and equally important, all viewers participate in the society and culture on an ongoing basis and are able to understand it, whether or not it directly serves their interests. The process of having been raised and educated under the sway of certain dominant meanings and beliefs (ideology) establishes certain norms and expectations for all viewers. Because, from this perspective, the economic base determines everything else, a transformation of television's ideological practices would require a shift in the mode of production—a total reorganization of ownership and control of the medium. The most rigid and extreme versions of this approach do not even allow the possibility that nondominant views might find expression within commercial broadcast media; nor do they admit the importance (in some cases even the possibility) of alternative or counterreadings on the part of the mass audience.

Classical Marxism, as this view is sometimes called, tends to define ideology as *false consciousness*, or a complex production of illusory ideas about the way society works and in whose benefit. According to this view, the ruling class promulgates systems of meaning to promote its own interests and works to generalize and universalize them, so that oppressed or subservient classes mistakenly adopt the ruling-class ideas as their own. This, then, is ideology: beliefs that are taken as "natural" when in fact they perpetuate the status quo and continue the class system of oppression. In adopting the values and beliefs of the ruling classes as their own, individuals participate in their own oppression. Materialist (Marxist) analysis of the economic base reveals the actual class dynamics at stake in a given institution or system and allows an understanding of the truth of class oppression to replace the false consciousness of ideology. Political activism and social transformation can occur when ideology is exposed as such through the insight of materialist analysis. Ideological analysis is empowering insofar as it helps lift the blinders of false consciousness and enables people to understand the way the system—even, perhaps, their favorite television shows—help perpetuate their oppression.

A rather simple example of classical Marxism applied to television might argue that the mass audience believes that television is harmless entertainment, offering a pleasant way to relax at the end of a hard work day. But in actuality the medium lulls the mass audience into passive inaction and indeed instills bourgeois aspirations and values, promising that personal fulfillment can come through the practices and products of current consumer society. Thus, this mass audience exists in a state of false consciousness; by failing to recognize how their ideas and values are formed for them to serve the interests of others, they are dupes of ideology. Corrective political action would involve educating the mass audience to understand how the medium instills values at odds with their real, material interests. For example, having more control over their own productive work might be more fulfilling than an evening watching television and might yield more concrete rewards than drinking a particular brand of beer, driving a certain car, or using a specific brand of lipstick.

Within Marxism, the theory of ideology as false consciousness has been subject to criticism and revision. In the first place, it does not explain how or why people so readily adopt ideas that would seem to be at odds with their own interests in society, especially their material interests. Furthermore, if one follows this argument, one would assume that television expressed a highly restricted range of beliefs and ideas. However, this does not seem to be the case with contemporary commercial television. Although the range of opinions and values allowed on television is by no means entirely open, television does seem to allow for the expression of a range of beliefs and ideas. Because it emphasizes institutional and economic analysis of media organizations and concentrates on the expression of overtly political ideas through the media, the classical Marxist approach is limited by its inability to account for the fact that, as Robert Allen notes in the introduction, most people watch television, most of the time, because they find it enjoyable. In this sense, classical Marxism does not provide sufficiently subtle critical and theoretical perspectives for dealing with the pleasures of contemporary culture, including watching TV.

Because of these problems and limitations, many theorists have acknowledged the inadequacy of a definition of ideology as merely false consciousness and have developed alternative ideas about ideology and how it functions. These alternative approaches variously stress contradictions within society (and within individual social subjects), the coexistence of competing ideological positions, and the ways in which individuals assume positions in relation to their social world—the very formation of subjectivity as a process. _Subjectivity_ refers to the understanding of individuals as a composite effect of forces and structures that constitute them as individuals, centrally including language, social (class) organization, and family relations. Theories of subjectivity argue that the very ideas of individuality and the self are built upon, and chronologically come after, one's participation in complex networks of social and cultural processes that inform the unconscious as well as the conscious being. These ideas are centrally developed in the context of psychoanalysis and will be discussed more fully in the next chapter by Sandy Flitterman-Lewis. Some Marxist scholars have felt that an adequate theory of ideology requires understanding social subjectivity in these terms. Such approaches offer a basis for understanding ideology and ideological criticism that does not reduce plea-surable participation in everyday entertainment to the effects of false consciousness.

Still working within the base/superstructure model, other theorists have emphasized the principle of *uneven development* present in Marxist thought from its inception. This involves the recognition that social transforma-tion is a constant but inconsistent process. All parts of the social system —the mode of production and the superstructure—may be dominated by ruling-class interests. But traces of earlier social forms and practices co-exist alongside the dominant along with more progressive elements and forces. Moreover, these contradictory and conflicting perspectives are not evenly distributed. Certain cultural practices may express issues and ideas from a prior social formation, whereas other artifacts embody progressive elements that look forward to future forms of social and material practice. In this context, cultural artifacts and texts have the potential to criticize and challenge the status quo by carrying ideological positions that are out of phase with the current, dominant mode of ideological production. The video artwork of Cecilia Condit, including such pieces as "Beneath the Skin" (1981) and "Possibly in Michigan" (1983), offer a feminist vision and critique of relations between the sexes, especially focusing on the vio-lence that underwrites them, while citing forms of popular fiction.[2] Yet especially in a medium like television, which normally requires substan-tial financial investment to produce and air programs, the expression of values and beliefs would tend to line up with dominant interests more often than not. Nonetheless, the emphasis on uneven development allows for a more complex understanding of society and ideology. In particular, it foregrounds the fact that a variety of voices may express conflicting class interests, although the ruling class interests will prevail in most contexts.

Italian Marxist Antonio Gramsci used the term *hegemony* to explain the complex ways in which the dominant class maintains its control over society. Hegemony describes the general predominance of particular class, political, and ideological interests within a given society. Although soci-ety is composed of varied and conflicting class interests, the ruling class exercises hegemony insofar as its interests are recognized and accepted as the prevailing ones. Social and cultural conflict is expressed as a strug-gle for hegemony, a struggle over which ideas are recognized as the pre-vailing, commonsense view for the majority of social participants. Hege-mony appears to be spontaneous, even natural, but it is the historical result of the prestige enjoyed by the ruling class by virtue of their position and function in the world of production. With this concept, it is possible to argue that television programs express a range of positions and ideas. From this perspective, the medium functions as a forum for negotiating hegemony, although dominant interests will prevail most of the time and may even restrict the range of competing voices that get heard.

A more thoroughgoing reformulation of ideology was developed by the French Marxist philosopher Louis Althusser, who reconceptualized society through a revision of the base/superstructure model itself. As a Marxist, Althusser recognized the importance of the mode of production in determining the nature of society. But rather than arguing that the mode of production is a *base* that by itself determines the rest of the *superstructure,* he proposed that society is comprised of a variety of interrelated social and intellectual activities or practices, including the economic, the political, and the ideological. Together these different practices make up the *social formation.* These areas of social practice—economic, political, and ideological—do not exhaust human experience but designate key arenas within which individuals find their identity in the social formation.

Economic practice involves the mode of production—the nature of productive forces and relations of production. Political practices describe social relations and specific forms of social organization. Economic and political analyses are therefore concerned with the nature and relations of power as expressed in particular economic and social systems. Ideological practice refers to systems of representation (images, myths, and ideas) in which individuals experience and express their relation to their material world.[3] Ideological analysis, then, aims to understand the ways in which meanings are produced by and for individuals within a social formation. Economic, political, and ideological practice are distinct but coexisting arenas of human activity. They exert mutual influence and pressure on one another but also operate with *relative autonomy.*

The idea of relative autonomy is a crucial revision that Althusser introduced in relation to the classical Marxist base/superstructure conception of society. Although economic practice ultimately determines all other practices (or, as Althusser puts it, the economic determines all other social practices "in the last instance"), political and ideological practice are not necessarily direct reflections of economic practice but have a life of their own. That is, each sphere of social practice has its own structures, dynamics, and history. Because of this relative autonomy, political and ideological practices are important arenas for contestation, along with economic practices.

Moreover, all spheres of the social formation are characterized by disunity and contradiction. Social practices are complex and heterogeneous structures. For example, the very idea of social identity (who we understand ourselves to be in relation to others in society) is a complex construction and may include different sets of interests. One crucial term of distinction—class—is established as a function of economic practice, but other terms may emerge specifically within the contexts of political or ideological practice. National identity, for example, is produced in the context of political practice. A given individual may be defined and positioned by a variety of categories, including class, nation, race, gender, age, profession, and so forth. At times the various interests of an individual, defined as an effect of these intersecting categories, may work in concert, whereas at other times they may be divided or come into conflict with one another.

Althusser's understanding of ideology also covers the idea of social subjectivity. Systems of representation—including language, myths, religion, and so on—function to construct individuals as social subjects, contributing to the production and recognition of one's very sense of identity. In this area Althusser drew on psychoanalytic ideas about individual self-recognition to develop his theories of subjectivity as a social process. In this instance, ideology is seen to function as a system that *interpellates* individuals, or hails them. That is to say, ideology asks us to recognize and position ourselves within its terms of reference. Ideology, like the character Ernestine in a Lily Tomlin sketch, asks, "Is this the party to whom I am speaking?" Once the question is heard, it is hard to just say, "no." In other words, ideology functions as a system of address, and individuals are positioned as social subjects through their responses in this system.

The Althusserian conception of society and ideology is not without problems and has been subject to substantial criticism and revision.[4] But the basic terms of his understanding of ideology are important. Because Althusser defined ideology in terms of both systems of representation and individuals' relations to their material world, his theories have been useful and influential in film, media, and cultural studies. The relative autonomy of ideological practice signals the importance of studying individual modes of representation, recognizing that they are socially determined but are not necessarily simple or direct reflections of dominant economic interests. Furthermore, because ideological practice concerns relations between the individual and the social formation via interpellation, it focuses attention on individuals as social subjects who not only construct but are also constructed by systems of representation.

Both Gramsci and Althusser open the way for the analysis of culture as a set of practices instead of seeing artifacts as fixed entities with specific, hidden ideological meanings waiting to be exposed by the Marxist critic. Indeed, insofar as ideological practice concerns ways in which individuals experience and contest meaning—and how they produce representations and meanings—there is no such thing as being "outside" ideology. As cultural theorist Stuart Hall has said, "The notion that our heads are full of false ideas which can, however, be totally dispersed when we throw ourselves open to 'the real' as a moment of absolute authentication, is probably the most ideological conception of all."[5] Hall points to the way in which ideology presents itself as natural or serves to naturalize a given system of representation. "When we contrast ideology to experience, or illusion to authentic truth, we are failing to recognize that there is no way of experiencing the 'real relations' of a particular society outside of its cultural and ideological categories."[6] In other words, ideology is not a "message" hidden within a text or system of representation, it is the very system of representation itself and the commonsense principles that endow the system with meaning for those who participate in it.

Because ideology involves a complex set of practices and relations, ideological criticism includes a variety of procedures and methods that emphasize different aspects of the intersections among individuals, systems of representation, and the social formation. A mass art form like television provides a crucial arena for ideological analysis precisely because it represents the intersection of economic-industrial interests, an elaborate textual system, and a leisure-entertainment activity. Marxist scholarship in mass communication, especially before 1980, overwhelmingly centered on economic and institutional analysis of media systems. This includes, centrally, the work in political economy outlined in the introduction to this book. This work is crucial to understanding the economic complexity of the television industry and has implications for the ideological understanding of the medium. But ideological analysis must also focus on television as a system of representation through which individuals experience and understand their world. Ultimately the goal is to understand how textual systems, with their relative autonomy and structuring contradictions, also function within the dynamics of the larger social formation.

The Viewer as Consumer and as Commodity

Even a cursory glance at American television reveals that advertising occupies a central position in terms of both textual system and economic support. Networks and individual stations earn profits by selling time to commercial sponsors. In the United States, television followed the model of the radio industry in developing networks and commercial sponsorship and from the start considered the viewer/consumer on a national scale.[7] The position and functioning of advertising is a crucial aspect of ideological analysis, because it is the place within television's textual system where the economics of the system are made manifest. With the prominent and regular display of commercials on television, the source of network and station income is not hidden but becomes, on the contrary, an integral part of the television program flow. The importance of commercial sponsorship and the relation of viewership to station and network revenue are underscored in popular television magazines and newspaper columns that regularly report on ratings and the competition for audiences.

American commercial television is "free." Viewers do not pay for broadcasting through a license fee (as is the case in Britain) because advertisers pay for air time to promote their products. Because commercial television is first and foremost a mass-advertising medium, viewers are positioned as potential consumers. This does not mean that every viewer is in the market for everything advertised on television. Rather, this address to viewers as consumers means that they are regularly subjected to a range of appeals for a variety of products. Even viewer-supported cable services (Home Box Office, Showtime, and others) include promotional spots for their own programs. In these cases, the viewer is addressed as a potential consumer for the station itself and its services. Because they are "sold" to advertisers, viewers themselves become commodities in the act of watching television. An elaborate apparatus of ratings is in place—the Nielsen and Arbitron systems being the most prominent—to measure the audiences for specific programs and stations. Ratings are used by the television industry to determine network and local advertising rates. The viewer-as-consumer is thus abstracted into an object of exchange value that the network or station offers to a commercial sponsor—literally sold to advertisers in lots of one thousand.

This understanding of the viewer as at once a consumer and a commodity provides a basis for analysis that draws together the culture industry on the one hand and consumer society on the other. One does not normally decide to watch television in order to look at products for possible future purchase or to become a token in the system of exchange between networks, stations, ad agencies, and commercial sponsors. Yet both of these positions are inevitably at stake, supporting and sustaining the activity of watching television, which is undertaken for a variety of other reasons—to relax, to see how a favorite sports team is doing, to learn about the day's events, or because there is nothing better to do. Ideological analysis emphasizes the commercial message as the linchpin between television as information-entertainment and television as an industry, with the viewer as the place where these meanings or forces converge. An awareness of how the material interests of the industry are most directly expressed on television leads to an understanding of the viewer as a consumer and a commodity. But it does not exhaust the work of ideological analysis. On the contrary, it becomes the grounds for raising a range of issues focused on texts and readers.

However abstract or impersonal the implications of commodification may be, it is important to realize that viewers are not forced to watch television but choose to do so freely, as individuals. This choice takes place, by and large, with some awareness of the process by which one becomes a consumer/commodity in the very act of viewing. With this understanding, ideological criticism turns its attention to the nature of the meanings and pleasures that television offers through its programs. For in the absence of force, one assumes that the medium itself offers attractions to its audience—that it is, in some sense, familiar, meaningful, and perhaps even enjoyable.[8] Indeed, despite being derided as "couch potatoes" by too many media critics, people still watch television in large numbers and with great frequency. The medium's convenience and accessibility furnish a partial explanation for its popularity, because television programs are quite literally at one's fingertips. But this is a necessary precondition of television's effectiveness as an agency of consumerism; it is not sufficient to account for the values and meanings the medium may hold for its viewers or for the pleasures those viewers might derive from it. For an explanation of these, we must turn our attention to the programs themselves, to see what they have to offer, individually and as a group.

Ideology in Narrative

The analysis of individual programs, groups of programs, and viewer-text relations is central to understanding the ideology of television. Here ideological criticism draws on the methods and insights of different approaches to textual analysis—semiotics, genre study, narrative analysis, psychoanalysis, and others—to discern what meanings are made available through the medium and its programs and the nature of viewer engagement. In drawing on these various methods of analyzing texts, the ideological perspective assumes that television offers a particular construction of the world rather than a universal, abstract truth. In other words, ideological criticism examines texts and viewer-text relations to clarify how the meanings and pleasures generated by television express specific social, material, and class interests. This is not to say that a given program or episode directly expresses the beliefs of a particular producer, writer, director, or network programmer—though obviously these may be contributing influences and viewpoints. Nor does it mean that there is some conspiracy among television executives to control the ideas expressed through the medium. Rather, ideological analysis focuses on the systematic meanings and contradictions embodied in textual practices. This includes the way familiar narrative, visual, or generic structures orient our understanding of what we see and how they naturalize the events and stories on television.

Narrative and generic conventions are crucial ways in which television handles social tensions and contradictions. At the level of the individual episode, ideological criticism can begin with narrative analysis to see how the structural and functional logic of plot development explains and naturalizes a sequence of events. Discussion of a specific episode of the American situation comedy *Webster* may clarify this point.[9] The program is a family sitcom centered on a young black boy, Webster Long, and his white foster parents, George and Katherine Papadopoulous. George is a sportscaster, a former professional football player whose best friend and teammate was Webster's father. Katherine is an upper-middle-class woman who works in the city government. In the premiere episode, George and Katherine return home from their honeymoon to discover that Webster's parents have been killed in a car accident and that Webster is now legally in their custody. In a subsequent episode originally broadcast in 1986, Webster becomes excited by the state lottery, convinced that he can become a millionaire if allowed to play. George tries to persuade him that gambling is a waste of money but finally lets him spend his allowance on a lottery ticket. Webster chooses his six numbers with his family; the digits are to consist of each person's lucky number and age. Katherine goes last, and instead of announcing her age, she volunteers to buy the ticket and fill in the last number herself.

The night before the drawing, Webster dreams that he wins the lottery. His dramatized fantasy is a parodic version of excessive wealth. Servants lead him around his mansion on a horse for amusement and do his homework for him. Webster sits amid ornate antiques, dressed in a red silk robe trimmed with gold sequins. He offers lavish gifts to his parents and their friends, including an immense pearl left over from a necklace he designed for the Statue of Liberty. It is too large to wear, but the perfect size for bowling in the mansion's bowling alley. As Webster revels in his wealth, noting that the U.S. government has put his face on a new trillion-dollar bill, Katherine reminds him that "When you give out of love, you're rich even without money." The next day, the whole family watches the lottery drawing on television. As the numbers are called one by one, they directly follow Webster's ticket, ending with Katherine's age, thirty-nine. George begins to celebrate until Katherine reads the ticket she purchased, where the sixth number is thirty-six. She confesses that she lied about her age when she finished filling in the ticket. As a result, Webster does *not* win millions of dollars. In the final scene, the family is commiserating with one another over their loss. Webster seeks to console George and Katherine, who in turn notes that it doesn't matter if they have money. "If you've got what we've got, you can be rich without money." Webster repeats her statement, revealing that Katherine had said the same thing in his dream. "We could have all the money in the world and not be as rich as we are," he affirms.

In this episode we are presented with an obvious moral tale about the value of gambling, even in legal forms. George insists that no one ever really gets rich through games of chance and that the lottery is a waste of time. This in fact proves to be the case and is the meaning of the episode as summarized in the weekly *TV Guide* listing for the show: "To teach Webster how hard it is to get rich playing the lottery, George buys him a ticket." Yet this linear and predictable development is cut across and displaced by another logic that promotes Webster as a privileged, almost magical agent. His scheme for picking numbers proves effective: the family members' lucky numbers and ages *are* the winning numbers for the one week that he plays the lottery. His childlike faith in his ability to win is thus confirmed by the narrative outcome of the lottery drawing, producing an effect strong enough to supersede the "adult" message about the serendipity of gambling.

Indeed Webster would have won millions if Katherine had not betrayed his scheme by misrepresenting her age, which she does by claiming to help Webster achieve his goal in the first place by actually purchasing the ticket. This particular narrative move relies on a cultural stereotype —women lie about their ages—to naturalize an outcome that sustains the double logic indicated above. Gambling is shown to be a waste of money, proving George's point; and yet Webster maintains his privileged status in surmounting the odds in principle, if not in fact. George and Webster are both proved "right" by the narrative because Katherine toys with Webster's formula for picking numbers, which she does even though, within the fiction, only three characters would even know that the "39" on the ticket referred to her age—which they all know anyhow. To reinforce the idea that women naturally lie about their ages, she offers the following by way of apology: "I don't know what got into me. It was like a reflex." An additional implied aspect of this sequence of events is that Webster's magical faith can only work once, in the context of his initial naive belief in his ability to win. From now on George's perspective on gambling will prevail. In the process, Webster shifts his interest in wealth as money to an emotional investment in wealth as familial love.

On a weekly basis, the general lifestyle of the family—their house, clothing, occupations—represents a recognizable upper-middle-class image. In this episode, the dream of becoming an instant millionaire is first endorsed only by Webster but is adopted by George and Katherine in the course of the actual lottery drawing. As the numbers are drawn, they all become increasingly excited, so that they are all profoundly depressed when they realize that they "lost" by one number. In this way the episode implies that the style of living it regularly represents is simply normal, that the lure of millions of dollars offered by the lottery is a fantasy shared by everyone—all families, all conceivable viewers—in the same way. The ideological significance of the "taken-for-grantedness" of the family's social and economic position may well be lost on many U.S. viewers, not because they share this position but because the lifestyle represented pervades media representations as an average standard of living. But it is immediately revealed when the program, and others like it, are shown in countries where, for the average viewer, achieving the Papadopoulous's standard would itself be beyond imagination. Structurally, then, the aspiration to wealth embodied in this particular episode diverts attention from the fact that this family is in fact already very well off within the context of American society and fabulously wealthy in relation to families in the Third World.

To complicate matters, within this context of upwardly mobile class aspirations Webster's dream is obviously parodic, a conglomeration of *media* representations of the very rich—lots of servants, a live horse —with childlike additions.[10] The pearl, above all else, condenses the admixture of imagery insofar as it represents a precious gem (an object representing a certain investment value), jewelry (though not usable as such), a sport (to link up with George's profession), and a toy all at the same time. It is also merely a fantasy object, because no real pearl could ever be that size. Webster's fantasy of riches is constructed strictly *as a* fantasy, and a child's fantasy at that. It is not "really" how rich people live. The absurdity of Webster's dream image of wealth helps soften the blow of not winning the lottery, as does the repeated dictum that love, especially familial love, itself constitutes wealth. This homily would seem to be the "message" of the episode, especially when it is repeated by Webster as the final agent of authority as he explicitly shifts his privileged, magical faith in the lottery to faith in the family.

But a more detailed analysis of the episode's narrative indicates that this message and confirmation of faith in the family is only one stage or moment in a more intricate scheme of values and meanings that includes linking the value of familial love to *honesty* in order to promote the realization of fantasies. This is expressly at issue in the program's subplot. At the opening of the episode, George is depressed because his favorite Greek restaurant is closed, and he can no longer spend Friday afternoons eating his favorite dish prepared by his "Yaya" (as he calls the grandmother-figure who ran the restaurant). Katherine traces this woman and invites her over to teach her how to prepare the dish for George. The Yaya proposes that she do the cooking herself, while Katherine can impress George by pretending she prepared the dish. Katherine refuses to go along with this idea, not because George would not believe her (although throughout the series she is depicted as being incompetent in the kitchen), but because she could not lie to George about something as meaningful as his Friday afternoon repast. In this case honesty wins out; Katherine successfully prepares George's favorite dish and is able to restore his Friday afternoon ritual. These narrative developments are embedded in, but secondary to, the lottery story in which Katherine lies about her age "like a reflex" and thereby fails Webster.

The theme of familial love thus supports or frames the overall logic of the episode's narrative development, but it hardly begins to contain the network of ideological values. Rather, the above analysis suggests the importance of recognizing a combination of narrative functions as the work of ideology. Some of these are specific to this particular show — for example, sustaining the privileged status of the character for whom the program is named. Others have more to do with typical practices of representation within the medium, such as implying that an upper-middle-class lifestyle is "average." At other moments, the show relies on broader cultural and social myths, in this case the belief that women do not like to admit their ages, especially as they approach forty. All of these strands are drawn together and activated in this specific episode to naturalize and give sense to a story with a more overt moral message about gambling, wealth, and the family.

In analyzing this episode, ideological criticism discerns the overall inter-action of meanings and the logic of how they are structured. This includes a certain degree of contradiction and instability, for example in the fact that Webster could have won the money had his formula been followed. But if this had happened in the narrative, the message about the impor-tance of family love would have been lost, or certainly muted. At the same time, a narrative development of this sort would have profound im-plications for future episodes of the program, including the necessity of transforming the family's week-to-week lifestyle image. Katherine's "be-trayal" of Webster's magical formula is in some sense a logical necessity within this episode—to prove the importance of familial love—and for the program in general. However, it functions at the expense of women, both in general as a cultural truth, and in specific when Katherine herself fails to follow Webster's wishes. Understanding the ways in which all of these countervailing forces balance and naturalize one another in the epi-sode is precisely the point of ideological analysis of specific programs on television.

This approach is not limited to dramatic narrative programs but is equally applicable to game shows, news, documentaries, sports, and other kinds of television programming. In each case, one chooses a specific set of episodes or programs and analyzes them with the goal of understand-ing the cultural logic that sustains them. Like commercials, game shows dramatize the consumerist ethic that underwrites so much of television by offering structured and formulaic arenas for competition, often with the goal of winning lavish prizes. A program such as *The Price Is Right* di-rectly involves consumer knowledge as the basis of competition, with a person's success or failure as a contestant based on his or her ability to assess the retail market value of a wide range of products including cars, jewelry, household cleansers, groceries, and appliances. In the course of proceeding to the grand prize competition that caps each episode, partici-pants are subjected to a variety of competitive games that require them to demonstrate their skills as consumers. In a crucial sense, the whole show becomes a sort of continuous advertisement as each new object and product within these games is described in detail by brand name.

Although money and prizes remain the goal of most game shows, they do not all so blatantly proclaim consumerism as the specific terms of com-petition, only as the goal. Most game shows structure knowledge within a restricted field. In programs like *Password Plus*, *Wheel of Fortune*, *Scrab-ble*, and *The $100,000 Pyramid*, the ability to guess the correct word, phrase, or category on the basis of the least information defines the competition. How many letters, words, or definitions are required before you can properly identify the correct answer? These structures are charged with significance in the context of game show competition, as players strive to fill in the blanks first to reap the rewards of winning.

At the same time, most game shows integrate elements of chance into the course of play. Some level of skill is always necessary, but skill alone is rarely adequate for achieving success. Contestants on *The Price Is Right* are selected from the studio audience. Whether or not one even gets to compete is a matter of luck. In other game shows, the amount of money to be won is determined by the spin of a wheel or the press of a button at the right time. Chance is also incorporated into game shows that emphasize specific kinds of knowledge or skill in that contestants usually have to pick categories blindly, without full knowledge of the kinds of information that will be required. On *Wheel of Fortune*, a variation of Hangman, contestants not only compete to correctly identify the phrase or name featured on the game board, but they also spin a wheel every time they request a new letter to plug into the empty spaces on the board. The wheel determines the amount of money each letter earns but also introduces opportunities to lose a turn or to go bankrupt, thus losing all the money one has accumulated. A player proceeding with all due skill can suddenly be eliminated in a crucial round of the game. In other words, a double narrative logic is at work, one combining knowledge and luck.

Although the balance between elements of chance and skill may vary, this dual logic is typical of most game shows. It provides a context for evoking familiar adages or versions thereof: life isn't fair; success is a question of being at the right place at the right time; it's not what you know; and so on. At the same time, one can admire skillful players, compare contestants in terms of how well they play the game, and even measure oneself against them. But all this occurs against a backdrop of acknowledged serendipity. One can aspire to the prizes and simultaneously console oneself: I may be a better/worse player; but I might have better/worse luck if I were actually competing. In other words, in most game shows neither sheer skill nor sheer luck prevails, and this balance contributes to the shows' effectiveness and appeal. Viewers can enjoy the adeptness of the players without feeling hopelessly stupid, recognizing that luck has something to do with their success; and viewers can maintain feelings of superiority over lesser players, whether or not the game's elements of chance work in their favor. This sustains a viewer's pleasure while that person is watching a particular show, mentally participating in the play, or rooting for a particular contestant. The important point is that through the balance of skill and chance, which is also a tension, there is always an available space for identification with and distance from the players, so that viewers can be as involved or disaffected as they like and still continue to watch.

An ideological approach to game shows, as to dramatic programs, aims at an understanding of the underlying narrative logic and patterns that structure the games. Such an approach acknowledges from the very start that the structure and appeal of game shows is a question of consumer rewards, with large sums of money, new cars, appliances, vacations, and so forth held out as the desired rewards for properly negotiating the range of skill and chance proposed by each program. But it is also instructive to specifically examine both the ways in which these rewards are achieved in a regulated field of competition and the nature of the rules of the game. What kind of knowledge is at stake in the show in the first place? What sort of competition is involved? How are these factors incorporated and intertwined in a series of steps en route to the grand prize?

Ideology and Contradiction in the Texts of Television

The discussions of *Webster* and of game shows indicate that ideological analysis is not necessarily a simple or self-evident practice. This is true in at least two senses. In the first place, the underlying theoretical perspectives that support ideological analysis, outlined earlier in this chapter, encourage an understanding of the contradictions and instabilities in culture as the places where the dominant system is most clearly exposed. In this regard it is important to recall the ideas of uneven development and of hegemony as a negotiated terrain. It is also necessary to remember that ideology is not a fixed set of beliefs, but an arena of representational practice (and therefore a site of struggle and contestation). Taken together, these ideas suggest that the expression even of dominant ideology necessarily includes tensions and contradictions. Indeed, in some sense dominant ideology can be seen as the effort to contain or smooth over points of contention and contradiction in the process of promoting a more unified idea of social subjectivity. But it is only more or less successful, never finally achieving a homogeneous set of representational practices or a unified social subject. Ideological criticism aims to expose the fault lines within the system.

To further complicate matters, television as a textual system is itself dense and complex. As a medium that usually aims to attract the largest possible audience for any given program, television's ideological system is relatively diffuse. Moreover, especially with the growth of cable services and home videocassette recorders, the competition for audiences has involved not only aiming for the largest mass audience, but also the targeting of specific subaudiences by specific cable channels, networks, or programs. Television in general aspires to attract the largest possible audience at all times. It achieves this in practice by aiming its programming at specific core audiences. The kind of programming one sees on Saturday morning is decidedly different from what airs on most stations on Thursday evening or Sunday afternoon. The differences occur because, even though one individual may watch television at all of those times, the core mass of viewers for each of those time periods is seen as demographically distinct. At the same time, a variety of interests are balanced in the production and programming of any single show. These include the interests and needs of the network as a corporate entity, of individual stations, and of sponsors and advertising agencies; the concerns of the creative personnel who actually create the programs; awareness of the audience, which is perceived as increasingly fragmented owing to a proliferation of new technologies for delivering entertainment into the home via video and television; and reaction to a range of activist pressure groups representing different political positions and agendas. If all of these institutional and interpersonal relations are considered together, ideological pluralism and dispersion can be seen as an institutional imperative, even within the confines of a medium that, at least in the United States, is thoroughly entangled with the demands of consumer culture.

Moreover, the production of multiple ideological positions can be viewed as an effect of programming practices, as individual episodes and programs are situated within the larger system of program flow. The creators of a program do not usually have any say over the kinds of ads that air during their show; nor do they determine where their show will air in the programming schedule. Similarly, viewers watch when they want to, perhaps turning on the television in the middle of an hour-long dramatic episode, flipping through other channels on the remote control when they get bored, and so on. Whatever the institutional imperatives that generate a context for ideological dispersion—and there are many countervailing forces—the texts that comprise television are not discrete and delimited but are juxtaposed with and bump up against one another. In other words, individual episodes are segmented and interspersed with commercials, news briefs, and program previews, all of which are themselves sequences of mininarratives. These sequences are, in turn, positioned within an unceasing flow from program to program.

This appearance of an endless text, extended and reduplicated from station to station, is regulated through various kinds of repetition: shows air on the same night and time each week, genres maintain certain conventions, and so forth. This kind of regularity provides a sense of segmentation within program flow. One can reserve Thursday night for *Knots Landing* and be sure of seeing it (if it is not preempted). Similarly, fans of *Dallas* and *Dynasty*, if they happened to be home on Thursday night, might choose to sample *Knots Landing* based on the knowledge that it was a prime-time serial melodrama. In this context, a given program may develop variable perspectives and issues over time. And the perspectives put forth in one scene or episode may be repeated, fragmented, and even contradicted by the next program or the commercial that follows. Thus, within a single episode, across an evening of viewing, or over a season's worth of episodes of a particular program, the production of ideology may emerge as variable, slippery, or even contradictory.

The American crime drama *Cagney and Lacey* offers striking examples of this point, but the show is hardly singular in offering heterogeneous ideological meanings to its viewers. The program features two female police detectives as the center of narrative interest and espouses a sympathetic liberal feminism. Individual episodes frequently foreground personal and professional issues that are perceived as being of particular concern to women—sexual harassment, problems of working mothers, child abuse, and so forth. Yet the visual and narrative strategies engaged in individual episodes may work to undercut or contradict the ostensible progressive orientation of the show by relying on traditional plot structures and conventional modes of visual representation that have conventionally worked to undermine the power and effectiveness of women. For example, framing and mise-en-scène are sometimes used in ways that imply that one or the other of the central characters is caged or trapped. This may produce an impression of weakness or helplessness on the part of that character, even though within the narrative she is supposed to be an active, competent detective.

In one episode, Christine Cagney is physically threatened by a suspect in a murder to which she was witness. He follows her around in an effort to persuade her not to testify against him through sheer threat of force. This episode includes repeated shots of Cagney isolated in her apartment, almost cowering, trapped by the camera as well as by the suspect who watches her through the rooftop skylight of her apartment. In this case

her usual ability to perform as a cop—aggressive, strong, and confident
—is displaced by conventions for representing women as subject to the
menacing threat of a narrative character and the look of the camera. In
another episode, Cagney initiates a sex discrimination suit against a superior officer, against the wishes of her New York City police department
superiors. When she resolves to pursue the case, she is seen in a close-up
framed against the barred windows of the precinct interrogation room.
Thus, even as the program offers a portrait of two strong, professional
women, it deploys familiar visual and narrative conventions, using an already established visual and narrative language, that restrict women's
ability to control their own fates and subjugate them to the control of the
camera, forcefully identified with the male gaze.

Of course, in these examples there is also room for alternative interpretations. When Cagney is framed against the barred windows of the precinct interrogation room, the scene could be taken as just another familiar
image of a weak woman or as a self-conscious comment by the program
itself on the way in which women, however competent, are framed by
social constraints. This example underscores how television must be analyzed in terms of disunity and contradiction in at least two senses: first, as
the codes of narrative and visual construction come into conflict at particular moments within the program; and second, as these forms of disjunc-
tion open the possibility of a range of interpretive positions. Ideological
criticism aims precisely at understanding these contradictions as constitutive of the text's *ideological problematic*. The ideological problematic
refers to the field of representational possibilities offered by a text and the
structuration of issues in particular ways. In this vein, ideological criticism is less concerned with finding a specific message in a text than with
delineating the range of issues and questions raised within a program or
across a set of texts (a number of episodes, or a program and the advertisements, or an evening of programming).

The ideological problematic refers to the nature and range of issues
raised and *how* they are raised and to the systems of representation that
are thereby promoted or excluded, in implicit or explicit terms. David
Morley explains: "The problematic is importantly defined in the negative
—as those questions or issues which cannot (easily) be put within a particular problematic—and in the positive as that set of questions or issues
which constitute the dominant or preferred 'themes' of a programme."[11]
What are the constitutive issues at stake in the first place, especially when
it comes to asserting important categories of social subjectivity? What
range of possibilities for meaning are promoted by the text? What areas of

meaning are staked out as significant for discussion? What is implicitly or explicitly left out? These are the kinds of questions that are raised—and answered with the help of other critical methodologics.

In the case of *Cagney and Lacey*, the problematic is initially established as a function of a number of generic and discursive systems. On the one hand, the program combines the police drama with aspects of domestic melodrama. As a police show, the focus on urban crime and police procedures provides a context for a certain range of issues within the context of "law and order": the ethics of dealing with informants, the role of the press in reporting crime, and the impact of crime on its victims, among others. On the other hand, the presence of two women detectives —one married with children, the other single, and both nearing forty —allows for the examination of a particular range of domestic and interpersonal issues. With this emphasis the problems involved in raising children or of balancing careers and families can be raised. Simultaneously, a feminist discourse cuts across both of these others and at times offers an explicit connection between them, because the show quite consciously addresses issues of concern to women in a progressive spirit. For example, it may include concerns of pornography or child abuse as part of its police plots, but these issues also have implications for the characters as women and mothers.

Together, these areas begin to define the ideological problematic of *Cagney and Lacey*, circumscribing the kinds of plots it includes and the nature of the issues it raises on a weekly basis. The combination establishes its similarities to other programs within television but also differentiates it on the one hand from other police shows, which may not share its domestic and feminist concerns, and on the other hand from shows that share its domestic or feminist concerns but are not police shows (for example, *Kate and Allie* or *Designing Women*). Within the defined ideological problematic, which can expand and mutate over time, the program may orchestrate a variety of perspectives without clearly insisting that only one position is acceptable. For example, in one episode Cagney thinks that she might be pregnant. She is therefore forced to consider an array of options—whether to tell the potential father, whether to try and marry, whether to have the baby—and decide on a course of action. She explicitly raises these possibilities and their implications, often in discussion with Lacey, while the two of them pursue the police subplot. In the end, it turns out that she is not pregnant after all. Thus all the choices prove to be hypothetical options rehearsed by the program but not requiring a decisive course of action—one way of addressing issues of concern to contemporary women in the abstract, combining the program's feminist and domestic voices.

At the same time, in the elaboration of the ideological problematic, the field of choice is circumscribed; although different perspectives may be introduced, the range is not infinite. In *Cagney and Lacey*, feminism is explored in the context of the traditional, middle-class, nuclear family. Although Christine Cagney has no husband or children, her familial situation is explored through her relationships with her father and brother. Similarly, the police system itself and its hierarchy of authority at times causes problems for the protagonists, not only in the episodes dealing with Cagney's sexual harassment suit, but also, for example, in conflicts over areas of jurisdiction between precincts. This allows the program to raise questions about the police system and to suggest that it has problems, especially when it comes to questions of the sexual division of labor and power. But the program never poses a thoroughgoing challenge to the system as a whole. Instead, such problems are portrayed as weaknesses or aberrations in a fundamentally good system, within which the characters of Cagney and Lacey represent an ideal.

The latitude of competing voices and positions constructed within the particular problematic presents itself as a totality precisely because different points of view are incorporated. In other words, the very incorporation of different positions and points of view conveys an impression of completeness, as if anything that might be said on the issue has been covered. But often only a delimited or circumscribed range of choices is in fact presented to begin with. Moreover, the presentation of multiple positions and points of view is often regulated or controlled by an implicit hierarchy that privileges certain positions over others. This hierarchy is established in a number of ways, including the positions that are most frequently represented and the framing narrational logic within which a limited plurality of voices is allowed to speak. For example, on *The 700 Club*, TV minister Pat Robertson's forum for representing his conservative, evangelical position, a wide range of social and cultural issues are raised. A viewer casually flipping through the channels might chance on the program just as someone was describing a life of debauchery. But this person's story would only be presented in the program in order to be condemned as ungodly; it would most likely occur in the context of a confessional narrative wherein the individual in question subsequently experienced a spiritual rebirth of the kind celebrated by Robertson and his evangelical organization.

This is an extreme example of a show's introducing a range of voices and perspectives in order to reframe them according to a preestablished and clearly delineated set of ideological values. But in many instances television can be seen as working to contain minority positions or deviations from the mainstream by first providing a context for their expression. With regard to *Cagney and Lacey*, the roles held by the program's title characters are hardly aberrant, but they are not typical within the context of television. The women are presented as having an unusual degree of strength and independence in their narrative roles and might be viewed as a challenge or threat to traditional gender roles. In this context, the use of conventional visual strategies for representing women —such as positioning them from the point of view of a male spectator, either explicitly within the fiction (as when Cagney is stalked and watched through her skylight window) or implicitly, by depicting them in typically feminine poses and behaviors—along with the domestic plots that emphasize the more traditional roles of wife, mother, and daughter, can be seen as working to contain the potential threat.

On television, the movement between program plot segments and commercial breaks may exacerbate the sense of contradiction. In an episode initially broadcast during the 1983–84 season, the professional plot concerns the illegal adoption market. The parallel personal subplot focuses on Mary Beth Lacey and her family as she arranges to get temporary custody of the abandoned infant whose plight has prompted the police investigation. (A wealthy couple who had purchased the child through a private adoption has abandoned her at a hospital after discovering that she is deaf.) During the course of the investigation, the baby's real mother is located. In a confrontation with Lacey, she explains that she sold the baby out of economic hardship, but now regrets her actions and hopes to reclaim custody. The episode concludes with Lacey returning the infant to a child welfare officer in an extremely emotional scene, on the heels of the Laceys' decision to look into the possibility of adopting her.

The commercial that directly followed this scene was one for Hallmark Mother's Day cards, featuring a baby and a jingle about a first Mother's Day. The highly sentimental Hallmark version of motherhood was jarring in the face of the program's portrayal of the same thing. Indeed, the episode offers three representations of motherhood, each involving a specific set of problems: a wealthy woman who can't bear children and turns to the marginally legal private baby market; a welfare mother who feels pressured to sell her third child for economic reasons—to help the rest of her family and the baby enjoy better living conditions; and a professional experience a loss. The discrepancies in conception and representation between the program and the commercial seem irreconcilable. But they are mutually interdependent, as the troubled versions of motherhood represented in the episode appear to be more realistic, complex, and progressive in contrast to the more traditional, sentimental representation offered by Hallmark. Moreover, all of these representations work together to define the contours of the problematic of "motherhood," with the ad serving to provide a necessary supplement in the overall concert of voices.

Contradictions—and confirmations—between juxtaposed segments of television flow are not necessarily systematic in the sense of being willfully or consciously planned by programmers or sponsors. However, they occur regularly through the course of television programming as an effect of the structure of the system, in which continuous programming is the rule and flow is a principal characteristic of the system. Almost everyone can cite his or her own striking examples. Public service messages about health and nutrition air on Saturday morning, embedded among ads for candy, cookies, snack foods, and sweetened cereals aimed at children. A news story about new research linking smoking with some illness can be followed by an ad for smoker's tooth polish.

At the same time, with regard to *Cagney and Lacey*, some feminists have stressed the importance of female bonding, represented in the relationship between the two main characters, as an important aspect of the show. Although the two characters bring different and often conflicting perspectives to bear on issues of personal and professional life within the fiction, they work successfully as a team and provide one another with support. They do not compete against one another but negotiate and combine viewpoints in order to work together. The narrative occasions that foreground this sort of interaction are seen as privileging women's perspectives and as offering the possibility of concerted action grounded in different aspects of women's experience. In these instances, it is possible to argue that the program goes beyond simply presenting a strong image of women to offer a nascent feminist ideology within the context of mass art. Similar arguments may be made regarding other programs that feature women constituting a community (personal or professional) as the center of narrative interest, such as *Kate and Allie, Designing Women, The Golden Girls*, and *Heartbeat*.

Thus over time, both within individual shows and across several episodes, a program may produce a range of ideological effects and meanings. The contradictions and multiplicity of views help explain a program's appeal to a broad potential audience. In the case of *Cagney and Lacey*, one can recognize progressive, liberal, and traditional values working at once through the fabric of the show, often as competing and contradictory positions. Depending on where and how one focuses one's attention, a range of belief systems can be partially satisfied and fulfilled, though they are received in a context of contestation, moderated by the other perspectives that accompany them. An awareness of this field of multiple meanings as the work of ideology is crucial in understanding the effectiveness and appeal of television as a mass medium.

The Pleasures of Consumption

So far this chapter has focused on more familiar and conventional forms of television programming. This focus is based in the common assumption that programs are what attract viewers in the first place; they are the major source of the pleasure, entertainment, and information that accounts for why viewers watch television. Within the course of the programming flow, viewers are then subjected to other appeals of a promotional nature, not only advertisements, but promotions for other programs and episodes that are not on now but will be shown later (this evening, next week, etcetera). Promotional and advertising appeals are recognized as the sites where television's consumerist mission is obvious—not only to political economists but to all viewers—and where the dominant ideology of the medium is baldly exposed. Programming is then seen as the area in which more complex and subtle meanings, effects, and pleasures are generated.

Shop-at-home television programs and stations that have emerged in the course of the past decade can be analyzed as a limit or test case in this regard.[12] In shop-at-home television the programming *is* sales—a flow of products offered directly to the viewer for purchase, one at a time, twenty-four hours a day. The programming provided by television shopping stations is not differentiated from the commercial appeals of advertisements. Instead, programming is a continuous segmented sales pitch. Television's force as an apparatus and agency of consumer culture is fully and explicitly expressed by this kind of programming. At the same time, the shopping channels raise questions about the very nature of television programming in the first place. How much, or how little, programming does it take to entice viewers to watch the television for more than a few minutes? If someone watches shop-at-home programs for hours on end, is it simply because that person likes commercials? Would he or she also watch hours of nonstop television advertising? Shop-at-home programming allows us to interrogate the minimal requirements of programming and representational practices on television. For the structure of such programs precludes regular rules of shopping: they are not interactive catalogs from which viewers pick what they want to buy and when.

The Home Shopping Network (HSN) is one of the first and most successful of the shop-at-home channels. It is widely available on cable systems throughout the United States and also runs on a number of broadcast stations. On HSN certain forms of meaning and pleasure seem to persist even in the absence of conventional entertainment and information. This includes appeals to viewers as members of a community, even as a family of consumers, who are connected through exchanges of confession and testimonials between program hosts and call-in purchasers. In the process of selling its products, HSN provides appropriate terms and guidelines for its own use by the viewer, with a particular emphasis on the female as the ideal consumer and on domestic space as the ideal site of consumption. Because both a television and a telephone are necessary to shop with HSN, the home is very nearly the only location from which one can avail oneself of the service.

The network provides its shop-at-home services under the name of the Home Shopping Club (HSC), which individuals automatically join with their first purchase. The club offers items for purchase one at a time, and they can only be bought during the time they are displayed on the television, usually five to ten minutes. Each item is shown in a series of close-up shots, with information about price, number sold, and so on included in accompanying graphics. A wide range of products is sold on the club, but certain kinds of products dominate. These include jewelry, collectibles, clothing, and small electric appliances. A program host describes the item at length as it is displayed and then takes calls from buyers who discuss their purchase. Over the course of the programming, an overarching discourse of consumption is constructed through these phone exchanges: people discuss what they buy, why they buy, how they buy, and for whom they buy.

Most of the merchandise offered by HSC could be categorized as the conspicuously consumed trinkets of working-class and lower-middle-class lifestyles and taste cultures within American consumer society.[13] Many of the products, especially the jewelry and collectibles, are imitations or cheaper versions of the fine china and crystal figurines or jewelry one might find in upscale department stores or specialty shops like Tiffany's. The HSC products offer an image of wealth, but they lack the manufacturer and designer imprimatur that would constitute value in the way of the upscale, properly bourgeois products that are their model. At the same time, all HSC viewers are addressed and presented as knowledgeable and informed shoppers in general. In conversations between program hosts and shoppers, there is a constant dialogue about the quality and value of the products being sold, including comparison of commercial retail values and the bargain prices offered by the club. The program projects its viewers as experts who fully understand the larger world of consumerism and the merchandise that circulates within it. Thus the program offers the image of a working-class taste culture, with the subjects who populate it constructed as discerning, active, and educated consumers.

Moreover, as Robert Allen points out in his chapter, the club represents the exemplary viewer-consumers that have made it successful as members of a larger community of desire that everyone can join. Shoppers are applauded for acting to fulfill their desires, though the process of accumulation will never be complete because there is a constant stream of products waiting to be purchased. With consumption literally based in the home, the female consumer becomes the focus for regenerating consuming desires. Through phone calls, viewers learn how shopping with the club also consolidates and confirms domestic and social relations, because often the product is purchased as a gift for someone else—a daughter, spouse, parent, or neighbor.

The Home Shopping Club and its parent network, HSN, represent the pleasures of buying in the very process of selling their merchandise. The program constantly reconfirms the value of staying home and watching television—HSC in particular—as the best way to secure family and community relations. It also validates the position of women as the center of these relations. Given these emphases, conventional forms of entertainment and information programming are not necessary as the lure to situate viewers as virtual subjects of consumption. For in the world according to HSC, television affords direct participation in the pleasures of personal and economic exchange to consolidate the family as the subject of an improved standard of living. In these terms, even despite the direct sales pitch and the programming that is indistinguishable from a direct commercial appeal, there are complex ideological meanings to be derived about consumption, the family, pleasure, values, and gender. This discussion of HSC only initiates consideration of the density of class and gender positions generated through the course of its programming, which at first may seem to be nothing more than a blatant advertising gimmick.

Television as a Heterogeneous Unity

The ideological meanings and positions produced on television—in episodes, series, or whole networks—are not unified or monolithic, but that does not imply that television can mean anything you want it to or has something for everyone. Rather, a range of intersecting and at times even contradictory meanings runs through the course of programming, offering some things for most people, a regulated latitude of ideological positions meeting the interests and needs of a range of potential viewers. This means that the medium does not often encompass extreme positions and places a strong emphasis on balance and even-handedness when it does present a range of opinions and perspectives to hedge against offending any moderate position. It is useful to approach this heterogeneity in terms of the idea of the ideological problematic.

Within individual programs, between programs and commercials, and across a variety of programs, television is highly fragmented and heterogeneous, allowing for the orchestration of a variety of issues, voices, positions, and messages. None of these on its own accounts for the ideology of the medium. Instead, the aim of ideological analysis is to understand their coexistence and contradiction through the medium in systematic and social terms. Above, this point was illustrated in relation to ideas about maternity and motherhood presented on *Cagney and Lacey*. What became clear was that the concept "motherhood" was important enough to warrant exploration and narrative exposition through the course of the show, but that this concept itself involved complex and contradictory positions. It is not enough to conclude that "motherhood" is an important idea, in the absence of a concrete analysis of the multiple representations that comprise it. In the case in question, this included a consideration of one of the advertisements that aired during the program.

In the process of offering a concert of voices, and with its strong links to consumerism, television works to sustain the dominant social-cultural ideology while allowing that this ideology itself involves a series of values and attitudes. Yet the recognition of a whole range of perspectives—including the possibility of opposing and contradictory ideas—does not mean that everything can be said in the context of television. There are social and cultural attitudes that lie beyond the multiplicity of dominant ideological expressions. At times such positions may find an outlet on television, but these occasions are rare, and they do not necessarily, or usually, occur in the context of network prime-time programming. In other words, however complex and contradictory, the range of ideological positions to be found on television is ultimately limited to sets of cultural and social beliefs that are not extreme—positions that, from the perspective of the mainstream, could still be considered reasonable and widely held.

The recognition of television's regulated ideological plurality (the inclusion of a range of perspectives with minimal attention to extreme or minority positions) raises the question of viewers—how they engage and are engaged by the medium and how they are situated in relation to its production, ideological positions, and meanings. Some of these issues are more fully addressed in the context of psychoanalytic criticism, feminism, and British cultural studies. With respect to the ideological functioning of the medium, it is nonetheless crucial to understand that, as a site of textual activity, television is the locus of intersection and coexistence of varying narratives, genres, appeals, and modes of address. Viewers consent to watch, and to submit to its array of appeals, in exchange for the text and the possibility of identifying particular meanings, mobilizing the voices that seem to speak "to them."

This interpretation in turn raises the possibility of alternative or subversive reading strategies, because particular marginalized or disempowered social groups (women, African Americans, gays, and others) may develop strategies for focusing on isolated moments within the textual flow that offer the possibility of disrupting and destabilizing the dominant ideology. The whole issue of reading practices, especially in the context of *identity politics* (the idea of building a coalition based on emphasizing a particular aspect of one's social identity, defined in terms of race, sexual preference, etcetera), is more central to the questions raised by British cultural studies. But it is a useful issue to bring up in the context of ideological criticism because it points to the ways in which individuals can recognize and use the meanings made available through the heterogeneity of television's systems of representation, however much the system may strive to "contain" extreme or disruptive meanings. Feminist approaches to daytime soap opera, for example, have suggested that the traditional villainess transforms feminine weakness into a source of power and strength and offers viewers a figure of female vengeance against patriarchal restraint.[14]

Focusing our attention on readings highlights the fact that a dominant ideology is less a fixed set of meanings and beliefs than it is a negotiated position within a system of contradictory and contestatory meanings that are expressed in cultural texts, including television. These readings are carried out in the interest of a willful subversion of dominant ideology by social and cultural groups whose interests are not centrally addressed, or are largely ignored, by television's system of representation and its plurality of voices. Readings "against the grain" are interested in the latent possibility of alternative viewpoints erupting within the multiple strategies of appeal that are normally at work in the medium. For example, in the discussion of *Cagney and Lacey*, we saw how a variety of perspectives and topics were expressed in the show but were ultimately contained by dominant conventions and norms. A subversive reading emphasizes a marginal voice or position and brackets off the dominant context that presumably holds it in place, or it demonstrates how the marginal voice exposes the contradictions of the dominant context within which it emerges. These alternative readings become a way of turning the medium on its head, allowing various subcultural voices to initiate breakdowns and reversals of meanings of television's dominant ideological practices through the medium's own texts.

In part, alternative readings are possible because of the overriding contradiction that characterizes contemporary social practice in general and television in particular. In striving to represent itself as a totality that speaks for and to us all, the medium inevitably raises issues and points to values and ideas that are problematic or disruptive and that cannot be neatly or easily subsumed in general social consensus. The combined texts of television nevertheless work to hold themselves together as the diversified expression of dominant ideology. This struggle for unity occurs not only at the level of ideas and issues, but also at the level of genre and mode of address, as television attempts to fashion a unified "world" out of discontinuous textual fragments. Regularity and repetition are important strategies for ordering the unending flow of television's images and sounds. The same shows, featuring the same characters, air at the same time each week; reruns and syndicated repeats provide frequent returns to already known material; news and talk show hosts are promoted as familiar (even familial) personalities. All of this contributes to an overall sense of regularity and stability, as part of television's appeal across the variety of program flow.

Within this context, the production of the celebrity personality as a commodity can be seen as a crucial strategy that works to hold the diversity of television's textual flow in place for the viewer, because the celebrity is a product circulated through a system of textual segments. In American television, the figure of Ed McMahon is prototypical in this respect. His prominent status as a nationally recognized figure is anchored in his multiple appearances within television: as Johnny Carson's "second banana" on *The Tonight Show* (over a period of thirty years); as the commercial spokesman for a variety of advertised products (including, for example, Alpo dog food); as the promoter for the Publisher's Clearinghouse Sweepstakes; and as the host of the syndicated show *Star Search*. McMahon's career is typical of the way the medium produces familiar individuals in the form of celebrities. The habitual regularity of the medium is not limited to programs, genres, and scheduling, but embraces the individuals who populate it.

The proliferation of appearance as a form of regularity on television signals the status of the celebrity as a commodity, a figure of circulation that allows viewers to find unity in relation to the celebrity persona across a range of genres, programs, and audiences. It is not simply coincidental that made-for-TV movies frequently star actors who are well known for their other work on television. The medium counts on the recognition of the television star from a series to draw an audience for the made-for-TV movie. Although specific commercials, program episodes, and programs (series, serials, and specials) maintain their integrity and impact as individual texts, they also constantly refer to one another.[15] In the case of the made-for-TV movie with its stars drawn from daytime and prime-time television dramas, the movie may be perfectly entertaining to someone unfamiliar with the specific cast. But it will presumably attract a ready-made audience and will be even more meaningful to the viewer who already knows and admires the actor and the character he or she plays on another TV program. Moreover, having watched the actor in the movie, the viewer may decide to become a regular watcher of a previously unviewed series. The recognition and enjoyment of intramedium connections and references at this level means that any given text or textual segment makes sense on its own but also may evoke additional fields of signification. On the one hand, a text may be provisionally excised from the flow of television and analyzed on its own terms, according to a variety of methods. On the other hand, the rest of the medium becomes the representational context that grounds the program within television as a self-defined textual field.

This process of multiple referentiality is not limited to the deployment of celebrity figures but increasingly becomes the rule as self-reflexivity and intertextual references proliferate through the medium. These are found in almost any program and genre, including *Saturday Night Live*, *Late Night with David Letterman*, *St. Elsewhere*, *Moonlighting*, *Murder, She Wrote*, *thirtysomething*, and *The Simpsons*, among other programs. The final episode of the situation comedy *Newhart* ended by suggesting that the whole program had been a dream of the main character on the earlier *Bob Newhart Show*, thereby referencing the popular situation comedy with which it shared a star. The final episode of *Dallas* in 1991 offered a version of *It's a Wonderful Life*, as the central character, J. R. Ewing, gets to see what the world of *Dallas* would have been like if he had never been born. (Although this episode references a popular film rather than a television program, properly speaking, it is a film whose popularity has grown in direct proportion to its numerous television screenings, which in fact proliferated when the copyright was not renewed and the film entered the public domain.) The range of self-reflexivity and self-referentiality encompasses a wide range of genres.

A full understanding of television's ideological production must take account of this aspect of the meanings generated through the medium. For it leads to a certain limited sense of meaning and logic, whereby the terms of clarity and understanding are contained by the medium itself rather than by reference to the "real world." It promotes recognition and understanding of the medium and its texts as constructions, allowing the audience to participate in the inside jokes and artifice that seem to permeáte and at times even overtake it. This can reach extremes, as it did when, for example, Mickey Mouse—the animated figure—appeared "live" at the 1988 Academy Awards show to present the award for best animated short. Obviously, the animated cartoon figure was not actually there on stage but was technologically inserted for the (international) television audience viewing the event. He even brought his own guests: Minnie Mouse, Donald Duck, and Daisy Duck were shown sitting in the audience, among the other celebrities, as Mickey shared the stage with Tom Selleck.

Murphy Brown, an American situation comedy, provides another example, this time in a more conventional narrative context. The eponymous heroine of the program (played by Candice Bergen) is a reporter on a weekly television news magazine show. In one episode, Morgan Fairchild plays an actress starring in a new situation comedy in which the main character is a prominent celebrity investigative reporter on a weekly television news magazine show. In preparation for her role, she spends time with Murphy Brown and her coworkers and ends up asking Murphy to do a walk-on during the premiere episode of her show. Murphy agrees, although the show turns out to be awful, Murphy herself included. At the end of the episode, Murphy is in the offices for her own program when Connie Chung (a well-known, real television news reporter) walks in —playing herself, "Connie Chung," within the fiction. She and Murphy discuss Murphy's role on the situation comedy, and Connie says that she would never do anything like that because it could damage her credibility and integrity as a recognized news personality. When Murphy protests that Connie is only saying that because she did not actually have an opportunity to make such a choice, Connie explains that she was in fact asked first but turned down the offer.

What sense is a viewer to make of this? On the one hand, we have a highly typical moment of television's self-reflexivity in the form of a cute joke that most *Murphy Brown* viewers will readily get. On the other hand, any attempt to unpack the joke demonstrates that conventional terms of referentiality no longer function. Instead, representation is stretched to the limits of signifying logic. As a character in the fiction of *Murphy Brown*, Connie Chung is telling the truth—she did not appear on the sitcom within the sitcom. Yet here she is, Connie Chung herself, portraying herself and doing a walk-on for a fictional situation comedy, in which she says she would not compromise her integrity by doing such a thing. To complicate matters even further, this cameo appearance coincided with the introduction of Connie Chung's own prime-time news show, which was receiving extensive press coverage, and criticism, for its own "confusions" of fiction and nonfiction through the use of dramatic reenactments of the events being reported. Yet even at this limit point of meaning, the episode also presumes a set of given categories and identities as reference points to make meaning, even non-sense, out of this turn of events. These reference points include recognition of the distinctions between news and entertainment, however tenuous the dividing line, and of the celebrity figures who forcefully represent the different modes of television (Morgan Fairchild, Candice Bergen, and Connie Chung), as well as the confusions between them.

At this point it is possible, even necessary, to return to the cough medicine commercial discussed at the start of this chapter and consider an additional possible reading. At one extreme we might assume that the ad is hermetically self-referential and that the actor, who is not a doctor, plays a doctor *only* in this ad and nowhere else on television. In this case the interplay of extratextual and intertextual reference is caught up in a sort of mirror logic, signaled by the declaration, "I'm not a doctor, but. . . ." The verbal message implies that the actor plays a doctor in a different (fictional) television text. But if we assume, even playfully, that he plays a doctor *only in this commercial*, then we may conclude that the ad is referring to itself and to all of the times it is broadcast. Intertextuality becomes self-conscious self-referentiality, because the implied reference to *another* text is actually only a reference to *this* text. Television hereby exhibits its own fictionality, but in terms that insist that this fictionality exercises affective and intellectual appeal. In this extreme interpretation, television is at once completely artificial and completely meaningful to its viewers. We know that the ad does not really convey the voice of medical authority—it is only an actor playing a doctor in a commercial. Moreover, the ad tells us that it knows that we recognize this artificiality. But we may still follow its lead and buy the product to alleviate a cough, which is also something the ad wants us to do.

Because the commercial so clearly sets up the terms of its functioning within the conventions of the medium—including self-consciousness about its own fictionality and self-referentiality—it is easy, even effortless, to watch it and follow its logic as long as we already understand the medium's norms, its regular practices and strategies. Even at its points of minimal referentiality, with its self-reflexive acknowledgement of its own fictionality this particular commercial, along with many other television texts, fits into the world constructed on television and works to position us as potential consumers in a real marketplace beyond the confines of the television screen (but also active within it, as we have seen). Ideological analysis allows us to understand the strategies and mechanisms of television that produce these paradoxical and contradictory positions of knowledge within contemporary culture.

Finally, ideological criticism is concerned with texts as social processes and as social products. Given television's prominent position in contemporary social life, its dense network of texts, and its pervasive implication in a larger consumer culture, it constitutes a major arena of contemporary ideological practice. It is thus clearly important to subject the medium to ideological investigation. This is especially the case as the expansion of cable and other alternative choices to network and broadcast programming proliferate and fragment the audience, offering a wider range of programming but also reduplicating much of what already exists. At the same time, these characteristics make the project of ideological analysis a complex task. Because of its fragmentation and heterogeneity, television constantly draws viewers into its world of representation, but it does so in uneven or variable ways. This representational heterogeneity mainly functions as a limited and regulated pluralism, striving to hold things in balance and to develop all subjects and points of view in relation to normative frames of reference.

Dominant ideological interests may constitute this normative frame and prevail in the last instance. But along the way we are confronted with a variety of issues, ideas, and values that cannot easily be subsumed under the heading of "ruling ideology," which is itself constructed in contradiction. The process is further complicated by the fact that, in the current social formation, television itself contributes to and exists in highly fragmented and dispersed systems of representation, so that it is difficult to identify a single normative or dominant voice. In the face of this heterogeneity, it is all the more crucial that we directly confront and analyze the mobilization of multiple perspectives and contradictions, through and across the texts that comprise television, in order to develop our understanding of ideological practice in all its complexity.

NOTES

1. The discussion of Marxist theory developed here is intended as a general and introductory overview. In the process of summary, I inevitably and unfortunately simplify an important and complex body of literature, conflate a broad range of diverse thought, and elide refinements and subtleties within Marxist theory. This chapter is not an appropriate context for detailed elaboration of these positions; however, I have included key texts on Marxist theories of ideology in the supplemental bibliography.

2. For a detailed discussion of this work, see Patricia Mellencamp, "Uncanny Feminism," in *Indiscretions: Avant-Garde Film, Video, and Feminism* (Bloomington: Indiana University Press, 1990), pp. 126–39.

3. This formulation is borrowed and paraphrased from several theorists who have discussed Althusser's theory of ideology, in particular Stuart Hall, "Signification, Representation, Ideology: Althusser and the Post-Structuralist Debates," *Critical Studies in Mass Communication* 2 (June 1985): 103; and Rosalind Coward and John Ellis, *Language and Materialism* (London: Routledge and Kegan Paul, 1977), p. 67. Althusser explains ideology in these terms in "Marxism and Humanism," in *For Marx*, trans. Ben Brewster (New York: Vintage Books, 1970), pp. 221–47.

4. Stuart Hall's "Signification, Representation, Ideology" offers what I would consider a revision or reappraisal of Althusser that draws heavily, but not uncritically, on his theory. A more thoroughgoing critique can be found in Simon Clarke et al., *One-Dimensional Marxism* (London: Allison and Busby, 1980).

5. Hall, "Signification, Representation, Ideology," p. 105.

6. Ibid.

7. James Schwoch, "Selling the Sight/Site of Sound: Broadcast Advertising and the Transition from Radio to Television," *Cinema Journal* 30, no. 1 (Fall 1990): 55–66.

8. There have developed a variety of alternative perspectives on how the

medium engages its viewers. Some of these are summarized by William Boddy, "Loving a Nineteen-Inch Motorola: American Writing on Television," in *Regarding Television—Critical Approaches: An Anthology*, ed. E. Ann Kaplan, American Film Institute Monograph Series, vol. 2 (Frederick, Md.: University Publications of America, 1983), pp. 1–11. In particular, Boddy provides an overview of the so-called "pessimistic" culture theorists who perceived mass media as organizing popular taste "along the demands of the consumer market" (p. 4) and offering a false sense of community to the alienated, fragmented masses of industrial society.

Others have discussed the medium's appeal in terms of its utopian kernel. This position proposes that mass culture generally succeeds when it responds to *real* social needs, but that it fulfills these needs in imaginary terms and in highly delimited ways. Here, the goal of analysis is to discern the utopian/liberating aspirations expressed in television, as well as to describe how these aspirations are channeled and delimited. See Hans Magnus Enzensberger, *The Consciousness Industry* (New York: Seabury Press, 1974), and Richard Dyer, *Light Entertainment* (London: British Film Institute, 1973), esp. pp. 39–42.

9. Although no longer in its first run on prime-time television, *Webster* enjoyed a long run in prime time and remains popular in syndication. It is discussed here as a relatively available and familiar show.

10. Interestingly enough, the behavior of George and Katherine in this dream is clearly modeled on "the millionaire and his wife" from *Gilligan's Island*. George wears yachting clothes and affects the speech patterns of Mr. Howell, while Katherine dresses over-formally—in an elaborate gown and fur coat—and behaves like the empty-headed Mrs. Howell.

11. David Morley, *The "Nationwide" Audience: Structure and Decoding* (London: British Film Institute, 1980), p. 139.

12. This discussion is based on a longer analysis of the Home Shopping Club in Mimi White, *Tele-Advising: Therapeutic Discourse in American Television* (Chapel Hill: University of North Carolina Press, 1992). Also see Jane Desmond, "How I Met Miss Tootie: The Home Shopping Club," *Cultural Studies* 3, no. 3 (October 1989): 340–47.

13. Pierre Bourdieu, *Distinction: A Social Critique of the Judgment of Taste* (Cambridge, Mass.: Harvard University Press, 1984).

14. Tania Modleski, *Loving with a Vengeance: Mass-Produced Fantasies for Women* (London: Methuen, 1982), pp. 95–98.

15. For a more systematic analysis of how television constructs these unities and continuities as a mechanism of viewer engagement see Mimi White, "Crossing Wavelengths: The Diegetic and Referential Imaginary of American Commercial Television," *Cinema Journal* 25, no. 2 (Winter 1986): 51–64.

FOR FURTHER READING

The suggestions for further reading are divided into three broad areas, beginning with Marxist theories of ideology and concluding with analyses of television that incorporate ideological perspectives. In the process of organizing particular selections, I have not always maintained firm boundaries. For example, I have included an article on television by Theodor W. Adorno in section 2, along with readings by the Frankfurt School theorists. Similarly, Raymond Williams's book on television also appears in section 2, along with other works by Williams on culture and society.

Marxist Theory of Ideology

One of the earliest elaborations of ideology in the writings of Marx is Karl Marx and Friedrich Engels, *The German Ideology* (Moscow: Progress Publishers, 1976), pt. 1. See also the collection of Marx and Engels, *On Literature and Art*, ed. Lee Baxandall and Stefan Morawski (New York: International General, 1973).

The work of Antonio Gramsci is available in *Selections from the Prison Notebooks*, ed. and trans. Quentin Hoare and Geoffrey Nowell-Smith (New York: International Publishers, 1971), and *Selections from Cultural Writings*, trans. William Boelhower (Cambridge, Mass.: Harvard University Press, 1985).

Louis Althusser develops his theory of ideology in a number of essays in *For Marx*, trans. Ben Brewster (New York: Vintage Books, 1970), and in *Lenin and Philosophy*, trans. Ben Brewster (New York: Monthly Review Press, 1971). The Althusserian position on ideology is elaborated in relation to semiotics, psychoanalysis, and the theory of the subject in Rosalind Coward and John Ellis, *Language and Materialism* (London: Routledge and Kegan Paul, 1977). A critique of the Althusserian position, in particular in relation to understanding culture, is offered by Simon Clarke et al., *One-Dimensional Marxism* (New York: Allison and Busby, 1980).

Ideology and Culture

The Frankfurt School offers Marxist perspectives on sociology and culture that were not developed in this chapter. Their contributions to Marxist theories of mass culture have been significant. In particular, see Max Horkheimer and Theodor W. Adorno, *Dialectic of Enlightenment*, trans. John Cumming (New York: Seabury Press, 1972), esp. "The Culture Industry: Enlightenment as Mass Deception." Also see Andrew Arato and Eike Gebhardt, eds., *The Essential Frankfurt School Reader* (New York: Urizen Books, 1978); and Theodor W. Adorno, "Television and the Patterns of Mass Culture," in

Television: The Critical View, ed. Horace Newcomb, 1st ed. (New York: Oxford University Press, 1976), pp. 239–59. (Note: Adorno's essay is not included in more recent editions of the Newcomb anthology.)

Raymond Williams is a crucial figure in the debate over theories of ideology and culture, elaborating sociological perspectives on literature and culture within the context of Marxist theory. In *Keywords* (New York: Oxford University Press, 1976) he traces key terms and concepts in culture and society. Also see *Culture* (London: Fontana, 1981) and *Problems in Materialism and Culture* (London: Verso, 1980). Williams also wrote one of the earliest books on television in the tradition of British cultural studies, *Television: Technology and Cultural Form* (New York: Schocken Books, 1975). Williams's work in this area is discussed in Stuart Laing, "Raymond Williams and the Cultural Analysis of Television," *Media, Culture, and Society* 13, no. 2 (April 1991): 153–69. Alan O'Connor, ed., *Raymond Williams on Television* (London: Routledge, 1989), includes articles that Williams wrote from 1968 to 1972 for a regular television column in *The Listener*, a weekly magazine published in England by the BBC.

Within the context of literary theory, Althusserian perspectives are developed in Pierre Macherey, *A Theory of Literary Production*, trans. Geoffrey Wall (London: Routledge and Kegan Paul, 1978); and in Fredric Jameson, *The Political Unconscious: Narrative as a Socially Symbolic Act* (Ithaca, N.Y.: Cornell University Press, 1981). Jameson has also published a collection of his writings on film, entitled *Signatures of the Visible* (New York: Routledge, 1990). A theoretical discussion of the arts and mass culture within the Marxist tradition, including extensive discussion and critique of Althusser, is available in Terry Lovell, *Pictures of Reality* (London: British Film Institute, 1980).

Approaches to art as a social product, including Marxist theories of ideology, can be found in Janet Wolff, *The Social Production of Art* (New York: New York University Press, 1984). A summary of different methodological approaches to culture in the Marxist tradition is provided by Lawrence Grossberg, "Strategies of Marxist Cultural Interpretation," *Critical Studies in Mass Communication* 1 (December 1984): 392–421.

Ideology, Mass Media, and Television

Useful chapters or essays on ideology and culture, including film, television, and mass media, are collected in Michele Barrett et al., eds., *Ideology and Cultural Production* (New York: St. Martin's Press, 1979). A collection of essays from the Birmingham Centre for Contemporary Cultural Studies that includes Marxist approaches to culture is Stuart Hall, Dorothy Hobson, Andrew Lowe, and Paul Willis, eds., *Culture, Media, Language* (London: Hutchinson, 1980). Leftist perspectives on American mass media are offered in

Donald Lazere, ed., *American Media and Mass Culture: Left Perspectives* (Berkeley: University of California Press, 1987). Issues of popular culture, politics, and gender are raised in Colin MacCabe, ed., *High Theory/Low Culture: Analyzing Popular Television and Film* (New York: St. Martin's Press, 1986). Media systems, institutional analyses, and the mediation of culture in particular texts are all covered in James Curran et. al., eds., *Mass Communication and Society* (Beverly Hills, Calif.: Sage, 1979). Gaye Tuchman, ed., *The TV Establishment: Programming for Power and Profit* (Englewood Cliffs, N.J.: Prentice-Hall, 1979), offers essays on media structures and practices based on the reflection hypothesis that the content and structure of the media reflect social values and needs.

International perspectives and issues in mass media and television are addressed in: Therese Daniels and Jane Geson, eds., *The Colour Black: Black Images in British Television* (London: British Film Institute, 1990); Ariel Dorfman and Armand Mattelart, *How to Read Donald Duck: Imperialist Ideology in the Disney Comic* (New York: International General, 1975); Conrad Phillip Kottak, *Prime Time Society: An Anthropological Analysis of Television and Culture* (Belmont, Calif.: Wadsworth, 1991); Edward W. Said, *Covering Islam* (New York: Pantheon, 1981); Cynthia Schneider and Brian Wallis, *Global Television* (New York: Wedge Press, 1988); and Alessandro Silj et al., *East of Dallas: The European Challenge to American Television*, (London: British Film Institute, 1988).

Books on mass culture, media, and video culture that incorporate issues of ideology include: Sean Cubitt, *Timeshift: On Video Culture* (London: Routledge, 1991); Henry Giroux et al., *Popular Culture, Schooling, and Everyday Life* (Granby, Mass.: Bergin and Garvey, 1989); Fred Inglis, *Media Theory: An Introduction* (Oxford: Basil Blackwell, 1990); Len Masterman, *Teaching the Media* (London: Comedia, 1985), esp. chap. 6, "Ideology"; and James Schwoch, Mimi White, and Susan Reilly, *Media Knowledge: Readings in Popular Culture, Pedagogy, and Critical Citizenship* (Albany: State University of New York Press, 1992). Historical perspectives, with especial attention to issues of class in television, are addressed by George Lipsitz, *Time Passages: Collective Memory and American Popular Culture* (Minneapolis: University of Minnesota Press, 1990). Todd Gitlin, *Inside Prime Time* (New York: Pantheon, 1985) looks at the organization and practices of the American network television industry in relation to the kinds of programs that appear in prime time.

Books that offer analyses of various forms and modes of programming from an ideological perspective include: Hal Himmelstein, *Television Myth and the American Mind* (New York: Praeger, 1984); Len Masterman, ed., *Television Mythologies: Stars, Shows, and Signs* (London: Comedia, 1984); Elayne Rapping, *The Looking Glass World of Nonfiction TV* (Boston: South End Press, 1987); Ella Taylor, *Prime Time Families: Television Culture in Postwar America* (Berkeley: University of California Press, 1989); John Tulloch, *Television Drama: Agency, Audience, and Myth* (London: Routledge, 1990); and Mimi White, *Tele-Advising: Therapeutic Discourse in American Television* (Chapel Hill: University of North Carolina Press, 1992). A range of books dealing with audiences and reception have been written; I cite one here because it so centrally raises issues of gender and class: Andrea Press, *Women Watching Television: Gender, Class, and Generation in the American Television Experience* (Philadelphia: University of Pennsylvania Press, 1991).

Anthologies with articles incorporating questions of ideology and television include: Manuel Alvarado and John O. Thompson, eds., *The Media Reader* (London: British Film Institute, 1990); Tony Bennett et al., eds., *Popular Television and Film: A Reader* (London: British Film Institute/Open University Press, 1981); Todd Gitlin, ed., *Watching Television* (New York: Pantheon, 1986); Andrew Goodwin and Garry Whannel, eds., *Understanding Television* (London: Routledge, 1990); E. Ann Kaplan, ed., *Regarding Television —Critical Approaches: An Anthology*, American Film Institute Monograph Series, vol. 2 (Frederick, Md.: University Publications of America, 1983); and Patricia Mellencamp, ed., *Logics of Television: Essays in Cultural Criticism* (Bloomington: Indiana University Press, 1990). The January 1988 special issue of *Camera Obscura* is devoted to "Television and the Female Consumer" and includes a number of articles that situate television in relation to issues of gender and American consumer culture. An interesting book-length study of political campaign films made for television is offered in Joanne Morrelae, *A New Beginning: A Textual Frame Analysis of the Political Campaign Film* (Albany: State University of New York Press, 1991).

6 : PSYCHOANALYSIS,
FILM,
AND
TELEVISION

sandy flitterman-lewis

fter a day's work at the film studio, Alfred Hitchcock used to doze off in front of the TV screen; "Television," he said, "was made for that purpose." For film theorists, psychoanalysis has provided a useful way of discussing our relationship with the cinema. It has done this primarily through an analogy between film and that product of slumber, the dream —tracing the relationship between films themselves and the dream-work, that unconscious process of transformation that permits us to relate "stories told in images" to ourselves while we sleep. But if the dreamer and the film spectator are kindred spirits in some ways, what kinds of conclusions can we draw when we apply this analogy to the study of television, a medium whose very techniques and processes, while similar in some ways to film, are vastly different in crucial ways? In what follows, I will discuss the principles of psychoanalytic criticism as they have devel- oped in film studies, the main features that differentiate television from film in this regard, and, finally, the ways in which psychoanalytic theory must be modified when applied to TV, through a discussion of the soap opera—considered by many to be the "quintessential televisual form." However, from the very outset it is important to emphasize that cinema and television are two completely distinct media; as textual systems, and in the manner by which we engage with them as viewers, film and televi- sion are profoundly different. The conditions that produce visual/auditory images and that shape our viewing experience in the cinema are simply not the same when we watch TV. For this reason, where psychoanalysis is

[handwritten marginalia: psychoanalysis / cinema / as / dream... / , as re- / creation of / Lacan's / Imaginary / stage.]

concerned, there can be no simple exchange of method from one medium to the other. Rather, what the psychoanalytic approach might provide, in its application to television studies, is the definition and description of an entirely new type of social subject, part viewer, part consumer—the "tele-spectator" (to use French filmmaker Jean-Luc Godard's evocative term).

Psychoanalysis as a Cultural Theory

In order to analyze the ways in which this *different* TV spectator is constructed and engaged, I will begin by summarizing the basic tenets of psychoanalysis. This will necessarily require a certain amount of over-simplification on my part, for the argument is complex and fairly resistant to summary. What I intend here is simply to trace the broad outlines of psychoanalytic theory so that its relation to a critical understanding of both film and television will become clear; readers who would like to pursue this line of argument in depth should consult the bibliography for further reading. Psychoanalysis, as a theory of human psychology, describes the ways in which the small human being comes to develop a specific personality and sexual identity within the larger network of social relations called culture. It takes as its object the mechanisms of the unconscious—resistance, repression, sexuality, and the Oedipus complex—and seeks to analyze the fundamental structures of desire that underlie all human activity.

Sigmund Freud, who discovered and theorized the unconscious, believed that human life is dominated by the need to repress our tendencies toward the gratification of basic desires and drives (the "pleasure principle") in favor of delayed and more socially acceptable means of gratification (the "reality principle").[1] We come to be who we are as adults by way of a massive and intricate repression of those very early, very intense expressions of libidinal (sexual) desire. The *unconscious* is what Freud designates as that place to which unfulfilled desires are relegated; as such, it has been referred to as that "other scene" where the "drama of the psyche" is played out. In other words, beneath our conscious, daily social interactions there exists a dynamic, active play of forces of desire that is inaccessible to our rational and logical selves.

The unconscious, however, is not simply a ready-and-waiting place for repressed desire—it is *produced* by the very act of repression. In describing the process by which the unconscious is formed, Freud takes the hypothetical life of the infant as it develops from an entity entirely absorbed by the need for immediate gratification into an individual capable of establishing a position in a social world of men and women. Freud's theory of the human mind is not simply a parable of individual development, but a general model for the way all of human culture is structured and organized. One of Freud's major contributions to the theory of human personality was his discovery of *infantile sexuality*—there is eroticism in the earliest of our childhood experiences. From the very first moment in an infant's life, the small organism strives for satisfaction of those biological needs (food, warmth, and so on) that can be designated as instincts for self-preservation. Yet at the same time, this biological activity also produces experiences of intense pleasure (sensuous sucking at the breast, a complex of satisfying feelings associated with warmth and holding, and the like). To Freud, this distinction indicates the emergence of sexuality; desire is born in the first separation of the biological instinct from the sexual drive. It is important to note that the element of fantasy is already present, for all the infant's future yearnings for milk will be marked by a need to recover that *totality* of sensations that goes beyond the mere satisfaction of hunger and includes physical pleasure—Freud would say sexual pleasure as well. In other words, there is a process of hallucinating—a *fantasmatic* process—going on; each time the child cries for milk, we can say that the child is actually crying for "milk" (milk-in-quotes)—that hallucinated image of the bonus of satisfaction that came when the need of hunger was fulfilled.

As the child grows, there is a gradual organization of the libidinal drives that, although still centered on the child's own body, channels sexuality toward various objects and aims. The first phase of sexual life is associated with the drive to incorporate objects (the oral stage); in the second, the anus becomes the sexualized zone (the anal stage); and in the third, the child's libido is focused on the genitals (the phallic stage). What is important here is that the child does not yet experience itself as a unified self, nor is it able to distinguish between itself and the outer world. Rather, the child is like a field across which the libidinal energy of basic drives plays.

In Freud's view, the Oedipus complex marks a decisive moment in the child's development, for it defines the individual's emergence into sexually differentiated selfhood. In the pre-Oedipal stages, both the male and the female child are in a dual, reciprocal relation with the mother; with the Oedipal moment, this two-sided relation becomes three, and a triangle is formed by the child and both parents. The parent of the same sex becomes a rival in the child's desire for the parent of the opposite sex. The boy gives up his incestuous desire for the mother because of the threat of punishment by castration perceived to come from the father. The child copes with this threat by identifying with his father (he symbolically becomes him). He thereby learns how to take up a "masculine" role in society. The forbidden desire for the mother is driven into the unconscious, and the boy learns to accept substitutes for the mother/ desired object in his future as an adult male. For the female, the Oedipal moment is not one of threat, but of realization—she recognizes that she has *already* been castrated and, disillusioned in the desire for the father, reluctantly identifies with the mother. In addition, the Oedipus complex is far more complicated for the girl, who must change her love object from mother (the first object for both sexes) to father, whereas the boy can simply continue loving the mother (or her stand-in).

Such schematizing probably makes this process sound rather far-fetched to some readers. You might also see why some have claimed Freud's theories to be inherently sexist. For the moment, I simply wish to describe the general outlines of the theory and to point out that Freud did not create but merely described the mechanisms of consciousness prevalent in the patriarchal society in which we live. What is relevant for this essay, however, is the work of the unconscious, the production of fantasy, and the erotic component of desire present in all of our activities (including watching film and TV). In discussing the Oedipal moment, we should remember that these are *symbolic* structures found at the level of the unconscious rather than of felt experience. Although we might remember feelings of hostility or intense love for one parent, we cannot remember the Oedipal situation as such, for it is precisely because of *repression* that these experiences become part of our unconscious psychic makeup. The important point is that the Oedipus complex signals the transition from the pleasure principle to the reality principle, from the child's exclusive focus on its relations with mother and father to its assimilation within the larger society. The threat of castration and the Oedipus complex are less important as *literal* processes than they are as *symbols* for the way in which a given culture imposes its rules and order on all of us. It is through these processes that the child develops a unified sense of self (an ego) and takes up a particular place in the cultural networks of social, sexual, and familial relations.

For Freud, the individual (or subject) who emerges from this process is irrevocably split between two levels of being—the conscious life of the ego, or self, and the repressed desires of the unconscious. This unconscious is formed by repression, for it is guilty desires, forced down below the surface of conscious awareness, that cause it to come into being. Thus it is radically distinct from rational conscious life—it is utterly *other*, strange, illogical, and contradictory in its instinctual play of the drives and ceaseless yearning for gratification. According to Freud, dreams are the "royal road to the unconscious." This is because dreams are actually symbolic fulfillments of unconscious wishes. (The Disney song "A Dream Is a Wish Your Heart Makes" was not too far off. Or—to take a televisual example—Dr. Zachary Smith from *Lost in Space* says, "Dreams are the true interpreters of our desires.") In order for the unconscious subject to produce a dream—a symbolic "text" that can be understood by unraveling the various threads of dream-imagery to get to the "dream-wish" itself —the unconscious engages in something called the *dream-work*. Various operations such as *condensation* (in which a whole range of associations can be represented by a single image), *displacement* (in which psychic energy is transferred from something significant to something banal, conferring great importance on a trivial item), *conditions of representability* (in which it becomes possible for certain thoughts to be represented by visual images), and *secondary revision* (in which a logical, narrative coherence is imposed on the stream of images) combine to transform the raw materials of the dream (bodily stimuli, things that happened during the day, dream-thoughts) into that hallucinatory "visual story" that is the dream itself.

With the transforming work of the dream as an example, we can see that the workings of the unconscious find no *direct* expression in conscious life (because these workings are the result of an initial repression). However, the complicated pathways between conscious activity and unconscious desire are made evident through the vehicle of language. As dreams, neuroses (the result of an internal conflict between a defensive ego and unconscious desire), slips of the tongue, failures of memory, and jokes and puns indicate, unconscious wishes and desires—with a logic of their own —underlie even the most apparently "innocent" activity. Even the simple acts of filmgoing or watching TV are shaped by unconscious desires. This fact implies that there can never be a one-to-one relationship between language and the world; meaning always *exceeds* its surface, and things do not always "mean" what they appear to. We can never say with any certainty that the speaking subject says exactly what it means or means what it says; we can never possess the "full" meaning of any of our actions.

Thus we know of the existence of the unconscious when it "speaks" to us through the language of dreams, neuroses, and the like. This emphasis on expression has led French psychoanalyst Jacques Lacan to say that the unconscious is "structured like a language." Lacan is credited with reinterpreting Freud in the context of structural linguistics, and it is the work of Lacan upon which psychoanalytic film theory is based. Because of his emphasis on language, Lacan rereads the Oedipus complex along these lines: the child moves out of the pre-Oedipal unity with the mother not only through fear of castration, but through the acquisition of language as well. Thus the moment of linguistic capability (the ability to speak, to distinguish a speaking self) is the moment of one's insertion into a social realm (a world of adults and verbal exchange). All of us learn to speak in the language and customs of our particular culture; Lacan inverts this to say that we are in fact *spoken* by the culture itself. Our sense of self is formed through the perception and language of others, and this formation takes place even at the deepest levels of the unconscious. In other words, we can speak only using a language that is foreign to us when we come into the world. Someone else gives us our names, and we learn who we are through the responses of others.

Lacan presents a theory in which the questions of the human subject (individual), its place in society, and its relationship to language are all interconnected. He charts the development of the self and the formation of the psyche in terms of psychoanalytic "registers" that are roughly equivalent to Freud's pre-Oedipal and Oedipal phases. In what Lacan calls the "Imaginary," the child's first development of an ego—an integrated self-image—begins to take place. It is here in the "Mirror Phase," Lacan says, that this ego comes into being through the infant's identification with an image of its own body. Between the ages of six and eighteen months, the human infant is physically uncoordinated; it perceives itself as a mass of disconnected, fragmentary movements. It has no sense that the fist that moves is connected to the arm and body, and so forth. When the child sees its image (for example, in a mirror—but this can also be the mother's face, or anyone perceived as whole), it mistakes this unified, coherent shape for a superior self. The child *identifies* with this image (as both reflecting the self and as something *other*), and finds in it a kind of satisfying unity that it cannot experience in its own body. The infant internalizes this image as an "ideal ego," and this process forms the basis for all later identifications, which are imaginary in principle. Simply put, in order for communication to occur at all, we must at some level be able to say to each other, "I know how you feel." The ability to temporarily—and imaginatively —*become* someone else is begun by this original moment in the formation of the self.

↘ unified mirror image (both self & other) = img, ideal ego

Lacan's "Symbolic" register is roughly equivalent to the Oedipal process and encompasses all discourse and cultural exchange. A third term, symbolized by the father and signifying the Law (of culture), disrupts the harmony of the dual relation between (m)other and child in the Imaginary. The Symbolic Order concerns preestablished social structures (Lacan uses language as his model) such as the taboo on incest, which regulates relations of marriage and exchange. In this schema, the figure of the father represents the fact that a wider familial and social network exists and that the child must seek a position in that context. The child must go beyond the dual identifications of the Imaginary, in which the distinction between "me"/"you" is always blurred, to take a position as someone who can designate himself or herself as an "I" in a world of adult third persons ("he," "she," and "it"). The appearance of the father thus prohibits the child's total unity with the mother and, as noted before, causes desire to be repressed in the unconscious. Lacan's contribution to psychoanalytic theory involves his rethinking of the Oedipal process in terms of language: when we enter the Symbolic Order we enter language/culture itself. (In fact, Lacan uses the term *symbolic* to indicate an emphasis on systems of meaning, the use of symbols, and symbolic relations.)

But because, as we have seen, the unconscious is the site of repression, we are never entirely in control of our meanings. Although, in conscious life, we have some idea of ourselves as reasonably unified and coherent, this self-perception is in some sense an illusion. The ego is simply a function or "effect" of that which is always beyond our grasp in the unconscious. Thus when we speak, our conscious, intended meanings always bear the traces of what we have repressed. This is what Lacan means when he says that the subject is always split in language. You the subject, as in the subject of a sentence, always take up a somewhat arbitrary position when speaking. The pronoun "I" *stands in* for the ever-elusive subject, the speaking self. When I say "I am lying to you," the "I" in the sentence is fairly stable and coherent; but the "I" that pronounces the sentence (and throws its truthfulness into question to boot) is an always changing, shifting force. For the sake of understanding, the "I" of the sentence and the one who produces/pronounces it are put into a unity that is of an imaginary kind. Thus, there is a certain level of illusion about identity; we stabilize the shifting that happens in speaking in order to make communication possible.

Lacan's work demonstrates an alliance among language, the unconscious, parents, the Symbolic order, and cultural relations. Language is what internally divides us (between conscious and unconscious), but it is also that which externally joins us (to others in culture). By reinterpreting Freud in linguistic terms, Lacan emphasizes the relations between the unconscious and human society. We are all bound to culture by relations of desire; language is both that which speaks from deep within us (in patterns and systems that preexist our birth), and that which we speak in our continual network of relations with others. It is in this sense that psychoanalysis can be interpreted as a social theory.

Psychoanalysis and Film Studies

Early in "The Imaginary Signifier," his classic study of film spectatorship, Christian Metz poses a founding question: "What contribution can . . . psychoanalysis make to the study of the cinematic signifier?"[2] In other words, how can the theory of the unconscious help us to understand what happens when we watch a film—how we interact with it, how it creates its meanings, what pleasures we derive from it, what we come away with? This question echoes throughout Metz's work, emphasizing that: (1) we can't discuss the film spectator without taking the processes of the unconscious into account; and (2) psychoanalysis brings something to the study of film that other types of study leave out. This is because a psychoanalytic approach to the cinema shifts its emphasis away from the film itself —that discrete, formal entity on the screen—toward the spectator, or more precisely, toward the spectator-text relations that are central to the process of meaning-production in film.

Film theory looks to psychoanalysis to understand why the cinema so immediately became such a pervasive and powerful social institution. For this reason, it is at the level of the cinema's institutional form that Metz first stakes his argument for psychoanalysis; he speaks of the "dual kinship" between the psychic life of the spectator and the financial or industrial mechanisms of the cinema. The cinema reactivates—in ways that are pleasurable—those very deep and globally structuring processes of the human psyche. As Metz puts it:

> The cinematic institution is not just the cinema industry (which works to fill cinemas, not to empty them). It is also the mental machinery —another industry—which spectators "accustomed to the cinema" have internalized historically, and which has adapted them to the consumption of films. (The institution is outside us and inside us, indistinctly collective and intimate, sociological and psychoanalytic, just

as the general prohibition of incest has as its individual corollary the Oedipus complex . . . or perhaps . . . different psychical configurations which . . . *imprint* the institution in us in their own way.) The second machine, i.e., the social regulation of the spectator's metapsychology, like the first, has as its function to set up good object relations with films. . . . The cinema is attended out of desire, not reluctance, in the hope that the film will please, not that it will displease. . . . [T]he institution as a whole has filmic pleasure alone as its aim.[3]

Differing from the models of mass audience offered by empirical or socio-logical approaches to the cinema ("real" people who go to movies) and the notion of a consciously aware viewer provided by formalist approaches (people have conscious artistic ideas about what they see), psychoanalytic film theory discusses film spectatorship in terms of the circulation of de-sire. That is, it considers both the viewing state and the film text alike as in some way mobilizing the structures of unconscious fantasy. More than any other form, the cinema is capable of actually reproducing or approxi-mating the structure and logic of dreams and the unconscious. From Freud, we know that *fantasy* refers to the fulfillment of a wish by means of the production of an *imaginary scene* in which the subject-dreamer, whether depicted as present or not, is the protagonist. To paraphrase French post-Freudians Jean Laplanche and J-B Pontalis, we organize our unconscious ideas into fantasies—imaginary scenarios or stagings of desire in which our deepest wishes are dramatized or "performed."[4] The important point here is that psychoanalytic film theory emphasizes the notion of *production* in its description, considering the viewer as a kind of *desiring producer* of the cinematic fiction. According to this idea, then, when we watch a film it is as if we were somehow *dreaming* it as well; our unconscious desires work in tandem with those that generated the film-dream.

This dreamlike process implies that the spectator is actually a central part of the entire pleasure-producing machinery of the cinema. Jean-Louis Baudry calls this machinery the *cinematic apparatus*,[5] and it is roughly defined as a complex, interlocking structure involving: (1) the technical base (specific effects produced by the various components of the film equip-ment, including camera, lights, film, and projector); (2) the conditions of film projection (the darkened theater, the immobility implied by the seat-ing, the illuminated screen in front, and the light beam projected from behind the spectator's head); (3) the film itself as a "text" (involving vari-ous devices to represent visual continuity, the illusion of real space, and the creation of a believable impression of reality); and (4) that "mental machinery" of spectatorship (including conscious perceptual as well as unconscious and preconscious processes) that constitutes the viewer as a desiring subject. From this it should be clear that there are both technological *and* libidinal/erotic components that intersect to form the cinematic apparatus as a whole. And at the very center of the cinematic apparatus, there is the spectator, for without this viewing subject the entire mechanism would cease to function.

But can we say with any certainty *who* this spectator is? What exactly defines the spectator's "fictive participation," and what specific psychoanalytic processes are engaged? The first thing we can note about the cinema spectator is his/her capacity for belief. Metz tells us that belief in the cinema involves a basic process of denial *and* acceptance.[6] Behind every incredulous spectator (who *knows* the events taking place on the screen are fictional) lies a credulous one (who nevertheless accepts these events as if they *were* true); the spectator thus *disavows* what s/he knows in order to maintain belief in the cinematic illusion (that what the cinema shows us is true). The whole effect of the film viewing situation turns on this continual back-and-forth of knowledge and belief, this split in the consciousness of the spectator between "I know full well . . ." and "But, nevertheless . . . ," this "no" to reality and "yes" to the dream. The spectator is, in a sense, a double spectator whose division of the self is uncannily like that, as we have seen, between conscious and unconscious. So even at the very basic level of belief in the cinematic fiction, something akin to unconscious desire is at work.

Now we come to what is perhaps the trickiest notion in psychoanalytic film theory's conception of film spectatorship. For film theory sees the viewer not as a person, a flesh-and-blood individual, but as an *artificial construct*, produced and activated by the cinematic apparatus. The spectator is discussed as a "space" that is both "productive" (as in the production of the dream-work) and "empty" (anyone can occupy it); the cinema in some sense *constructs* its spectator through what is called the *fiction effect*. There are certain conditions that make film viewing similar to dreaming: we are in a darkened room, our motor activity is reduced, our visual perception is heightened to compensate for our lack of physical movement. Because of this, the film spectator enters a "regime of belief" (where everything is accepted as real) that is like the condition of the dreamer. The cinema can achieve its greatest power of fascination over the viewer not simply because of its impression of reality, but more precisely because this impression of reality is intensified by the conditions of the dream. The cinema thus creates an impression of reality, but this is a total *effect*—engulfing and in a sense "creating" the spectator—which is much more than a simple replica of the real.

Psychoanalytic film theory goes to great lengths to distinguish between the real person and the film viewer, drawing on operations of the unconscious for its description. Three factors go into the psychoanalytic construction of this viewer: (1) regression; (2) primary identification; and (3) the concealment of those "marks of enunciation" that stamp the film with authorship. First, those conditions of the dream state that we've just discussed also produce what Baudry calls "a state of artificial regression."[7] The totalizing, womblike effects of the film viewing situation represent, for him, the activation of an unconscious desire to return to an earlier state of psychic development, one before the formation of the ego, in which the divisions between self and other, internal and external, have not yet taken shape. Baudry sees this condition, in which the subject cannot distinguish between perception (of an actual thing) and representation (an "image" that stands in for it), as being like the earliest forms of satisfaction of the infant, in which, as you remember, the boundaries between itself and the world are confused. Baudry says that the cinema situation reproduces the *hallucinatory* power of a dream because it turns a perception into something that looks like a hallucination. But he notes an important difference. Whereas Freud says that the dream is a "normal hallucinatory psychosis" of every individual, Baudry points out that film offers an "artificial psychosis without offering the dreamer the possibility of exercising any kind of immediate control."[8]

Yet in order for the slippage from dreamer to viewer to occur—a slippage that defines the peculiar situation of cinema viewing—and in order for the film spectator to actually become the subject of someone else's dream (the film), a situation must be produced in which the viewer is "more immediately vulnerable and more likely to let his own fantasies work themselves into those offered by the fiction machine."[9] This has already been prepared for by the heightened receptivity (a state something like the suggestibility of hypnosis) produced by the "artificial regression" of the fiction effect.

Metz defines primary cinematic identification as the spectator's identification with the act of looking itself. He calls the spectator "*all-perceiving*" and says it is s/he who literally makes the film happen. For this reason, "the spectator *identifies with himself*, with himself as a pure act of perception"; without the spectator, the film cannot exist.[10] This type of identification is considered *primary* because it is what makes all secondary identifications with characters and events on the screen possi-

ble. This process, both perceptual (the viewer sees the object) and unconscious (the viewer participates in a fantasmatic or imaginary way), is at
once constructed and directed by the look of the camera and its stand-in,
the projector. From a look that seems to proceed from the back of the
head (from the projector behind us in the theater)—"precisely where fantasy locates the 'focus' of all vision"—the spectator is given that illusory
capacity to be everywhere at once, that power of vision for which the
cinema is famous.[11] Baudry describes this arrangement in a slightly more
technological way: "[T]he spectator identifies less with what is represented,
the spectacle itself, than with what stages the spectacle, makes it seen,
obliging him to see what it sees; this is exactly the function taken over by
the camera as a sort of relay."[12]

Metz says that this type of identification is possible because the viewer
has already undergone that formative psychic process called the Mirror
Phase (discussed earlier). The film viewer's fictional participation in the
unfolding of events is made possible by this first experience of the subject,
that early moment in the formation of the ego when the small infant begins to distinguish objects as different from itself. Just as the infant sees
in the mirror an ideal image of itself, the film viewer sees on the movie
screen larger-than-life, idealized characters with whom s/he is encouraged to identify. Film theory has been quick to appreciate the correspondence between the infant in front of the "mirror" and the spectator in
front of the screen, both being fascinated by and identifying with an im-
aged ideal that is viewed from a distance. This early process of ego construction, in which the viewing subject finds an identity by absorbing an
image in a mirror, is one of the founding concepts in the psychoanalytic
theory of cinema spectatorship and the basis for its discussion of primary
identification. Part of the cinema's fascination, then, comes from the fact
that while it allows for the temporary loss of ego (the film spectator "becomes" someone else), it simultaneously reinforces the ego. In a sense,
the film viewer both loses him/herself and refinds him/herself—over and
over—by continually reenacting the first fictive moment of identification
and establishment of identity.

You will remember that the third element in this construction of the
cinematic viewer (after regression and primary identification) has to do
with "authorship" (who or what produces the cinematic world) and its
effacement. In our discussion of the viewer as dreamer, I noted that a
number of conditions combine to give the spectator the impression that it
is he or she who is dreaming the images and situations that appear on the
screen. Dream and fantasy have this in common with fiction: they are all

imaginary productions that have their source in unconscious desire. Freud is very concise when he summarizes this function of the desiring subject: "His Majesty the Ego, the hero of all day-dreams and all novels."[13] Obviously, however, although the dreaming subject is the "author" of his or her own dreams, the viewing subject is pulled into an imaginary world produced *for* but not *by* him or her. The film works to hide its "real" author, thereby encouraging the viewer to forget that s/he is watching someone else's "dream," a story that is the result of someone else's desire.

Whereas all fantasies originate from the subject who produces them, film obviously involves a more complicated process that takes into account the unconscious desire of *both* filmmaker and spectator. I pointed out earlier that the viewer's position is produced as an "empty space" so that the viewer is more susceptible to having his/her own fantasies interact with the film. This interaction is achieved by shifting the terms of what film theory calls the "system of enunciation." The concept is borrowed from structural linguistics and (if you remember our earlier example) implies the position of the speaking subject. Every time we speak there is both the statement (what is said, the language itself) and the process that produces the statement (how something is said, from what position). Film theory applies this concept to the cinema. In every film there is always a place of enunciation—a place from which the cinematic discourse proceeds. This is theorized as a *position*, not to be confused with the actual individual, the filmmaker, and is related to the distribution of looks (who sees, and where they see it from). Metz connects the process of enunciation to *voyeurism*, the erotic component of seeing that founds the cinema.[14] In psychoanalytic terms, voyeurism applies to any kind of sexual gratification obtained from vision, and is usually associated with a hidden vantage point. Metz shows how the space of cinematic *enunciation* becomes the position of cinematic *viewing*: "If the traditional film tends to suppress all the marks of the subject of enunciation, *this is in order that the viewer may have the impression of being that subject himself*, but an empty, absent subject, a pure capacity for seeing."[15]

For his model of the cinema, Metz changes the linguistic emphasis into a concept of the enunciator as "producer of the fiction," calling attention to the way that every filmmaker organizes the image flow, choosing the series of shots that make up the relay between the one who looks (the camera, the filmmaker) and what is being looked at (the scene of the action). But this organizing process must be hidden, and this is achieved by disguising the *discourse* (in which an enunciative source is present, its reference point is the present tense, and the pronouns "I" and "you" are engaged) in order to present itself as impersonal *history* [*story*] (in which the source of enunciation is suppressed, the verb tense is an indefinite past of already completed events, and the pronouns engaged are "he," "she," and "it"). Discourse emphasizes the *relation* between speaker and addressee, whereas in history the address is impersonal. For the spectator to have the impression that it is his/her own story being told, it must appear as if the fiction on the screen comes from nowhere. Since history is, by definition, "a story told from nowhere, told by nobody, but received by someone," the invisible style that hides the work of the enunciator makes it *seem* like "it is . . . the receiver (or rather the receptacle) who tells it."[16]

Psychoanalysis and Television

I have explained the model for viewer participation in the cinema in such detail because the argument in psychoanalytic film theory is extremely complex; each interlocking part depends on its relation to the others. A whole constellation of factors works together to produce what we call the film spectator: the technology of cinema; the nature of filmic enunciation; the characteristics of the viewing situation; and the psychic processes that link viewer with film. But clearly television, in many of these respects, is quite different. Psychoanalytic film theory cannot simply be *applied* to television. Its insights must be adapted and its account of viewer/text relations reformulated. This process is further complicated by something I noted in the first edition of this book: compared to the extensive amount of work done in psychoanalytic film theory, there was relatively little work on television from a psychoanalytic perspective. Not much has changed in the intervening years; although refinements of psychoanalytic film theory have occurred (particularly in terms of the female spectator and precise definitions of the gaze in psychoanalysis), psychoanalytic television theory remains largely untheorized, at least in terms of the model that I've outlined. And although there has been a significant amount of interesting work on television utilizing other methodologies, psychoanalysis per se has not received the same attention in television studies.

From the very start, then, television requires that the spectator-dreamer analogy be rethought. Because there is no "artificial regression," primary voyeuristic identification is not engaged. The source of enunciation is dispersed (and made problematic), and with that, its terms of address. And, as we shall see, three of the most important ways that the classical fiction film binds its viewer into the text—the point-of-view and reverse-shot structures and secondary identification with characters—are detached, reorganized, and complicated in television. A "fascination in fragments" is all that remains.

Let's start with some of the more obvious differences between film and television in terms of the way each organizes its texts and engages its viewers; these features will lead to very different psychoanalytic consequences and effects. Films are seen in large, silent, darkened theaters, where intense light beams are projected from behind toward luminous surfaces in front. There is an enforced and anonymous collectivity of the audience because, for any screening, all viewers are physically present at the same time in the relatively enclosed space of the theater. In contrast to this cocoonlike, enveloping situation is the fragmentary, dispersed, and varied nature of television reception. The darkness is dissolved, the anonymity removed. As Roland Barthes has pointed out (in considering television to be "the opposite experience" of cinema), the site of television reception is the home: "[T]he space is familiar, organized (by furniture and familiar objects), tamed. . . . Television condemns us to the Family, whose household utensil it has become."[17]

Cinema depends on the sustained and concentrated *gaze* of the spectator and the continuous, uninterrupted unfolding of its stories on the screen. Television, on the other hand, merely requires the *glance* of the viewer. Whereas the aura of cinema spectatorship produces hypnotic fascination, the atmosphere of television viewing enables just the opposite—because the lights are more likely to be on, one can get up and return, do several things at once, watch casually, talk to other people, or even decide to turn the television off. The stories commercial television tells us are constantly interrupted by advertisements, station identifications and promos, and the like. In addition, the TV viewer can switch channels at will, enabling him or her to watch several shows simultaneously. As Robert Stam puts it, television "is not Plato's cave for an hour and a half, but a privatized electronic grotto, a miniature sound and light show to distract our attention from the pressure without or within."[18]

Technological innovations have widened this breach between the conditions of reception in film and TV. The proliferation of Watchman pocket TVs, home video cameras, and VCRs allows for the infinite availability of the video image, just as digital monitors that make possible the simultaneous viewing of two programs, the ubiquity of remote control, and the expansion of cable and satellite broadcasting allow for its multiplicity. And further compounding the complexity of the viewing situation in TV is the fact that we watch Hollywood movies *on* television—either via broad-casts or on videocassette.

Cinema and television also involve different technologies, which in turn produce different psychoanalytic effects. A film is a strip of autonomous still images that appear to move when projected in rapid succession on the screen. The moving television image, on the other hand, is generated by the continuous scanning of whatever is in front of the camera by an elec-tronic beam. An endless series of horizontal lines replaces the intermit-tent stillness of the single image, creating what Stephen Heath and Gillian Skirrow call a "perpetual present" that can always be changed in the very moment of its transmission.[19] Technological differences between film and television encourage different spatial relationships between viewer and image. A film is always distanced from us spatially (we sit "away" from it in the theater), making the screen image seem inaccessible, beyond our reach. The television set occupies a space that is nearby—just across the room, at the end of the bed, in the palm of our hand, or elsewhere. The television screen thus takes up a much-reduced, and more intimate, part of the spectator's visual field and seems available (the TV set is a control-lable possession) at a moment's notice. It does not fascinate in quite the same way. In fact, because *we go* to the cinema, whereas TV *comes to us*, we can talk about two very distinct *kinds* of fascination or absorption. In cinema, the viewer is absorbed, taken up by the film from afar, positioned and controlled. In TV, it is the viewer who does the absorbing, taking in the programs like a sponge, in an attitude of distraction that allows the viewer to be everywhere at once. An explosion of stimulation replaces directed fascination.

And it is precisely with regard to TV's quality of "immediacy" that we can make some fundamental distinctions between psychoanalysis in film and television. A film is always distanced from us in time (whatever we see on the screen has always already occurred at a time when we weren't there), whereas television, with its capacity to record and display images simultaneously with our viewing, offers a quality of *presentness*, of "here and now" as distinct from the cinema's "there and then." It is television's peculiar form of presentness—its implicit claim to be live—that founds the impression of immediacy. In the words of Heath and Skirrow, TV's electronically produced, present-tense image suggests a "permanently alive view on the world; the generalized fantasy of the television . . . image is exactly that it is *direct*, and direct for *me*."[20] Television produces a sort of "present continuous" that confuses the immediate time of the display of the image with the time when the events shown actually took place. It hardly matters what content is communicated by the television, so long as the "communicating situation" created by this sense of presentness is maintained.

Although this argument is based on Heath and Skirrow's comments on live transmission and has been equally analyzed in Stam's work on television news and Jane Feuer's work on live TV, it is the *effect* of "liveness"—an illusory feeling—that I want to emphasize.[21] Whether live or on tape, much of television—from news programs and talk shows to soap operas and situation comedies—creates the impression that we are watching events as they take place. Whatever the format, television's "immediate presence" invokes the illusion of a reality presented directly and expressly for the viewer (though this is less so for prime-time serials which more closely resemble the cinema).

Thus television substitutes liveness and directness for the cinematic dream-state, immediacy and presentness for regression. It also modifies primary identification in ways that support its more casual forms of looking. The television viewer is a *distracted* viewer, one whose varied and intermittent attention calls for more complex and dispersed forms of identification. As we have seen, the cinema bases its primary identification on the association of the spectator's look with that of the camera. Television breaks down the voyeuristic structure of primary identification —there is no camera position to be occupied in the same way. But if the position is dispersed, voyeurism remains; it increases and amplifies as its focus perpetually shifts. Television's fractured viewing situation explodes the singular vision of cinema, offering instead numerous partial identifications, not with characters but with "views." The desire to see and the desire to know, wedded in the cinema by the spectator's guided gaze, find themselves liberated in TV and intensified because of this. Voyeuristic pleasure is not bound to a single object, but circulates in a constant exchange.

Remember that the psychoanalytic differences between film and television are rooted in technology. When we examine TV closely, we see that there can be a number of possible "looks," not of one camera but of many. Three *different* types of camera looks ensure that the "constructed spectator" of television will be different from that of film. For example, think of the different camera looks operating in a simple local television news story. We see the news anchor as s/he introduces a "live" report from a reporter "on the scene." We then see the reporter as he or she addresses us directly. During the reporter's account, we may be given another "look" as we see footage *of* the event being described but recorded earlier. The number of "looks" may be further multiplied in more complicated stories: shots from helicopters, "live" reports interspersed with footage shot months earlier, footage of eyewitnesses to the event reported, etc.[22] Thus television generates a variety of perspectives and camera positions with which to identify.

Scholars disagree over how television's fragmented and multiple looks affect our relationship with TV. John Caughie discusses this dispersal not in terms of camera positions but of television's fragmented broadcast flow. Each little narrative unit, each little "drama" (and this includes such diverse elements as commercials, news briefs, and the like) provides the viewer with a sense of coherence that is only momentary before being disrupted by the switch to the next TV segment.[23] However, both Robert Stam and Mimi White conclude that television does precisely the opposite. According to Stam, the variety of television's views gives the spectator an exhilarating sense of being everywhere at once. The viewer is endowed with a masterful sense of visual power and omnipotence.[24] White maintains that television's constant blending of fictional programs and accounts of actual events creates a totalizing world that binds the diverse material of TV (and the reality of actual events) into one continuous whole. Television addresses us, she says, as an ideal spectator, presenting us with a world that is "progressively all-encompassing, self-defining, and continuous."[25] Lynne Joyrich adds consumerism and melodrama into the equation of television spectatorship, enriching this discussion with a social dimension. In her view, television draws us all into a shared bond of consumerism and, because of its location in the home, combines passivity with domesticity in its most prevalent form, the melodrama.[26]

Yet it is not simply the unifying effect, the imaginary coherence, that links primary identification to the apparatus in cinema. As we have seen, cinematic processes of identification are connected to authorship, because the viewer takes up the position, the "look," offered him/her by the filmmaker. Such a concept of authorship is literally nonexistent in television, where the practical implications of programming make such centrality impossible. Who is the author of *Murphy Brown*, or of *Jeopardy!*, or of the *CBS Evening News*, for that matter? The television apparatus makes us redefine the notion of "author"—and with it the "enunciative source" in television. How can we speak of the "producer of the fiction" in television? Whose unconscious desires do we share in television and how does "it" (television's enunciator) address us differently than we are addressed in film?

You will remember that in the theory of cinematic enunciation, each filmmaker possesses and then delegates *the look* (what the camera sees). We might in one shot see what no character in the film can see, and in another shot see *only* what a particular character sees. This is what characterizes a particular director's system of enunciation—the organization of a system of looks across the viewer's visual field. In television, by contrast, the look is much more qualified and diffuse. In many forms of television—game shows, talk shows, television news, to name but a few —our view is almost never limited to that of a particular character. But even with forms of television that seem to be most like cinema in style, the prime-time serial for example, this system of looking is complicated. If the enunciative source is conceived of as a site of unconscious desire that we are made to share, where is this "site" in *Knots Landing*, for example? Is the authorial subject-position held by David Jacobs (the series' cocreator), by Lawrence Kasha (co-executive producer), by Bernard Lechowick, Mary-Catherine Harrold, or Lynn-Marie Latham (producers), by writers such as Parke Perrine or Mimi Kennedy? Is it held by the directors of individual episodes (who are, at times, the actors themselves) or their writers? How does E. Robert Rosenbaum, the executive in charge of production, or Lorimar, the production company, fit into this conception of authorial desire? And—especially with television—couldn't the sponsor be considered the author as well?

It is only possible to say, then, that the look that hovers over the television text is disembodied and dispersed and therefore doubly difficult to designate. Because we only sometimes see through the eyes of a character (proportionally speaking, the bulk of TV programming gets along quite well without these constructions), our look is most often *not* taken up in an exchange between fictional characters. Heath and Skirrow say that television constructs a situation of looking itself, apart from any specific individual (author or character).[27] The "who speaks" (or "whose desire is articulated") of cinematic enunciation becomes the position of the spectator as a look.

This issue might be made a little clearer if we look at some recent remarks by French filmmaker Jean-Luc Godard. In an hour-long video entitled *Soft and Hard* (1985), Godard and his collaborator, Anne-Marie Mieville, discuss their work, the differences between film and television, the language of visual images, and so forth. This discussion is all juxtaposed with clips from classical Hollywood films and contemporary TV programming. At one point near the end, Godard speaks of his work as a filmmaker and of his frustrations in television. When seen in the light of film theory's argument about enunciation—and the changes called for by the different enunciative structure of TV—his comments seem remarkably astute. Enunciation is a concept *linked* to authorship, but it is not exactly the same thing. The notion of the unconscious as a productive source is what marks the difference between the two. Godard says:

> When one says "I," you can see that . . . "I" projecting itself towards others, towards the world. . . . The cinema has shown that quite clearly, more than all other forms. . . . The "I" could be projected, enlarged, and could get lost. But its idea could be traced back. Television, on the other hand, can project nothing but *us* [elle *nous* projette], so you no longer know where the subject is. In cinema, in the very idea of the large screen, like in the myth of Plato's cave, [we have] the idea of "project," "projection," which in French, at least, have the same roots. Project, projection, subject. With TV, on the other hand, you feel that you take it in [on la reçoit]—you're subjugated by it, so to speak. You become its subject . . . like the subject of a king.[28]

Another difference between film and television that is partly related to this issue of enunciation has to do with the television "text." It involves both the form and content of the "classical cinema," whose aim is the construction of a fictional world in which the illusion of reality is provided by the fluid continuity of seamless editing. In a very basic sense, there is nothing that corresponds to the feature-length film in television. Even the miniseries and the made-for-TV movie (which are organized pretty much along the lines of the dominant fiction film) are marked by the segmentation, variety, and (commercial) interruption characteristic of television. At the same time, the serial form of soap operas and prime-time dramas implies that we will always be frustrated in our desire for narrative closure. In television, our need for such completion becomes reorganized; elements of the story are partially resolved in a way that inevitably permits the continuation of the text. For example, whereas classical Hollywood cinema almost always leads to marriage (the formation of the couple being seen as synonymous with resolution), marriage in most television narrative forms (especially soap operas and prime-time dramas) is a major mode of complication, a site of disruption rather than resolution.[29] The unstable, reversible, and circular movement of this type of program thus frustrates our desire for closure, for it embeds interruption into the very heart of the discursive structure. Therefore, even in TV's most fictional forms—those places to which we would most readily look for the similarities between television and film —the TV apparatus organizes spectatorship quite differently, relying on proliferation rather than plenitude, perpetual deferral rather than ful-fillment.

Finally, one of the most important differences between film and televi-sion, when analyzed in terms of psychoanalysis, involves the way that our identification is negotiated through the point-of-view and reverse-shot structures. Historically, it was through editing, the joining of shot to shot in the creation of a fictional world, that the cinema came to have its own method of constructing not only "reality" but its spectator as well. A Hollywood movie is made up of thousands of individual pieces of film, thousands of shots, dozens of "looks." A single conversation scene may involve numerous shots and several camera positions. One character's lines might have been shot one day, another's the next. While one character's lines are being shot in close-up, the character to whom she is speaking might not even be on the set. Hollywood cinema has devised elaborate strategies to ensure that the viewer perceives a succession of individual shots and looks as a coherent whole. Furthermore, it produces this coher-ence while hiding the strategies that accomplish it. Hollywood editing is sometimes called "invisible" editing, because we are not supposed to con-sciously notice the transition from one shot, one look, to the next. In this way, we are made to believe in the reality of the constructed world. Again, the hand of the "author," the force that produces the looks we share and binds them together into a seamless whole, remains hidden as we are pulled into the "realistic" scene unfolding on the screen.

Most often, the spectator's ability to construct a mentally continuous time and space out of fragmentary images is based on a "suturing" (sew-ing together) of looks, a structured relay of glances: (1) from the filmmaker/ enunciator/camera toward the profilmic event (the scene observed by the camera); (2) between the characters within the fiction; and (3) across the visual field from spectator to screen—glances that tie the scene together and bind the viewer to the film. Central to the process of tying the look of the camera, the look of the characters, and the look of the spectator to-gether are the reverse-shot and the point-of-view shot; these are the main means by which "the look" is inscribed in the cinematic fiction and the experience of the characters is shared. Shot/reverse-shot sequences are common in conversation scenes, where by looking over the shoulder or from the position of one character we see who that character is talking/ listening to. A reverse-shot taken from behind or beside the second char-acter reveals the first character. In point-of-view shots, our look becomes that of a particular character—we are put *in* that character's visual posi-tion and view the world of the film through his/her eyes during that shot.

In both cases, the spectator therefore identifies, in effect, with someone who is always off-screen, an absent "other" whose main function is to signify a space to be occupied. In psychoanalytic terms, the spectator is inserted into a logic of viewer/viewed that evokes certain unconscious fantasy structures such as the primal scene (an early "scenario of vision" in which the unseen child observes the parents' lovemaking). Film theory suggests that just such a combination of vision and desire lays the groundwork for a comparison between film viewing and unconscious activity.

Therefore, in the cinema, the reverse-shot structure enables the spectator to become a sort of invisible mediator between an interplay of looks, a fictive participant in the fantasy of the film. From a shot of one character *looking*, to another character *looked at*, the viewer's subjectivity is bound into the text. However, this positioning of the spectator as a sort of ideal voyeur is totally broken down in television. Most often in television, the expected responding shot of the reverse-shot structure is denied, and therefore the spectator is placed *outside* of the fictional world instead of within it. Whereas in the cinema the reverse-shot structure works together with the point-of-view system to bind the spectator into a position of coherence and fictive participation, in television the effect is just the opposite. Voyeurism is engaged precisely because of the *refusal* of such a binding operation.

As we shall see, even the reverse-shot structure, the staple of soap opera—whose continual exchange of dialogue often provides the only basis for the drama—is drastically changed in television because of the fragmentation and dispersion I've already discussed.[30] In the cinema this binding operation has been used to perpetuate what Noël Burch has called the cinema's "greatest secret"—in which the fragmented space is recombined through editing to preserve an illusory, fictive continuity—but television needs no such disguise.[31] In fact, it thrives on just the opposite, keeping the look forever in circulation and fantasy always deferred. In the soap opera, it is never a question of "creating" a coherent space, of concealing the activity of an organizing principle outside the text, because the spectator is never *moved* through space. Nor is there a strong distinction between the space of the fiction and the space of daily life. Paradoxically, TV's hold is much stronger precisely because of the easy conduct from one "world" to another. Likewise, a belief in the fictional totality is not necessary, for what the reverse-shot accomplishes in the soap opera is something altogether different. The quality of viewer involvement, instead, is one of continual, momentary, and constant visual repositioning, in keeping with television's characteristic "glance." The look is not focused, as it is in a classical film by a director such as Alfred Hitchcock or Fritz Lang, for example; there is no enunciator to transform the discourse into an apparently self-generating story.

"Another" Kind of Pleasure

Psychoanalytic film theory has much to tell us about the meanings and pleasures that the cinema affords its spectators, and we have just seen how it can help us elucidate the differences between film and TV. From these discussions it should be clear that psychoanalysis can also tell us precisely how television viewing offers us "another" kind of pleasure, how it maintains its fascinating hold on us even in the absence of those elements that are central to cinematic fascination. This has to do, particularly, with the way in which psychoanalytic theory constructs its spectator (in both television and film), keeping in mind that this viewer is a theoretical construct, related—but not reducible—to actual viewers in the theater or in the home. The following examples will demonstrate how television's production of "another" kind of pleasure is based on the creation of a televisually specific "subject-effect" in which both primary and secondary identifications are reorganized, multiplied, and intensified. Once we have an understanding of how these unconscious processes are engaged, our knowledge of specific historical, economic, and cultural differences among audiences can be significantly grounded in the fantasy structures that underlie all viewing pleasures.

My examples are all taken from the daytime soap opera *All My Children* and occur on episodes broadcast in 1990. First, though, a short description of some of the residents of Pine Valley is necessary to clarify the situations from which these examples come. Natalie Hunter Chandler (Kate Collins) is currently involved in a steamy affair with the local police detective, Trevor Dillon (James Kiberd) and seeking a divorce from the manipulative scoundrel Adam Chandler (David Canary). Dixie Cooney Martin (Cady McClain) is a feisty, independent young woman from Pigeon Hollow who married the love of her life, Tad Martin (Michael E. Knight), but only after bearing Adam Chandler's illegitimate heir. Due to the machinations of her uncle Palmer Cortlandt (James Mitchell) and Tad's mother Opal Purdy (Jill Larson), Tad and Dixie separated long enough for Tad to have an affair with Adam's former wife, Brooke English (Julia Barr), the only woman Adam Chandler ever truly loved. This separation enabled the kidnapping of Dixie by the arch-villain Billy Clyde Tuggle (Matthew

Cowles) and her subsequent rescue by Tad, as a result of which they both recognized the depth of their love. Their remarriage, however, was stopped short by Tad's untimely death (actually, his disappearance) at the hands of Billy Clyde.

Let's look first at a brief sequence from an episode that aired in September 1990. The opening scene of that episode is an exchange between Trevor, Natalie, and Adam. Natalie, having suppressed her feelings for Trevor, has just made a marriage of (financial) convenience with Adam; Trevor is trying to convince her to follow her heart, get an annulment, and marry him—the only man who can make her "happier than [she's] ever been in [her] whole life." The scene is interrupted by the *AMC* title sequence, dividing the action into two large segments. The first section lasts 48 seconds and is comprised of 15 shots, basically alternating between Trevor and Natalie (for 12 shots), then Adam (arriving in the twelfth shot) alternating with Trevor & Natalie (together in the alternating shot). Trevor pleads with Natalie ("We can be married. Just say the word.") until Adam bursts in ("All right, Trevor. I want you out of here. Now!"), and the segment ends on a zoom-in to Natalie in close-up (she spins around wide-eyed) while the first strains of the *AMC* theme song beat time. The section following the title sequence is much longer (1 minute and 14 seconds), but has roughly the same number of shots (17). It depicts Trevor and Adam arguing in the background, while in the foreground Natalie listens, increasingly frustrated. Finally, she turns and tells them both to shut up; then, saying that she's made up her mind, she looks ambiguous, expectant, in close-up as the music punctuates the suspension of the sequence.

The sixth shot, in which Natalie listens in the foreground to the two men arguing behind her, is the longest shot of the segment and the most "theatrical" (in that it is "staged" to permit us to watch Natalie's expression while the two men argue). Yet it defies its theatricality by having the camera move, almost imperceptibly, closer in to Natalie as she listens. This allows the camera to amplify the subtle conflict playing across Natalie's face and demonstrates, in a very striking way, the centrality of the close-up to soap opera style. As Jeremy Butler points out, "If soap opera sound is structured around dialogue, the image is predicated upon the importance of the close-up . . . [which] privileges facial signs of performance."[32] In fact, the entire sequence just discussed could be described as "the drama of Natalie's face," as minimal dialogue (for her) and maximum facial expression intensify the narrative significance of the moment.

But most important, for our purposes, is the way in which this sequence

1

2

3

4

5

6

7

8

9

10

Natalie-Trevor-Adam confrontation

demonstrates the specificity of the soap opera's televisual style in terms of its rupture and dispersion of primary (and later, secondary) identifications, processes that at once secure the unconscious participation of the spectator and point to the difference of the televisual text. Within the space of any soap opera program hour (minus the fifteen minutes for commercials) we can find an incredible variety and complexity of both shot setups and narrative subsegments (even in our brief sequence, the variations in type of shot, camera angle, character movement, and camera movement demonstrate this). Our vision is thus dispersed, fragmentary, and amplified; this quality of viewing is both characteristic of the soap opera form, and central to the peculiar kind of spectatorship in television that I want to describe.

As typified by this sequence, there is an astounding variety of shot setups within the confined world of the soap opera. Even though action takes place in a limited number of locations (in *AMC*, the various places where the characters live, the hospital and offices where they work, the restaurants and burger joints where they relax, the health club where they work out, and so forth), scenes are marked by a constant diversity of camera angles and distances within a single space. Camera distance is further complicated by a continually moving (or zooming) camera that often rests only momentarily on a conversation before moving again. For this reason, there is a perpetual "fracturing" of the televisual space. For example, in this sequence of limited activity, the background/graphic elements of the shot are always changing, as the camera follows the transition caused by a character's movement or slightly modifies the close-up from shot to shot. And these are almost never simply a repetition of a single glance, but involve a constant diversion of the eyes or a reframing of the space (to include a portion of another character, a different angle, etcetera). From this constant movement, a visual rhythm that depends on fragmentation is built. Within a single sequence there is never any *sustained* camera work (the camera seems to hop about from place to place), nor any sustained focus of the representation. Rather, we find a parallel on the formal level (*how* we are shown the world of the soap opera) to what occurs *in* that world (at the level of the narrative content). The complexities of the soap opera form confirm the fact that TV viewing is never static. The eye is constantly in movement, never resting; it always has something new to see.

In terms of primary identification, this constant motion clearly implies that there is no "unifying presence" at the site of spectatorship, thereby demonstrating just how powerfully television reorganizes our patterns of looking. Soap opera, as an exemplary television text, mobilizes different relations of desire and vision than those that operate in the Hollywood film. Even when it uses the structures of Hollywood cinema (point-of-view and reverse-shot, the flashback, systems of continuity and alternation, patterns of secondary identification, and a focus on the image over dialogue/sound), the daytime drama has to modify these, reworking them to fit in with the televisual system of enunciation. And it is precisely this reorganization—particularly, as we shall see, in terms of dispersion and amplification of the desiring gaze—that produces the peculiar multiple pleasures of television.

The first point to be made concerns the construction of an imaginary space. As I noted, the cinema spectator's participation depends on the illusion of spatial coherence produced by invisible editing and a carefully regulated interaction of looks, all subordinated to the logic of the narrative. Stephen Heath refers to this process as "the conversion of seen into scene," in which vision itself is dramatized, staged as a narrated spectacle before the viewer.[33] However, the soap opera's form disturbs such a narrative binding, giving us not a dramatic "scene" but an infinite variety of autonomous "seens," partial views of interrupted exchanges. Soap opera scenes are shot in "real time," the actors performing before three television cameras that record the action simultaneously. Editing involves switching between cameras *as the scene unfolds*. Thus, whereas cinema must *construct* a spatially and temporally continuous scene from bits and pieces of film, soap operas *start* with "whole" space and "real" time, then proceed to fragment that space, move around it, reorganize it, and single out aspects of it for our detailed examination. Because of the way that space is repeatedly dispersed and fragmented here, we do not find the same illusory space construction that was such a central part of the *film* viewer's role.

In soap operas, space is continually *redefined* by camera movement within and across shots, with background elements helping to keep us oriented to the space as a whole. This means that there is a subtle (but undeniable) variation in shots that only *appear* similar, due to the actions of secondary characters, the placement of objects, and the changing shape of background space. Two shots of the same scene of a soap opera are almost never from exactly the same camera position. At any given moment, two of the three cameras shooting a soap opera scene are not being "taken." They are being repositioned, their images reframed as the characters move around the set, so that when the director switches back to one of them it shows the spectator a somewhat different view of the scene from the one it offered when last we saw through its lens. Thus soap operas do not employ the standard conventions of "invisible" editing to hide transitions between shots or require their viewers to construct a total imaginary space. Rather than the continuous move to incorporate space, suppress difference, and totalize viewing, what the viewer of the soap opera sees is a scene in constant flux.

A corollary to what I am calling the specifically televisual reorganization of vision, and equally disturbing to primary cinematic identification, are the peculiar variations of the reverse-shot and point-of-view structures that we find in even the most simple soap opera dialogue. For rather than a systematic volley of alternated looks from static camera positions, most often we have a close-up of one character followed by a more distant shot of the other (which provides a slight, but perceptible, variation in the background). Furthermore, the soap opera viewer is never given a responding shot that would indicate the *perceptual* point of view of the person speaking. Thus close-ups often appear from nowhere, or seem to without the spatial anchoring we find in classical film. In addition, characters' glances frequently appear somehow curiously askance rather than directed at another character. This dislocation of the gaze, this displaced eyeline structure, can be explained in part by production circumstances. Television cameras cannot penetrate the space of the scene without being seen by the viewer. However, it is the production of *effects* that concerns me here. And in these terms, the spectatorial position produced by soap opera's visual style is very different from the bound, coherent, integrated position of viewing produced by Hollywood cinema.

One final feature that reworks primary identification involves the point-of-view shot. A mainstay of cinematic identification, the traditional point-of-view shot is rarely found in the soap opera. Conventionally, in the cinema, the point-of-view shot, often in combination with the subjective image (for example, distortions to convey dizziness), is one of the primary ways of drawing the spectator psychologically into the world of the film. It anchors cinematic identification by making the spectator's glance coincide with that of a specific character. However, the "live-tape" shooting style of the soap opera does not accommodate the point-of-view shot very well. Because the action of a soap opera scene unfolds in real time within the restricted space of an interior set, it would be very difficult to reposition a TV camera for a point-of-view shot without that camera being seen by the viewer. To use our example, as we view the conversation/confrontation between Trevor, Natalie, and Adam, we look *at* their faces, but we do not look through their eyes or otherwise experience the scene from their perspectives. As noted, this dialogue is represented in two sequences containing a multitude of separate shots, but rather than conveying any character's subjective view (and thereby locating them—and the spectator—as points of coherence that anchor the vision), these shots simply fragment and complicate the space.

When Trevor makes his first appeal to Natalie, each of them is shown looking in a direction that makes the camera's placement *outside* of their consciousness obvious. Even at the moment of greatest intensity (Trevor in voice-over: "I love you, Natalie. And I know you love me"), Natalie is decidedly *not* seen from Trevor's viewpoint. Her close-up, in fact, is tightly cropped (each shot of her in this sequence is a tiny variant on this close-up) such that her expression is emphasized, but not her (or Trevor's) subjectivity. When Adam enters and looks at them, we expect to see their reactions from his point of view. We do see their startled looks, but not from where he's standing. In fact, it is the *camera* that takes over the function of vision as it emphatically closes in on Natalie's face—in a look that is neither anchored in nor mediated by any of the characters.

In the second segment of this sequence, the pattern is repeated. The "theatrical" shot discussed above (shot six) presents another way of avoiding subjective point of view. The spatial placement of the characters in the frame (Natalie in the foreground, Trevor and Adam visible behind her) gives us a vision *of* them rather than *from* them. This shot is followed by medium close-ups of Natalie alternating with medium shots of Trevor and Adam together in the frame. The climax of this segment (Trevor in voice-over, again: "Say what you want, doll") is also a close-up of Natalie. But, characteristically, we are given no responding shot to reveal her point of view. We are thus left to contemplate her ambiguous expression (as the music encourages us to do), while the drama moves on to two other characters completely unrelated to the Trevor/Natalie/Adam triangle—Palmer Cortlandt and his nephew Will (Dixie's uncle and brother). These instances graphically illustrate the way in which the soap opera's televisual structure frustrates any possibility of anchoring spectator-identification within the subjective vision of its characters and the way in which it perpetually offers a fragmented subjectivity dispersed across numerous views.

Perhaps we can best see the different pleasures of plurality and dispersion that television provides in the way that it reorganizes, and thereby reconstitutes, secondary identifications. Unlike feature films, with their relatively self-contained worlds and limited number of characters, soap operas typically present large communities of regularly appearing characters. In fact, as David Jacobs, cocreator of *Knots Landing*, contends,

"The story is just a clothesline to hang the relationships on. It's not about the story—or plot—but around the relationships between the characters [that the interest develops]."[34] And most critics who write about soaps agree. Emphasizing the importance of character interaction, Robert Allen asserts that our viewing pleasure in the soaps can be attributed as much to the relationships as to the characters as individuals.[35] Jane Feuer relates this amplification to the family, claiming that the "implied spectator" for television is not the isolated individual (as film theory assumes), but rather a fully socialized family member. She then generalizes about the "familialised viewing subject" created by the episodic series and the continuing serial, showing how TV works to break down any barriers between the fictional world, the world of advertising, and the actual world of the viewing family.[36] As Ann Kaplan notes in her chapter, Tania Modleski puts this "familialization" in a feminist context, arguing that the utopian vision of the extended family generated by the soap opera is a positive collective fantasy for women: "What the spectator is looking at and perhaps longing for, is a kind of *extended* family, the direct opposite of her own isolated nuclear family. . . . The fantasy here is truly a 'collective fantasy'—a fantasy of community, but put in terms with which the viewer can be comfortable. . . . The fantasy of community is not only a real desire . . . it is a salutary one."[37]

Due to this multiplicity of characters, secondary identifications in the soap opera are both fractured and extended over time. A film actor preparing for a role does so with the knowledge of how the film will end, and thus what the fate of his/her character will be. To a degree, who that character is will be determined by how the drama ends. Similarly, our relationship to that character is inevitably conditioned by how s/he figures in the film's narrative resolution. But there is no ending point in soap operas, no moment of ultimate closure in light of which an actor can gauge his/her performance or the viewer can locate a relationship with that character. Soap operas encourage multiple identifications with characters by keeping those characters perpetually open to change. Several examples will demonstrate how (1) the open-ended narrative structure of the soap opera increases this plurality by allowing characters to both transform their interactions and change over time; and (2) how the dispersal and variety of identifications both generates more complex imaginary processes and further blurs the distinctions between fictive and real, a blurring that is central to TV's particular conjunction of fantasy, desire, and belief.

Two more examples from *All My Children* will show how the soap opera's open-ended structure adds to this complication of identification processes, making any identification with characters fragmented, momentary, and partial and at the same time intensifying the quality of our interest in their lives.[38] Both instances concern the wedding of Dixie and Tad Martin, first as it was aired in January 1990, and then as it occurs in flashback some ten months later in November of that same year. On each occasion we are made to identify with a variety of characters as we trace their changing (and ambiguous) desires across time.

An entire segment between commercials is devoted to Tad and Dixie's wedding. While the ceremony celebrates their union, we are guided through the conflicting thoughts and reactions of the numerous characters present. Uncle Palmer escorts Dixie down the aisle, and once Donna Sago and her daughter, Emily Ann, begin to sing, the music accompanies a series of glimpses at the attending guests. First a close-up of Palmer signals a flashback in which he remembers scheming with Opal Purdy, Tad's (estranged) mother, to break up the relationship that is now being celebrated: "I never give up," he says to Opal on learning of their defeat. "If worst comes to worst, I'll make sure that that marriage is short and sweet." The next close-up is Opal's, as she remembers a scene in Palmer's study (the site of his flashback as well) where Dixie's reaction to the falsely discredited Tad allows Palmer and Opal to play good cop/bad cop. Palmer tells a distraught Dixie that her fiancé is the "Casanova of the nineties," and Opal later recalls this phrase, congratulating him: "Casanova of the nineties—that's a touchdown! We have won the game!!"

A return to the wedding discloses a general shot of the guests; Natalie and Trevor are seated together, but she looks across the room at Jeremy Hunter (her first love and husband from another time), who looks longingly back at her. Then a sequence of close-ups that zoom in and dissolve, each into the next, pairs other lovers, both secret and revealed. Jackson Montgomery looks adoringly at Erica Kane, who turns around and smiles; Cecily smiles at her husband Nico; then two additional shots pair older, established couples, Phoebe and Langley Wallingford and Ruth and Joe Martin. Neither the editing nor the glances of the characters indicate *where* they are located in the crowd, but the shots tell us everything about *who* they are (how they feel). Each shot is thus a little vignette, a silent discourse on the narrative threads that involve and connect the different characters.

A return to the happy wedding couple establishes them in profile close-up at the altar, a shot that will become crucial in the subsequent flashback months later. The song now concludes as various shots depict the ceremony, including exquisite tight close-ups of both Tad and Dixie as

Tad and Dixie's wedding

1

2

3

4

5

6

7

8

9

10

11

12

they exchange their vows. One close-up each of Palmer and Opal serve as reminders of their discontent, but for the most part, the sequence radiates with the beauty of the ceremony and closes on the kiss as the camera moves subtly forward.

This brief description makes clear that the wedding is a privileged instance, embedding flashbacks and complications in its resolving form. Multiple and perpetually threatened, each resolution contains seeds of its undoing, promising future unions and new configurations and complicating the possibility of varied identifications. And this is precisely what occurs some ten months later as Dixie, now divorced from Tad and prisoner of the evil Billy Clyde (Emily Ann's father, before Donna adopted her), remembers her wedding. In the intervening time, in fact, it is Palmer and Opal who have become a romantic pair, while Palmer's nephew Will tries everything to separate the two. Dixie's flashback occurs in a seedy shack as Billy Clyde prepares to marry her against her will. Dressed in the wedding gown that he has forced her into and terrified by his crazed declarations of love, she conjures up an image of her past happiness and thereby realizes (as do we) how deeply she still loves Tad. Tad, meanwhile, is on Billy Clyde's trail, searching for clues with the aid of Donna (who hates Billy Clyde for what he did to Emily Ann's mother, Estelle) and Trevor (a police detective by profession); Tad, too, has recognized his feelings.

Billy Clyde advances toward Dixie with a bunch of flowers, and as he kneels, the camera moves in. As it advances to a large close-up of Dixie's frightened face, she takes the flowers, while the voice of the minister at her and Tad's wedding signals a dissolve. As can be expected, the image that follows is a direct visual "quote" from the wedding: the altar profile close-up of the pair that initiated their vows. Then, in exact duplication, the exchange of exquisite tight close-ups of each of them underscores the irony of their current situation. The dissolve back to the present occurs right before Tad pronounces his fervent affirmation, leaving the silent image of his loving look inscribed in Dixie's memory. The remainder of the sequence depicts Billy Clyde's malicious rambling, the arrival of the phony "reverend," and Dixie's plan to hide the ring in her flowers. It ends on a close-up of her praying for rescue, her desperation a vivid reminder of all the changes that have occurred in the intervening months.

In keeping with this pattern, after the commercial break Opal and Palmer affirm their love for each other in a strong embrace (in the same study where both of their interruptive flashbacks had occurred during Tad and Dixie's wedding). Thus the displacement and transformation of the flashbacks, indicative of the infinitely variable and open-ended structure

Dixie's flashback

of the soap, confirm the ever-shifting temporalities and circumstances that constantly vary our identifications with the characters. Our attention is as intense as it is partial, as we participate in the multiple and changing fictions that each character evokes.

In addition to these transformations over time, soap opera's characteristic and constant plurality of secondary identifications intensifies the viewer's imaginary activity, enabling the slide from fictive to real in order to solidify the connections between the characters' world and ours. As Tania Modleski asserts, "[Although] soap operas invite identification with numerous personalities . . . the spectator is never permitted to identify with a character completing an entire action. . . . [Therefore, they] present us with numerous limited egos, each in conflict with the others, and continually thwarted in its attempts to control events because of inadequate knowledge of other people's plans, motivations, and schemes."[39] Certainly this ability to interact imaginatively with a number of competing lives is amplified by the soaps' variety of fictions, but here it is important to make a distinction between *identification*, as a specific imaginary process, and *sympathy* (or empathy), as a condition of cognitive choice. Janet Bergstrom clarifies this difference by emphasizing the unconscious nature of identification: "Freud's case studies provide rich examples of the ways in which imaginary identifications (through dreams, day-dreams, and fantasies) are formed in tandem with the storehouse of moments and affects that govern an individual's unconscious life. Imaginary identifications, and the affect tied to them, have a history which is specific to the individual; these identifications are subject to fluctuations, but they are bound by a logic of association that is never arbitrary."[40]

Because psychoanalytic identification is concerned with unconscious processes of the psyche rather than with perception and cognition, consciously felt sympathy has little to do with identification in the psychoanalytic sense and thus even less to do with identification in the cinema or TV. Empathy concerns a particular level of experience, but we must go deeper to understand its imaginary component. Identification involves the ability of the subject *of fantasy* to occupy a variety of roles—continually sliding, doubling, and exchanging numerous fictive positions. Soaps allow us to assume the intensity of identification in a completely transitory way; we are able to alternate fictions (often between character and star) with the ease characteristic of the process of dreams. The dispersal of looking that dominates the daytime drama's visual style and the fragmentation of its narrative mode produce the peculiar form and intensity of the soap opera's mobile identifications. And it is this sense of connection to the characters and their worlds—this amplification of belief—that produces the "other" pleasures and fascinations of television viewing in the soap.

Conclusion

I have tried, in this analysis, to show how the cinematic apparatus is a machine of fascination, luring the spectator into desire for the image. The apparently innocent act of cinema viewing involves unconscious factors of which we may not even be aware, for it engages multiple processes of the psyche in its task. The television apparatus is equally fascinating, yet it provides a very different kind of lure. Blurring the categories of fiction and nonfiction, embedding distraction in its very core, fragmenting vision into a plurality of views, rupturing primary identification and amplifying secondary identifications, instilling a desire for continual consumption (not only of its programs but of the products that it sells), and trading on the powerful sense of immediacy that it creates, the television apparatus is in many ways more pervasive than its cinematic kin. Both the cinema and television are combined technological and libidinal institutions, creating spectators insistent on perpetual return. Yet in television, a complex network of ratings, consumption, and economic exchange requires ever more powerful psychic mechanisms, reduplicating structures of fascination to compensate for its appeal to a dispersed and fractured subjectivity. The very nature and function of our fantasmatic participation in the televisual situation must be redefined.

Early in this essay I cited Christian Metz's formulation of the cinematic institution as a form of "mental machinery" that has adapted spectators to the consumption of films. He sees its function as the production of pleasure, for "the cinema is attended out of desire, not reluctance." With a few modifications, this description could apply to television as well. And yet psychoanalysis, which provides a way of understanding how the cinema operates, can only provide us with a series of questions where television is concerned. The mechanisms that produce and regulate desire in television are infinitely varied, multitudinous, and complex. When I originally wrote this conclusion in 1986, I stated that the field was open, with everything yet to be developed. Very little has changed since then; although an elaborate psychoanalytic model of film spectatorship exists, the work in this area of television still remains to be done. By tracing out the terms of psychoanalysis in film studies and by offering a suggestive example of television's differences, I have hoped to indicate some of the things we need to think about in developing our own theories of spectatorship in TV. For as Metz points out, all of us—analyst, critic, and spectator alike—are fueled by the workings of unconscious desire.

NOTES

1. This discussion relies in part on Terry Eagleton's very useful summary discussion of psychoanalysis in *Literary Theory: An Introduction* (Minneapolis: University of Minnesota Press, 1983), pp. 151–93. For another general introduction to psychoanalysis, particularly as it relates to film theory, see my chapter, "Psychoanalysis," in *New Vocabularies in Film Semiotics*, coauthored with Robert Stam and Robert Burgoyne (London: Routledge, 1992), pp. 123–83.

2. Christian Metz, "The Imaginary Signifier," *Screen* 16, no. 2 (1975): 14–76. This article also appears in a book of collected essays by Metz, *The Imaginary Signifier: Psychoanalysis and the Cinema* (Bloomington: Indiana University Press, 1982), pp. 3–87. The quote is from p. 17 of the book; all subsequent references will be to this book.

3. Ibid., p. 7.

4. Jean Laplanche and J-B Pontalis, *The Language of Psychoanalysis* (New York: W. W. Norton, 1974), p. 475.

5. Both of Baudry's essays, "The Ideological Effects of the Basic Cinematographic Apparatus" and the more fully psychoanalytic "The Apparatus: Metapsychological Approaches to the Impression of Reality in the Cinema," are found in *Narrative, Apparatus, Ideology: A Film Theory Reader*, ed. Philip Rosen (New York: Columbia University Press, 1986), pp. 286–98, 299–318. They appear in a slightly different (earlier) translation in *Apparatus*, ed. Theresa Hak Kyung Cha (New York: Tanam Press, 1980), pp. 25–37, 41–62. The latter collection is illustrated with a conceptual piece by Cha herself (who was a video and performance artist) intended to demonstrate the psychoanalytic underpinnings of the concept of the cinematic apparatus. Subsequent references to Baudry's essays will be taken from Rosen's collection.

6. Metz bases his discussion of belief in the cinema on the work of psychoanalyst Octave Mannoni, *Clefs pour l'Imaginaire* (Paris: Editions du Seuil, 1969), pp. 9–33.

7. Baudry, "The Apparatus," p. 313.

8. Ibid., p. 315.

9. Bertrand Augst, introduction to *Christian Metz: A Reader* (n.p., 1981), p. 3.

10. Metz, "Imaginary Signifier," pp. 48, 49.

11. Ibid., p. 49.

12. Baudry, "Ideological Effects," p. 295.

13. Sigmund Freud, "The Poet's Relation to Day-Dreaming," in *On Creativity and the Unconscious* (New York: Harper and Row, 1958), p. 51.

14. Christian Metz, "History/Discourse: A Note on Two Voyeurisms," originally published in *Edinburgh 76 Magazine #1: Psychoanalysis and Cinema* (1976): 21–25, which is the text I am citing. It appears in Metz, *Imaginary Signifier*, under the title "Story/Discourse: A Note on Two Kinds of Voyeurism." The original version can also be found in John Caughie, ed., *Theories of Authorship* (London: Routledge and Kegan Paul, 1981).

15. Metz, "History/Discourse," p. 24 (italics mine).

16. Ibid.

17. Roland Barthes, "Upon Leaving the Movie Theater," in Cha, *Apparatus*, p. 2.

18. Robert Stam, "Television News and Its Spectator," in *Regarding Television—Critical Approaches: An Anthology*, ed. E. Ann Kaplan, American Film Institute Monograph Series, vol. 2 (Frederick, Md.: University Publications of America, 1983), p. 27.

19. Stephen Heath and Gillian Skirrow, "Television: A World in Action," *Screen* 18, no. 2 (1977): 54.

20. Ibid.

21. Jane Feuer, "The Concept of Live TV," in Kaplan, *Regarding Television*, pp. 12–22.

22. This is adapted from Robert Stam's discussion in "Television News."

23. John Caughie, "The 'World' of Television," *Edinburgh 77 Magazine #2: History/Production/Memory* (1977): 81.

24. Stam, "Television News," p. 24.

25. Mimi White, "Crossing Wavelengths: The Diegetic and Referential Imaginary of American Commercial Television," *Cinema Journal* 25, no. 2 (Winter 1986): 62.

26. Lynne Joyrich, "All That Television Allows: TV Melodrama, Postmodernism, and Consumer Culture," *Camera Obscura* 16 (January 1988): 129–53.

27. Heath and Skirrow, "Television," p. 46.

28. Thanks to Janet Perlberg and Karen Cooper of the New York City Film Forum for making the tape available to me.

29. See my "All's Well That Doesn't End—Soap Opera and the Marriage Motif," *Camera Obscura* 16 (January 1988): 118–27, for a detailed discussion of these issues.

30. See Jeremy Butler's excellent "Notes on the Soap Opera Apparatus: Televisual Style and *As The World Turns*," *Cinema Journal* 25, no. 3 (Spring 1986): 53–70, for an extremely useful and detailed discussion of the soap opera's fragmented visual form.

31. Noël Burch, "Film's Institutional Mode of Representation and the Soviet Response," *October* 11 (Winter 1979): 82.

32. Jeremy Butler, "'I'm Not a Doctor, But I Play One on TV': Characters, Actors, and Acting in Television Soap Opera," *Cinema Journal* 30, no. 4 (Summer 1991): 19.

33. Stephen Heath, "Narrative Space," in *Questions of Cinema* (New York: Macmillan, 1981), p. 37.

34. Quote from David Jacobs, appearing as a guest on *The Sally Jessy Raphael Show*, 12 November 1990.

35. See Robert C. Allen, *Speaking of Soap Operas* (Chapel Hill: University of North Carolina Press, 1985), pp. 61–95.

36. Jane Feuer, "Narrative Form in American Network Television," in *High Theory/Low Culture: Analyzing Popular Television and Film*, ed. Colin MacCabe (New York: St. Martin's Press, 1986), pp. 103, 105.

37. Tania Modleski, *Loving with a Vengeance: Mass-Produced Fantasies for Women* (Hamden, Conn.: Archon, 1982): 108.

38. For interesting discussions of soap opera's refusal of narrative closure, see the articles by Feuer and Modleski cited above, as well as Jane Feuer, "Melodrama, Serial Form, and Television Today," *Screen* 25, no. 1 (1984): 4–16.

39. Modleski, *Loving with a Vengeance*, pp. 88, 91.

40. Janet Bergstrom, "The Spectatrix," *Camera Obscura* 20/21 (May/September 1989): 98. See also the section on primary and secondary cinematic identification in "Psychoanalysis," my chapter in *New Vocabularies*.

FOR FURTHER READING

There are a number of primary texts in psychoanalytic film theory; all are central to formulating key concepts in the relationship between psychoanalysis and the cinema (apparatus, gaze, identification, split belief, mirror stage, etc.).

Christian Metz, *The Imaginary Signifier: Psychoanalysis and the Cinema* (Bloomington: Indiana University Press, 1982), contains the following relevant essays by Metz: "The Imaginary Signifier," pp. 3–87; "Story/Discourse: A Note on Two Kinds of Voyeurism," pp. 91–98; "The Fiction Film and Its Spectator," pp. 101–47; "Metaphor/Metonymy," pp. 151–211. "The Imaginary Signifier," perhaps the most comprehensive "statement of purpose" in the field, discusses the unconscious structures that underlie our experience of film, noting how the powerful impression of reality in cinema is first and foremost an illusion. "The Fiction Film and Its Spectator" explores the analogies and disanalogies between film and dream. All the essays use concepts from

Lacanian psychoanalysis, but "The Imaginary Signifier" contains the most complete application.

The anthology *Apparatus*, edited by performance artist Theresa Hak Kyung Cha (New York: Tanam Press, 1980), contains several of the founding articles of psychoanalytic film theory. Many of the essays deal with the spectator's experience as a semihypnotic trance; with the similarities and differences between film and dream; and with the notions of regression, identification, and the cinematic apparatus. All are important, but among the most significant are: Bertrand Augst, "The Lure of Psychoanalysis in Film Theory," pp. 415–37; Roland Barthes, "Upon Leaving the Movie Theater," pp. 1–4; Jean-Louis Baudry, "Ideological Effects of the Basic Cinematographic Apparatus," pp. 25–37, and "The Apparatus: Metapsychological Approaches to the Impression of Reality," pp. 41–62; Thierry Kuntzel, "The Defilement: A View in Close-Up," pp. 233–47. Metz's "The Fiction Film and Its Spectator" is also included in this anthology, pp. 373–409. In addition, there are highly interesting articles by filmmakers Dziga Vertov, Maya Deren, Jean-Marie Straub, and Daniele Huillet and a conceptual piece by Cha. Philip Rosen, ed., *Narrative, Apparatus, Ideology: A Film Theory Reader* (New York: Columbia University Press, 1986), contains revised translations of both Baudry articles, as well as excerpts from "The Imaginary Signifier" and landmark articles by Laura Mulvey, Nick Browne, and Stephen Heath. Rosen's introductory material is useful for the advanced student, and the anthology is wide-ranging in its overview of major theoretical trends in film.

Robert Lapsley and Michael Westlake, *Film Theory: An Introduction* (Manchester, Eng.: Manchester University Press, 1988), is also for the advanced student, containing chapters on politics, semiotics, psychoanalysis, authorship, narrative, realism, and the avant-garde. More explanatory, and more geared to the general student, is *New Vocabularies in Film Semiotics* (London: Routledge, 1992), with sections on semiotics and intertextuality by Robert Stam, narratology by Robert Burgoyne, and psychoanalysis by Sandy Flitterman-Lewis, presented in a lexicon format with an eye toward the definition of terms and their use in film studies.

Janet Bergstrom's interview with the cine-semiologist Raymond Bellour, "Alternation, Segmentation, Hypnosis," *Camera Obscura* 3/4 (Summer 1979): 70–103, is a useful explanatory article that describes key concepts in a conversational tone. Stephen Heath's collection of essays, *Questions of Cinema* (New York: Macmillan, 1981), is more difficult reading but combines important psychoanalytic generalizations with textual analysis; see especially the essay entitled "Narrative Space," pp. 19–75 (reprinted in the Rosen collection). Laura Mulvey's central article, "Visual Pleasure and Narrative Cinema," *Screen* 16, no. 3 (1975): 6–18 (reprinted in many anthologies), discusses the psychoanalysis of spectatorship in terms of sexual difference. The most lucid explication of feminist film theory from a psychoanalytic standpoint is Mary Ann Doane, *The Desire to Desire: The Woman's Film of the 1940s* (Bloomington. Indiana University Press, 1987), which discusses the "women's films" of the forties within this framework.

There are a number of critical overview articles that summarize the issues in psychoanalytic film theory. The most useful collection, though often extremely difficult reading, is one put out by the British Film Institute for the Psychoanalysis and Cinema Event in Edinburgh in 1976, *Edinburgh 76 Magazine #1: Psychoanalysis and Cinema*. Among the articles included are Rosalind Coward, "Language and Signification: An Introduction," pp. 6–20; Stephen Heath, "Screen Images, Film Memory," pp. 33–42; Claire Johnston, "Toward a Feminist Film Practice: Some Theses," pp. 50–57; Christian Metz, "History/Discourse: A Note on Two Voyeurisms," pp. 21–25; and Geoffrey Nowell-Smith, "A Note on History/Discourse," pp. 26–32. A slightly different perspective, and one more accessible to the general student, is found in E. Ann Kaplan's anthology, *Psychoanalysis and Cinema* (New York: Routledge, 1989), in which fifteen scholars apply psychoanalytic criticism to a variety of films.

Janet Bergstrom, "Enunciation and Sexual Difference," *Camera Obscura* 3/4 (Summer 1979): 32–69, offers another useful discussion of important concepts. For more critical (and sometimes skeptical) perspectives on psychoanalysis, see Dudley Andrew's chapter entitled "Identification" in *Concepts in Film Theory* (New York: Oxford University Press, 1984), pp. 133–56; Charles Altman, "Psychoanalysis and Cinema: The Imaginary Discourse," *Quarterly Review of Film Studies* 2, no. 3 (1977): 257–72; and Christine Gledhill, "Developments in Feminist Film Criticism," in *Re-Vision: Essays in Feminist Film Criticism*, ed. Mary Ann Doane, Patricia Mellencamp, and Linda Williams (Los Angeles: American Film Institute, 1984), pp. 18–48.

Individual articles that describe the psychoanalytic method or concentrate on particular textual analyses can be useful in clarifying the major points. Some of these are: Raymond Bellour, "Hitchcock: The Enunciator," *Camera Obscura* 2 (Fall 1977): 66–91, and Sandy Flitterman, "Woman, Desire, and the Look: Feminism and the Enunciative Apparatus of Cinema," in *Theories of Authorship*, ed. John Caughie (London: Routledge and Kegan Paul, 1981), pp. 242–50, which both discuss Hitchcock's *Marnie*; two articles by Thierry Kuntzel that discuss *The Most Dangerous Game* ("The Film-Work, 2," *Camera Obscura* 5 [Spring 1980]: 6 69, and "Sight, Insight, and Power: Allegory of a Cave," *Camera Obscura* 6 [Fall 1980]: 90–110); and Stephen Heath's detailed and complicated analysis of Welles's *Touch of Evil* ("Film and System, Terms of Analysis," Parts 1 and 2, *Screen* 16, nos. 1–2 [1975]: 7–77, 91–113).

In "The Order of [Cinematographic] Discourse," *Discourse #1* (1979): 39–57, Bertrand Augst applies Foucault to discussions of the cinema. Mary Ann Doane discusses identification in "Misrecognition and Identity," *Cine-tracts* 11 (Fall 1980): 25–32; and Lesley Stern discusses point of view in "Point of View: The Blind Spot," *Film Reader*, no. 4 (1979): 214–36.

I indicated in the original edition of this work that there had been relatively little written in the field of psychoanalytic television studies. Since that time, there still has not been very much specifically psychoanalytic work done; most writers seem to concentrate on other approaches, often pointing to the limitations they see in the psychoanalytic method. Still, there are a number of articles that take important steps in that direction, and John Ellis, *Visible Fictions: Cinema, Television, Video* (London: Routledge and Kegan Paul, 1982), is an exemplary book in this respect. Ellis is one of the first to describe in detail both the similarities and differences between the cinema and television institutions. The forthcoming special issue of *Quarterly Review of Film and Video*, a tribute to Beverle Houston, contains articles by Thomas Elsaesser, Nick Browne, and Marsha Kinder, among others, that suggest new and exciting ways in which television can be theorized along psychoanalytic lines.

In *The "Nationwide" Audience: Structure and Decoding* (London: British Film Institute, 1980), David Morley begins the work on how a TV text "inscribes" its viewers, positioning its audience through various modes of address. But Morley takes a much more critical position toward psychoanalysis in his excellent overview article "Changing Paradigms in Audience Studies," in *Remote Control: Television, Audiences, and Cultural Power*, ed. Ellen Seiter, Hans Borchers, Gabriele Kreutzner, and Eva-Maria Warth (London: Routledge, 1989), wherein a number of articles by top television scholars mention but never directly deal with the psychoanalytic method. Robert Deming discusses the different theories of "spectator-positioning" in television in "The Television Spectator-Subject," *Journal of Film and Video* 37, no. 3 (Summer 1985): 49–63; and John Caughie, in "The 'World' of Television," *Edinburgh 77 Magazine #2: History/Production/Memory* (1977): 73–83, and "Rhetoric, Pleasure, and Art Television—Dreams of Leaving," *Screen* 22, no. 4 (1981): 9–31, deals with subject-positioning in relation to television's regulated "flow" and with the "televisual look." These essays, though, are more complex and difficult for the beginning reader.

Among the works on individual programs (or types of programming) that rely on a psychoanalytic approach, Stephen Heath and Gillian Skirrow, "Television: A World in Action," *Screen* 18, no. 2 (1977): 7–59, analyzes how a particular type of viewer is constructed by the documentary/interview format. Margaret Morse and Sandy Flitterman discuss relations of sexuality and desire in televised sports (Morse, "Sport on Television: Replay and Display," in *Regarding Television—Critical Approaches: An Anthology*, ed. E. Ann Kaplan, American Film Institute Monograph Series, vol. 2 [Frederick, Md.: University Publications of America, 1983], pp. 44–66) and in a particular detective series (Flitterman, "Thighs and Whiskers: The Fascination of *Magnum, P.I.*," *Screen* 26, no. 2 [1985]: 42–58). Robert Stam's excellent article "Television News and Its Spectator," also in Kaplan, *Regarding Television*, pp. 23–43, uses Metz's "imaginary signifier" in a detailed and highly readable discussion of televised news. Both Stam's and Morse's articles are wonderful examples of the psychoanalytic method as applied to TV. Another article by Morse, "Talk, Talk, Talk—the Space of Discourse in Television," *Screen* 26, no. 2 (1985): 2–15, discusses TV news, as well as sportscasts and talk shows, in terms of the relations of subjectivity and discourse.

Two articles by Jane Feuer, although not specifically psychoanalytic, have psychoanalytic applications and refer to some of the theory: "Melodrama, Serial Form, and Television Today," *Screen* 25, no. 1 (1984): 4–16; and "Narrative Form in American Network Television," in *High Theory/Low Culture: Analyzing Popular Television and Film*, ed. Colin MacCabe (New York: St. Martin's Press, 1986), pp. 101–14. This is also the case with Annette Kuhn's important article, "Women's Genres: Melodrama, Soap Opera, and Theory," *Screen* 25, no. 1 (1984): 18–28.

Equally focused on women's genres, but more specifically psychoanalytic, are articles by Lynne Joyrich ("All That Television Allows: TV Melodrama, Postmodernism, and Consumer Culture") and Sandy Flitterman-Lewis ("All's Well That Doesn't End: Soap Opera and the Marriage Motif"), both in *Camera Obscura* 16 (January 1988): 128–53, 118–27, in a special issue on TV and the female consumer. This special issue is forthcoming as a book from the University of Minnesota Press in 1992, entitled *Private Screenings: Television and the Female Consumer* and edited by Denise Mann and Lynn Spigel. The *Camera Obscura* anthology is joined by two other new collections that have articles relevant to, if not explicitly about, psychoanalytic theory in its application to television: Patricia Mellencamp, ed., *Logics of Television: Essays in Cultural Criticism* (Bloomington: Indiana University Press, 1990), and James Naremore and Patrick Brantlinger, eds., *Modernity and Mass Culture* (Bloomington: Indiana University Press, 1991).

Two articles that apply psychoanalysis to TV, but in ways different from those outlined in this chapter, are Beverle Houston, "Viewing Television: The Metapsychology of Endless Consumption," *Quarterly Review of Film Studies* 9, no. 3 (Summer 1984): 183–95; and Marsha Kinder, "Music Video and the Spectator: Television, Ideology, and Dream," *Film Quarterly* 38, no. 1 (Fall 1984): 3–15. The former uses Lacanian theory to analyze the way in which television's lack of spectacle works against producing a unifying experience for the viewer, instead instilling in its audience the desire to consume. The latter article discusses the form and institutional setting of music television, focusing on the relations between video and dreaming.

This list of works on television that use psychoanalysis is intended to be suggestive rather than exhaustive; there are other articles that, though not developing a psychoanalytic theory of television viewing, make use of some of the concepts. The most important point to consider with any articles referring to psychoanalysis is whether they support a belief in the unconscious and its functioning or not. Often articles will cite psychoanalysis only to note its limitations as a method or a theory; less frequent, but more relevant to this chapter, are articles that are concerned with the workings of the unconscious in the televisual text and situation.

General works on psychoanalysis that are relevant to this kind of work are, of course, Sigmund Freud, *The Interpretation of Dreams*, *Three Essays on the Theory of Sexuality*, *Jokes and Their Relation to the Unconscious*, *The Psychopathology of Everyday Life*, and a collection of essays entitled *General Psychological Theory*. Terry Eagleton's chapter on psychoanalysis in *Literary Theory: An Introduction* (Minneapolis: University of Minnesota Press, 1983) provides a useful overview, as does Juliet Mitchell's founding work, *Psychoanalysis and Feminism* (New York: Vintage Books, 1975). Jacques Lacan's writings, *The Four Fundamentals of Psychoanalysis* (London: Hogarth Press, 1977) and *Ecrits: A Selection* (New York: W. W. Norton, 1977), are notoriously difficult, but there are some texts that go a long way toward clarifying the issues. Jean Laplanche and J-B Pontalis use an extended dictionary format in their extremely useful book, *The Language of Psychoanalysis* (New York: W. W. Norton, 1973); Rosalind Coward and John Ellis's *Language and Materialism* (London: Routledge and Kegan Paul, 1977) has a more difficult prose style but provides helpful discussions on "developments in semiology and the theory of the subject"; and Kaja Silverman's *The Subject of Semiotics* (New York: Oxford University Press, 1983) and Linda Williams's *Figures of Desire* (Champaign: University of Illinois Press, 1981) contain excellent summaries of Lacanian concepts, particularly in their relation to film.

FEMINIST CRITICISM AND TELEVISION

e. ann kaplan

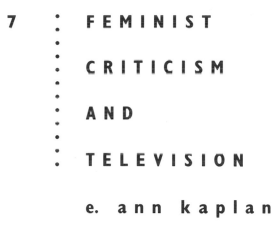

he two parts of my title, "feminist criticism" and "television," require brief discussion individually before I link them together. I need to say something about the contexts in which television studies developed in order to account for the paucity of feminist approaches before the 1980s, and, since *feminism* does not have a single meaning, I need to discuss the ways in which I define the term.

I will focus mainly on U.S. television studies, but a contrast with the British approach is important to illuminate, through the differences, developments in the United States. In this country, television studies have had even more difficulty than film in being accepted as an academic subject. Film finally obtained such acceptance through its claims to be "art," but no one was willing to make that argument for television. Thus, whereas film was able to find a place in various humanities departments in the 1960s and 1970s, television was taken up by the social sciences or in departments of journalism. Robert Allen, among others, has noted how difficult it was for television criticism to develop within the traditional mass communication research paradigm.[1]

In Britain, television study took a different tack in part because it was not developed in schools of communication, but rather through organizations like the British Film Institute and places other than the major universities: art colleges, further education colleges, and polytechnic institutes. British intellectuals outside of the university communities, then, originally developed methods for studying and criticizing television that were not dissimilar from those used in early cultural and film studies.[2]

It is thanks to the journals *Screen* and *Screen Education*, together with the University of Birmingham's Centre for Contemporary Cultural Studies, that critical work on television was developed and debated. Much of this early work focused on how to *teach* television and gave rise to methods of study closely related to the experiences of the student-spectators with whom teachers interacted. Thus television studies in Great Britain were concerned from the beginning (1970s) with the social contexts within which television was viewed and might be taught. Reception became a logical focus for studies of the relationship of viewers and televisual texts.

British media scholars were also interested in television as an institution and the ways in which television as institution raised larger social issues—particularly relations of social power and class and the psychological impact of mass culture. In the mid-1970s, work on television as an institution was further stimulated by the announcement of a new network, Channel 4, which was to address "minority" audiences and provide a venue for independent and experimental programming. While scholars at American universities were "objectively" measuring television's content, social effects, and patterns of individual use, British media teachers, scholars, and practitioners were engaged in far more polemical work on the role of television in British society.[3]

However, neither in America nor in Britain was there much feminist work on television throughout the 1970s. The gap was noticed in 1980 by Susan Honeyford, who suggested that perhaps the dearth of feminist criticism in television had to do, first, with "the massive dominance of the national broadcast television institutions with their insistence on large audiences" and, second, with "the relatively little academic work or serious critical writing" on television.[4] A later article by Gillian Skirrow discussed efforts to get TV unions to agitate for more jobs for women,[5] but otherwise *Screen* articles on television, until 1981, dealt mostly with broad issues—defining TV studies, teaching strategies—or with the contents of specific programs.[6]

How do we explain this gap, particularly at a time (1970s) when feminists were developing important and suggestive theories for analyzing the classical Hollywood cinema? Perhaps one reason is that American scholars who were both female and feminist tended to work in the humanities rather than in the social sciences. If TV studies concentrated on the (traditionally male-dominated) production sphere and involved social science methods (again largely male dominated), then the lack of feminist work in those areas is understandable. For instance, between 1940 and 1970 there were very few studies of soap operas—an obvious TV genre for feminist analysis—even from a quantitative perspective; what studies there were did not foreground gender issues.[7] One of the problems with quantitative research is precisely that it pretends to take an "objective" stance, that is, to provide empirical data untainted by any particular set of concerns or interests. By definition, as we'll see, feminism is a "political" position, and feminist research (no matter what type) must look for issues having to do specifically with women and the place they are assigned in society. For this reason, most of the quantitative content analyses of soaps do not constitute *feminist* research, although their results may be useful for feminist scholars.

In Britain, the feminists interested in television were more activist-oriented and thus focused on changing the institution itself rather than on developing feminist readings of TV texts. Fewer women in Britain than America have academic positions that give them the privileged time to write; much of the film theory developed in Britain, for instance, was the work of women actually engaged in independent filmmaking, so that theory was closely linked to practice. But, as I discuss further below, there was no analogous independent television production with the same possibilities for exhibition, because the nature of television as an institution makes such independent production enormously difficult.[8]

In general, a circular effect was set in motion, such that the more feminist theory was developed for film studies, the more it absorbed the interests of scholars who might have pioneered feminist approaches to TV. It is also possible that the low academic standing of television, together with the frequent disregard in which American programming was held, made women—who already had a difficult time getting ahead in academic humanities departments—reluctant to engage with the form. Women were interested in and constantly watched films, but these same women scholars did not necessarily watch television.

But in the early 1980s things changed dramatically in the wake of the maturation of cinema studies. A significant number of female film scholars on both sides of the Atlantic finally began to work on female representation in television. An article by Stephen Heath and Gillian Skirrow, published in *Screen* in 1977, that discussed the British program *World in Action* was one of the first to apply British theoretical approaches from the 1970s, first worked out for the classical Hollywood film, to television. A model for any future close-reading analysis, Heath and Skirrow's essay focused on "the fact of television itself" and on "the ideological operations developed in that fact" rather than on discussion of any particular (political) positions that the "content" might reveal.[9]

Meanwhile, various American graduate programs in film began to turn their attention to critical analysis of television, and graduate students produced some of the first interesting work.[10] Young scholars in other disciplines, notably literature, also began to apply their critical approaches to related kinds of popular women's TV programs such as soaps. A television conference held in New York in 1980—to which few, if any, women critics were invited—first made me realize the necessity for more work by women on television and female representation, and also how little recognized was the work that had been done. In response I organized a conference at Rutgers University entitled "Perspectives on Television," which showcased approaches to female representation on television informed by psychoanalysis and semiology.

The 1980s saw a dramatic increase in feminist television studies, as will be clear below. Today we are witnessing an explosion in feminist approaches to television that builds on, and would have been impossible without, two previous decades of research and debates.[11] Because new research now takes for granted (and has integrated) earlier work, a review of some of that work is necessary. Students may have difficulty confronting recent research unless they are familiar with what went before. Research is always collaborative, always cumulative: an understanding of prior arguments is essential in order to comprehend new ones.

Let me, then, turn briefly to my second term requiring definition, *feminist criticism*. This needs special clarification given the contemporary reaction against 1970s ideas and movements. In the areas of literature and film, feminist criticism already had quite a long history by 1980. Contemporary feminist literary criticism dates from the late sixties and the pioneering work of Betty Friedan, Germaine Greer, and Kate Millett, all of whom drew upon the insights of Simone de Beauvoir, whose 1949 book, *The Second Sex*, was way ahead of its time.[12] The study of images of women in film dates back to work by the National Organization of Women in the late 1960s; to the pioneering journal, *Women and Film*, published from 1970 to 1972; to film journals like *Jump Cut* that made feminist approaches a central part of their format; and, finally, to the emergence in 1976 of a journal, *Camera Obscura*, specifically devoted to feminist film theory. This journal, influenced by French and British film theory, was a major conduit for that work to American students and film researchers.

Along with this critical work, there were in the 1970s a whole host of film conferences and screenings through which women could familiarize themselves not only with recent independent work being done by women, but also with the work of women directors in Hollywood and throughout the world. These events, together with the development of critical research, enabled a subfield of feminist theory to emerge within film studies. Similar conferences and screenings were not set up around television, largely because of its specific institutional mode: its forms of production and exhibition; its situatedness as a predominating commercial mode within the private home; its lack of historical documents by or about women; the paucity of *alternate* modes of expression such as there had always been in film. Partly because of these realities, a similar set of "feminist" approaches to television were not readily developed.

By the 1980s, the word *feminist* had come to mean a variety of things in literary and film research. I will briefly detail these meanings in both film and allied humanities fields because understanding the different kinds of feminist work will both explain some of the work that scholars have been doing and suggest future work that will need doing in television. I want to emphasize, however, that although there is a rough chronological sequence to my discussion of types of feminism, I do not view later methods as necessarily replacing earlier ones. Certain developments naturally challenge what went before (they only arise, of course, because of earlier work), but these challenges can, in turn, be answered. Feminisms "mutate," as it were, and it is important to follow these mutations. A second caveat has to do with the inevitably archetypal nature of any attempt at categorizing. Very rarely will any piece of feminist criticism offer a pure illustration of a particular category; I will discuss theories that combine types or do not fit neatly into any one type. The categories are useful merely as a charting of the terrain—for purposes of clarification and illustration.

From a *political* perspective, one might isolate in the 1970s a *bourgeois feminism* (women's concern to obtain equal rights and freedoms within a capitalist system); a *Marxist feminism* (the linking of specific female oppressions to the larger structure of capitalism and to oppressions of other groups—gays, minorities, the working classes, and so on); a *radical feminism* (the designation of women as different from men and the desire to establish separate female communities to forward women's specific needs and desires); and, as the 1980s got underway, a *post-structuralist feminism* (the idea that we need to analyze the language order through which we learn to be what our culture calls "women"—distinct from a group called "men"—as we attempt to bring about change beneficial to women). By the late 1980s, in the wake of research by such scholars as Jean Baudrillard,

Jean-François Lyotard, Fredric Jameson, and Arthur Kroker and David Cook, feminists were confronted by a new concept, *postmodernism*. The conjuncture of postmodernism and feminism has produced its own strand of theory and research, as I will discuss later with regard to MTV and Madonna.[13] By briefly reviewing examples of these different kinds of feminist work on television, I will show that scholars have developed critical methods according to their *political* definition of feminism.

But first a word about the *philosophical* definition of feminism. In the 1980s, the two main philosophical positions were, for good or ill, labeled "essentialist" and "antiessentialist" and were much debated in relation to feminist research. Although the distinction was always seen as problematic, it was also useful at the time. The first three political definitions of *feminist* were seen as falling under the category of "essentialist" feminism, whereas the fourth, post-structuralist feminism, was usually said to reflect an "antiessentialist" position.

Essentialist feminism assumes there is a basic "truth" about woman that patriarchal society has kept hidden. It argues that there is a particular group—"women"—that can be separated from another group—"men"—in terms of an identity that precedes or is outside of culture and that ultimately has to have biological origins. The essential aspects of woman, repressed in patriarchy, are assumed to embody a more humane, moral mode of being that, once brought to light, could help change society in beneficial directions.

Few, if any, feminists now would argue for such a biologically essential view of women. Rather, they would distinguish specifically *female* values from *male* values, recognizing, however, that all values are socially constructed rather than "innate." These female values become a means for critiquing the harsh, competitive, and individualistic male values that govern society; they offer an alternate way not only of *seeing* but of *being*, which threatens patriarchy. Feminists who subscribe to this theory believe that female values, because of their essential humaneness, should be resurrected, celebrated, and revitalized. Marxist feminists would, in addition, focus on the way social structures and the profit motive have prevented humane female values from becoming dominant, and radical feminists would emphasize that the silencing of the female voice results from male domination, forced heterosexuality, the insistent emphasis on the bourgeois nuclear family, and so forth. Liberal feminists remain largely reformist rather than revolutionary and are content merely to assert women's rights to whatever our society has to offer them.

Antiessentialist feminists view things rather differently, although the philosophical approaches are not necessarily as incompatible as they might at first seem. Antiessentialist theorists attempt to understand the processes through which female subjectivity is constituted in patriarchal culture, but they do not find an "essential" femininity behind the socially constructed subject. In this view, the "feminine" is not something outside of, or untouched by, patriarchy, but integral to it. Antiessentialist theorists are concerned with the links between a given sex identity and the patriarchal order, analyzing the processes through which sexuality and subjectivity are constructed at the same time. Most feminists agree that we can change *sex roles*—many Western societies were catching up with the Eastern block in enacting such changes before the Berlin Wall (and others) fell. But antiessentialists argue that for such changes to take a firm hold—to have anything more than merely a local, fashionable, and temporary change—we have to understand more about how we arrive at sex identity in the first place. (The fact that sexism long remained a problem in Eastern Europe and persists still in other Communist countries attests to the fact that social changes are not sufficient in and of themselves.) If the goal is to get beyond the socially constructed definitions of man/woman or masculine/feminine, then, antiessentialists argue, we need to know precisely how those social constructions are inscribed in the processes of becoming "human."[14]

Although the essentialism/antiessentialism polarity has been quite useful, it is now being replaced by a concentrated effort to understand the different versions of the "self" and its relations with the world that the feminisms outlined above constructed and then relied upon. Such an understanding entails a move into psychoanalytic terrain in an attempt to theorize the complex links between two different, but both socially constructed, concepts of the "self."[15]

It is significant that, between 1963 and about 1980, American feminists in most disciplines found useful a binarism between female and male values and ways of seeing. This can be accounted for in terms of women's need to resist the long-standing male tradition of defining woman only in relation to male needs and desires. Feminists wanted to break down this marginalization and silencing of women: one way of doing so was to assert women's ways of being as different from men's ways of being and from male configurations of women. The research produced within the frame of the first three political positions noted above was extremely useful, because it made possible the new kinds of work feminists are able to do today. I will distinguish three broad kinds of feminist work, each of which provides an example of the political and philosophical definitions of feminism. To clarify differences among approaches, I will draw examples from studies of prime-time serials and soap operas. Note that although there is a broad developmental aspect to my account of feminist critical methods—a particular kind, as I have mentioned, may be seen as arising out of questions not answered by a previous approach—it is also true that a new approach does not invalidate or eliminate earlier ones. In fact, in the 1990s we can find examples of most types of feminist criticism still being produced concurrently; they have not been incorporated into methods that combine earlier approaches with new ones. The process is synthetic or dialectical rather than negational.

The first kind of feminist research implicitly demands equal access to the (patriarchal) symbolic order; the idea is that women desire equality rather than subjugation. This approach has two possible results. The first is what historians have called "domestic feminism" (largely characteristic of the nineteenth century), in which women valorized the patriarchally constructed "feminine." However, they were likely to see this "feminine" as "natural," and they celebrated the qualities assigned to women as morally higher or better than the male values of competition and aggressive individualism. A second is what, above, I have called "liberal" feminism (more characteristic of recent times), in which women strive for equality with men in the public work sphere. That is, women demand equal access to jobs and institutional power (of whatever kind), equal pay for equal work, equal benefits across the board, and changes in family routines to accommodate their demanding careers.

Liberal feminism leads to a type of television criticism that is heavily dependent on content analysis. TV programs are analyzed in terms of the kinds and frequency of female roles they contain. Such studies might examine the degree to which dramas reflect recent changes in the status of women, their movement out of the home and into the work sphere, the characteristics working women are perceived to have, the quality of family life and the involvement (or not) of men in domestic chores.

An example of this type of feminist criticism is Diana Meehan's *Ladies of the Evening: Women Characters of Prime-Time Television*.[16] Meehan's aim is to provide "specific and accurate descriptions of television characters and behaviors and some index of change over time" (p. vii). She assumes that television's presentation of women characters encompasses "reflections of women's lives, implicit endorsement of beliefs and values about women in a very popular forum" (p. vii). She combines a quantitative approach—"counting the number of female characters or female heroes, the numbers of times that situation comedy jokes were at the expense of a female or that dramatic acts of violence were committed by women or against women"—with a more qualitative approach that allows her to address "questions about women characters' power and powerlessness, vulnerability and strength" (p. viii). In addition, Meehan uses what might be called a comparative approach to determine the degree to which female characters are representative of the female population in society. This involves "considering female characters as real people" (p. viii). Later, Meehan explains her assumption that "viewers . . . evaluate the behavior of others as appropriate or inappropriate compared with television models, and life and its television versions become even more interrelated" (p. 4).

The heart of Meehan's book is her ambitious attempt, not only to isolate and study occurrences of a whole series of female roles (the imp, the good-wife, the harpy, the bitch, the victim, the decoy, the siren, the courtesan, the witch, the matriarch), but also to show the changes in each image from 1950 to 1980. One of her many conclusions is that "the composite impression of the good-bad images was a forceful endorsement of a secondary position for women, a place in the world as selfless, devoted adjuncts to men" (p. 113). In addition, Meehan notes that "any other female stance was, at best, an irritation, an interruption, and at worst a threat to world order, a destructive force." She concludes that "except in the rarest of cases, expression of female autonomy, even expression of her own sexuality, was potentially harmful or dangerous" (p. 113).

Another of Meehan's findings concerns occupational role models other than the housewife. Women on television, Meehan shows, were nearly always in service occupations, whereas males were shown in "controlling occupations." In effect, "the television rendition of the working woman's role is a copy of its portrayal of the housewife." Like the housewife, the working woman is dependent on a male for supervision and direction, and further, she mirrors the domestic model in the kinds of work activities she performs. Finally, there is the familiar dichotomy between homemaker and wage earner, "relegating the home to the housewife and leaving the workplace a single's domain" (p. 123).

Meehan concludes that "American viewers have spent more than three decades watching male heroes and their adventures, muddied visions of boyhood adolescence replete with illusions of women as witches, bitches, mothers and imps. Television has ignored the most important part of women's lives—their concepts, sensations, aspirations, desires, and dreams. It's time to tell the stories of female heroes—heading families, heading corporations, conquering fears, and coping with change.

Good models are needed to connect women to each other and to their society" (p. 131).

This kind of feminist criticism is important in documenting what we have come to understand as a prevalent way of imaging women in popular culture, but unfortunately it does not tell us much about how these images are produced (a study that might help us understand their continuity —with small changes—over a thirty-year period) or about exactly how these images *mean*, how they "speak" to the female viewer. We are left with vague notions of "positive" as opposed to "negative" images of women and of a standard—the autonomous, self-fulfilling, self-assertive, socially and financially "successful" woman—against which the images are judged to be either positive or negative. It was to counter just such a way of reading images of women in film that Laura Mulvey, Claire Johnston, and others referred to below undertook their work.

Meehan's model has serious problems. First, it represents the human consciousness as a tabula rasa upon which TV images are graven. Images are seen as models that viewers imitate because they are "read" by them as real people. Second, it assumes that this process of imitation is analogous to that which takes place in the family, where the child models its personality on those of its parents. What this view obviously leaves out is that fictional characters are *not* real people, and therefore viewers are forced to take a different position toward them. Also, the processes through which children "identify" with significant adults in their lives is enormously complicated and involves (as will be clear from my discussion of Lacan below) the unconscious and the language order in which children are placed. The viewer exists in a dynamic relationship to other people and to the screen image. He/she brings to reception an already complex unconscious and in a certain sense is "constructed" as a subject in the processes of reception.

Occasionally, Meehan's discussion points to a more nuanced understanding of subjectivity, as when she notes that "television has never been simply a reflection of society, as evident by the variety and abundance of content which grossly distorts the experience of viewers. The distortion can be attributed to the aspect of television content that is fantasy" (p. 113). She talks briefly about fantasy as an expression of myth, with a brief reference to Carl Jung, and mentions that the fantasies shown on TV are basically male ones, although she notes, without exploring the idea, that they also appeal to women (p. 125). But this insight emerges at the very end of Meehan's study and stands in opposition to her main theory that "the reality of the images is evident in the recognizable similarities between the action and events of characters and the experiences of the viewers; the goodwife, harpy and bitch display social behaviour we encounter in society" (p. 113).

It is clear that such work shows women demanding equal access to the (patriarchal) Symbolic. The "stories" Meehan says it is time "to tell" envision a society in which women are incorporated into the masculine public sphere as "heading families, heading corporations." Women are not to be seen as different from men, but this really means that women are "to become men." This position fails to acknowledge that such a move demands woman's complete surrender to patriarchy and its values, norms, and ways of being. As I will explain later, it implies that woman must replace being defined *by* the phallus with her identification *with* the phallus. Although this may be an important transitional phase, it should not be seen as an end in itself.

The second kind of feminist work exemplifies what we might call pre-Althusserian Marxist feminism. It looks at how television's status as an explicitly capitalist institution affects which images of women are portrayed. Such Marxist-feminist researchers stress the production of the woman-viewer as a consumer, a process that emerges from television's need—as a commercial, profit-making institution—to sell objects along with providing entertainment. But television's reliance on constructing numbers of viewers as commodities involves reproducing female images that accommodate prevailing (and dominant) conceptions of "woman," particularly as these satisfy certain *economic* needs.

Pre-Althusserian Marxist feminists, then, are interested in how women as a group are manipulated by larger economic and political concerns outside their control. Thus narratives might construct images of the working woman if society needs women in the work force; alternatively, they might represent woman as content to be a housewife when that is economically beneficial. The approach involves content analysis not that dissimilar from the previous "liberal" or "reformist" feminism, but the ends are different because the Marxist discussion, unlike others, always takes place within the context of television as a profit-making, capitalist concern.[17]

Lillian Robinson's "What's My Line? Telefiction and Women's Work" is an excellent example of this approach to television. Written in 1976, before there was much feminist work on television at all, the article deals with the contrast between the image of working women in television serials (including soaps) and the actual situation of women as workers in society. "TV fiction," Robinson argues, "has developed a set of myths specific to women and work elaborating on the themes of whether and why women enter the job market, what occupations they engage in, how they typically perform there, how they interact with the people with and for whom they work."[18] Turning, like Meehan, to "actual working women" to "test" the images, Robinson also finds distortions; whereas TV images collapse women's work identity and situation into sexuality, the real working woman sees herself as a person, "both worker and woman—with a job, a boss, a paycheck, and a set of working conditions, not a complex of sex roles involved in a workplace" (p. 312).

Unlike Meehan, however, Robinson accounts for these distortions by defining television as "a branch of something called the entertainment industry," which, Robinson says, "implies [that] something is manufactured here, mass-produced by alienated labor for the consumers who constitute its mass audience" (p. 313). But Robinson refuses to fall into Meehan's trap of conceiving her audience as completely vulnerable to the images provided. She argues, rather, that women do not necessarily accept what they are shown, and that the images are merely "one of the factors that *influence* the consciousness of women" but do not provide the whole story (p. 313).

Robinson contrasts the statistics relating to women's work in society with TV images of working women. She finds that, despite the trend away from family-based situations in comedy and drama, "the probability of a TV woman's being employed is about half what it would be for her real-life counterpart." In addition, "Motherhood almost always means leaving the work force, which is not too surprising, but marriage itself tends to have the same result" (p. 315). Robinson gives examples from shows like *Days of Our Lives*, *All in the Family*, and *One Day at a Time* to prove her points, and she demonstrates that, in addition to the distorted proportion of women working on TV, there is a large difference between the kinds of work women are seen to do on TV and the work they do in real life.

Robinson first looks at the low-status jobs that TV women do, pointing out that "TV women, both in offices and outside them, tend to be assigned what I think of as 'cutesy jobs,' occupations that require human contact and that place the woman in a series of potentially colorful situations" (p. 324). These jobs, Robinson notes, often entail silly costumes, animals, children, or humiliating situations, and they "create a climate of inference about the general silliness of women's reasons for working, women's jobs, and women's characteristic performance at them" (p. 324). Her Marxist-feminist point of view leads her to comment that TV shows carefully do not foreground the fact that these jobs "are normally unproductive and often socially useless" and "that most of them pay minimal wages . . .

those jobs arranged through a temporary agency [creating] double exploitation" (p. 324).

Robinson concludes by examining images of professional women, and she finds, interestingly, that such images are definitely there, "larger than life size and in far greater numbers than the real world, in which most of us still work as typists, waitresses, and saleswomen, would admit." (p. 335). Robinson assumes that the drastic fates that befall these TV professional women are meant as some kind of a warning to real women not to aim so high. This warning, she feels, is premature except insofar as it contributes to three interconnected myths: "that women enjoy a higher status than we feminists claim; that this status has been and may be achieved without fundamental social upheaval; and that having a career nonetheless poses a very real threat to female nature, to individual women's stability, and to institutions like the family that are built on these twin foundations" (p. 335).

Robinson's essay has many of the same strengths and limitations as Meehan's, but it differs in not demanding equal access to the (capitalist) patriarchal Symbolic. Rather, Robinson attempts (although she would not use this language) to show how that very Symbolic exploits and manipulates women workers and, further, constructs images that either belittle women's work or warn women of the deleterious effects of aiming too high. Her objective is to expose the workings of the patriarchal Symbolic rather than to argue for woman's access to it. But like Meehan, Robinson assumes an essentialist notion that women can resist their exploitation —that they are not socially constructed through the processes of their positioning.

A third type of feminist research emerges from the politics I have called radical feminism. This position rejects the male symbolic order in the name of difference. Femininity is not just celebrated by radical feminism; it is seen as better and essentially *different*. This approach focuses on women-identified women and on striving for autonomy and wholeness through communities of women, or at least through intense relationships with other women. Radical feminist criticism might be concerned with TV's depiction of traditional family life as the solution for all ills, with the forced heterosexual coupling in most popular narratives, or with the discrepancies between images of marriage in popular culture and in real life. The failure of popular culture to address women's positive ways of relating to one another and the portrayal of men as "naturally" dominant may also be issues.

Carol Aschur's pioneering essay "Daytime Television: You'll Never Want to Leave Home," written in 1976 (under the name "Carol Lopate"), shows traces of this radical position. Aschur's opening discussion of game shows exposes the infantilized positioning of women vis-à-vis the "inevitable male M.C."[19] "The M.C.," Aschur notes, "is the sexy, rich uncle, the women, preadolescent Lolitas," and she comments on the way the emcee exploits his position by fondling the women and receiving their embraces for the free gifts they get in this unreal, bountiful world (p. 72). The game shows, Aschur reveals, "recreate and transform women's general economic powerlessness as well as their role as consumers." They are shown as dependent for money on men, who control the spending power although women actually make the purchases. Women's decision-making power is limited to choosing which commodities to buy with the money men give them.

Turning to soap operas, Aschur illustrates the two important myths that they propagate: the idea of America "as a country where almost everyone is middle class" and the idea that "the family can be, and is, the sole repository of love, understanding, compassion, respect, and sexuality" (p. 74). Soap opera families "portray the idealized lives of families economically headed by professional men," while most women are housewives. Even when women work, they are rarely seen on the job. Aschur objects to the way that the family is set up as central; people, she says, are never allowed to leave the family or to "be alone long enough to develop a real self and thus have a personality that can be known" (p. 79). Furthermore, soap operas do not reveal "the nonbenign aspect of the power that men hold over women" (p. 81). Soaps misrepresent "real life" by portraying men, like the game show emcee, as "having the capacity to assist, protect, and give, without retaining the power to dominate that most men potentially have over most women. No soap opera father is a disciplinarian; no husband a wife beater" (p. 81). Although Aschur concludes that there is more equality between women and men in soaps than in real life or any other dramatic form, she argues that soaps ultimately function to promise the housewife, confined to her home, that "the life she is in can fulfill her needs." They repress her actual loneliness and isolation, as well as the possibility that, through her solitude, "she has the possibility for gaining a self" (p. 81).

In accord with this type of feminism, Aschur suggests a need for women to reject the male symbolic order, although again she does not use this terminology. That order, as revealed in popular TV shows that address women, exploits and infantilizes women on the one hand and idealizes the (in fact oppressive) patriarchal family on the other. The implication is that women can, and should, reject such debasing images, and indeed such degrading life scenes, in order to find themselves. Autonomy, independence from men, and bonding with other women are suggested, parenthetically, as both possible and desirable. Aschur's essentialism is evident, but it is important to note that she arrives at very different conclusions than does Meehan and differs also from Robinson in suggesting individual rather than social alternatives.

The fourth kind of feminism I noted, namely post-structuralist feminism, is that in which women reject the dichotomy between masculine and feminine as metaphysical or biological and aim at transcendence of the categories of sexual difference — or at least at recognition of their cultural construction. This feminism is only possible in the wake of the great twentieth-century modernist movements and the postmodernist theories that followed upon them. In this stage, scholars analyze the symbolic systems — including the filmic and televisual apparatuses — through which we communicate and organize our lives in an attempt to understand how it is that we learn to be what our culture calls "women" as opposed to what are called "men."

Post-structuralist feminism is often antiessentialist in contrast to the essentialism of the previous three types discussed, although, as we'll see, some of the work combines essentialist and antiessentialist assumptions. In the late 1970s and 1980s, one important influence on these post-structuralist American feminist television critics was that of the various French feminisms, which in turn were influenced by French psychoanalysis, semiotics, deconstruction, and Althusserian Marxism. A brief detour into the main theories that had this impact is, then, in order.

Especially important were Jacques Lacan's theories of the way in which the subject is constructed in a patriarchal language order (which Lacan calls "the Symbolic") and in which woman is normally relegated to the position of absence, or lack. As Sandy Flitterman-Lewis discusses, for Lacan the Imaginary *proper* lacks gender specificity — or rather, it brings both genders into the feminine through the illusory sense of being merged with the mother. What Lacan calls the "Mirror Phase" (the moment when the child first sets up a relationship to its image in the mirror) marks an awareness that the sense of oneness with the mother is illusory. The child begins to be aware of the mother as an object distinct from itself (the mirror contains an image of the mother holding the child); it also recognizes its "mirror" self (which Lacan calls an Ideal Imago) as an entity distinct from itself. The subject is thus constituted as a *split* subject (that is, both mother and nonmother, this side of the mirror and within the mirror). It is important that the Ideal Ego constructed during this

mirror-phase is not entirely on the side of the Imaginary; the child unconsciously incorporates the image of the mother as *another image*. It begins
to symbolize its own look as that of the Other and to set in motion the
desire for the mother (displaced into a desire for what she desires) that
will persist throughout its life.

This recognition of the mother as Other is, according to Lacan, a universal experience and one that is essential in order for the human-to-be
to, in fact, become *human*. The mother-child dyad must be interrupted by
the language order ("me"/"not me") if the child's development is to move
beyond the level of the Imaginary. The Mirror Phase thus prepares the
child for its subsequent entry into the realm of the Symbolic (by which
Lacan means language and other signifying and representational systems
such as images, gestures, and sound), in which the child takes up its position as a "sexed" being (it recognizes various subject positions such as
"he," "she," "you," "it"). Because signifying systems are organized around
the phallus as the prime signifier, the woman occupies the place of lack or
absence. The boy and girl, thus, find themselves in vastly different positions vis-à-vis the dominant order once they enter the realm of the
Symbolic.

The problem for the girl is in being positioned so as to identify with the
mother, which means desiring what the mother desires: the phallus. This
desire has nothing to do with anything essential or biological, but everything to do with the way that the Symbolic is organized. Lacan's system,
in fact, frees us from the tyranny of the biological. It also enables us to see
that some conventions, conceived of by certain stages of feminism as due
to "nature," are in fact socially constructed.

A second major French influence on post-structuralist feminist television research is that of Michel Foucault. Interestingly, Foucault's works,
unlike those of Lacan, are rarely cited explicitly, yet their influence is
pervasive. Foucault's theories—first, of how objects of knowledge are constituted in the very processes of their articulation, and second, of how
knowledge is organized *discursively*—have changed the face of television
criticism.[20] According to Foucault, discourse is power, or rather, power
operates in culture through discourse. He understands the discursive construction of sexuality and the policing of desire through dominant discourses. Feminist television critics use this concept of the discursive constitution of cultural objects for analyzing the ways in which television is
constructed as an object or the ways in which ads and other commercial
products construct cultural discourses that become pervasive—that function as power. Perhaps the best example of this kind of work is Lynn

Spigel's analysis of popular discourses on television and domestic space between 1948 and 1955.[21]

As noted earlier, feminist television criticism has been greatly influenced by feminist film theory, especially the work of Laura Mulvey and Claire Johnston.[22] Most important for psychoanalytic issues is Mulvey's crucial —and by now much discussed—essay "Visual Pleasure and Narrative Cinema," written in 1975.[23] Mulvey's interest in the commercial Hollywood film as an embodiment of the patriarchal unconscious provoked new interest by women in dominant popular forms. Drawing on Freud's twin mechanisms of voyeurism and fetishism, Mulvey shows that the dominant Hollywood cinema is built on a series of three basic "looks," all of which satisfy desire in the male unconscious. There is, first, the look of the camera in the filming situation (called the profilmic event); although technically neutral, this look is inherently voyeuristic and usually "male," in the sense that a man is generally doing the filming. Second, there is the look of the male figures within the film narrative, and these are organized through shot-countershot so as to make the woman the object of their gaze. Finally, there is the look of the spectator, which imitates (or is necessarily in the same position as) the first two looks. That is, the spectator is forced to identify with the look of the camera, to see as it sees.

Voyeurism and fetishism are mechanisms that the Hollywood cinema uses to construct the (presumedly male) spectator in accordance with the needs of *his* unconscious. Voyeurism is linked to the scopophilic instinct (that is, the male's pleasure in his own organ is transferred to pleasure in watching other people have sex). Mulvey argues that cinema relies on this instinct, making the spectator essentially a voyeur. Fetishism also comes into play in the cinema, where the whole female body may be "fetishized" in order to counteract the male fear of sexual difference, that is, of castration. Mulvey originally argued that if the spectator is a woman, she has to assume the male position and participate in both mechanisms.

Many critics agree that the Hollywood cinema lays out, for our contemplation, unconscious processes that are inaccessible except through psychoanalysis. These theories led to a set of concerns on the part of feminist scholars employing them that were different from those undertaken by previous essentialist feminists. Following Mulvey, feminist film critics became interested in what she had theorized as an exclusively "male" gaze and in discussing what possible "female" gaze there might be. Soon realizing that the theory applied mainly to the central "male" genres—the Western, gangster, adventure, and war films—women scholars turned to the one film genre that specifically addresses the female spectator—the melodrama—and issues relating to this genre and women viewers are still being actively pursued.[24] These scholars began to think about the text-spectator relationship, about how exactly the actual (historical) female viewer (or subject) sitting in the cinema is related to the screen images passing in front of her. Some of this work, which takes a direction similar to the reader-response criticism discussed in Robert Allen's chapter in this volume, contains some sociological aspects. That is, it still assumes an interaction between two given entities—the text on the one hand, the reader on the other—whereas other psychoanalytically oriented approaches assume that the reading subject is created (or constructed) in the very act of reading—that there is no reader outside of the text and no text, for that matter, outside of the reader.[25]

Some of the most interesting new feminist work on television uses methods developed for studies of the Hollywood film. This work examines the ways in which television functions as *apparatus*. This apparatus involves the complex of elements including the machine itself (its technological features—the way it produces and presents images); its various "texts" —ads, commentaries, and displays; the central relationship of programming to the sponsors, whose own texts—the ads—are arguably the *real* TV texts; and the now various sites of reception, from the living room to the bathroom. Scholars working along these lines might focus on problems of enunciation, that is, of who *speaks* a text and to whom it is addressed; the role of TV in domestic life; or the ideology embedded in the forms of production and reception. As Sandy Flitterman-Lewis discusses in her essay in this volume, still unclear is the degree to which film theories apply to the very different "televisual" apparatus. Because feminist film theory evolved in relation to the classical Hollywood cinema, it is particularly important for women who study television to consider to what extent the television spectator is addressed in the same manner as the film spectator. Do the same kinds of psychoanalytic processes of subject construction apply? Is there a different form of interaction between the television text and the female viewer than that between the cinema screen and its spectator? What might that relation be?

Let's consider an essay on soap operas that addresses this last question. Written by Tania Modleski in 1981, this essay established a set of interests for much of the work on soaps that followed, even that of scholars who took rather different approaches. Modleski's essay was the first to develop Carol Aschur's suggestion of a relationship between the structure/rhythm/mode of the soap opera and women's work. Recent theoretical developments enabled Modleski to take the argument further into the realm of the particular psychic demands on woman in the family. Using psychoanalytic arguments from both Nancy Chodorow and Luce Irigaray, Modleski theorizes that "soap operas tend . . . to break down the distance required for the proper working of identification. . . . They point to a different *kind* of relationship between spectator and characters that can be described in the words of Irigaray as 'nearness.'"[26] Modleski uses Chodorow and Irigaray's theories about the mother-daughter relationship to describe how the female spectator is socialized to relate to fictional texts: just as a relationship of "nearness" is inevitable in the mother-daughter bonding, which involves a kind of symbiosis, a difficulty of knowing where mother begins and daughter ends, so the female spectator will tend to overidentify with fictional characters and will not observe the boundaries that in fact separate her from the image.

Soaps, Modleski goes on to argue, at once rely upon woman's socialized skills in attending to the needs and desires of others and further develop those skills. They have an episodic, multiple narrative structure that accommodates woman's need to be "interruptible" (she must answer the phone, speak to the neighbor, take in the delivery, attend to the baby, see to the cleaning, ironing, food preparation, and so on) while providing pleasure within the act of teaching "the art of being off center" (p. 71).

Finally, in discussing the alternation between soap narratives and those of commercials (only hinted at by Aschur), Modleski suggests that the two modes address woman's dual function as both "moral and spiritual guides and household drudges" (p. 72). Soaps both accommodate the nature of woman's work in the home and make distraction or interruption pleasurable. A woman's entertainment, unlike a man's, must be consumed on the job because her "job" is neverending. Modleski claims that "woman's popular culture speaks to woman's pleasure at the same time that it puts it in the service of patriarchy, keeps it working for the good of the family" (p. 69).

Just as Modleski makes use of the new interest in psychoanalysis and the screen-spectator relationship to build on work done before, so other scholars have built on her essay. Sandy Flitterman-Lewis, for instance, uses the semiotics developed by Christian Metz for film analysis to discuss, in more detail than Modleski or Aschur, the precise nature of the relationship between commercials and the soap drama. She focuses on the processes of enunciation, asking: Who speaks the text? To whom is it addressed? Her examination of commercials as texts—that is, as modes of meaning production—reveals that each corresponds to one syntagm (the basic unit of narrative construction that Metz postulated). Soaps themselves, she notes, like any narrative, consist in many syntagms, but *formally* the two kinds of text are similar. Her point is that, "far from disrupting the narrative flow of daytime soap opera, commercials can be seen to *continue* it."[27] Commercials, that is, prolong and maintain the overall impulse for narrative that soaps fulfill while providing units of satisfying closure in an overall form that itself frustrates closure.

In terms of social meanings, Flitterman-Lewis reveals the idealized family present in the commercials, as opposed to the families in soaps who are overwhelmed with apparently unresolvable problems. The commercials thus function interactively with the soaps, setting up a "dialectical alternation between the vision in the soaps and that in the ads" (p. 94). It is this interaction between social meanings in the two sets of narratives that results in commercials having "an important function in shaping society's values" (p. 95).

Flitterman-Lewis does not explore exactly what values the soaps help to shape, but Charlotte Brunsdon, in an analysis of the British soap opera *Crossroads*, tries to identify them, relying implicitly on Foucaultian discourse theory and Althusserian concepts of ideology. Brunsdon discovers that instead of being "in the business" of "creating narrative excitement, suspense, delay and resolution," as is the classical Hollywood film, *Crossroads* is concerned with the ideology of "personal life." In other words, the coherence of the soap does not come from "the subordination of space and time to linear narrativity," but rather from "the continuities of moral and ideological frameworks which inform the dialogue." The serial takes place within a very circumscribed set of values that provide the norms for everyone's lives; even as people violate those norms, they are nonetheless constrained by them and ultimately have to learn to adjust to them or suffer the consequences. According to Brunsdon, *Crossroads* is "in the business" of "constructing moral consensus about the conduct of personal life. There is an endless unsettling, discussion and resettling of acceptable modes of behavior within the sphere of personal relationships."[28]

In addition, Brunsdon is interested in the tension between the subject positions that a text constructs "and the social subject who may or may not take up these positions" (p. 76). Following Paul Willemen, David Morley, and Steve Neale (and there are others, like Tony Bennett), Brunsdon stresses that the historical spectator is constructed by a whole range of other discourses, including motherhood, romance, and sexuality, that will determine her reactions to a text. Brunsdon shows that program publicity, scheduling, and ads all imply a female audience for *Crossroads*. She concludes that the address of the soaps is a gendered one that relies on "the traditionally feminine competencies associated with the responsibility for 'managing' the sphere of personal life" (p. 81). Brunsdon is careful to avoid the essentialist trap of claiming that such competencies are "natural" to women; rather, she sees women as being socially constructed to possess such skills through inscription in "the ideological and moral frameworks [the rules] of romance, marriage and family life" (p. 81).

Brunsdon's essay is important because it focuses explicitly on the difference in narrative conventions between soaps and the classical Hollywood cinema, and on the ideological implications of those differences. The structure of the soap, an endless dialogue about personal lives, inscribes the viewer in a particular ideological framework regarding the family. This positioning is quite different from that in the Hollywood film.

It seems to me that exploring these differences in relation to all kinds of TV programs is an important future task. As feminists, we need to explore the degree to which theories worked out for the dominant Hollywood narratives apply to what, above, I called the "televisual apparatus," because the representation of women is produced by the apparatus as much as by the narrative. Indeed, much recent film theory has argued that one cannot make any distinction between the apparatus and the narrative, because it is the apparatus itself that produces certain inevitable "narrative" effects (such as, in film, the forced identification with the look of the camera). But this argument, a very complex one, goes beyond the confines of this paper.[29] I introduce it here only to highlight a crucial area for future feminist television research. We need to know how the televisual apparatus is used in any one TV genre to represent the female body—to see what possibilities there are for different kinds of female representation and how the limits of the apparatus restrict images of woman on TV. But critics also need to analyze TV texts in relation to other prevailing discourses that constitute the performers, the spectators, and television itself, as found in ads, in discourses about sexuality, in the gender sign-system. That is, issues relating to consumer culture and mass society always need to be addressed along with individual texts. For now, I will refer to my recent work on music television (MTV) and Madonna as an example of a feminist approach that combines analysis of female images in individual TV texts with attention to their context of production/exhibition, to the televisual apparatus, and to discursive frameworks that constitute texts as *texts* and that also constitute performers like Madonna in specific ways.

In a brief discussion of feminist "Madonna politics," I will distinguish my approach from that of scholars who do audience analysis in the British cultural studies tradition discussed by John Fiske in this volume. Not that one approach cancels out the other—one would hope that the methods are complementary rather than contradictory. But the theoretical differences of the approaches have important political implications.

Let me begin by discussing the implications of the televisual apparatus for the representation of women on music television (MTV). MTV is an advertiser supported, twenty-four-hour cable service available on most U.S. cable systems and now available in Europe and South America as well. MTV was launched in 1981 as a vehicle for promotional videos provided free to the network by record companies—just as radio stations play free records with which they are provided. Confined to a short, four-minute format inserted within the twenty-four-hour flow, rock videos are a unique artistic mode (their song-image form has links with opera and the Hollywood musical, but it differs from both in central ways briefly alluded to below). I am interested in the spectator-screen relationship as it is produced both by the visual strategies of individual videos and by the juxtaposition of four-minute texts with a series of other four-minute texts within a flow that includes other *kinds* of texts. These can include not only sponsor's ads, ads for MTV itself, contests, interviews, music news, and the veejay's comments, but recently also MTV game shows and special comedy slots. How does this "flow" affect the spectator? Is there any particular gender address in it? How does the flow particularly affect the *female* spectator?

Let me first say something about the construction of what I have elsewhere called the "decentered" MTV spectator: this is a *fragmented* spectator: someone who is not asked to concentrate for very long on any particular material and who is produced through the rapid flow of comparatively short segments within a continuous, twenty-four-hour flow of texts.[30] The spectator's attention is constantly diverted to something else instead of being absorbed for a long time, as it might be by a film (shown in a cinema) or by a novel. MTV shares this fragmentation of viewer attention with other forms of television such as continuous weather and news channels and other "serialized" forms that contain continuous segments intended to be viewed daily (soaps, news, and game shows, for example).[31]

These kinds of programs are very different from films. They are not discrete units consumed within a fixed two-hour limit, presented on an unmovable screen and out of the spectator's control. Nor are they comparable to the novel, which is also clearly bounded or limited by a different sort of "frame" (although one more within the reader's control than is the film). Margaret Phelan has argued that TV is like Foucault's Panopticon, in which the guard surveys a series of prisoners through their windows. In this model, the TV producer is the "guard" and the individual TV viewer the "prisoner" who watches in "a sequestered and observed solitude."[32] But the metaphor also works well for the spectator's relationship to the various episodes that represent, in Foucault's words, "a multiplicity that can be numbered and supervised." In fact, the TV viewer's desire for plenitude, for complete knowledge and pleasure, is forever delayed, forever deferred.[33] TV is seductive precisely because it speaks to a desire that is insatiable—it promises complete knowledge and pleasure in some far distant and never-to-be-experienced future. Its strategy is to keep us endlessly consuming in the hopes of fulfilling our desire; it hypnotizes us through addressing this desire; it keeps us returning for more.

This strategy is particularly evident in MTV, where the spectator watches an endless succession of four-minute videos, forever hoping to fulfill his/her desire in the next text that comes along. The lure of the "coming up next" trailer, which all programs employ and which is the staple of the serial, is an intricate aspect of the minute-by-minute watching of MTV. The spectator is trapped in the constant hope that the next video will be one to somehow ultimately satisfy, and so he/she goes on watching and hoping, enticed by the constant and seductive promise of immediate plenitude. But all these spectators are actually doing is consuming endlessly.

The question is, to what degree does this decentering televisual apparatus specifically position women? Are women necessarily addressed differently by the apparatus, as was argued (initially, at least) for the classical Hollywood film? Is there something inherent in the televisual apparatus that addresses woman's social positioning as absence or lack, as was also the case with the Hollywood film?

This question takes me beyond the confines of my topic, but it is possible that TV programs including MTV construct, not the male gaze of the Hollywood film, but a wide range of gazes with different gender implications. This means that the apparatus itself, in its modes of functioning, is not gender specific. But across its "segments"—be they soap operas, crime series, news, or morning shows—one finds a variety of "gazes" that indicate an address to a certain kind of male or female "Imaginary." In addition, there is also a kind of genderless address, so that people of both genders are able to undertake multiple identifications, depending on the program involved.

What this lack of gender specificity implies is that the televisual Imaginary is more complex than the cinematic one and does not involve the same regression to the Lacanian Mirror Phase. In the case of MTV, for example, rather than evoking aspects of Lacan's Ideal Imago—a process that depends on sustained identification with a central figure in a prolonged narrative—the channel instead evokes issues of split subjectivity and the alienation that the mirror image involves. Whereas filmic processes seek (especially for the male viewer) to heal, for the duration of the movie, the painful split subjectivity instituted during the Mirror Phase, MTV produces the decenteredness that is our actual condition and that is especially obvious to the young adolescent.

MTV addresses the desires, fantasies, and anxieties of young people growing up in a world in which all traditional categories and institutions are being questioned. I have elsewhere argued that there are five main types of videos on MTV and that these involve a whole series of gazes instead of the broadly monolithic Hollywood gaze.[34] The plethora of gender positions on the music channel arguably reflects the heterogeneity of current sex roles, and the androgynous surface of many star images indicates the blurring of clear lines between genders that is characteristic of many rock videos. But, as we will see, Madonna takes things even further.

This phenomenon makes MTV an especially appropriate proving ground for some postmodern theories. Because of the sophisticated, self-conscious and skewed stance that the texts assume toward their own subject matter, it is often difficult to know precisely what a rock video actually means; its signifiers are not linked along a coherent, logical chain that produces an unambiguous message. The mode, to use Jameson's contrast, is that of pastiche rather than parody. By this expression, Jameson means that whereas modernist texts often took a particular critical position vis-à-vis earlier textual models, ridiculing specific stances or attitudes or offering a sympathetic, comic perspective, postmodernist works tend to take the form of pastiche, which lacks any clear positioning toward what it shows or toward any earlier texts that are used.[35]

Jameson's analysis of pastiche has implications for gender representations in rock videos, in which it is often unclear who is speaking the text and therefore whether the male or the female discourse dominates. One finds oneself not knowing, for instance, whether videos like Billy Idol's "Cradle of Love" or Poison's "Unskinny Bop" are virulently sexist or are merely pastiching an earlier Hollywood sexism. Even in videos that fall into the category I call "classical," wherein the gaze is clearly voyeuristic and male, there is a studied self-consciousness that makes the result quite different from that in the dominant commercial cinema.

Textual analyses need to be combined with more general studies of the ways performers are constituted and their personae constructed. Let's take the specific example of Madonna, a television rock star whose phenomenal rise to success, largely through MTV, makes her an appropriate object of study. Madonna is the site of whole series of discourses, many of which contradict each other but which together produce the divergent images in circulation.[36] Here I will explore differing feminist constructions of Madonna, along with Madonna's constructions of herself. For it is precisely Madonna's intuitive grasp of the televisual world in which we live — of the medium's possibilities for engaging spectators in diverse ways — that in part accounts for her success. She is the supreme television heroine.

Two main feminist approaches to the "Madonna phenomenon" (henceforth called the MP) may be characterized as representing, first, a feminist identity politics, and second, a feminist politics of the signifier. Each of these approaches harks back to 1970s and 1980s "feminisms" outlined earlier in this chapter. Now, however, the terms of the argument are more self-consciously located in implications of female subjectivity for political strategies. The first approach is linked to British cultural studies and audience research, whereas the second comes out of post-structuralist feminism and is linked to a politics that focuses on the body as text.

Because John Fiske's essay in this volume more or less exemplifies that first approach, I will deal with it only briefly. As Fiske puts it, "culture is a process of making meanings in which people actively participate. . . . [T]he mass-produced text can only be made into a *popular* text by the people, and this transformation occurs when the various subcultures can activate sets of meanings and insert those meanings into their daily cultural experience." Building on Angela McRobbie's theory of "girl culture," several scholars have examined Madonna as a fascinating example of, as Fiske puts it, "the permeability of the boundary between television and other forms of cultural experience."[37] Fiske argues that "[Madonna] enables girls to see that the meanings of feminine sexuality *can* be in their control, *can* be made in their interests, and that their subjectivities are not necessarily totally determined by the dominant patriarchy." As Lisa Lewis has written, "Female address videos reclaim style for girls and richly articulate style as a symbolic vehicle for female expression." In relation to Madonna specifically, Lewis notes that "at least part of the appeal of Madonna's overtly sexual image for adolescent girls lies in the way it can be used to counter feminine ideals of dependency and reserve."[38]

One of the values of an audience-centered approach like this one is its materiality—it keeps close to the experiences of the young women who watch Madonna or the fans who celebrate her. A problem is that it leaves intact given gender binarisms and notions of individual subjects. Madonna's image may be empowering for some young women, and this is a good thing; but the MP may be far more generally subversive if one considers how Madonna's recent work challenges constructs of *both* genders because it understands gender as a *sign-system* that does not necessarily coincide with *identity*.

Judith Butler's theory of parodic performance gives us a starting point for such a perspective. In Butler's argument, gender is a particular and prevailing cultural sign-system that involves subjects repeating gender signs as constitutive of a specific identity.[39] Butler's notion of challenging binary constructs through parodic play with gender stereotypes in gay, transsexual, and carnivalesque reversals is attractive. In many ways, Madonna would seem precisely to embody what Butler believes is the most useful future strategy for avoiding oppressive binary "engendering." Having investigated "the political stakes in designating as an *origin* and *cause* those identity categories that are in fact the *effects* of institutions, practices, discourses with multiple and diffuse points of origin," Butler goes on to "think through the possibility of subverting and displacing those naturalized and reified notions of gender that support masculine hegemony and heterosexist power, to make gender trouble . . . through the mobilization, subversive confusion and proliferation of precisely those constitutive categories that seek to keep gender in its place" (pp. x–xl, 33–34).

Engaged as she is in self-consciously philosophical discourse, Butler does not read cultural texts (fiction, TV, film) and thus is unable to flesh out her abstract argument with concrete examples. But much of what Madonna does can be read, via Butler, as mobilizing for the purposes of subversion the constitutive categories of gender.

I will briefly illustrate what I mean by reference to two videos, "Express Yourself" and "Justify My Love," and to Alex Keshishian's 1991 documentary about Madonna, *Truth or Dare*. All of these materials must be located within Madonna's "Blond Ambition" phase—her most daring to date and the one that offers the greatest challenge to the dominant gender sign-system. All three texts need situating within a network of discourses: prevailing conservative discourses about Madonna (to which Madonna's videos deliberately respond), that of her worshipful fans, the discourse of television and show business, the promotional discourses of the MP's own business enterprise, and the discourses that relate the MP's specific texts to earlier texts.

In the cases of both "Express Yourself" and "Justify My Love," those other texts/contexts are German expressionistic films and film directors/ actresses and the decadent Germany of the 1920s immediately preceding the Nazi period. "Express Yourself," in addition, is specifically modeled on the German director Fritz Lang's 1927 film *Metropolis*, although it also contains references to Josef Von Sternberg's *The Blue Angel*. But it completely rewrites these patriarchal narratives. The heroine of the video presides over the text before it begins, heralding it as dedicated to women (in contrast to the male address of both Lang's and Von Sternberg's films) and—in the fashion of the circus *metteur en scène*—conjuring up her audience.

Here Madonna works, even more explicitly than in other videos, against the "sacred image of the same": her image is not set up in every frame as focus of the camera, audience, and male gazes; even when her figure is central, it adopts many different subject-positions, so that identification is dispersed, multiple, constantly changing, never fixed, never one. Body-boundary maintenance is violated in "Express Yourself" not only through Madonna's cross-dressing (at one point, she "becomes" Fritz Lang, the director, on his *Metropolis* set—fuming, raging, commanding one moment, then revealing female underwear and masturbating the next), but also through Madonna's "becoming" the cat, which is seen ominously gliding through spare rooms or being stroked by insistent, changing hands. In this sequence Madonna locates her sensuality alongside that of animals; or perhaps she is asking to become the creature so stroked and loved by human hands—hands that do not stroke her until the end, when the worker (who longs for her) finally finds her. Such transgressions of normalized gender signs challenge the system. The video asks us to rethink the gender signs we repeat daily: it asks us to engage in the revolutionary act that Butler notes, namely to repeat gender constructs self-consciously and arbitrarily, thus subverting the given sign-system.[40]

"Express Yourself" has two aims: to alter gender relations and to destabilize gender altogether. The first aim is evident in the lyrics, which exhort the spectator to "make him express himself" so that *she* can get a sexual high, and further to "respect herself" and not settle for "second best." In this sense, the video apparently aims to empower women—to exhort them to take control.

But "Express Yourself" does not have the normalization of female identity or narrative as its main ends. Instead, the power of the video comes from the incredible series of images, edited to produce a rapidly moving, radically decentered, destabilizing experience. The destabilization results both from the violation of normal time/space relations, produced by the rapid-fire, nonclassical editing, and from the multiple subject positions through which the heroine (and "star" Madonna) moves during the course of the video. The spectator is unable to locate any secure position within the world of the video, whose logic is close to that of the dream. Glaring colors—the heroine's lurid green dress, bright yellow hair, black underwear, and too-red lips, the stark blackness of the cat—contrast with the soft browns and grays of the underworld and the opaque blue-white of the sets in which the heroine undresses and through which she crawls in the animal position.

The sets themselves are compelling: the claustrophobia of the upper-class world is conveyed through images of the heroine lounging in a room with high walls and only one opening; the oppressiveness of the workers' underworld is expressed in the rain-sodden steel frames and floors of the place where the lover sleeps and works. Close-ups of machines recall Eisenstein's factories, and the powerful male body resembles a Rodin sculpture.

Although in one sense the video evokes a dream space—a space of desire/longing pitted against power/domination—it also uses that space to challenge prevailing gender codes. The heroine uses her body as a text, a means of "writing" herself differently. She repeats traditional male/female gender signs but challenges them by mixing up the signs: for example, when the heroine is dressed as "Fritz Lang," she opens her jacket to reveal her brassiere; in the "Blond Ambition" performance version, the figure also has a suspender belt dangling outside its trousers. This is typical of Madonna's postmodern feminist daring in her "Blond Ambition" period —and it is a mixing of signs upon which many of the acts in the tour relied, as will be clear in my discussion of *Truth or Dare.*

"Justify My Love" perhaps carried Madonna's postmodern daring to its furthest extent. Although it was censored by MTV as obscene, the video is so stylized and so self-conscious as to hardly fall into any such category. It plays self-consciously with images familiar from depictions of decadent 1920s Germany and its homoerotic and orgiastic underworlds. Its terrain is clearly that of fantasy—something that U.S. reviewers misunderstood. The heroine (Madonna) is obviously having a lot of fun, a fact made clear by a shot of her giggling in the midst of all the too-posed, highly stylized, and too-serious sexual acts, and again as she runs off at the end. This video is beautifully photographed in black and white; dominating the images is the figure of the superb vogue dancer, whose lean, sinuous body is silhouetted in many scenes, his limbs twisting and turning rhythmically.

Gender signs again are deliberately played with, and the spectator is confused as to the gender of the various lovers who are either coupling or watching others' coupling. The video forces the spectator to question the boundaries of gender constructs and the cultural constraints on sexual themes and sexual fantasies.

Truth or Dare (released in Britain as *In Bed with Madonna*) pretends to reveal the "truth" about Madonna, and in doing so, the film exemplifies the "politics of the signifier." In the film, Madonna is seen in a startlingly diverse array of guises and poses, from a grainy, black-and-white image of her sitting in a bathrobe and shower cap, awkwardly sipping soup, to lush color images of performances which themselves challenge gender signs and identities. We are shown "surprise" encounters between Madonna and an old friend in grainy black and white; Madonna in bed with her black, gay male dancers; and the "truth or dare" game in which Madonna dares to perform fellatio with a bottle. Madonna assumes the role of Mother-Boss of the show, who nurtures her child-dancers and prays with them before each performance, as well as that of a more conventional boss, who bemoans the loss of a needed secretary.

Specific acts filmed for the documentary make a good case for the project as one that is engaged in challenging the dominant sign-system and normative modes of gender identification. For example, the "Cleopatra" act, in which Madonna reworks the Roman story, shows the heroine masturbating on a bed while her black male eunuchs, sporting huge conical breasts, encourage her and eye each other. Are the eyes male or female? Is it feminine to masturbate publicly, or does that action transgress feminine codes and reach over to masculinity? Such are the questions the performance provokes.

The questions feminists have been debating, and which I have discussed with respect to Madonna, in the end all have some validity. Following the British cultural studies approach, Madonna—especially in her early phases—has provided a useful, subversive role model for adolescent women with her self-generating, self-promoting image, her autonomy and independence, and her determined creativity. More recently, as in "Justify My Love," Madonna has explored female sexual fantasies about bondage, group sex, and sadomasochism. In this respect, if Madonna is not an artist who should be linked to avant-gardists, she is at least someone who pushes the limits of social codes through aesthetic expression, and this in a period when the dominant culture is reacting against the challenges of the 1960s. But what she does is not transcendent art, for all times and places. Hers is an expression linked to and best discussed within a specific, local, cultural context. For example, Madonna's version of "No Respect" demonstrates her increasing attention to the constraints of middle American sexual mores and to the inhibitions and repressions involved, especially in relation to gay/lesbian sexual alternatives and to the desires that emerge in sexual fantasies.[41]

The anti-Madonna media discourse serves those who feel threatened by her challenges to patriarchal heterosexual norms, and some positive overreaction to Madonna by women writers also assists dominant patriarchal culture in taking up its antifeminist, clichéd/archaic discourse.[42] I believe that the level of the politics of the signifier may make inroads on precisely such oppressive gender "identities" over time. Unfortunately, I have not been able to deal here with Madonna's complex relationship to consumerism—that is, with her phenomenal commercial success. It is certainly disingenuous to praise Madonna's shrewd business sense, as one critic does,[43] without recognizing the values involved in marketing oneself for huge profits or querying whether the best or only model for a young woman is that of a successful business woman. But the crucial issue of whether the MP must be seen as being in collusion with an oppressive late-capitalist phenomenon will have to be followed up elsewhere.[44] That the MP has been able to produce such complex debates—debates that have great implication for feminist television criticism as well as for cultural studies methods in general—attests to the dramatic impact of the phenomenon itself.

NOTES

1. See E. Ann Kaplan, introduction, and William Boddy, "Loving a Nineteen-Inch Motorola: American Writing on Television," in *Regarding Television—Critical Approaches: An Anthology*, ed. E. Ann Kaplan, American Film Institute Monograph Series, vol. 2 (Frederick, Md.: University Publications of America, 1983), pp. xi–xxiii, 1–11; Robert C. Allen, *Speaking of Soap Operas* (Chapel Hill: University of North Carolina Press, 1985), chap. 2, esp. pp. 40–44; David Morley, *The "Nationwide" Audience: Structure and Decoding* (London: British Film Institute, 1980), pp. 1–5.

2. Recently a few scholars (such as Charlotte Brunsdon) have been able to undertake work on television from within the university.

3. For British work of this kind, see Morley, *The "Nationwide" Audience*; and the Glasgow University Media Group, *Bad News* (London: Routledge and Kegan Paul, 1976), and *More Bad News* (London: Routledge and Kegan Paul, 1980). For typical American work in the social science mode, see G. Com-

stock, Steven Chaffee, N. Katzman, M. McCombs, and D. Roberts, *Television and Human Behaviour* (New York: Columbia University Press, 1978).

4. Susan Honeyford, "Women and Television," *Screen* 21, no. 2 (1980): 49.

5. Gillian Skirrow, "Representations of Women in the Association of Cinematograph, Television and Allied Technicians," *Screen* 22, no. 3 (1981): 94–102.

6. See, for example, John Caughie, "Progressive Television and Documentary Drama," *Screen* 21, no. 2 (1980): 9–35; Mike Poole, "The Cult of the Generalist: British Television Criticism, 1936–83," *Screen* 25, no. 2 (1984): 41–62; Tony Pearson, "Teaching Television," *Screen* 24, no. 3 (1983): 35–43.

7. It was only in the wake of the work by feminist theorists in the 1980s that a book on soaps did emerge from a "communications" scholar, who happened also to be male: Robert Allen's *Speaking of Soap Operas* (Chapel Hill: University of North Carolina Press, 1985). I will discuss this work later on. An example of more traditional work on soaps is Bradley S. Greenberg, Kimberly Neuendorf, Nancy Buerkel-Rothfuss, and Laura Henderson, "The Soaps: What's On and Who Cares?," *Journal of Broadcasting* 26, no. 2 (Spring 1982): 519–35.

8. Helen Baehr, "The Impact of Feminism on Media Studies: Just Another Commercial Break," *Medie Kultur*, no. 4 (November 1986): 132–54.

9. Stephen Heath and Gillian Skirrow, "Television: A World in Action," *Screen* 18, no. 2 (1977): 7–59.

10. I am thinking here of the work by Cathy Schwichtenberg on *The Rockford Files*, Rebecca Baillin on *Charlie's Angels*, and others. Ellen Seiter at Northwestern University was another "pioneer" in the area of soap operas.

11. See the special issue of *Camera Obscura* 16 (January 1988), the theme of which is "Television and the Female Consumer." Patricia Mellencamp and Kathleen Woodward organized a conference on television in 1989 that featured a series of lectures, some of which dealt with female issues.

12. See Simone de Beauvoir, *The Second Sex*, trans. H. M. Parshley (1949; reprint, Harmondsworth, Eng.: Penguin, 1972); Kate Millett, *Sexual Politics* (New York: Doubleday, 1969); and Germaine Greer, *The Female Eunuch* (London: MacGibbon and Kee, 1970).

13. See E. Ann Kaplan, *Postmodernism and Its Discontents: Theories and Practices* (London: Verso, 1988); Craig Owens, "The Discourse of Others: Feminists and Postmodernism," in *The Anti-Aesthetic: Essays on Postmodern Culture*, ed. Hal Foster (Port Townsend, Wash.: Bay Press, 1983), pp. 57–77; and Meaghan Morris, *The Pirate's Fiancé: Feminism, Reading, Postmodernism* (London: Verso, 1988). On the issue of feminism and postmodernism, see the discussion of my recent work on MTV and Madonna below.

14. See E. Ann Kaplan, "The Hidden Agenda: A Review of *Re-Vision: Essays in Feminist Criticism*," *Camera Obscura* 24/25 (Fall 1985): 235–49,

and "Feminist Film Criticism: Current Issues," *Studies in the Literary Imagination* 19, no. 1 (Spring 1986): 7–20. The latter article is reprinted in R. Barton Palmer, ed. *The Cinematic Text: Contemporary Methods and Practice* (Atlanta: Georgia State University Press, 1989), pp. 155–71.

15. See Teresa de Lauretis, "Fantasy and Female Subjectivity: A Feminist Reevaluation of Freud's Theory of Sexuality" (tentative title), publication forthcoming.

16. Diana Meehan, *Ladies of the Evening: Women Characters of Prime-Time Television* (Metuchen, N.J.: Scarecrow Press, 1983). Page references to this work will be cited in the text.

17. For an excellent example of this kind of work on media images before the invention of television, see Maureen Honeywell, *Creating Rosie the Riveter* (Amherst: University of Massachusetts Press, 1984).

18. Lillian Robinson, "What's My Line? Telefiction and Women's Work," in *Sex, Class, and Culture* (Bloomington: Indiana University Press, 1978), pp. 310–44. Page references to this work will be cited in the text.

19. Carol Lopate [Aschur], "Daytime Television: You'll Never Want to Leave Home," *Feminist Studies* 3, nos. 3/4 (Spring/Summer 1976): 69–82. Page numbers in the text refer to this version.

20. See Michel Foucault, *The History of Sexuality, Volume 1: An Introduction*, trans. Robert Hurley (New York: Vintage, 1980); *The Order of Things: An Archaeology of the Human Sciences* (New York: Vintage, 1973); and "Nietzsche, Genealogy, History," in *Language, Counter-Memory, Practice: Selected Essays and Interviews by Michel Foucault*, trans. Donald F. Bouchard and Sherry Simon, ed. Donald F. Bouchard (Ithaca, N.Y.: Cornell University Press, 1977). For discussions about Foucault, see Alan Sheridan, *Michel Foucault: The Will to Truth* (London: Tavistock, 1980); and Jonathan Arac, *After Foucault: Humanistic Knowledge, Postmodern Challenges* (New Brunswick, N.J.: Rutgers University Press, 1988).

21. See Lynn Spigel, "Installing the Television Set: Popular Discourses on Television and Domestic Space, 1948–1955," *Camera Obscura* 16 (January 1988): 11–46; see also Serafina Kent Bathrick, "The True Woman and the Family Film: The Industrial Production of Memory," Ph.D. diss., University of Wisconsin-Madison, 1981.

22. For overviews of feminist film theory, see: E. Ann Kaplan, *Women and Film: Both Sides of the Camera* (London: Methuen, 1983); and Annette Kuhn, *Women's Pictures: Feminism and Cinema* (London: Routledge and Kegan Paul, 1982).

23. Laura Mulvey, "Visual Pleasure and Narrative Cinema," *Screen* 16, no. 3 (1975): 6–18.

24. See, for example, the debates over various readings of *Stella Dallas* in

Cinema Journal 24, no. 2 (Winter 1985): 40–43; 25, no. 1 (Fall 1985): 51–54; and 25, no. 4 (Summer 1986): 49–53.

25. For details of work on female spectatorship, see the entire volume of *Camera Obscura* 21/22 (Spring 1990), edited by Mary Anne Doane and Janet Bergstrom.

26. See Tania Modleski, "The Rhythms of Reception: Daytime Television and Women's Work," in Kaplan, *Regarding Television*, pp. 67–75. Subsequent references are cited in the text. See also Modleski, *Loving with a Vengeance: Mass-Produced Fantasies for Women* (Hamden, Conn.: Archon, 1982).

27. Sandy Flitterman, "The *Real* Soap Operas: TV Commercials," in Kaplan, *Regarding Television*, pp. 84–96. Subsequent references are cited in the text.

28. Charlotte Brunsdon, "*Crossroads*: Notes on Soap Opera," in Kaplan, *Regarding Television*, p. 79.

29. For further discussion of these complex issues, see Sandy Flitterman-Lewis's chapter in this volume.

30. See E. Ann Kaplan, "A Postmodern Play of the Signifier? Advertising, Pastiche and Schizophrenia in Music Television," in *Television in Transition*, ed. Phillip Drummond and Richard Paterson (London: British Film Institute, 1985), pp. 146–63; Kaplan, "History, the Historical Spectator and Gender Address in Music Television," *Journal of Communication Inquiry* 10, no. 1 (Winter 1986): 3–14; and Kaplan, "Sexual Difference, Pleasure and the Construction of the Spectator in Music Television," *Oxford Literary Review* 8, no. 1/2 (1986): 113–22. Fuller discussion of the issues in these articles may be found in Kaplan, *Rocking around the Clock: Music Television, Postmodernism and Consumer Culture* (London: Methuen, 1987).

31. See Robert Stam, "Television News and Its Spectator," in Kaplan, *Regarding Television*, pp. 23–43.

32. Margaret Phelan, "Panopticism and the Uncanny: Notes toward Television's Visual Time," unpublished paper presented at the annual meeting of the Modern Language Association, December 1986.

33. For further discussion of these points, see my works cited in n. 30 above.

34. See Kaplan, *Rocking around the Clock*, chaps. 4 and 5.

35. See Fredric Jameson, "Postmodernism and Consumer Culture," in *The Anti-Aesthetic: Essays on Postmodern Culture*, ed. Hal Foster (Port Townsend, Wash.: Bay Press, 1983), p. 113.

36. See my essay, "Madonna Politics: Perversion, Repression, or Subversion? Or Masks and/as Master-y," in *The Madonna Connection*, ed. Cathy Schwichtenberg (London: Westview Press, 1992).

37. See Barbara Bradby, "Freedom, Feeling, and Dancing: Madonna Songs Traverse Girls' Talk," *One Two Three Four* (1991); Angela McRobbie, "Settling Accounts with Subcultures: A Feminist Critique," *Screen Education* 34

(1985): 37–49; Angela McRobbie and Mica Nava, eds., *Gender and Generation* (London: Macmillan, 1984); Lisa Lewis, *Gender Politics and MTV: Voicing the Difference* (Philadelphia: Temple University Press, 1990).

38. Lisa Lewis, "Being Discovered: Female Address on Music Television," *Jump Cut*, no. 35 (1990): 2–15; Lewis, *Gender Politics and MTV*, p. 123.

39. See Judith Butler, *Gender Trouble: Feminism and the Subversion of Female Identity* (London: Routledge, 1990).

40. Ibid., p. 147.

41. See Andrew Ross, *No Respect: Intellectuals and Popular Culture* (London: Routledge Chapman and Hall, 1989).

42. I have in mind here an article by Camille Paglia, "Madonna—Finally, a Real Feminist," *New York Times*, 14 December 1990; but see also Barbara Grizzuti Harrison, "Can Madonna Justify Madonna?," *Mademoiselle*, June 1991, pp. 80–81.

43. Paglia, "Madonna—Finally, a Real Feminist."

44. Kaplan, "Madonna Politics."

FURTHER READING

As noted in the essay, work on the representation of women in television has only recently grown into a sizable body of work. Some familiarity with 1970s and 1980s feminist film theory is essential for understanding current debates about feminist approaches to television and, indeed, the context for contemporary work itself.

Four recent books provide overviews of feminist film theory: Annette Kuhn, *Women's Pictures: Feminism and Cinema* (London: Routledge and Kegan Paul, 1982); E. Ann Kaplan, *Women and Film: Both Sides of the Camera* (London: Methuen, 1983); Mary Ann Doane, Patricia Mellencamp, and Linda Williams, eds. *Re-Vision: Essays in Feminist Film Criticism* (Los Angeles: American Film Institute, 1984); Mary Ann Doane, *The Desire to Desire: The Woman's Film of the 1940s* (Bloomington: Indiana University Press, 1987).

Equally important for research on women in television is an introductory understanding of developments in feminist theory and research methods from 1970 to the present, at least. For an overview of by-now-classic American feminist approaches, see Elaine Showalter, ed., *The New Feminist Criticism: Essays on Women, Literature, Theory* (New York: Pantheon, 1985); for an overview of feminist theories as they have developed in France, America, and Britain from 1970 to 1986, written from a position favoring European perspectives, see Toril Moi, *Sexual/Textual Politics: Feminist Literary Theory* (London: Methuen, 1986). Key texts for recent feminist approaches to television are Nancy Chodorow, *The Reproduction of Mothering: Psychoanalysis and the Sociology of Gender* (Berkeley: University of California Press, 1978); Julia Kristeva, "Women's Time," trans. Alice Jardine and Harry Blake, *Signs: A Journal of Women in Culture* 7, no. 1 (1981): 13–35; essays in *The Kristeva Reader*, ed. Toril Moi (Oxford: Blackwells, 1988); and Luce Irigary, "This Sex Which Is Not One" and "When Two Lips Speak Together," both collected in *This Sex Which Is Not One*, trans. Catherine Porter and Carolyn Burke (Ithaca, N.Y.: Cornell University Press, 1985). Judith Butler, *Gender Trouble: Feminism and the Subversion of Female Identity* (London: Routledge, 1990), usefully situates nearly all of the above feminist research within a Foucaultian discourse theory that is itself subordinated to performance theory and speech-act theory. Butler's work is especially useful for thinking about such marginalized communities as lesbians and gay men.

Some background knowledge about postmodernism is also useful. See E. Ann Kaplan, ed. *Postmodernism and Its Discontents: Theories and Practices* (London: Verso, 1988); Andrew Ross, *Universal Abandon?: The Politics of Postmodernism* (Minneapolis: University of Minnesota Press, 1988); and Stanley Aronowitz and Henry A. Giroux, eds., *Postmodern Education: Politics, Culture, and Social Criticism* (Minneapolis: University of Minnesota Press, 1991).

A good starting place for television analysis is the essays in E. Ann Kaplan, ed., *Regarding Television—Critical Approaches: An Anthology*, American Film Institute Monograph Series, vol. 2 (Frederick, Md.: University Publications of America, 1983; now published through Greenwood Press). The essays by Robert Stam and Jane Feuer provide excellent background for work on the televisual apparatus that is central to any specifically *feminist* analysis, and those by Tania Modleski, Charlotte Brunsdon, Sandy Flitterman, and Robert C. Allen provide models for different feminist approaches to the soap opera. Other essays providing background for feminist work in TV include Stephen Heath and Gillian Skirrow, "Television: A World in Action," *Screen* 18, no. 2 (1977): 7–59; Janice Winship, "Handling Sex," *Media, Culture and Society* 3, no. 1 (1981): 6–18; and, specifically on soaps, Ellen Seiter, "The Role of the Woman Reader: Eco's Narrative Theory and Soap Operas," *Tabloid* 6 (1981): 36–43. For a detailed analysis of soaps and a full bibliography, see Robert C. Allen, *Speaking of Soap Operas* (Chapel Hill: University of North Carolina Press, 1985). Chapters 3 and 4, in particular, contain material relevant to feminist criticism.

In the 1980s, some feminist scholars began to extend work being done on melodrama, in relation to the Hollywood film, to television serials. Work on cinematic melodrama includes: Laura Mulvey and Jon Halliday, eds., *Douglas Sirk* (Edinburgh: Edinburgh Film Festival, 1972); Laura Mulvey, "Afterthoughts on 'Visual Pleasure and Narrative Cinema,' Inspired by *Duel in the*

Sun," *Framework*, no. 15/16/17 (1981): 12–15; Mary Ann Doane, "The Woman's Film: Possession and Address," in Doane et al., *Re-Vision*, pp. 67–82; E. Ann Kaplan, "Theories of Melodrama," *Women and Performance* 1, no. 1 (Summer 1983): 40–48; and Christine Gledhill, ed., *Home Is Where the Heart Is: Studies in Melodrama and the Woman's Film* (London: British Film Institute, 1987). For applications to television, see Jane Feuer, "Melodrama, Serial Form, and Television Today," *Screen* 25, no. 1 (1984): 4–16; and Annette Kuhn, "Women's Genres: Melodrama, Soap Opera, and Theory," *Screen* 25, no. 1 (1984): 18–28.

The discourse analysis of Michel Foucault has been an important influence on feminist theory and on feminist analysis of television. On Foucault, see Paul Rabinow, ed., *The Foucault Reader* (New York: Pantheon, 1984). On the application of discourse analysis to television, see Lynn Spigel, "Installing the Television Set: Popular Discourses on Television and Domestic Space, 1948–1955," *Camera Obscura* 16 (January 1988): 11–46. Other relevant essays include Patrice Petro, "Mass Culture and the Feminine: The 'Place' of Television in Film Studies," *Cinema Journal* 25, no. 3 (Spring 1986): 5–21; and those on television in Tania Modleski, ed., *Studies in Entertainment: Critical Approaches to Mass Culture* (Bloomington: Indiana University Press, 1986). See also Patricia Mellencamp, ed., *Logics of Television: Essays in Cultural Criticism* (London: British Film Institute, 1991).

Discourse analysis is being taken up in another important area of research, namely that of audience response to television. The best work here is informed by neo-Marxist Althusserian ideas, sometimes together with Foucaultian theory; for a good example, see Tony Bennett, "Texts in History: The Determinations of Texts and Their Readings," in *Post-Structuralism and the Question of History*, ed. D. Attridge, G. Bennington, and R. Youngs (Cambridge: Cambridge University Press, 1987). This work is important for feminist criticism because it combines the problematic of subject formation crucial to gender issues with equally central issues of contextual and historical specificities. See David Morley, *Family Television: Cultural Power and Domestic Leisure* (London: Comedia, 1986); and Philip Simpson, *Parents Talking Television* (London: Comedia, 1987). Research on spectators from a different theoretical perspective may be found in Deidre Pribram, ed., *Female Spectators: Looking at Film and Television* (London: Verso, 1988), in which the essays deliberately confront the applicability of 1970s feminist film theory to television. See especially Jackie Byars, "Gazes/Voices/Power: Expanding Psychoanalysis for Feminist Film and Television Theory," pp. 110–31.

The *South Atlantic Quarterly* 88, no. 2 (Spring 1989), issue edited by Jane Gaines, contains several essays pertinent to work on women and television. See especially Gaines's own essay in the volume, "Dead Ringer: Jacqueline

Onassis and the Look-Alike," pp. 461–86; and Jane Feuer, "Reading *Dynasty*: Television and Reception Theory," pp. 443–60.

Feminist criticism of music videos is only just beginning. The earliest piece is E. Ann Kaplan, "A Postmodern Play of the Signifier? Advertising, Pastiche and Schizophrenia in Music Television," in *Television in Transition*, ed. Phillip Drummond and Richard Paterson (London: British Film Institute, 1985), pp. 146–63; a development of these ideas is available in Kaplan, "Sexual Difference, Pleasure and the Construction of the Spectator in Music Television," *Oxford Literary Review* 8, no. 1/2 (1986): 113–22. Further work on sexual difference in rock videos may be found in Kaplan, *Rocking around the Clock: Music Television, Postmodernism and Consumer Culture* (London: Methuen, 1987).

For an example of a quantitative approach to sex roles in MTV, see Jane D. Brown and Kenneth Campbell, "The Same Beat but a Different Drummer: Race and Gender in Music Videos," *Journal of Communication* 36, no. 1 (Winter 1986): 94–106. For a useful collection of essays on MTV relevant to a feminist analysis, see the *Journal of Communication Inquiry* 10, no. 1 (Winter 1986).

For work from the perspective of British cultural studies that has influenced American work on female rock stars, see Angela McRobbie and Mica Nava, eds., *Gender and Generation* (London: Macmillan, 1984); Angela McRobbie, "Settling Accounts with Subcultures: A Feminist Critique," *Screen Education* 34 (1985): 37–49; Barbara Bradby, "Freedom, Feeling, and Dancing: Madonna Songs Traverse Girls' Talk," *One Two Three Four* (1991); Lisa Lewis, *Gender Politics and MTV: Voicing the Difference* (Philadelphia: Temple University Press, 1990); and Susan McLary, *Feminine Endings: Music, Gender, and Sexuality* (Minneapolis: University of Minnesota Press, 1991).

8 : BRITISH CULTURAL STUDIES AND TELEVISION

john fiske

The term *culture*, as used in the phrase "cultural studies," is neither aesthetic nor humanist in emphasis, but political. Culture is not conceived of as the aesthetic ideals of form and beauty found in great art, or in more humanist terms as the voice of the "human spirit" that transcends boundaries of time and nation to speak to a hypothetical universal man (the gender is deliberate—women play little or no role in this conception of culture). Culture is not, then, the aesthetic products of the human spirit acting as a bulwark against the tide of grubby industrial materialism and vulgarity, but rather a way of living within an industrial society that encompasses all the meanings of that social experience.

Cultural studies is concerned with the generation and circulation of meanings in industrial societies. (The study of culture in nonindustrial societies may well require a different theoretical base, though Claude Lévi-Strauss's work has proved of value in studying the culture of both types of society.) But the tradition developed in Britain in the 1970s necessarily focused on culture in industrial societies. In this chapter I shall draw largely upon the work done at the University of Birmingham's Centre for Contemporary Cultural Studies (CCCS) under Stuart Hall, with some references to the works of Raymond Williams and those appearing in the journal *Screen*. The cultural studies developed at the CCCS is essentially

Marxist in the traditions of Louis Althusser and Antonio Gramsci, though this Marxism is inflected sometimes with a structuralist accent, sometimes with an ethnographic one.

Some basic Marxist assumptions underlie all British works in cultural studies. As Mimi White notes in her chapter, they start with the belief that meanings and the making of them (which together constitute culture) are indivisibly linked to social structure and can only be explained in terms of that structure and its history. Correlatively, the social structure is held in place by, among other forces, the meanings that culture produces; as Stuart Hall says, "A set of social relations obviously requires meanings and frameworks which underpin them and hold them in place."[1] These meanings are not only meanings of social experience, but also meanings of self, that is, constructions of social identity that enable people living in industrial capitalist societies to make sense of themselves and their social relations. Meanings of experience and meanings of the subject (or self) who has that experience are finally part of the same cultural process.

Also underlying this work is the assumption that capitalist societies are divided societies. The primary axis of division was originally thought to be class, though gender and race have now joined it as equally significant producers of social difference. Other axes of division are nation, age group, religion, occupation, education, political allegiance, and so on. Society, then, is not an organic whole but a complex network of groups, each with different interests and related to each other in terms of their power relationship with the dominant classes. Social relations are understood in terms of social power, in terms of a structure of domination and subordination that is never static but is always the site of contestation and struggle. Social power is the power to get one's class or group interest served by the social structure as a whole, and social struggle—or, in traditional Marxist terms, the class struggle—is the contestation of this power by the subordinate groups. In the domain of culture, this contestation takes the form of the struggle for meaning, in which the dominant classes attempt to "naturalize" the meanings that serve their interests into the "common sense" of society as a whole, whereas subordinate classes resist this process in various ways and to varying degrees and try to make meanings that serve their own interests. Some feminist work provides a clear example of this cultural struggle and contestation. Angela McRobbie and Lisa Lewis, for instance, both show how young girls are able to contest the patriarchal ideology structured into such films as *Flashdance* or the pop stars Madonna and Cindy Lauper and produce feminine readings of them.[2]

The attempt of the dominant classes to naturalize their meanings rarely, if ever, results from the conscious intention of individual members of those classes (though resistance to it is often, though not always, both conscious and intentional). Rather, it must be understood as the work of an ideology inscribed in the cultural and social practices of a class and therefore of the members of that class. And this brings us to another basic assumption: culture is ideological.

The cultural studies tradition does not view ideology in its vulgar Marxist sense of "false consciousness," for that has built into it the assumption that a true consciousness is not only possible but will actually occur when history brings about a proletarian society. This sort of idealism seems inappropriate to the late twentieth century, which appears to have demonstrated not the inevitable self-destruction of capitalism but its unpredicted (by Marx) ability to reproduce itself and to incorporate into itself the forces of resistance and opposition. History casts doubt on the possibility of a society without ideology, in which people have a true consciousness of their social relations.

Structuralism, another important influence on British cultural studies, also denies the possibility of a true consciousness, for it argues that reality can only be comprehended through language or other cultural meaning systems. Thus the idea of an objective, empirical "truth" is untenable. Truth must always be understood in terms of how it is made, for whom, and at what time it is "true." Consciousness is never the product of truth or reality but rather of culture, society, and history.

Althusser and Gramsci were the theorists who offered a way of accommodating both structuralism (and, incidentally, Freudianism) and the history of capitalism in the twentieth century with Marxism. For Althusser, ideology is not a static set of ideas imposed upon the subordinate by the dominant classes but rather a dynamic process constantly reproduced and reconstituted in practice—that is, in the ways that people think, act, and understand themselves and their relationship to society.[3] He rejects the old idea that the economic base of society determines the entire cultural superstructure. He replaces this base/superstructure model with his theory of overdetermination, which not only allows the superstructure to influence the base but also produces a model of the relationship between ideology and culture that is not determined solely by economic relations. At the heart of this theory is the notion of ideological state apparatuses (ISAs), by which he means social institutions such as the family, the educational system, language, the media, the political system, and so on. These institutions produce in people the tendency to behave and think in socially acceptable ways (as opposed to repressive state apparatuses such as the police force or the law, which coerce people into behaving according to the social norms). The social norms, or that which is socially acceptable, are of course neither neutral nor objective; they have developed in the interests of those with social power, and they work to maintain their sites of power by naturalizing them into the commonsense—the only— social positions for power. Social norms are ideologically slanted in favor of a particular class or group of classes but are accepted as natural by other classes, even when the interests of those other classes are directly opposed by the ideology reproduced by living life according to those norms.

Social norms are realized in the day-to-day workings of the ideological state apparatuses. Each one of these institutions is "relatively autonomous," according to Althusser, and there are no overt connections between it and any of the others—the legal system is not explicitly connected to the school system nor to the media, for example—yet they all perform similar ideological work. They are all patriarchal; they are all concerned with the getting and keeping of wealth and possessions; and they all endorse individualism and competition between individuals. But the most significant feature of ISAs is that they all present themselves as socially neutral, as not favoring one particular class over any other. Each presents itself as a principled institutionalization of equality: the law, the media, and education all claim, loudly and often, to treat all individuals equally and fairly. The fact that the norms used to define equality and fairness are those derived from the interests of the white, male, middle classes is more or less adequately disguised by these claims of principle, though feminists and those working for racial and class harmony may claim that this disguise can be torn off with relative ease.

Althusser's theory of overdetermination explains this congruence between the "relatively autonomous" institutions by looking not to their roots in a common, determining economic base but to an overdetermining network of ideological interrelationships among all of them. The institutions appear autonomous only at the official level of stated policy, though the belief in this "autonomy" is essential for their ideological work. At the unstated level of ideology, however, each institution is related to all the others by an unspoken web of ideological interconnections, so that the operation of any one of them is "overdetermined" by its complex, invisible network of interrelationships with all the others. Thus the educational system, for example, cannot tell a story about the nature of the individual different from those told by the legal system, the political system, the family, and so on.

Ideology is not, then, a static set of ideas through which we view the world but a dynamic social practice, constantly in process, constantly re-producing itself in the ordinary workings of these apparatuses. It also works at the micro-level of the individual. To understand this we need to replace the idea of the individual with that of the subject. The individual is produced by nature, the subject by culture. Theories of the individual concentrate on differences between people and explain these differences as natural. Theories of the subject, on the other hand, concentrate on people's common experiences in a society as being the most productive way of explaining who (we think) we are. Althusser believes that we are all constituted as subjects-in-ideology by the ISAs, that the ideological norms naturalized in their practices constitute not only the sense of the world for us, but also our sense of ourselves, our sense of identity, and our sense of our relations to other people and to society in general. Thus we are each of us constituted as a subject in, and subject to, ideology. The subject, therefore, is a social construction, not a natural one. A biological female can have a masculine subjectivity (that is, she can make sense of the world and of her self and her place in that world through patriarchal ideology). Similarly, a black person can have a white subjectivity and a member of the working classes a middle-class one.

The ideological theory of the subject differs in emphasis, though not fundamentally, from that developed in psychoanalysis by placing greater emphasis on social and historical conditions, particularly those of class. Althusser drew upon Freudian theory to develop his idea of the subject: As Ann Kaplan notes, feminists too have used psychoanalytic theory, though much more sophisticatedly, to theorize the gendered subject. This gendered subject is more rooted in psychological processes, the ideological subject of Althusser in historical and social ones.

But both theories stress the role played by the media and language in this constant construction of the subject, by which we mean the constant reproduction of ideology in people. Althusser uses the words *interpellation* and *hailing* to describe this work of the media. These terms derive from the idea that any language, whether it be verbal, visual, tactile, or what-ever, is part of social relations and that in communicating with someone we are reproducing social relationships.

In communicating with people, our first job is to "hail" them, almost as if hailing a cab. To answer, they have to recognize that it is to them, and not to someone else, that we are talking. This recognition derives from signs, carried in our language, of whom we think they are. We will hail a child differently from an adult, a male differently from a female, someone whose status is lower than ours differently from someone in a higher so-cial position. In responding to our hail, the addressees recognize the so-

cial position our language has constructed, and if their response is cooperative, they adopt this same position. Hailing is the process by which
language identifies and constructs a social position for the addressee. Interpellation is the larger process whereby language constructs social relations for both parties in an act of communication and thus locates them in
the broader map of social relations in general.

Hailing is obviously crucial at the start of a "conversation," though its
ideological work continues throughout. Look, for instance, at the opening
statements of the anchor and reporter on a U.S. network news report in
April 1991:

> *Anchor*: There is growing concern tonight about the possible eco-
> nomic impact that a nationwide railroad strike set for midnight
> tonight poses. The unions and the railroads remain deadlocked.
> Wyatt Andrews brings us up to date on what President Bush and
> Congress may do about it.
>
> *Reporter*: By morning 230,000 rail workers might not be working on
> the railroad and the strike threatens millions of Americans. Just
> as thousands of commuters may find no train leaving the station
> beginning tonight at midnight.

The word *strike* hails us as antiunion, for "striking" is constructed
as a negative action by labor unions that "threatens" the nation. By
ascribing responsibility to the unions, the word hides the fact that
management plays some role, possibly even a greater one, in the dispute. The report opposes the unions not to management but to "the railroads" and thus excludes the unions from them. This exclusion of the
unions from the railroads allows the unspoken management to become
synonymous with them, and ideology continues its work by constructing the railroads not as an industry but as a national resource and
so uses them as a metonym for the nation and, by extension, of "us."
Recognizing ourselves in the national "us" interpellated here, we participate in the work of ideology by adopting the antiunion subject position proposed for us. This subject-as-ideology is developed as the item
progresses:

> *Passenger A*: Gas, miles, time. The highways are going to be packed.
> Not much we can do, though.
>
> *Passenger B*: I'm going to stay home. I've got an office in my home
> and I'm going to just stay there and work.

Reporter: But the commuter inconvenience is nothing compared to the impact on freight trains. Up to half a million industrial jobs may be at stake. Whether it's cars in the heartland or chemicals in Kansas City, the railroads still carry more freight than either trucks or airplanes, meaning that the strike would threaten the heart of industrial America in the heart of this recession.

Railroad Official: If we don't get this strike settled quickly a lot more people are going to be out of work, a lot more product is not going to be shipped and this economy's recovery is going to be set back immensely.

Reporter: Negotiations meanwhile seem to be at bedrock bottom, on wages, on health care, and the number of workers per train. Both sides even late today were on opposite tracks. The unions complain the railroads blocked raises and stonewalled the negotiations for three years. The railroads accuse the unions of protecting legions of workers who essentially do nothing.

Railroad Official: The issue with our union is between who works and who watches. That's the issue of whether we have excess people in the cab who don't have anything to do.

The national "we" is constructed as hardworking producers at the personal level by the passengers and at the industrial level by the reporter. The repeated use of the "heart" metaphor not only makes "America" into a living, breathing body (like the one "we" inhabit), but it constructs the unions as a potentially lethal disease, if not a stiletto-wielding assassin! The railroad official continues to conflate "the railroads" (by which he means "the management") with the national subject of the hard-working producer.

So far, the dispute has been cast solely in terms of the bad effects the unions have upon this national "us," and only in the reporter's next segment do we receive a hint that there are causes of the dispute that may both justify it and implicate management in it. These hints are left floating, so we have no way of assessing the reasonableness of the wage claims, for instance. The generalized terms—"on wages, on health care, on the number of workers per train"—contrast with the concrete realities of 230,000 unionists not working and of the millions of Americans, thousands of commuters, and up to half a million jobs that are threatened. We might like to think about the ideological practice of not allowing the unions to speak for themselves "live," but of putting their case into the words of the reporter-management-"us." Unionists would not, for instance, describe their negotiating opponents as "the railroads," nor would they categorize their arguments as mere "complaints" while according management's the stronger status of "accusations."

The news item concludes by continuing the ideological practice that by now seems so natural and familiar:

> *Reporter*: What exactly happens in the morning? If you are a commuter, check locally. Some Amtrak and commuter trains will be operating and some of the unions say they will strike only freight lines and not passenger trains. In Washington, watch Capitol Hill. Tomorrow President Bush is likely to ask Congress to impose a solution: the move, the unions say, plays right into the railroad's hands. The unions have all along warned the railroads would stall the negotiations and force tonight's strike all in the snug belief that Congress would bail them out.

As Mimi White points out in her chapter, this view of ideology as a process constantly at work, constructing people as subjects in an ideology that always serves the interests of the dominant classes, found powerful theoretical support in Gramsci's theory of hegemony. Originally, *hegemony* referred to the way that one nation could exert ideological and social, rather than military or coercive, power over another. However, cultural theorists tend to use the term to describe the process by which a dominant class wins the willing consent of the subordinate classes to the system that ensures their subordination. This consent must be constantly won and rewon, for people's material social experience constantly reminds them of the disadvantages of subordination and thus poses a constant threat to the dominant class. Like Althusser's theory of ideology, hegemony does not denote a static power relationship but a constant process of struggle in which the big guns belong to the side of those with social power, but in which victory does not necessarily go to the big guns—or, at least, in which that victory is not necessarily total. Indeed, the theory of hegemony foregrounds the notion of ideological struggle much more than does Althusser's ideological theory, which at times tends to imply that the power of ideology and the ISAs to form the subject in ways that suit the interests of the dominant class is almost irresistible. Hegemony, on the other hand, posits a constant contradiction between ideology and the social experience of the subordinate that makes this interface into an inevitable site of ideological struggle. In hegemonic theory, ideology is constantly up against forces of resistance. Consequently it is engaged in a constant struggle not

just to extend its power but to hold on to the territory it has already
colonized.

This definition of culture as a constant site of struggle between those
with and those without power underpins the most interesting current work
in cultural studies. Earlier work in the tradition tended to show how the
dominant ideology reproduced itself invisibly and inevitably in the forms
of popular television.[4] Hall's influential essay "Encoding/Decoding" is often
seen as a turning point in British cultural studies, for it introduces the
idea that television programs do not have a single meaning but are relatively open texts, capable of being read in different ways by different
people.[5] Hall also suggests that there is a necessary correlation between
people's social situations and the meanings that they may generate from a
television program. He thus postulates a possible tension between the
structure of the text, which necessarily bears the dominant ideology, and
the social situations of the viewers, which may position them at odds with
that ideology. Reading or viewing television, then, becomes a process of
negotiation between the viewer and the text. Use of the word *negotiation*
is significant, for it implies both that there is a conflict of interests that
needs to be reconciled in some way and that the process of reading television is one in which the reader is an active maker of meanings from the
text, not a passive recipient of already constructed ones.

Hall developed his theory of the "preferred reading" to account for this
conflict of interests. He postulates three broad reading strategies produced by three generalized, not material, social positions that people may
occupy in relation to the dominant ideology. These are the *dominant*, the
negotiated, and the *oppositional*. The dominant reading is produced by a
viewer situated to agree with and accept the dominant ideology and the
subjectivity that it produces. A negotiated reading is one produced by a
viewer who fits into the dominant ideology in general but who needs to
inflect it locally to take account of his or her social position. This inflection
may contain elements of resistance deriving from the perception of areas
of conflict between the constructions of the dominant ideology and the
viewer's more materially based construction of social experience. And
finally there are readings produced by those whose social situation puts
them into direct opposition with the dominant ideology—these readings
are termed oppositional.

The preferred reading theory proposes that TV programs generally prefer a set of meanings that work to maintain the dominant ideologies but
that these meanings cannot be imposed, only preferred. Readers whose
social situations lead them to reject all or some constructions of the domi-

nant ideology will necessarily bring this social orientation to their readi
of the program.

Such negotiations of meaning occur not only with specific programs but
also with genres, for example that of the action-detective show (for decades common on U.S. television), which I propose to call "muscle drama."
I would include in this genre such hits of the 1970s and 1980s as *Starsky
and Hutch*, *The A-Team*, and *Magnum, P.I.*, as well as more recent vari-
ants, such as *Simon and Simon*, *Hunter*, and *Jake and the Fatman*. A
dominant reader of the genre would find pleasure in it because it reproduces in him/her a subject position that fits easily into the dominant ideology, bolsters that ideology as an adequate way of making sense of the
world, and therefore affirms the subject position as the natural one from
which to view the world. The typical male hero can be seen as literally
embodying patriarchal capitalism. The ideology works both through the
progress and resolution of each week's narrative and through the frame of
that narrative—that is, those elements of the program that are consistent from week to week. They are not part of the conflict to be resolved in
each episode and therefore form the basic, uninspected assumptions, or
common sense, through and in which the dominant ideology naturalizes
itself. The dominant ideology works in a number of overlapping specific
ideologies: masculinity, individualism, competition, all merge "naturally"
into the general (that is, the dominant) ideology of patriarchal capitalism.

This is a masculine genre, dominated by male heroes. Maleness is a fact
of nature, but masculinity is a cultural constraint that gives meaning to
maleness by opposing it to femininity. Shere Hite investigated men's opinions of what makes a man a man. The list of characteristics she generated
began with such qualities as self-assurance, lack of fear, the ability to take
control, autonomy and self-sufficiency, leadership, dependability, and
achievement. These qualities work along two main avenues: self-sufficiency,
which stresses the absence of a need to depend on others; and assertive-
ness, expressed as the ability to lead others and to influence events and
most readily experienced in performance and achievement.[6] Freudian explanations of how masculinity is achieved in childhood point to the boy's
rejection of his desire for his mother because it puts him into a position of
rivalry with his father. He then identifies with his father in order to gain
access to masculine power and authority. The price he pays, however, is
the guilt-producing rejection of his mother and the consequent suppression in himself of the feminine characteristics that threaten male power
and independence. These characteristics are essentially ones of nurturing
and of intimacy. The absence of women from significant roles in most mus-

cle drama represents the suppression and devaluation of feminine characteristics in patriarchal constructions of masculinity.

Like all ideological constructs, masculinity is constantly under threat—it can never rest on its laurels. The threats come internally from its insecure bases in the rejection of the mother (and the guilt that this inspires) and the suppression of the feminine, and externally from social forces, which may vary from the rise of the women's movement to the way that the organization of work denies many men the independence and power that their masculinity requires. Thus masculinity constantly has to be reachieved, rewon. This constant need to reachieve masculinity is one of the underlying reasons for the popularity of the frequent televisual display of male performance. Masculinity forms a link between muscle drama and pornography. For, as Andrew Moye points out, pornography reduces masculinity to performance—in this case, the performance of the penis.[7] In a patriarchy, masculinity must be able to cope with any situation; it becomes less a construction of man than of superman. It is the perpetual gap between the actual male performance and the supermale performance proposed by patriarchy that these programs are striving to close. Similarly, it is the gap between the penis and the phallus that pornography strives to close. The penis is the natural sign of maleness; the phallus is the cultural sign of masculinity—the totality of meanings, rights, and power that a culture ascribes to maleness. Hence these shows, in their role as "masculine definers," are full of phallic symbols, particularly guns as agents of male power (think how rare it is for a female on TV to use a gun successfully, particularly to kill a male). They are also full of machinery, particularly cars, as extensions of the masculine body in powerful, spectacular action.

This male power must be tempered with notions of duty and service; it must be used in the interest of the weak or of the nation. If used for personal gain, it becomes the mark of the villain. So masculine power involves both exerting and submitting to authority. This is one of the reasons why the male team or duo is such a popular formation of the masculine hero, and why this hero formation so commonly works on the side of, but in tension with, an institution of official authority. Another reason is that the male bonding inherent in such a formation allows for an intimacy that excludes the threat of the feminine. Feminine intimacy centers on the relationship itself and produces a dependence on the other that threatens masculine independence—consequently, any woman who attracts a hero has to be rejected at the end of the episode. Male bonding, on the other hand, allows an interpersonal dependency that is goal-centered, not relationship-centered, and thus serves masculine performance instead of threatening it. The hero team also compensates for male insecurity: any inadequacies of one team member are compensated by the strengths of another, so the teams become composite constructions of masculinity. All the traits embodied in one man would make him into an unbelievable superman, and ideology — closely connected to fantasy though it be — has to be grounded in credibility, that is, in a conventional construction of the realistic. If it were not, it would be unable to work on, and be put to work by, the viewers.

I have concentrated on how the ideology of masculinity is actively at work in the muscle drama. It is comparatively easy to see how this merges indistinguishably into the overlapping ideologies of individualism, competition, and a form of "social Darwinism" that proposes that morality is always on the side of eventual winners. These ideologies, in turn, merge into a particular construction of American and Western nationalism — a right-wing version of the nation that sees it as masculine (exerting in the international sphere power over others in the service of the weak or of a higher morality), based on competitive individualism and social Darwinism. Such an ideology serves, at the broader level, to link this genre with the rehabilitation of the Vietnam war that occurred during the 1980s. Heroes like Magnum, T. J. Hooker, one of the Simon brothers, and the whole A-Team developed their masculinity in Vietnam. Their popularity was part of the remasculinization of Reagan's America after its "softness" under Carter and served to underwrite ideologically Reagan's Granada "rescue" and, more recently, Bush's invasions of Panama and Iraq. Ideologically, this genre as it developed in the 1980s worked to ground problematic political acts in the much-less-questioned and therefore more natural-seeming construction of masculinity.

The generic hero team is conventionally constructed to embody, not just the ideologies of masculinity and nation, but also the overlapping ones of race. In *Magnum, P.I.*, for instance, T. C., the driver/pilot and engineering expert, represented masculinity as physical power and its mechanical extensions. His blackness (like that of B. A. in *The A-Team*, who performed a similar ideological role) introduces the racial dimension: physical power may be the basis of masculinity, but because it needs leadership and social control to be acceptable, it therefore ranks low in the hierarchy of masculine traits. It is noticeable how often the hero team contains a nonwhite in a subordinate position, from Ahab and Queequeg in *Moby-Dick*, through the Lone Ranger and Tonto, to the television hero teams of *Ironside*, *The A-Team*, and *Magnum, P.I.* In *Starsky and Hutch*,

Starsky, the dark Jewish one, was the driver; Hutch, the blond, college-educated Aryan, was the leader. Their superior officer may have been black, but, as is often the case, the role of the official superior was narratively subordinated to the hero team. In *Miami Vice* Crockett was blond and white, while his partner Tubbs was a black-looking cocktail of non-white races.

The reader whose social position is one of ease with the dominant ideology, who works *with* the genre, will use its foregrounded ideology to reaffirm his (gender deliberate) ideological frame, through which he views the world and makes sense of both himself and his social experience. In responding to the program's interpellation, he adopts the subject position it constructs for him. Althusser's account of the power of the dominant ideology working through language and texts to construct the reader as a subject in ideology can really only account for Hall's "dominant reading." Gramsci's notion of hegemony, with its emphasis on the dominant ideology's constant struggle to win the consent of the subordinate and to incorporate or defuse oppositional forces, underlies Hall's next two reading strategies—those that produce negotiated and oppositional readings.

A negotiated reading is one that inflects the dominant ideology toward the social experience of a particular viewing group. Thus, boys watching a muscle drama might concentrate on the performance side. Their social situation denies them the ability to exert the power (either physically, because their bodies are still immature, or socially, because of their low hierarchical position in the family or school) that society tells them they should if they are to be "masculine." We know that B. A., the muscular black driver and mechanic in *The A-Team*, was particularly popular with white youths. Presumably they foregrounded his strength, engineering expertise, and low rank in the hero team over his race and therefore made sense of his subordinate position as a way of articulating their subordination in society, not the powerlessness of blacks in a white hegemony. Black youths, however, would have been more likely to use B. A.'s blackness, his strength, and the gold chains he always wore (which Mr. T said were symbols of his people's slavery) to make sense of their constant struggle to assert and extend their own position in society.

Female viewers of the genre will also negotiate it toward their interests. The physical attractiveness of Hunter, Jake, Magnum, or Crockett may be read as an integral part of their protection of the weak. Their rejection of intimacy with any one woman would not be seen as a latent recognition of women's threat to masculinity, nor as a representation of the suppression of the feminine in the masculine psyche and therefore of the subordination of women in a patriarchal society (for the two are structural reflections of each other). It would rather be seen as a means of maintaining their masculine freedom to serve all women and provide them with the security and justice that their material social position may deny them. Masculinity in heroes like these can be read, then, not as the embodiment of masculine oppression in patriarchy, but as the patriarchal agent that rights the wrongs and corrects the deficiencies of the system in practice.

These sorts of negotiated readings are ones produced by ideologically cooperative readers who read "with" the structure of the text and seek to match their social experiences with the ideology-in-the-text. Actually, they produce almost dominant readings, which may lead us to speculate whether the "pure" dominant reading is ever achieved. There is probably no one audience group positioned in perfect ideological centrality. All groups will need to "shift" the text slightly to fit their social positions, in which case all readings become, as Horace Newcomb suggests, negotiated ones.[8] But if this is so, it is still valuable to recognize that negotiated readings can occur on a scale stretching from the ideologically central to the deviant. Thus a macho teenager, at the point of maximum opposition to authority, may read the violence in the genre as justified masculinity that overrides the "weakness" of its use in the service of the weak or of "natural justice." Such a reading may see the failure of the police or official authorities as a criticism of them and of the society they stand for, and in this way may veer toward the oppositional because it plays down the contextual ideologies within which that of masculinity operates and from which it acquires its social and moral acceptability.

Readings at this end of the scale stop being negotiated and become oppositional when they go "against" the text to deconstruct the dominant ideology. Thus, a feminist could read the genre as a blatant display of patriarchal chauvinism and how it sells itself to society. This reading would produce, not pleasure (except the wry pleasure of recognizing that patriarchy is up to its tricks yet again), but annoyance. That annoyance could be used to incite political action, either in the form of consciousness-raising or more directly. Similarly, a black activist could find the subordinate positions of T. C., B. A., and Tubbs in the hero formation a perfect example of white hegemony at work and a spur to further oppositional practice.

We have already traced the dominant or preferred reading of the TV news report on the railroad dispute. An oppositional reading, possibly by an Amtrak blue-collar worker, might read in the mediated versions of the union case what has been repressed or distorted and would thus make sense of the story not as an account of the dispute but as a representation of "what we unionists are always up against in this society."

A negotiated reading, however, might pick up the same hints but would use them to mean something like, "I bet there's more to this than they're telling us here: Amtrak management is not exactly the most efficient or progressive in the country." Although such a reading does not accept the preferred reading of the story, neither does it challenge the dominant ideology that such a reading prefers. It negotiates a position for this specific occasion.

The typical reading of television is probably, as Newcomb argues, a negotiated one.[9] This is an underlying assumption of the cultural studies approach. For if our society is seen not as homogeneous but as a structure of different interest groups, and if television is to appeal to a large number of people in our society, then it follows that the television audience must not be seen as a homogeneous mass but as a mix of social groups, each in a different relationship to the dominant ideology. However complex and difficult it might be to describe these relationships, they can always be placed on a scale that ranges from *acceptance of* to *opposition to* the dominant ideology. The television text can only be popular if it is open enough to admit a range of negotiated readings through which various social groups can find meaningful articulations of their own relationships to the dominant ideology. Any television text must, then, be polysemic to a certain extent, for the structured heterogeneity of the audience requires a correspondingly structured heterogeneity of meanings in the text. The hero team is a significant ideological formation here, as it provides for a greater "openness" than the single hero. Its greater variety of opportunities for identification enables various social groups to negotiate appropriate points of entry into the dominant ideology.

This polysemy is never free but is constrained and structured, for it exists always against the dominant ideology, which works to close off alternate or resisting meanings and to homogenize the preferred ones around its own interests. Mikhail Bakhtin's theory of heteroglossia is an attempt to explain this process.[10] Bakhtin analyzes the difference between heteroglossic or multitongued texts, which contain the many voices of subordinated groups, and monoglossic or more homogeneous ones, which carry only the voice of the dominant. He uses the metaphor of a spinning wheel to illustrate the difference: at the center is a relatively homogeneous hub of domination and control, and around the circumference are multiple, heterogeneous points of subordination that form potential points of resistance. Centripetal forces, those tending toward the center, are ones of hegemony and domination working through homogenization, whereas centrifugal forces, those tending toward the circumference, are ones of resistance and difference working through heterogeneity. The two are always opposed to each other, and television texts are held in an unstable tension between them.

An earlier version of this theory, and one that has been very influential in British cultural studies, is Valentin N. Volosinov's account of "multi-accentuality."[11] This theory proposes that the prime determinant of the meaning of a sign is the social context of its use and not, as structuralism argues, its relationship to other signs in the structure of a sign system.

In capitalism the social context of a sign's use is typically one of social struggle, so the meaning of the sign becomes part of that social struggle. The same word can be spoken in different "accents" according to who is using it, and thus to "accent" a word is to inflect its meaning with the social interests of a particular group against those of others. When the word *nigger* is accented by contemporary black rap artists in their music videos, to take an example, they are giving it *their* meanings of blackness, racial subordination, and prejudice against the historically dominant white ones. In doing so, they are exploiting the multiaccentuality of the sign "nigger" and are thus politically engaging in racial relations. (They are also, incidentally, engaging in another struggle for meaning, this time within race relations but across class relations, with those who prefer to be called "African American" and those who prefer to be called "black.") The struggle over the sign "nigger"—and thus over the racial identities and politics of those categorized by it—is a more confrontational version of the racial struggle engaged in by the previous generation over the multiaccentuality of "black" in the "black is beautiful" movement. It is not just a struggle over the meanings of a word but over who has the power to control those meanings. This is important, for the power to control the meaning of social experience is a crucial part of controlling the social relations, identities, and behaviors of those (both blacks and whites) involved in that experience. The semiotic struggle does not reflect the social struggle but is part of it.

The interests of the socially dominant are served by "uniaccentuality," that is, by limiting the meanings of a sign to those that it bears when spoken with the dominant accent, thereby taking it out of the realm of struggle. The TV news report analyzed above, for instance, spoke the word *railroads* with a managerial accent and thus excluded the different and contradictory meanings that a union accent would have given it. Again, social and ideological domination is seen to work through homogeneity and the construction of social difference within this unity. So it is in the interests of dominant whites to construct both the blue-collar classes and other races as different from and subordinate to them and to contain this difference within a homogeneous ideology. The interests of subordinate groups, however, are served by exploiting multiaccentuality or heteroglossia, for this enables them to "speak" their difference from the dominant position in *their* accents and to engage in the struggle to make sense of social difference in their own terms rather than submitting to those proposed and preferred by the dominant group.

An important body of cultural studies work has derived from the recognition of the heteroglossia or multiaccentuality of TV texts and the heterogeneity of audiences, a strand that Robert Allen discusses in his chapter as "ethnographic audience research." Such scholars as David Morley, John Corner and his colleagues, Angela McRobbie, and Robert Hodge and David Tripp have set out to discover how actual audience groups actively use television as part of their own cultures—that is, use it to make meanings that are useful to them in making sense of their own social experiences and therefore of themselves.[12] These scholars are in opposition to the other main strand of British (and European) study of culture, which is centered around the journal *Screen* and has come to be known as Screen Theory. Screen Theory draws on a combination of structuralism and semiotics with psychoanalysis and Marxism to argue the power of the text over the viewing subject and to analyze, with great theoretical sophistication, the textual strategies that operate to position the viewing subject within dominant ideology. David Morley has clearly elaborated the theoretical and methodological differences between the two schools.[13]

Morley tested Hall's preferred reading theory in the field. He took a television program that he and Charlotte Brunsdon had previously subjected to detailed cultural analysis, showed it to groups of people, and then held discussions on their reactions to the program and its meanings for them.[14] He turned to groups rather than individuals because he was interested in the shared, and therefore social, dimensions of reading. The groups were defined largely by occupation—bank managers, apprentices, students, trade unionists, and so on—because occupation is a prime definer of social class, and class was, in Hall's theory, the prime producer of social difference and therefore of different readings. (A few of Morley's groups, however, were defined by gender or race—black unemployed women, for example.) What Morley found was that the preferred reading theory overemphasized the role of class in the production of semiotic differences and underestimated the variety of readings that could be made. Thus the readings showed some interesting and unexpected cross-class similarities: bank managers and apprentices, for example, produced broadly similar readings despite their class differences; so, too, did some university students and shop stewards. We could explain these apparent anomalies by suggesting that the apprentices and bank managers were similarly constructed as subjects of a capitalist ideology, in that both were inserting themselves into the dominant system (albeit at different points) and thus had a shared interest in its survival and success. Some university students (not all, by any means) and trade union officials, however, were in institutions that provided them with ways of criticizing the dominant system and they thus produced more oppositional readings.

Another interesting example of class difference emerged as one of the findings in a recent study by John Corner, Kay Richardson, and Natalie Fenton on the ways in which different audiences read different British TV programs dealing with nuclear power in the wake of the Chernobyl explosion in the Soviet Union.[15] The most "mainstream" of the programs contained reassurances by white-coated scientists as to the high safety standards of British installations. Middle-class and educated viewers tended to accept these assurances at face value: some working-class viewers, however, were much more skeptical and produced readings along the lines of, "Well, they would say that, wouldn't they?" This skepticism is a product of the constant experience of class difference in their workaday lives and was brought from there to contradict a TV text with a strongly preferred meaning. It was a social discourse in negotiation with a televisual one.

Morley's study led him to develop a theory of discourse rather than one of class to account for the different readings of television. A discourse is a socially produced way of talking or thinking about a topic. It is defined by reference to the area of social experience that it makes sense of, to the social location from which that sense is made, and to the linguistic or signifying system by which that sense is both made and circulated. When the media report, as they typically do, that management "offers" but trade unions "demand," they are using the mass media discourse of industrial relations, which is located in a middle-class position. They could equally well report (but never do) that the unions "offered" to work for an extra 5 percent, but management "demanded" that they work for 2 percent. The consistent ascription of the generous "offer" and the grasping "demand" to management and unions, respectively, is clear evidence of the social location of this particular discourse. A discourse, then, is a socially located way of making sense of an important area of social experience.

A television text is, therefore, a discourse (or a number of discourses if it contains contradictions), and the reader's consciousness is similarly made up of a number of discourses through which s/he makes sense of his/her social experience. Morley defines reading a television text as that moment when the discourses of the reader meet the discourses of the text. Reading becomes a negotiation between the social sense inscribed in the program and the meanings of social experience made by its wide variety of viewers; this negotiation is a discursive one.

But not all TV audiences read all the discourses in a TV text. For instance, a study in which I was recently involved showed how homeless men watched television in their church shelter.[16] They rarely watched broadcast television because the norms of domestic life and of work and leisure that were structured into the regular broadcast schedule were irrelevant to them; they expressed their opposition to the dominant ideology by avoiding expressions of it. Instead, they preferred to watch movies —almost always violent ones—on the VCR. In viewing these, they opposed the dominant ideology, or preferred reading, by avoiding those parts of the text that worked most actively to promote it and by paying greater attention to those parts that opposed it. So, while watching *Die Hard*, they cheered enthusiastically when the villains killed the company's chief executive officer and when they destroyed a police armored vehicle and its occupants, but they switched off the tape before the end, when the hero and the police force restored law and order and reconfirmed the dominant ideology.

A later study by David Morley found that the way in which TV was watched was as significant as the readings made from it.[17] In the lower-class households he studied, Morley found that the process of watching TV was a key site for the struggles of gender politics. The male of the household tended to dominate the selection of viewing and, in particular, to monopolize the remote control. He employed masculine values in this selection, so that programs appealing to masculine tastes (ones that showed "real life" outside the home—news, documentaries, sports, or the masculine muscle drama) were seen as "better" than ones appealing to feminine tastes (those concerned with people and relationships, such as soap operas). He also attempted to control the conditions of viewing and would shush his wife or children if they distracted him with noise or conversation.

Cultural studies sees the television experience (that is, the entity constituted by the text and the activity of viewing it) as a constant dynamic movement between similarity and difference. The dimension of similarity is that of the dominant ideology that is structured into the forms of the program and is common to all the viewers for whom that program is popular. The dimension of difference, however, accounts for the wide variety of groups who must be reached if the program is to be popular with a large audience. These groups will be positioned to the dominant ideology in different ways, and these ways will be paralleled in the different readings they make of the program and the different ways in which they watch it. The play between similarity and difference is one way of experiencing the struggle between hegemony and resistance.

This emphasis on the reader and the struggle for meaning necessarily reduces the prime position granted to the text by the cultural theorists of the 1970s. The text can no longer be seen as a self-sufficient entity that bears either the dominant ideology or its own meaning and exerts a similar influence on all its readers. Rather, it is seen as a potential of meanings that can be activated in a number of ways. Of course, this potential is proscribed and is thus neither infinite nor free; the text does not determine its meaning so much as delimit the arena of the struggle for that meaning by marking the terrain within which its variety of readings can be negotiated. This discursive negotiation that we now understand reading to be also means that the boundaries of the text are fluid and unstable. Raymond Williams suggested in the early seventies that television was not a discrete series of programs or texts but a "flow" in which programs, commercials, newsbreaks, and promotional spots all merged into a continuous cultural experience. More recently, John Hartley has suggested that television is a "leaky" medium whose meanings constantly spill over into other areas of life.[18]

Angela McRobbie has also explored the permeability of the boundary between television and other forms of cultural experience. Her study of girls and dance shows that girls derive similar pleasures and meanings from dancing in discos and from viewing films and television programs such as *Flashdance* or *Fame*.[19] On one level of reading, the narrative form and pleasure of *Flashdance* clearly work hegemonically—the female factory worker uses her dancing skills to win a place in a ballet company and marry the boss's son. In the process she displays her body for patriarchal pleasure; indeed, her beautiful body is crucial to her successful move up the social hierarchy (from breakdancing to ballet and marrying into management). Women, so the hegemonic reading would go, are rewarded for their ability to use their beauty and talents to give pleasure to men. But McRobbie has shown that this is not the only reading. She has found among teenage girls a set of meanings for dance and female sexuality that contest and struggle against the patriarchal hegemony. For these girls, dance is a form of autoeroticism, a pleasure in their own bodies and sexuality that gives them an identity not dependent upon the male gaze of approval. *Their* discourse of dance gives a coherent meaning to dancing in discos or to watching filmic and televisual representations of dance that asserts their subcultural identity and difference from the rest of society. This meaning is one that they have made out of the cultural forms provided for them by patriarchy.

McRobbie's study preceded the movie and TV series *Dirty Dancing* by some years, but her findings and analysis still apply if one major difference is taken into account. *Dirty Dancing* reverses the gender politics of the class relations between hero and heroine. In this scenario, the hero is of a lower class than the heroine, but it is still the socially subordinate person who uses the control of his body in dance not only to assert his own social worth but also to overcome his subordination. The upper-middle-class heroine finds, through dancing and through her relations with the working-class hero, an authenticity of identity and experience that is lacking in the masquerade necessary for her to conform to the version of femininity proposed by a patriarchal, bourgeois society. Exploring the strategies by which subordinate subcultures make their own meanings in resistance to the dominant is currently one of the most productive strands of cultural studies.

Madonna, who has been a major phenomenon of popular culture for almost a decade, can provide us with a good case study. Her success has arguably been due largely to television and to her music videos; most critics have nothing good to say about her music, but they have a lot to say about her image—"the Madonna look." The simple view of her success would attribute it to her skill in manipulating her sexuality to make as much money as possible, largely from one of the most powerless and exploitable sections of the community—young girls.

But such an account is inadequate (though not necessarily inaccurate as far as it goes) because it assumes that Madonna fans are, in Stuart Hall's phrase, "cultural dupes," able to be manipulated at will and against their own interests by the moguls of the culture industry.[20] Such a manipulation is not only economic but also ideological, because the economic system requires the ideology of patriarchal capitalism to underpin and naturalize it; economics and ideology can never be separated. There is plenty of evidence to support this view, too. Madonna's videos exploit the sexuality of her face and body and frequently show her in postures of submission ("Burning Up") or subordination to men. As Ann Kaplan points out in her chapter, Madonna's physical similarity to Marilyn Monroe is stressed (particularly in the video of "Material Girl"), an intertextual reference to another star commonly thought to owe her success to her ability to embody masculine fantasies. All this would suggest that she is teaching her young female fans to see themselves as men would see them—that is, she is hailing them as feminine subjects within patriarchy and as such is an agent of patriarchal hegemony.

But if her fans are not "cultural dupes"—if, rather, they actively choose to watch, listen to, and imitate Madonna rather than anyone else—there must be some gaps or spaces in her image that escape ideological control and allow her audiences to make meanings that connect with *their* social experience. For many of her audiences, this social experience is one of powerlessness and subordination, and if Madonna as a site of meaning is not to naturalize this, she must offer opportunities for resisting it. Her image becomes, then, not an ideological role model for young girls in patriarchy, but a site of semiotic struggle between the forces of patriarchal control and feminine resistance, of capitalism and the subordinate, of the adult and the young.

Cultural studies, in its current state of development, offers two overlapping methodological strategies that can usefully be combined to help us understand how this cultural struggle operates. One derives from ethnography and encourages us to study the meanings that the fans of Madonna actually *do* (or appear to) make of her. This involves listening to them, reading the letters they write to fan magazines, or observing their behavior at home or in public. The fans' words or behavior are not, of course, empirical facts that speak for themselves; they are, rather, texts that need "reading" theoretically in just the same way as the "texts of Madonna" do.

The other strategy derives from semiotic and structuralist textual analysis. This strategy involves a close reading of the signifiers of the text—that is, its physical presence—but recognizes that the signifieds exist not in the text itself but extratextually, in the myths, countermyths, and ideologies of their culture.[21] It recognizes that the distribution of power in society is paralleled by the distribution of meanings in texts, and that struggles for social power are paralleled by semiotic struggles for meanings. Every text and every reading has a social and therefore a political dimension, which is to be found partly in the structure of the text itself and partly in the relation of the reading subject to that text.

It follows that the theory informing any analysis also has a social dimension, which is a necessary part of the "meanings" that analysis reveals. Meanings, therefore, are relative and change according to historical and social conditions. What is constant is the ways in which texts relate to the social system. A cultural analysis, then, will reveal both the way in which the dominant ideology is structured into the text and into the reading subject and those textual features that enable negotiated, resisting, or oppositional readings to be made. Cultural analysis reaches a satisfactory conclusion when the ethnographic studies of the historically and socially located meanings that *are* made are related to the semiotic analysis of the text. Semiotics relates the structure of the text to the social system to explore how the economic and ideological system is reproduced in the text but also how the polysemy of the text exceeds this reproduction. Ethnographic studies can show us how this semiotic excess is exploited by specific audiences in specific social conditions as they struggle to make their meanings in relationship to those that work to reproduce the patriarchal capitalist system encompassing both the text and its readers.

Thus Lucy, then a fourteen-year-old Australian fan, said of an early Madonna poster: "She's tarty and seductive . . . but it looks alright when she does it, you know, what I mean, if anyone else did it it would look right tarty, a right tart you know, but with her it's OK, it's acceptable. . . . With anyone else it would be absolutely outrageous, it sounds silly, but it's OK with her, you know what I mean."[22] We can note a number of points here. Lucy could find only patriarchal words to describe Madonna's sexuality —"tarty" and "seductive"—but she struggled against the patriarchy inscribed in them. At the same time she struggled against the patriarchy inscribed in her own subjectivity. The opposition between "acceptable" and "absolutely outrageous" refers not only to representations of female sexuality but is also an externalization of the tension felt by adolescent girls trying to come to terms with the contradictions between a positive feminine view of their sexuality and the alien patriarchal one that appears to be the only one offered by the available linguistic and symbolic systems. Madonna's "tarty" sexuality is "acceptable"—but to whom? Certainly to her young female fans who are experiencing the problems of establishing a satisfactory sexual identity within an opposing ideology: at the moment when girls become aware of their potential as women, patriarchy rushes in to assert its control over their identities and social relations. At this moment, Madonna intervenes, for, as Judith Williamson points out, she "retains all the bravado and exhibitionism that most girls start off with, or feel inside, until the onset of 'womanhood' knocks it out of them."[23]

Further evidence to support the empowerment that Madonna can offer to girls comes from the reactions to her of some boys. Matthew, aged fifteen and not a particular fan of Madonna, commented that he wouldn't like to be married to her "because she'd give any guy a hard time." Matthew is not untypical in his opinion, for a 1990 poll showed that, when asked if they would like to sleep with Madonna, 60 percent of the boys questioned declined. Not surprisingly, a powerful female in control of her own sexuality appeals more strongly to girls than to boys. As we shall see later, Madonna often denies or mocks patriarchy's conventions for representing women. This might well be why, according to *Time*, many boys find her sexiness difficult to handle and "suspect that they are being kidded."[24] Lucy and Matthew both recognize, in different ways and from different social positions, that Madonna's sexuality can offer a challenge or a threat to dominant definitions of femininity and masculinity.

"Madonna's Best Friend," writing to the music magazine *Countdown*, also recognized Madonna's resistance to patriarchy:

> I'm writing to complain about all the people who write in and say what a tart and a slut Madonna is because she talks openly about sex and she shows her belly button and she's not ashamed to say she thinks she's pretty. Well I admire her and I think she has a lot of courage just to be herself. All you girls out there! Do you think you have nice eyes or pretty hair or a nice figure? Do you ever talk about boys or sex with friends? Do you wear a bikini? Well according to you, you're a slut and a tart!! So have you judged Madonna fairly? —Madonna's Best Friend, Wahroonga, New South Wales[25]

This praise for Madonna's "courage just to be herself" is further evidence of the difficulty girls feel in finding a sexual identity that appears to be formed in their interests rather than in those of the dominant male. Madonna recognizes—some might say overemphasizes—the importance of sexual identity in determining the sort of social relations we enter into and thus the social experience we undergo:

> People's sexuality and the way they relate to the world is very important. . . . It's so much more than just fornication. Your sexual identity is so important. The more you pay attention to it, the more you realize that just about everything in the world is centered around sexual attraction and sexual power. You also become aware of people who are not in touch with their own, or have the wrong idea about it or abuse it.[26]

If some girls feel that patriarchy promotes the "wrong idea" of their sexuality and leads them to "abuse it," then Madonna's invitation to them to get "in touch with their own" and to construct a gender identity (and the social relations that go with it) in their own interests is a politically positive one. Her fans are aware that she does indeed offer them this invitation: "She's sexy but she doesn't need men. . . . She's kind of there all by herself"; or "She gives us ideas. It's really women's lib, not being afraid of what guys think."[27]

This sense of their own identity is never, of course, constructed freely by the girls, for it can be achieved only by struggling against the identity proposed by patriarchy. This struggle, this fighting back, can be enjoyable, as evidenced by a student fan in an essay:

> There is also a sense of pleasure, at least for me and perhaps a large number of other women, in Madonna's defiant look or gaze. In "Lucky Star" at one point in the dance sequence Madonna dances side on to the camera, looking provocative. For an instant we glimpse her tongue: the expectation is that she is about to lick her lips in a sexual invitation. The expectation is denied and Madonna appears to tuck her tongue back into her cheek. This, it seems, is how most of her dancing and grovelling in front of the camera is meant to be taken. She is setting up the sexual idolization of women. For a woman who has experienced this victimization, this setup is most enjoyable and pleasurable, while the male position of voyeur is displaced into uncertainty.[28]

But, like all pop stars, Madonna has her "haters" as well as her fans: "When I sit down on a Saturday and Sunday night I always hear the word Madonna and it makes me sick, all she's worried about is her bloody looks. She must spend hours putting on that stuff and why does she always show her belly button? We all know she's got one. My whole family thinks she's pathetic and that she loves herself. —Paul Young's sexy sneakers."[29] Here again, the "hate" centers on her sexuality and her painting and displaying herself to arouse the baser side of man—expressed by detractors as her presenting herself in whorelike terms. But the sting comes in the last sentence, when the writer recognizes Madonna's apparent enjoyment of her own sexuality, which he (the letter is clearly from a masculine subject, if not an actual male) ascribes to egocentricity and thus condemns.

Madonna's love of herself, however, is not seen as selfish and egocentric by girls; rather, it is the root of her appeal, and its significance becomes clear in the context of the way they are addressed by the rest of the media. McRobbie has shown how the "teenage press" typically constructs a girl's body, and therefore her sexuality, as a series of problems: breasts the wrong size or shape, spotty skin, lifeless hair, fatty thighs, problem periods. The list is endless, of course, and the advertisers, the ones who really benefit from these magazines, always have a product that promises—at a price—to solve the problem.

Madonna is much loved or much hated, a not-untypical position for woman to occupy in patriarchy, whose inability to understand women in their own terms is evidenced by the way it polarizes femininity into the opposing concepts of Virgin-Angel and Whore-Devil.

Madonna consciously and parodically exploits these contradictions: "When I was tiny," she recalls, "my grandmother used to beg me not to go with men, to love Jesus and be a good girl. I grew up with two images of women: the virgin and the whore. It was a little scary." She consistently refers to these contradictory meanings of women in patriarchy. Her video of "Like a Virgin" alternates the white dress of Madonna the bride with the black, slinky garb of Madonna the singer; the name Madonna (the virgin mother) is borne by a sexually active female; the crucifixes adopted from nuns' habits are worn on a barely concealed bosom or in a sexually gyrating navel. "Growing up I thought nuns were beautiful. . . . They never wore any make-up and they just had these really serene faces. Nuns are sexy."[30]

But the effect of working these opposite meanings into her texts is not just to call attention to their role in male hegemony: woman may either be worshiped and adored by man or used and despised by him, but she has meaning only from a masculine subject position. Rather, Madonna calls into question the validity of these binary oppositions as a way of conceptualizing woman. Her use of religious iconography is neither religious nor sacrilegious. She intends to free it from this ideological opposition and to enjoy it, use it, for the meanings and pleasure it has for *her* and not for those of the dominant ideology and its simplistic binary thinking:

> I have always carried around a few rosaries with me. One day I decided to wear [one] as a necklace. Everything I do is sort of tongue in cheek. It's a strange blend—a beautiful sort of symbolism, the idea of someone suffering, which is what Jesus Christ on a crucifix stands for, and then not taking it seriously. Seeing it as an icon with no religiousness attached. It isn't sacrilegious for me.[31]

The crucifix is neither religious nor sacrilegious, but beautiful: "When I went to Catholic schools I thought the huge crucifixes nuns wore were really beautiful." In the same way, her adolescent fans find in Madonna meanings of femininity that have broken free from the ideological binary opposition of virgin/whore. They find in her image positive feminine-centered representations of sexuality that are expressed in their constant references to her independence, her being herself. This apparently independent, self-defining sexuality is only as significant as it is because it is working within and against a patriarchal ideology.

As Ann Kaplan argues in her chapter, Madonna's image is based in part on that of Marilyn Monroe, the great sex symbol of an earlier generation. But the differences between the two "blond bombshells" are more instructive than the similarities. In the video "Material Girl," Madonna goes through a dance routine with tuxedo-clad young men in a parody of Monroe's number "Diamonds Are a Girl's Best Friend" from *Gentlemen Prefer Blondes*. During the number, she collects jewelry from the men as she sings the refrain, "Cause we're living in a material world, and I am a material girl." But despite her whorelike gathering of riches from men and her singing that only boys with money have any chance with her (which is close to Monroe's performance in "Diamonds Are a Girl's Best Friend"), she toys with the boys, showing that their jewelry has bought them no power over her, but instead that extracting it is an expression of her power over them. This quite contradicts Monroe's performance. Madonna says about her image's more general reference: "I don't see myself as Marilyn Monroe, I'm almost playing with her image, turning it around. I don't claim to know her and can barely believe most of what's written about her. The impression I get is, she didn't know her own strength and didn't know how to nurture it."[32] Madonna clearly does know where her own strength lies and how to use it. Her accumulation of material goodies is not mere capitalist greed but a way of exerting power over men.

But even the materialist reading of the video is contradicted. The stage performance is embedded in a mininarrative in which she rejects a rich suitor and accepts a poor one. The conclusion of the video shows her driving off with him in an old workman's truck, in which they make love during a rainstorm. The material girl has fallen for the nonmaterial values of love after all. The undermining of the song by the mininarrative may not seem to offer much of a resistance; after all, the main narrative is a conventional romance in which the poor, sensitive man is finally preferred to the apparently more attractive rich one. The "true love" that triumphs is as much a part of patriarchal capitalism as the materialism it defeats. But this contradiction does not work alone—it is supported by parody, by puns, and by Madonna's awareness of *how* she is making an image, not just of *what* her image is.

Some of the parody is subtle and hard to tie down for textual analysis, but some, such as the references to Marilyn Monroe and the musicals she often starred in, is more obvious. The subtler parody lies in the knowing way in which Madonna uses the camera, mocking the conventional representations of female sexuality at the same time she conforms to them. Even *Playboy* recognizes her self-parody: "The voice and the body are her bona fides, but Madonna's secret may be her satirical bite. She knows a lot of this image stuff is bullshit: she knows that *you* know. So long as we're all in on the act together, let's enjoy it."[33] One of her former lovers supports this: "Her image is that of a tart, but I believe it's all contrived. She only pretends to be a gold digger. Remember, I have seen the other side of Madonna."[34]

Madonna knows she is putting on a performance. The fact that this knowingness is part of the performance enables the viewer to respond to a different interpellation from that proposed by the dominant ideology and thus to occupy a resisting subject position. The sensitive man watching her material girl performance knows as she does—as we might also—that this is only a performance. Those who take the performance at face value, who miss its self-parody, are hailed either as ideological subjects in patriarchy or else they reject the hailing, deny the pleasure, and refuse the communication:

> The *National Enquirer*, a weekly magazine devoted to prurient gossip, quotes two academic psychiatrists denouncing her for advocating teenage promiscuity, promoting a lust for money and materialism, and contributing to the deterioration of the family. Feminists accuse her of revisionism, of resurrecting the manipulative female who survives by coquetry and artifice. "Tell Gloria [Steinem] and the gang," she retorts, "to lighten up, get a sense of humour. And look at my video that goes with Material Girl. The guy who gets me in the end is the sensitive one with no money."[35]

Madonna consistently parodies conventional representations of women, and parody can be an effective device for interrogating the dominant ideology. It takes the defining features of its object, exaggerates and mocks them, and thus mocks those who "fall" for its ideological effect. But Madonna's parody goes further than this: she parodies, not just the stereotypes, but the way in which they are made. She represents herself as one who is in control of her own image and of the process of making it. This, at the reading end of the semiotic process, allows the reader similar control over her own meanings. Madonna's excess of jewelry, of makeup, of trashy style, offer similar scope to the reader. Excessiveness invites the reader to question ideology; too much lipstick interrogates the tastefully made-up mouth, too much jewelry questions the role of female decorations in patriarchy. Excess overspills ideological control and offers scope for resistance. Thus Madonna's excessively sexual pouting and overdone lipstick can be read to mean that she looks like that not because patriarchy determines that she should but because she knowingly chooses to. She wears religious icons (and uses a religious name) not to support or attack Christianity's role in patriarchy (and capitalism) but because she chooses to see them as beautiful, sexy ornaments. She constantly takes items of urban living, prizes them free from their original social, and therefore signifying, context, and combines them in new ways and in a new context that denies their original meaning. Thus the crucifix is torn from its religious context and lacy gloves from their context of bourgeois respectability—or, conversely, of the brothel. By wearing underwear as outerwear and taking it out of the boudoir and into the street (or even into church), she reconfigures it. With her, dyed blond hair with the dark roots deliberately displayed is no longer the sign of the tarty slut, and the garter belt and stockings no longer signify soft porn or male kinkiness.

This wrenching of the products of capitalism from their original context and recycling them into a new style is, as Iain Chambers has pointed out, a typical practice of urban popular culture.[36] The products are purified into signifiers; their ideological signifieds are dumped and left behind in their original context. These freed signifiers do not necessarily mean *something*, they do not necessarily acquire new signifieds. Rather, the act of freeing them from their ideological context signifies their users' freedom from that context. It signifies the power (however hard the struggle to attain it) of the subordinate to exert some control in the cultural process of making meanings.

Madonna's videos constantly refer to the production of the image, and they make her control over its production part of the image itself. This emphasis on the making of the image allows, or even invites, an equivalent control by the reader over its reception. It enables girls to see that the meanings of feminine sexuality *can* be in their control, *can* be made in their interests, and that their subjectivities are not necessarily totally determined by the dominant patriarchy.

The constant puns in Madonna lyrics work in a similar way. Puns arise when one word occurs in two discourses—in the case of "Material Girl," those of economics and sexuality: one signifier has simultaneous but different signifieds according to its discourse. The most obvious puns are "give me proper credit," "raise my interest," "experience has made me rich." Less obvious ones are "the boy with the cold hard cash" or "only boys that save their pennies make my rainy day" ("make" has only vestigial sexual meanings, and the homonym between "pennies" and "penis" is only faint). The puns perform typical ideological work by equating economic with sexual success, a common strategy of popular culture in patriarchal capitalism. But puns demand active readers and can never fully control the meanings that are provoked by the yoking of disparate discourses. These puns can expose and thus reject, or at least resist, the economic and sexual subordination of women and the way that each is conventionally used to naturalize the other. The first and last verses of the song are:

> Some boys kiss me some boys hug me
> I think they're OK
> If they don't give me proper credit
> I just walk away

> Boys may come and boys may go
> And that's all right you see
> Experience has made me rich
> And now they're after me.[37]

The puns here can be used, not to naturalize the dual subordination of woman, but to assert woman's ability to achieve sexual-economic independence. If a body is all that patriarchy allows a woman to be, then at least she can use it in *her* interests, not in men's.

The pun always resists final ideological closure: the potential meanings provoked by the collision of different discourses is always greater than that proposed by the dominant ideology. Thus "Boy Toy," the name that Madonna has given to her range of products and that the media apply to her, can be read as *Playboy* does when it calls her the "world's number one Boy Toy" or "the compleat Boy Toy."[38] In this reading, Madonna is the toy for boys, but the pun can also mean that the boy is her toy—as she toys with the boys in "Material Girl."

Puns are also at work in the word "material," which is located in the discourse of economic capitalism but which is often used to criticize that discourse either from a religious viewpoint or from one of a "finer sensibility." In rejecting the materialism of the song, Madonna may be read as proposing the values of a finer sensitivity and a more spiritual love, either secular-erotic or religious-erotic. Madonna's combining of secular and religious love makes explicit a powerful undercurrent of patriarchal Christianity in general—and Catholicism in particular—that traditionally has tried to mobilize man's lustful love for Mary Magdalene, displace it onto

Mary the Virgin, and spiritualize it in the process. With Madonna, however, the dualism of the love is denied; it does not fit an either/or dichotomy in which one sort of love is morally superior to the other. By denying the opposition and the moral hierarchy inscribed in it, she rejects the traditional patriarchal Christian evaluation of love and allows sexual or sentimental love to appear on the same level as religious love—certainly not as inferior to it. Her use of the cross as a beautiful ornament for the female body and her characterization of nuns as sexy are all part of her critical interrogation of a patriarchal Christian tradition that makes sense of love by means of a moralistic opposition between the spirituality of the virgin and the lust of the whore. Similarly, the video of "Like a Virgin" refuses to allow the viewer a moral choice between the white-robed, virginal Madonna bride and the black-clad, sexy Madonna singer. As she says, referring to the video: "Passion and sexuality and religion all bleed into each other for me. I think you can be a very sexual person and also a very religious and spiritual person. . . . I'm a very sexual, very spiritual person. What's the problem?"[39]

In "Like a Prayer" this spirituality and passion are brought together in a way so explicit as to have caused Pepsi to withdraw their TV commercial based on the video. The video consists of a complex montage that juxtaposes images of Madonna in her underwear in a black church, kissing the icon of a black saint and bringing him to life, with a narrative in which she secures the release of a young black man jailed for a crime he did not commit. Although there may be no preferred meaning to the video, its use of provocative images organized around the themes of sexuality, religion, race, gender, and justice offended many of the dominant groups in society. But whereas mainstream religious groups condemned the video as blasphemous, two students of mine could find no evidence of black churches that were offended.[40]

Madonna's ability to offend the socially dominant while appealing to the subordinate reached its peak (so far at least) at the end of 1990 with the release of her video "Justify My Love" (see below). The music television channel (MTV) refused to screen it, and a hostile, sexist interview on NBC's *Nightline* accused Madonna of overstepping acceptable limits of sexual representation. Her response was that, in her view, these conventional limits allow the degradation and humiliation of women and tolerate violence toward them, but do not allow two or more people, regardless of gender, to enter into a mutual exchange of the sensual pleasures of touching and looking. The conventional limits confine sexuality to patriarchal dominance, and by rejecting them and replacing them with ones of her own, Madonna was asserting her control over her own sexual politics, however offensive they might be to other people. The fact that the group offended was, again, the socially dominant one is a good indicator of the politics of this control.

An earlier video, "Open Your Heart," also centered its images around the control of sexuality. In it, Madonna plays a striptease dancer in a peep show. As her sexual and revealing dance progresses, we gradually realize that she is subverting the conventions of striptease by making her parody of it muscular, assertive, and sexually challenging instead of supplicating and appealing. She uses this "turned" striptease not to allure the male voyeurs watching her but to control them, and in doing so she reverses the power relations in Freud's theory of voyeurism.

The video explicitly shows us a number of the voyeurs, whereas, according to Freud, voyeuristic power depends upon a voyeur's invisibility. But these men are not only pulled into the light and made visible, they are mocked, parodied, and exaggerated. They are represented by a series of disempowering images such as coke-bottle spectacles or cardboard cut-outs (which Madonna kicks over); some are shown groveling downward to catch a final glimpse of her under the descending shutter of the booth. Outside, by the box office, is a young boy trying to get in—possibly to "become a man" in the conventional sense. Madonna "rescues" him from this fate, and in the final shot the two of them, androgynously dressed alike, dance away in a nonsexual, gender-equal dance of joy while the peep-show owner desperately begs Madonna to return to her role as sexual lure. The irony, of course, is that, in controlling the look of those she enticed, she was never the lure he thought she was.

Madonna knows well the importance of the look. This is a complex concept, for it includes how she *looks* (what she looks like), how *she* looks (how she gazes at others—the camera in particular), and how others look at her. Traditionally, looking has been in the control of men, and the male look has, following Freud's theory of voyeurism, been a central element in patriarchal control over women. But Madonna appropriates this control for herself and shows that women's control of the look (in all three senses) is crucial to their gaining control over their meanings within patriarchy.

One of the ways in which she gains this control is, paradoxically, by relinquishing it. She does not wish to restrict and tie down the meanings of gender and the identities that go with them, for to do so would be merely to reproduce the worst of patriarchal politics. Her aim is to open them up, to give those who are subordinated or marginalized by patriarchy —that is, those who are not heterosexual men—greater control over their own sexuality and thus to diversify sexual identities and sexual relations in our society.

Semiotic power is exerted by controlling the categorizations used to make sense of the world, and patriarchy constantly attempts to control sexual categories and their meanings. So Madonna's consistent refusal to accept or fit into those categories is a strategy of resistance. She deliberately promotes ambiguity and androgyny in her songs and videos, and her 1990 video "Justify My Love" is the most explicit of all her work in its refusal of conventional sexual categories.[41] Its sensuous, erotic representation of mutual love moves easily across the categories of the clearly heterosexual, the clearly homosexual, and the androgynous: it shows highly feminine women and men, as well as masculine men and women; its pleasures are extended beyond the confines of the traditional couple and include those of looking as well as those of touching. No wonder MTV refused to show it. The video became, for a short time, a cause célèbre of gender politics and was accused, predictably, of promoting pornography, perversion, and promiscuity while being defended, equally predictably, for being emancipatory, honest, and erotic. One of its defenders summed up the controversy thus:

> There's no mistaking this piece for porn, because it carries such a firm point of view. Madonna uses her portrayal of blurred genders to amuse and liberate, as well as to exploit. Her cheeky S&M fantasies wind up asserting the independence of the individual, and to make sure we don't miss the point, she spells it out with the lyrics printed on-screen at the clip's close: "Poor is the man whose pleasures depend on the permission of another."[42]

So far in this chapter I have focused on young girls as a typical subcultural audience of Madonna. But they are far from the only one. Madonna is also highly significant in gay culture.[43] A disc jockey at a gay bar in Madison, Wisconsin, calls her "an equalist who speaks to a generation who thirsts for diversity." For him, Madonna's diversification of patriarchy's restricted sexual categories is appealingly progressive. Other members of Madison's gay community find a real attraction in her campy, playful control over her own image and in her ability to change that image at will. There is little explicit evidence that her image control appealed to the need experienced by some gay people to masquerade in order to reduce the problems of living in a heterosexual society; rather, the appeal lay in her honesty and power in rejecting sexual stereotyping. Her emphasis that "Justify My Love" is about "being truthful and honest with our partners" carries the implication that conventional sexuality often involves dishonesty and the attempt to fit one's own sexuality into a category already constructed, thereby submitting oneself to the control inherent in that categorization.[44] As one gay magazine puts it:

> She helps us confront religious guilt, purges us of libidinal inhibitions and forces us to rethink the limitations of gender, intercourse and responsibility—all with a good beat that you can dance to. . . . Her pride, flamboyance and glamour reach out to gay guys as much as her butch/fem dichotomy and her refusal to be victimized strikes a chord in lesbians.[45]

Madonna herself justifies her video by saying: "It's a celebration of sex. It is about two people regardless of gender displaying affection for each other, there's nothing wrong with that." To those who claim she is demeaning herself and women in her work, she replies confidently that they "are missing a few things. I am the one in charge. I put myself in these situations. There isn't a man making me do these things. I am in charge."[46]

This sense of power and control in sexual relations appeals equally, if differently, to both young girls and to the gay and lesbian communities. A final, if extreme, endorsement of this appeal is provided by Michael Musto of *Outweek*: "Despite the government's attempt to render some of Madonna's themes invisible, as a role model and evocator of change, Madonna is right now more powerful than the government."[47]

Cultural studies does not try to understand Madonna simply either as a bearer of meanings and ideology or as an agent of commodification and profit making, though she is clearly both of these. By stressing her multiaccentuality, it reveals her as a terrain of struggle upon which various social formations engage in relations with the dominant social order. Her meanings and their politics cannot be evaluated in terms of what she *is*, but only in terms of what people make of her in their social contexts. The controversy she provokes is evidence not only of how open a terrain she is for this struggle over meaning, but also of people's desire to seize what opportunities they can find to engage in it.

What I have tried to do in this chapter is to demonstrate some of the methodology and theoretical implications of British cultural studies. I shall now try to summarize these.

The television text is a potential of meanings. These meanings are activated by different readers in their different social situations. Because the television text is produced by a capitalist institution, it necessarily bears that ideology. Any subcultural or resistant meanings that are made from it are not "independent" but are made in relation to the dominant ideology. Because subcultures are related in various ways to the social system, they will produce an equivalent variety of ways in which to relate their subcultural readings of television to those preferred by the dominant ideology. Social relations in capitalism always involve a political dimension (because all such relations are determined more or less directly by the unequal distribution of power), and so all meanings arise, in part, from a political base. For some, the politics will be those of acceptance, for others, those of rejection or opposition, but for most the politics will be a base for the negotiation of meaning or for resistance.

Cultural analysis can help us to reveal how the television text serves as an arena for this struggle over meanings. It treats television as part of the total cultural experience of its viewers; the meanings of television are always intertextual, for it is always read in the context of the other texts that make up this cultural experience. These intertextual relations may be explicit and close or implicit and tenuous. All muscle dramas share many generic characteristics, but they also bear less obvious—though not necessarily less significant—relations with the Vietnam veterans' parade held in New York ten years after the war ended and with the unveiling of the Vietnam Memorial in Washington, D.C.

Critical and journalistic comments on television programs, fan magazines, and gossip publications are examples of other types of significant intertextuality. Criticism is, according to Tony Bennett, a series of ideological bids for the meaning of a text, and studying which interpretations are preferred in which publications and for which audiences can help us to understand why and how certain meanings of the text are activated rather than others.[48] We must be able to understand how that bundle of meanings that we call "Madonna" allows a *Playboy* reader to activate meanings of "the compleat Boy Toy" at the same time that a female fan sees her as sexy but not needing men, as being there "all by herself." Publications reflect the meanings circulating in the culture, and these meanings will be read back into the television text as an inevitable part of the assimilation of that text into the total cultural experience of the reader.

For culture is a process of making meanings in which people actively participate; it is not a set of preformed meanings handed down to and imposed upon the people. Of course, our "freedom" to make meanings that suit our interests is as circumscribed as any other "freedom" in society. The mass-produced text is produced and circulated by capitalist institutions for economic gain and is therefore imprinted with capitalist ideology. But the mass-produced text can only be made into a *popular* text by the people, and this transformation occurs when the various subcultures can activate sets of meanings and insert those meanings into their daily cultural experience. They take mass-produced signifiers and, by a process of "excorporation," use them to articulate and circulate subcultural meanings.[49]

Gossip is one important means of this active circulation of meanings. The "uses and gratifications" theorists of the 1970s recognized how commonly television was used as a "coin of social exchange," that is, as something to talk about in schoolyards, suburban coffee mornings, coffee breaks at work, and the family living room.[50] Dorothy Hobson has shown the importance of gossip among soap opera fans, and Christine Geraghty has called it the "social cement" that binds the narrative strands of soap opera together and that binds fans to each other and to the television text.[51] This use of television as a cultural enabler, a means of participating in the circulation of meanings, is only just becoming clear, and gossip or talk about television is no longer seen as the end in itself (as it was in the "uses and gratifications" approach), but rather as a way of participating actively in that process of the production and circulation of meanings that constitutes culture.

The cultural analysis of television, then, requires us to study three levels of "texts" and the relations between them. First, there is the primary text on the television screen, which is produced by the culture industry and needs to be seen in its context as part of that industry's total production. Second, there is a sublevel of texts, also produced by the culture industry, though sometimes by different parts of it. These include studio publicity, television criticism and comment, feature articles about shows and their stars, gossip columns, fan magazines, and so on. They can provide evidence of the ways in which the potential meanings of the primary text are activated and taken into their culture by various audiences or subcultures. On the third level of textuality lie those texts that the viewers produce themselves: their talk about television; their letters to papers or magazines; and their adoption of television-introduced styles of dress, speech, behavior, or even thought into their lives.

These three levels leak into one another. Some secondary texts, such as those of official publicity and public relations, are very close to primary texts; others, such as independent criticism and comment, attempt to "speak for" the third level. Underlying all this, we can, I think, see an oral popular culture adapting its earlier role to one that fits within a mass society.

This social circulation of meanings always entails struggle and contestation, for those with social power constantly attempt to repress, invalidate, or marginalize meanings that are produced by and serve the interests of subordinate groups and that therefore conflict with their own. This foregrounding of conflict, which informs the realm of culture just as it does that of social relations, is the key difference between the development of cultural studies in Britain and in the United States. Britain, like most of continental Europe, has never doubted that it is a society structured around class conflict; as a result, Marxist modes of analysis, which developed to explain capitalist societies as necessarily ones of conflicting social interests and therefore of constant social struggle, were particularly pertinent to cultural studies as it developed in Britain in the 1970s and 1980s.

Cultural criticism in the United States, however, has quite a different history. Its major concern has been to forge a national unity or consensus out of widely differing immigrant, enslaved, and native social groups. Its industrialization did not grow from a society of agrarian capitalism with an already politicized peasant class—which is one root reason for both the instability of the labor movement and the invisibility of the class system in the United States compared with Britain. U.S. cultural studies, then, tended toward liberal pluralist theories in which different social groups were seen to live together in relative harmony and stability. The models to which U.S. cultural theory turned were ones derived not from Marxism and the analysis of social conflict but from anthropology and the analysis of social consensus. Drawing on notions of ritual and mythology, they stressed what different social groups had in common, which was a form of *communitas* produced by a shared language and culture into which all entered freely and from which all derived equal benefits. The dominant ideology thesis, of course, differs diametrically while still stressing what people have in common: in its case, what is common to all is the dominant ideology, which is far from equal in the distribution of its benefits.

The growth of interest in British cultural studies in the United States during the 1980s may well be related to the rise of Reaganism. Reaganism rolled back the progress made during the 1960s and 1970s toward reducing inequalities in gender, race, and class; it widened the gap between the privileged and the deprived and concentrated power in the white, male, upper middle classes. Under such conditions, models of cultural consensus proved less convincing than ones of cultural conflict. British cultural studies, with its focus on struggle and its commitment to promoting the interests of the subordinate and critiquing the operations of the dominant, seemed to be tailor made for importation. But the theory should not be allowed to emerge unchanged from its transatlantic crossing. The different histories of the United States and Britain, particularly in race and class relations, require its models to be modified. Such differences, though, significant as they are, are still differences within the commonality of a white, patriarchal capitalism whose enormous benefits, rewards, and resources are unfairly distributed among its members. If an American adaptation of British cultural studies can provide a critically engaged theory that critiques the culture of domination and endorses those cultures of the subordinate that work against social inequality, and if by so doing it contributes to a more equal but diverse society, its importation will have been well justified. If it doesn't, the sooner it's dumped the better.

NOTES

1. Stuart Hall, "The Narrative Construction of Reality," *Southern Review* 17 (1984): 1–17.

2. Angela McRobbie, "Dance and Social Fantasy," in *Gender and Generation*, ed. Angela McRobbie and Mica Nava (London: Macmillan, 1984), pp. 130–61; Lisa Lewis, *Gender Politics and MTV: Voicing the Difference* (Philadelphia: Temple University Press, 1990).

3. Louis Althusser, "Ideology and Ideological State Apparatuses," in *Lenin and Philosophy and Other Essays* (London: New Left Books, 1971), pp. 127–86.

4. Stuart Hall et al., "The Unity of Current Affairs Television," in *Popular Television and Film: A Reader*, ed. Tony Bennett et al. (London: British Film Institute/Open University Press, 1981), pp. 88–117; Stephen Heath and Gillian Skirrow, "Television: A World in Action," *Screen* 18, no. 2 (1977): 7–59; John Fiske, "Television and Popular Culture: Reflections on British and Australian Critical Practice," *Critical Studies in Mass Communication* 3 (September 1986): 200–216.

5. Stuart Hall, "Encoding/Decoding," in *Culture, Media, Language*, ed. Stuart Hall et al. (London: Hutchinson, 1980), pp. 128–39.

6. Shere Hite, *The Hite Report on Male Sexuality* (London: Macdonald, 1981).

7. Andrew Moye, "Pornography," in *The Sexuality of Men*, ed. Adrian Mctcalf and Martin Humphries (London: Macmillan, 1985), pp. 44–69.

8. Horace Newcomb, "On the Dialogic Aspect of Mass Communication," *Critical Studies in Mass Communication* 1 (March 1984): 34–50.

9. Ibid.

10. Mikhail Bakhtin, *The Dialogic Imagination* (Austin: University of Texas Press, 1981).

11. Valentin N. Volosinov, *Marxism and the Philosophy of Language* (New York: Seminar Press, 1973). There is a well-grounded theory that Volosinov and Bakhtin were the same writer.

12. David Morley, *The "Nationwide" Audience: Structure and Decoding* (London: British Film Institute, 1980); McRobbie, "Dance and Social Fantasy"; Robert Hodge and David Tripp, *Children and Television* (Cambridge: Polity, 1986).

13. Morley, *The "Nationwide" Audience*.

14. Ibid. See also Charlotte Brunsdon and David Morley, *Everyday Television: "Nationwide"* (London: British Film Institute, 1978).

15. John Corner, Kay Richardson, and Natalie Fenton, *Nuclear Reactions: Form and Response in Public Issue Television* (London: John Libbey, 1990).

16. See Robert Dawson, "Culture and Deprivation: Ethnography and Everyday Life," paper presented at the International Communication Association Conference, Dublin, Ireland, July 1990; John Fiske, "For Cultural Interpretation: A Study of the Culture of Homelessness," *Critical Studies in Mass Communication* (forthcoming); John Fiske and Robert Dawson, "Audiencing Violence," in *Toward a Comprehensive Theory of the Audience*, ed. Lawrence Grossberg and Ellen Wartella (Champaign: University of Illinois Press, 1992).

17. David Morley, *Family Television: Cultural Power and Domestic Leisure* (London: Comedia, 1986).

18. Raymond Williams, *Television: Technology and Cultural Form* (London: Fontana, 1974); John Hartley, "Television and the Power of Dirt," *Australian Journal of Cultural Studies* 1, no. 2 (1983): 68–82.

19. McRobbie, "Dance and Social Fantasy."

20. Stuart Hall, "Notes on Deconstructing the Popular," in *People's History and Socialist Theory*, ed. Raphael Samuel (London: Routledge and Kegan Paul, 1981).

21. See Roland Barthes, *Mythologies* (London: Paladin, 1973); John Fiske, *Introduction to Communication Studies* (London: Methuen, 1982); John Fiske and John Hartley, *Reading Television* (London: Methuen, 1978).

22. Interview by John Fiske, December 1985.

23. Judith Williamson, "The Making of a Material Girl," *New Socialist*, October 1986, pp. 46–47.

24. *Time*, 27 May 1985, p. 47.

25. *Countdown*, December 1985, p. 70.

26. *US*, 13 June 1991, p. 23.

27. *Time*, 27 May 1985, p. 47.

28. Robyn Blair, student paper, School of Communication and Cultural Studies, Curtin University, November 1985.

29. *Countdown Annual*, 1985, p. 109.

30. Madonna, quoted in *National Times*, 23/29 August 1985, p. 9.

31. Ibid., p. 10.

32. *Star*, 7 May 1991, p. 7.

33. Ibid., p. 127.

34. Professor Chris Flynn, quoted in *New Idea*, 11 January 1986, p. 4.

35. *National Times*, 23/29 August 1985, p. 10.

36. Iain Chambers, *Popular Culture: The Metropolitan Experience* (London: Methuen, 1986), pp. 7–13.

37. From "Material Girl," lyrics by Peter Brown and Robert Raus (Minong Publishing Company, B.M.I., 1985).

38. *Playboy*, September 1985, pp. 122, 127.

39. *US*, 13 June 1991, p. 23.

40. David Brean and Chad Dell, "Like a Prayer," unpublished paper, University of Wisconsin-Madison, April 1989.

41. *US*, 13 June 1991, pp. 20–23.

42. Jim Farber in *Entertainment Weekly*, 14 December 1990, p. 19.

43. The research into Madonna's appeal to Madison's gay and lesbian communities was conducted by a student of mine, Jennifer Alterman. For a fuller account, see her "Madonna: A Visual Illusion," unpublished paper, University of Wisconsin-Madison, May 1991.

44. Madonna, speaking on *Nightline*, NBC, 3 December 1990.

45. *Outweek*, March 1991, pp. 35–41.

46. *Nightline*, NBC, 3 December 1990.

47. *Outweek*, March 1991, p. 62.

48. Tony Bennett, "The Bond Phenomenon: Theorizing a Popular Hero," *Southern Review* 16, no. 2 (1983): 195–225.

49. Lawrence Grossberg, "Another Boring Day in Paradise: Rock and Roll and the Empowerment of Everyday Life," *Popular Music* 4 (1984): 225–57.

50. Denis McQuail et al., "The Television Audience: A Revised Perspective," in *The Sociology of Mass Communications*, ed. Denis McQuail (Harmondsworth, Eng.: Penguin, 1972), pp. 135–65.

51. Dorothy Hobson, *"Crossroads": The Drama of a Soap Opera* (London: Methuen, 1982); Christine Geraghty, "The Continuous Serial—a Definition," in *Coronation Street*, by Richard Dyer et al. (London: British Film Institute, 1981), pp. 9–26.

FOR FURTHER READING

Graeme Turner, *British Cultural Studies: An Introduction* (Boston: Unwin Hyman, 1990) is a well-written account of the development and main issues of this school. P. Brantlinger, *Crusoe's Footprints: Cultural Studies in Britain and America* (New York: Routledge, 1990), is more illuminating than its title; its account of the theoretical debates is particularly good, though set within the framework of literary studies. Also recommended is a book of essays from the Birmingham Centre for Contemporary Cultural Studies that provides good examples of founding work in Marxist, structuralist, and ethnographic studies: Stuart Hall, Dorothy Hobson, Andrew Lowe, and Paul Willis, eds., *Culture, Media, Language* (London: Hutchinson, 1980). A general overview of this school's work on television is given in John Fiske, *Television Culture* (London: Methuen, 1987).

The first book in cultural studies to deal specifically with television is Raymond Williams, *Television: Technology and Cultural Form* (London: Fontana, 1974). Its historical overview argues that cultural needs determine technological development, and its contemporary analysis attempts, sometimes a bit uncertainly, to clarify television's cultural role. John Fiske and John Hartley, *Reading Television* (London: Methuen, 1978) brings European semiotics, particularly the work of Barthes, to bear upon television and links this to British cultural studies. The approach is less historical than Williams's, but the authors give more detailed analysis of programs. Roger Silverstone, *The Message of Television: Myth and Narrative in Contemporary Culture* (London: Heinemann, 1981), gives a very detailed theoretical analysis, drawing largely upon Lévi-Strauss, of a thirteen-part TV miniseries. Silverstone's book is more anthropological and less political than Williams's or Fiske and Hartley's.

An early American work that is in tune with the British approach and uses hegemony theory to analyze how the media covered the student unrest in the late 1960s is Todd Gitlin, *The Whole World Is Watching* (Berkeley: University of California Press, 1980). John Hartley, *Understanding News* (London: Routledge, 1983), which is one of the few culturalist studies of news, shows how the news makes meanings of events and how these meanings are located within the social system.

A number of recent collections of essays, although not exclusively British, have been strongly influenced by the British cultural studies approach. Manuel Alvarado and John O. Thompson, eds., *The Media Reader* (London: British Film Institute, 1990), has good sections on cultural identity (race, gender, and nation), political economy, and textual theory. Andrew Goodwin and Garry Whannel, eds., *Understanding Television* (London: Routledge, 1990), contains a wide selection of essays written for an undergraduate audience. John

Downing, Ali Mohammadi, and Annabelle Sreberny-Mohammadi, eds., *Questioning the Media: A Critical Introduction* (Newbury Park, Calif.: Sage, 1990), is not limited to television but devotes more attention to it than to any other medium. The historical inflection of cultural studies is well illustrated in John Corner, ed., *Popular Television in Britain: Studies in Cultural History* (London: British Film Institute, 1991). More focused collections are Mary Ellen Brown, ed., *Television and Women's Culture* (London: Sage, 1990); and Helen Baehr and Gillian Dyer, eds., *Boxed In: Women and Television* (London: Pandora Press, 1987). Selected papers from the first two London-based International Television Studies conferences have been edited by Philip Drummond and Richard Paterson and published by the British Film Institute under the titles *Television in Transition* (1985) and *Television and Its Audience* (1988).

Two good examples of ideological analysis of television programs are Stephen Heath and Gillian Skirrow, "Television: A World in Action," *Screen* 18, no. 2 (1977): 7–59; and Stuart Hall, Ian Connel, and Lydia Curti, "The Unity of Current Affairs Television," in *Popular Television and Film*, edited by Tony Bennett et al. (London: British Film Institute/Open University Press, 1981). The first shows the close analysis typical of screen theory, with its emphasis on the power of television to make meanings for the viewer and position him or her as a reading subject. The second has an equally detailed analysis, but its theory allows for more negotiated readings. Angela McRobbie, "*Jackie*: An Ideology of Adolescent Femininity," in *Popular Culture: Past and Present*, ed. Bernard Waites, Tony Bennett, and Graham Martin (London: Croom Helm, 1982), pp. 263–83, gives another excellent example of this school of ideological analysis applied not to television but to teenage girls' magazines — well worth reading.

Charlotte Brunsdon and David Morley, *Everyday Television: "Nationwide"* (London: British Film Institute, 1978) applies discourse theory to a detailed and lively analysis of television's way of addressing and interpellating its audience.

The ethnographic work illustrated in Hall et al., *Culture, Media, Language* is developed more fully by David Morley, *The "Nationwide" Audience: Structure and Decoding* (London: British Film Institute, 1980), using an open interview approach; and by Dorothy Hobson, *"Crossroads": The Drama of a Soap Opera* (London: Methuen, 1982), using the participant observer method. Cultural approaches to the audience form the focus of Ellen Seiter, Hans Borchers, Gabriele Kreutzner, and Eva-Maria Warth, eds., *Remote Control: Television Audiences and Cultural Power* (London: Routledge, 1989). A detailed ethnographic study of particular television audiences is Andrea Press, *Women Watching Television: Gender, Class, and Generation in the American Television Experience* (Philadelphia: University of Pennsylvania Press, 1991), an American study inflected with political concerns similar to those of British cultural studies—highly recommended.

Ien Ang, *Watching "Dallas": Soap Opera and the Melodramatic Imagination*, trans. Della Couling (London: Methuen, 1985), is a study based on letters from Dutch fans—mainly women—of *Dallas*. It is both influential and readable, a none-too-common combination of qualities. John Tulloch, *Television Drama: Agency, Audience, and Myth* (London: Routledge, 1990), is also highly recommended for its combination of textual analysis with ethnographic studies of both television producers and audiences. Australian books in this tradition are Patricia Palmer, *The Lively Audience: A Study of Children and the TV Set* (Sydney: Allen and Unwin, 1986); and Robert Hodge and David Tripp, *Children and Television: A Semiotic Approach* (Cambridge: Polity, 1986); both of these deal with children as culturally competent audiences and both are highly recommended. A useful international perspective informs James Lull, ed., *World Families Watch Television* (Newbury Park: Sage, 1988). Two other books, one Australian and one British, that combine ethnography with textual and production studies are John Tulloch and Albert Moran, *"A Country Practice": Quality Soap* (Sydney: Currency Press, 1986); and David Buckingham, *Public Secrets: "EastEnders" and Its Audience* (London: British Film Institute, 1987).

The most influential Marxist theory is found in Louis Althusser, "Ideology and Ideological State Apparatuses," in *Lenin and Philosophy and Other Essays* (London: New Left Books, 1971), pp. 127–86—a crucial essay. Antonio Gramsci's work is published in the long "prison notebooks," which are for the advanced student only (Gramsci, *Selections from the Prison Notebooks*, ed. and trans. Quentin Hoare and Geoffrey Nowell-Smith [New York: International Publishers, 1971]). A good selection is available in Tony Bennett, Graham Martin, Colin Mercer, and Janet Woollacott, *Culture, Ideology and Social Process* (London: Batsford/Open University Press, 1981), which contains essays commenting on and applying Gramsci's theory. The book also has an excellent selection of essays on structuralist and cultural theory, though not applied specifically to television.

9 : TELEVISION AND POSTMODERNISM

jim collins

The development of some kind of working relationship between television and postmodernism within the realm of critical studies is inevitable, almost impossible, and absolutely necessary. Inevitable, because television is frequently referred to as the quintessence of postmodern culture, and postmodernism is just as frequently written off as mere "television culture." Close to impossible, because of the variability of both television and postmodernism as critical objects; both are currently undergoing widespread theorization in which there are few, if any, commonly agreed-upon first principles. Necessary, because that very lack, the absence of inherited critical baggage, places television studies in a unique position vis-à-vis postmodernism. Unlike the critical work devoted to other media, television studies does not have to "retrofit" critical paradigms developed in modernist or premodernist periods and therefore should ideally be able to provide unprecedented insights into the complex interrelationships between textuality, subjectivity, and technology in contemporary cultures.

There is no short definition of *postmodernism* that can encompass the divergent, often contradictory ways the term has been employed. One reason for this divergence is that the term is used to describe: (1) a distinctive style; (2) a movement that emerged in the sixties, seventies, or eighties, depending on the medium in question; (3) a condition or milieu that typifies an entire set of socioeconomic factors; (4) a specific mode of philosophical inquiry that throws into question the givens of philosophical discourse; (5) a very particular type of "politics"; and (6) an emergent form of cultural analysis shaped by all of the above.

This terminological confusion is exacerbated by the contentiousness of the various definitions. As Jonathan Arac has written, "It remains even now typically the case that to 'have a position' on postmodernism means not just to offer an analysis of its genesis and contours, but to let the world know whether you are for it or against it, and in fairly bold terms."[1] One could argue that the chief drawback of most of this work is that the latter inevitably takes precedence over the former, producing little in the way of actual description but a great deal in the way of critical ax grinding. But although easy moralizing about postmodernism may often reveal little besides the presuppositions of the critical languages used to demonize or valorize it, the contested nature of the term—the fact that no definition of contours can ever be ideologically neutral, that description is inseparable from evaluation—reveals one of the most significant lessons of postmodern theory: all of our assumptions concerning what constitutes "culture" and "critical analysis" are now subject to intense debate.

If there is a common denominator in all of these contentious definitions of postmodernism, it is the determination to define it as something other than *modernism*, a term that is likewise given variable status. Modernism is generally characterized in one of two ways, depending on the individual critic's perspective on postmodernism: as a heroic period of revolutionary experimentation that sought to transform whole cultures, in which case postmodernism is seen as a neoconservative backlash; or as a period of profound elitism, in which case postmodernism signals a move away from the self-enclosed world of the avant-garde back into the realm of day-to-day life. John Barth, for example, in developing his operating definition of postmodernism, cites Gerald Graff's list of tell-tale characteristics of modernism as a suitable point of departure.[2] Graff argued that modernism began as a criticism of nineteenth-century bourgeois culture, a rejection of both its values and its most favored style, namely realism. This rejection involved a highly self-conscious overturning of the conventions of realist representation: a move away from "objective" depiction of the world to various forms of abstraction and symbolism that emphasized subjective inward consciousness; the frustration of expectations concerning the coherence of plot and character; the disruption of linear narrative; and the employment of a variety of stylistic strategies that stressed that the "truth" of human experience was not accessible through simple documentation because it was not a well-ordered, rational machine waiting to be cataloged.

Barth adds to Graff's list two more features that he sees as central to modernism: the role of the artist as self-exiled hero; and the foregrounding of language and technique, not as a means to an end, but as ends in themselves, the real "content" of art. These latter two characteristics are vitally important to Barth because they involve not just the stylistic/ideological features of modernism, but also the eventual fate of modernist art. The willful self marginalization on the part of the artist class, coupled with its fascination with purity of technique, led to the self-enclosure of experimental art within the rarefied realms of the museum and the university. This process culminates in the "metafiction" of the 1960s, in which the problems involved in the act of creation become the primary content of the work—for example, in texts like William Gass's "In the Heart of the Heart of the Country" or Barth's own *Lost in the Funhouse*, Federico Fellini's *8½* or Michelangelo Antonioni's *Blow-Up*.

Charles Jencks makes a similar argument about modernist architecture, specifically about what is called the International Style, which was developed by Mies van der Rohe and others in the 1920s.[3] Jencks sees the same insularity in these stark geometric structures, constructed of glass-and-steel I-beams, which banished any trace of the nineteenth century or of specific regional characteristics. The International Style resulted from the same fetishizing of technique as an end in itself; it contended that by changing structural conventions one could alter consciousness and produce social change, even if the inhabitants of these glass towers were unable to comprehend the political significance of these radical innovations.

Barth and Jencks both emphasize the paradoxical development of modernism, wherein the need to develop radically different styles that would provide the shock of the new, and thereby transform consciousness, depended on the rejection of the familiar (specifically nineteenth-century realism and twentieth-century mass culture). Yet that very rejection led to a semiotic/ideological impasse. The avoidance of the familiar and the celebration of innovation produced bold new forms of personal expression, but these styles failed to be very effective forms of communication. In trying to keep their distance from the familiar, modernists also kept their distance from the public they hoped to transform. The failure of modernism, according to this argument, can be traced directly to the collision of two priorities—the cultivation of radical forms of personal expression on the one hand, and the need to bring about sweeping social change by developing a revolutionary mass consciousness on the other. These priorities proved to be mutually contradictory, primarily because the former was founded on a romantic conception of the artist as an enlightened outsider who minimized or ignored the masses, whereas the latter depended on a socialist conception of the state that made the masses (and not the genius-artist) the agent of historical change. These conflicting priorities resulted in the abandonment of modernism's political agenda and the development of ever more daring forms of radical formal expression. By the 1960s, modernism was thoroughly institutionalized, no longer "revolutionary" except within the self-enclosed worlds of the art market and academia.

Postmodernism was, in varying ways, a reaction against the self-enclosure, the profitable marginalization that provided modernist artists with a guaranteed but increasingly smaller audience and orbit of influence. The alternative advocated by Jencks and Barth was not simple revivalism, in which modernism would be abandoned and older styles reinstated. The effort to reconnect with an audience outside galleries and scholarly journals involved a number of different strategies. One of the most common was to destabilize the relationship between high art and mass culture, primarily through the appropriation of signs drawn from mass media.

Robert Venturi and Denise Scott Brown's *Learning from Las Vegas* was massively influential in this regard.[4] They called for a new architecture that would communicate with contemporary audiences through the use of signs that were decidedly "impure," inartistic, and mass-produced. The "pop art" phenomenon of the 1950s and 1960s, specifically the work of Andy Warhol, Roy Lichtenstein, Richard Hamilton, and others, likewise depended on the appropriation of popular icons and symbols (Campbell soup cans, Marilyn Monroe, etc.) and their "rearticulation"—giving them different significance within the context of museum art. In the process, pop art contested the limits of both museum art and popular art. This process of appropriation involved a fundamental shift with regard to the production of meaning, in which meaning was not a matter of pure invention on the part of the individual artist but more a matter of customizing or rearticulating previously existing signs. The combination of signs drawn from different periods, styles, and institutions has been called *radical eclecticism*, in which a text, whether a building by Charles Moore or a popular song by Living Colour, tries to represent the discontinuity of the messages that surround us but also their simultaneity.

Although it is possible to list the tell-tale stylistic features of postmodern design—the move away from abstraction and geometrics to the overly familiar and mass-produced; the replacement of purity with eclecticism, internationalism with cultural specificity, and invention with rearticulation—the cultural significance of these changes and their ideological ramifications remains a matter of intense debate. It is also especially difficult to relate television to these debates in any kind of one-to-one correspondence. Television, unlike architecture, literature, or painting, never had a modernist phase that could serve as a point of departure for postmodern television. The emergence of postmodernism is decidedly an "uneven" development; its appearance and eventual impact vary from one medium to another.

Because neither an etymology, nor an evolutionary schema, nor an all-encompassing theoretical paradigm can provide an adequate working definition of postmodernism that allows for diverse applications to television, I will set forth a series of recurring themes developed by theoreticians working in different media that, in aggregate, provide a sense of the conflictedness but also the potential cohesiveness of postmodern theory. These themes, considered together, allow for a reconsideration of the semiotic, technological, and ideological dimensions of television.

A Semiotics of Excess: "The Bombardment of Signs"

One of the key preconditions of the postmodern condition is the proliferation of signs and their endless circulation, generated by the technological developments associated with the information explosion (cable television, VCRs, digital recording, computers, etcetera). These technologies have produced an ever increasing surplus of texts, all of which demand our attention in varying levels of intensity. The resulting array of competing signs shapes the very process of signification, a context in which messages must constantly be defined over and against rival forms of expression as different types of texts frame our allegedly common reality according to significantly different ideological agendas.

Television is obviously a central factor in this information explosion. Many critics on both the left and the right insist that television is likewise instrumental in the devaluation of meaning—the reduction of all meaningful activity to mere "non-sense," to a limitless televisual universe that has taken the place of the real. Such critics as Allan Bloom and Jean Baudrillard have made grandiose claims about the destructive power of mass culture (most especially television).[5] The former has claimed that television has brought about the ruination of true learning and morality. The latter has claimed that contemporary culture *is* television culture —endless simulations in which reality simply disappears. In Bloom's view, the culprit is not television alone, but the more general democratization of culture, which threatens the elite values that once formed the basis of real learning: the acquisition of Truth. But to Baudrillard (who is no more a postmodernist than Bloom), television is cause as well as symptom, allegedly constructing a seamless realm of simulations that hinder our acquisition of the *really real.*

The problem with these critiques is their contention that all signs are encoded and decoded according to exactly the same logic, or encoded so differently that, as a whole, they produce one and only one effect. They insist that the technological developments of the recent past have made "meaning" an antiquated concept, because all signs are supposedly exhausted, mere electronic pulses disconnected from any referent. The chief limitation of these critics who are so anxious to demonize television is that they insist on making dire predictions about the devastating effects of this technological explosion (which alters everything, everywhere, in the same way), but they fail to recognize that the rate of absorption of those technological changes has increased commensurately. The medium may indeed be the message, but twenty minutes into the future the technological novelty is already in the process of being absorbed. In the same way that a figure of speech enjoys a certain novelty at its initial appearance but then begins to become absorbed into the category of the already familiar, the "figures of technology" that produce an initial disorientation are quickly made manageable (*secondarized*) through different strategies of absorption as they are worked over by popular texts and popular audiences. This absorption/secondarization process involves the manipulation of the array by texts operating within it—television programs (as well as rock songs, films, bestsellers, and so forth) that demonstrate an increasingly sophisticated knowledge of the conditions of their production, circulation, and eventual reception.

A recent episode of *Northern Exposure* illustrates this absorption process quite clearly. When Holling, the local tavern owner, acquires a satellite dish that receives two hundred worldwide channels, his girlfriend Shelley quickly becomes a television addict, her entire life suddenly controlled by the new technology. She becomes maniacal in the process, and we see her calling the shopping channel to order thousands of dollars worth of kitsch items. The determination of her character by television programs is stressed repeatedly, as she dances to music videos or dresses up as a Vanna White wannabe to watch *Wheel of Fortune.* But by the end of the program she has confessed her televisual sins, in a mock confessional to the local disk jockey–priest, and resolves to watch selectively. Meanwhile the central character, Dr. Joel Fleischmann, envisions his failed love affair in terms of old black-and-white Hollywood films, including a silent-movie version of the final scene from *The Graduate,* with himself as the star. Other characters recognize his need for what they call "closure" in his relationship, and they decide to provide this by enacting a movie fantasy of how his relationship should have ended. The closure of both plot lines epitomizes the absorption of media culture, not just through parody but through its secondarization by texts and audiences that rearticulate it according to their own needs, a process thematized by the program itself.

Irony, Intertextuality, and Hyperconsciousness

The all-pervasiveness of different strategies of rearticulation and appropriation is one of the most widely discussed features of postmodern cultural production. Umberto Eco has argued that this ironic articulation of the "already said" is the distinguishing feature of postmodern communication. In his often-quoted example, he insists that we can no longer make innocent statements. A lover cannot tell his beloved, "I love you madly," because it would very probably produce only a laugh. But if he wants to make such a declaration of love, he could say, "As Barbara Cartland would put it, 'I love you madly.'" The latter indicates a mutual awareness of the "already said," a mutual delight in ironically manipulating it for one's own purposes.[6] This emphasis on irony is often written off as mere "camp" recycling, but such a view fails to account for the diversity of possible strategies of rearticulation, which range from the simple revivalism found in the buildings of Robert Stern, the interior design collections of Ralph Lauren, or the clothing of Laura Ashley to the more explicitly critical reworking of the "already said" in films like *Thelma and Louise*, the photographs of Barbara Kruger, or the radicalized cover versions of pop standards by the Sex Pistols or The Clash, in which the past is not just accessed but "hijacked," given an entirely different cultural significance than the antecedent text had when it first appeared. What is postmodern in all of this is the simultaneity of these competing forms of rearticulation—the "already said" is being constantly recirculated, but from very different perspectives ranging from nostalgic reverence to vehement attack or a mixture of these strategies. Linda Hutcheon argues very convincingly that what distinguishes postmodern rearticulations of the past is their ambivalent relationship to the antecedent text, a recognition of the power of certain texts to capture the imagination, but at the same time a recognition of their ideological or stylistic limitations (this ambivalent parody will be discussed in more detail below).[7]

There is no other medium in which the force of the "already said" is quite so visible as in television, primarily because the already said is the "still being said." Television programming since the fifties has depended on the recycling of Hollywood films and the syndication of past prime-time programs. The proliferation of cable channels that re-present programs from the past four decades of television history marks the logical extension of this process, in which the various pasts and presents of television now air simultaneously. Television programming as accessing of the accumulated past of popular culture ranges from K-Tel offers for old *Honeymooners* and *I Love Lucy* episodes to the explicitly parodic demolitions of television programs to be found on *In Living Color, David Letterman,* and *Saturday Night Live.* This diversity in the forms and motivations of televisual rearticulation is even more apparent in the simultaneous but conflictive "re-presentations" of early sitcoms on rival cable networks. The Christian Broadcasting Network and Nickelodeon both broadcast series from the late fifties and early sixties, but whereas the former presents these series as a model for family entertainment the way it used to be, the latter offers them as fun for the contemporary family, "camped up" with parodic voice-overs, super-graphics, and reediting designed to deride their quaint vision of American family life, which we all know never really existed even "back then."

The foregrounding of intertextual references has become a marker of "quality television" (for example, prime-time network programs like *Hill Street Blues* and *St. Elsewhere*, which reflect a more sophisticated "cinematic style," feature ensemble casts, etc.) as well. Jane Feuer has traced this self-conscious intertextuality as it developed in the MTM style, but more recently, as "quality television" has developed across production companies and networks, the explicit referencing has played a vital role in situating a given program in relation to other forms of quality and nonquality programs.[8] During the 1990 fall season, for example, Michael and Hope of ABC's *thirtysomething* referred to watching *L.A. Law*, while on NBC's *L.A. Law*, attorney Anne Kelsey spoke of wanting to get home and watch *thirtysomething* because it was "responsible television."

This sort of referencing-as-positioning is not restricted to quality TV. On a recent episode of *Knots Landing* (a nighttime soap that airs opposite *L.A. Law* and makes no claims whatsoever to be quality television), two minor characters argue about their favorite TV programs. One states that he has to turn down a dinner invitation because "I forgot to set my VCR. I gotta see what Corbin Bernsen is wearing tonight." When his friend states that he "never watches that show" because he's a "newshound," the *L.A. Law* fan says derisively, "News my foot. You're crazy about Diane Sawyer." When his colleague protests that "she's very intelligent," his friend responds, "Right, you're in love with her mind." The referencing here, within the context of an evening soap, presupposes three important factors: (1) that viewers will possess a televisual literacy developed enough to recognize programs from the actors' names and that they will know the television schedule well enough to appreciate the reference to the programs that air opposite *Knots Landing* on the two other major networks (*L.A. Law* and *Prime Time Live*); (2) that VCR time-shifting is now commonplace, especially for dedicated viewers of *L.A. Law* but also for those fans who exist within the fictional world of programs that air on competing channels; and (3) that the "irresponsible," nonquality program informs us why viewers *really* like quality television—for the wardrobes and the sexiness of the stars involved, which, as the characters of *Knots Landing* know, constitute the *real* pleasure of the televisual text.

These intertextual references are emblematic of the *hyperconsciousness* of postmodern popular culture: a hyperawareness on the part of the text itself of its cultural status, function, and history, as well as of the conditions of its circulation and reception. Hyperconsciousness involves a different sort of self-reflexivity than that commonly associated with modernist texts. Highly self-conscious forms of appropriation and rearticulation have been used by postmodern painters, photographers, and performance artists (David Salle, Cindy Sherman, Laurie Anderson, and others), and their work has enjoyed a great deal of critical attention. In the "meta-pop" texts that we now find on television, on newsstands, on the radio, or on grocery store book racks, we encounter, not avant-gardists who give "genuine" significance to the merely mass cultural, but a hyperconscious rearticulation of media culture by media culture.[9]

The self-reflexivity of these popular texts of the later eighties and early nineties does not revolve around the problems of self-expression experienced by the anguished creative artist so ubiquitous in modernism but instead focuses on antecedent and competing programs, on the ways television programs circulate and are given meaning by viewers, and on the nature of televisual popularity. A paradigmatic example of this is the opening scene of *The Simpson's Thanksgiving Special* (1990), in which Bart and his father, Homer, are watching television in their living room on Thanksgiving morning. *The Simpsons*, as a concept, is already a mean-spirited parody of the traditional family sitcom, and this particular scene adds an attack on the imbecilic chatter of "color commentators." But the scene goes beyond simple parody. As they watch the Thanksgiving Day parade, Bart keeps asking Homer to identify the balloon float characters, complaining that they could use some characters that "were made in the last fifty years." His father tells him that the parade is a tradition, that if "you start building a balloon for every flash-in-the-pan cartoon character, you'll turn the parade into a farce." At this point the television-within-the-television depicts a Bart Simpson balloon floating by while the "real" Bart Simpson looks on. Thus Bart watches himself as a popular phenomenon on television. *The Simpsons* television program thereby acknowledges its own characters' status as popular icons whose circulation and reception are worked back into the "text" itself.

Subjectivity, Bricolage, and Eclecticism

The "Bart watches Bart" example may be emblematic of a postmodern textuality, but what are the effects of this hyperconscious irony on television viewers? Is its ultimate effect emancipatory, leading to a recognition that television's representations are social constructions rather than value-neutral reflections of the "real" world? Or does this irony produce a disempowering apathy, in which no image is taken at all seriously? John Caughie has described this problem very effectively:

> The argument, then, is that television produces the conditions of an ironic knowingness, at least as a possibility . . . [which] may offer a way of thinking subjectivity free of subjection. . . . Most of all, it opens identity to diversity, and escapes the notion of cultural identity as a fixed volume. . . . But if it does all this, it does not do it in that utopia of guaranteed resistance which assumes the progressiveness of naturally oppositional readers who will get it right in the end. It does it, rather, with terms hung in suspension . . . tactics of empowerment, games of subordination with neither term fixed in advance.[10]

The crux of the matter here is the notion of the subject that is presupposed. Caughie's insightful point about irony vis-à-vis subjectivity suggests that television viewers are individual subjects neither completely programmed by what they are watching nor completely free to choose as self-determining individuals, captains of their fates, masters of their souls.[11] One of the significant developments in postmodern theory (put forward in an increasing number of disciplines) is the recognition that a new theory of the subject must be developed, one that can avoid the deterministic conception of the individual as programmable android without resurrecting a romantic "Self" that operates as a free agent, unfettered and uninfluenced by ideology.

w/: p.m,
identity= intersection of subject positions
conflicting

POSTMODERNISM : 337

The most productive attempts to develop a more nuanced understanding of the relationship between identity and cultural determination have argued that, within postmodern cultures, identity must be conceived as an intersection of conflicting subject positions. Chantal Mouffe asserts that accounting for the complexities of subjectivity is not a question merely of moving away from the notion of a unitary "free" self to a unitary determined self, but rather "the problem is the very idea of the unitary subject. . . . [W]e are in fact always multiple and contradictory subjects, inhabitants of a diversity of communities . . . constructed by a variety of discourses and precariously and temporarily sutured at the intersection of those subject positions."[12] The emergence within the past decade of "antiessentialist" or postmodern feminism has played a key role in these debates. Linda Nicholson and Nancy Fraser argue that "postmodern feminist theory would dispense with the idea of the subject of history. It would replace unitary notions of 'women' and 'feminine gender identity' with plural and complexly constructed conceptions of social identity, treating gender as one relevant strand among others, attending also to class, race, ethnicity, age and sexual orientation."[13]

The concept of the postmodern subject as multiple and contradictory, acted upon but also acting upon, has also led to reconsideration of the "effects" that popular culture, most especially television, has on its viewers. The *hypodermic* model of media effects (in which mass media allegedly "injects" values directly into passive viewers) has been challenged by John Fiske, Ien Ang, and others who share a cultural studies perspective.[14] Many of them use de Certeau's concept of "poaching" to characterize audiences' skillful abduction of televisual texts, focusing on the ways in which audiences make the meanings they want or need out of television programs.[15] It is at this point that British cultural studies begins to share a number of concerns with postmodern theory per se, positing a subject who operates as a technologically sophisticated *bricoleur*, appropriating and recombining according to personal need. The term *bricolage*, developed by anthropologists to describe the ways primitive tribespeople piece together a meaningful cosmogony (or simply a way of operating) out of random elements they encounter in their day-to-day lives, has recently been applied to the behavior of individuals in contemporary media cultures. The culturalist and postmodernist positions differ, however, in regard to "mass culture." The former presupposes that mass culture may still be pernicious and homogeneous, but that it may be transformed into something resembling a genuine folk culture at the moment of reception because viewers tend to disregard the intended effects of television and take from it what best fits into their lives. This is a very attractive political position in that it allows for the continued demonization of capitalism and mass culture while it celebrates the resourcefulness of·ordinary people. However, it fails to recognize the eclecticism of postmodern cultural *production*.

Many television programs, films, popular songs, and other manifestations of popular culture are already the result of sophisticated forms of *bricolage*, already conscious of the multiple ways they might be understood. As I have mentioned above, Charles Jencks insists that one of the distinguishing features of postmodern architecture is "radical eclecticism."[16] The work of Charles Moore, James Stirling, and Hans Hollein juxtaposes styles, materials, and conventions hitherto thought to be thoroughly incompatible. Michael M. J. Fisher and George Lipsitz contend very convincingly that this eclecticism, this creation as *bricolage*, is also a feature of the ethnic and racial subcultures that are so prominent in American popular culture. "It is on the level of commodified mass culture that the most popular, and often the most profound, acts of cultural *bricolage* take place. The destruction of established canons and the juxtaposition of seemingly inappropriate forms that characterize the self-conscious postmodernism of 'high culture' have long been staples of commodified popular culture."[17]

The eclecticism associated with postmodernism takes on a more complicated dimension in regard to television. Individual programs like *Pee-Wee's Play House, Max Headroom,* and *Twin Peaks* are as radically eclectic in their use of diverse stylistic conventions as any postmodern building. Furthermore, the eclecticism of television textuality operates on a technological/institutional level as well because it has been institutionalized by cable television and the VCR, which together produce infinite programming variations. Postmodernist eclecticism might only occasionally be a preconceived design choice in individual programs, but it is built into the technologies of media-sophisticated societies. Thus television, like the postmodern subject, must be conceived as a *site*—an intersection of multiple, conflicting cultural messages. Only by recognizing this interdependency of *bricolage* and eclecticism can we come to appreciate the profound changes in the relationship of reception and production in postmodern cultures. Not only has reception become another form of meaning production, but production has increasingly become a form of reception as it rearticulates antecedent and competing forms of representation.

Commodification, Politics, Value

Another major concern of postmodern cultural analysis has been the impact of consumerism on social life. Fredric Jameson argues that postmodernism is best understood as the end result of capitalism's relentless commodification of all phases of everyday existence. He sees pop culture's radical eclecticism as mere "cannibalization" of the past and as "sheer heterogeneity" without "decidable" effects.[18] For Jameson, all such cultural activity is driven by the logic of "late" capitalism, which endlessly develops new markets that it must neutralize politically by constructing a vision of success and personal happiness, expressible solely through the acquisition of commodities.

The relevance of Jameson's work for television studies has already been explored by a number of critics, not surprising given the advertiser-driven nature of the medium in the United States, where commercials not only interrupt programs but have actually emerged as a form of programming. The blurring of the distinction between programs and commercials has become even greater with the development of "infomercials," shopping channels, product lines generated by Saturday morning cartoons (as well as by evening soaps like *Dynasty*), and so on. If television is defined by its semiotic complexity, its intertextuality, and its eclecticism, it is also just as surely defined by its all-pervasive appeals to consumerism.

The problem for television studies, as it tries to come to terms with postmodernism, is how to reconcile the semiotic and economic dimensions of television. Stressing the semiotic to the exclusion of the economic produces only a formalist game of "let's count the intertexts," but privileging the economic to the point that semiotic complexity is reduced to a limited set of moves allowed by a master system is just as simplistic. The attempt to turn television into a master system operating according to a single logic is a fundamentally nostalgic perspective; the culture of the 1990s, though judged to be the sheer noise of late capitalism, is nevertheless expected to operate according to nineteenth-century models of culture as homogeneous totality.

Making postmodernism coterminous with late capitalism offers a theoretical neatness by providing an all-purpose, master explanation: postmodern culture is a symptom of more fundamental economic and political trends. But this position is fraught with a number of problems. The limitations of this view of postmodernism become especially apparent in Jameson's notion of "cognitive mapping."[19] He argues that a new aesthetics that will make sense of multinational capitalism has yet to emerge and that there exists as yet no way of mapping the chaotic spaces of postmodern cultures. But the "map" he hopes will be drawn will not be acceptable to him unless it envisions this space according to the contours of traditional Marxist theory.[20] Jameson doesn't entertain the notion that mere mass culture may itself provide a mapping function or that television is not just a chaotic terrain in need of mapping but is itself a proliferation of maps. Lifetime, MTV, Black Entertainment Television, and the Family Channel all envision contemporary cultural life from specific generational, racial, and gendered perspectives. Taken together, they don't coalesce into one big picture but rather a composite of overlapping views that visualize the terrain of contemporary life in reference to its specific uses. The desire to formulate one master map, despite the multiple ways that the terrain can be envisioned and put to use by individual subjects as *bricoleurs*, exposes not just the limitations of traditional Marxist paradigms, but also the need to develop far more sophisticated forms of materialist analysis that recognize the multiple uses and effects of consumerism.[21]

The question of whether postmodern cultures may be conceived of as totalities and therefore may operate according to a set of predictive "laws" involves another major issue in postmodern philosophy — specifically, the debate between foundational and antifoundational modes of critical analysis. *Antifoundationalism*, most often associated with Jean-François Lyotard, Richard Rorty, and Barbara Herrnstein Smith, involves the rejection of "master narratives," or any set of all-embracing laws governing human behavior, the science of history, or the ways and means of capital.[22] The antiessentialist feminism discussed earlier is likewise antifoundational in its move away from an absolute reliance on any universal metanarratives or "covering laws" to explain gender difference. Unfortunately, the move toward the relative and provisional (rather than the universal and predictive) as a way to formulate new notions of subjectivity and political effectivity has been mistaken for an abandonment of all value.

Christopher Norris, for example, contends that postmodern theory, specifically in the form Baudrillard presents, may be effective in diagnosing the simulated nature of contemporary life but becomes "muddled" and politically irresponsible when the postmodern condition is used "as a pretext for dismantling every last claim to validity or truth."[23] But Norris takes Baudrillard's nihilist abandonment of the issue of value and generalizes it into *the* postmodern theory of value and political action, a position allegedly held by all practicing postmodernists. Norris fails to make any mention of such postmodern political theoreticians as Chantal Mouffe or Ernesto Laclau or of postmodern feminism in this context. Dick Hebdige makes the crucial point that, in Baudrillard's universe, "postmodernity is associated with the annihilation of difference in the media age, the end of politics altogether," but on the other hand, "in those circles where politics of race and sexuality are taken seriously, critical postmodernism is identified with diversity and difference, a politics of contestation and change."[24]

Within this politics of diversity and difference, "value" is not abandoned —only absolute "truth values," or what Herrnstein Smith has called the automatic "axiomatics" of traditional critical theory that relied on transcendent, universal qualities as proof or verification for all evaluation. She insists that both value and evaluation are radically contingent. "That which we call 'value' may be seen neither as an inherent property of objects, nor an arbitrary projection of subjects but, rather, as the product of the dynamics of some economy or, indeed, of any number of economies (that is, systems of apportionment and circulation of 'goods') in relation to a shifting state, of which an object or entity will have a different (shifting) value."[25]

The ramifications of this point for television study—specifically for developing a theory of postmodern television—are far reaching, because Smith argues that we need to continue to debate the value of any given text but also insists on the contingent nature of those judgments. Evaluation always depends on criteria that are culturally determined and therefore culturally specific rather than transcendent. This is a vitally important point, because it allows for an analysis of television that recognizes the variable nature of televisual signs. Their value cannot be explained in reference to one logic but will be channel-, program-, and audience-sensitive. Even more important, by focusing on the dynamics of the economies that determine these shifting values, we can begin to understand the interconnectedness of the semiotic and the economic dimensions of postmodern television.

Twin Peaks

In order to demonstrate how the various themes of postmodern theory might be considered together in reference to a single television series, I will focus on *Twin Peaks*, because it became a cultural phenomenon that epitomizes the multiple dimensions of televisual postmodernism. *Twin Peaks* was not "postmodernist" just because it involved David Lynch, a bona fide postmodernist filmmaker, or because it depended on a number of postmodern stylistic conventions, or because it generated so many commodity intertexts (*The Secret Diary of Laura Palmer, Dale Cooper: My Life, My Tapes*, and a soundtrack album, among other things). Rather, the circumstances that allowed for its development and the ways in which it circulated are emblematic of postmodern culture and represent the confluence of a number of factors that give postmodern television its historical specificity.

The appearance of *Twin Peaks* on prime-time network television was due in large part to the impact of cable and VCR technology. The advent of cable systems that offer dozens of alternatives to the "big three" networks and the ubiquity of the VCR, which offers an even broader range of entertainment, led to a significant decline in the networks' share of the total viewing audience. In 1979, 91 percent of viewers were watching network programs during prime time, but by 1989 the number had dropped to 67 percent.[26] This viewer migration to cable and videocassettes has been portrayed in near-catastrophic terms by the networks, because those households that are able to afford cable and VCRs are precisely the households network advertisers most want to reach. Particularly prized within this audience segment are "yuppie" viewers, who not only purchase expensive consumer goods but also tend to consume other forms of entertainment—on broadcast television, videotape, cable, and pay-per-view and at movie theaters.

The development of *Twin Peaks* reflects a fundamental change in the way the entertainment industries now envision their publics. The audience is no longer regarded as a homogeneous mass but rather as an amalgamation of microcultural groups stratified by age, gender, race, and geographic location. Therefore, appealing to a "mass" audience now involves putting together a series of interlocking appeals to a number of discrete but potentially interconnected audiences. The promotion of *Batman: The Movie* by the various components of Warner Communications serves as the paradigmatic example here. D.C. Comics were used to secure the preteen and early teen audience, while MTV and Prince helped to lure the female teen audience. The original development of *Twin Peaks* involved exactly this sort of appeal to a number of distinct audiences. As producer Mark Frost himself acknowledged, he hoped the series would appeal to "a coalition of people who may have been fans of *Hill Street, St. Elsewhere*, and *Moonlighting*, along with people who enjoyed the nighttime soaps"— along with, of course, the people who watch neither anymore, now that cable and VCR have become household fixtures.[27] The emergence of "coalition audiences" as a marketing strategy parallels the development of "coalition politics" in contemporary political theory. Culture industries and

"'Twin Peaks'– the series that will change TV."

—CONNOISSEUR MAGAZINE

"Something of **a miracle. The most hauntingly original** work ever done for American TV." —TIME MAGAZINE

"The year's best show! **Grade: A+**"

—ENTERTAINMENT WEEKLY

" 'Twin Peaks' **extends the boundaries** of network television." —GQ MAGAZINE

" 'Twin Peaks' will **change television history.**" —LOS ANGELES DAILY NEWS

"**Unprecedented.** 'Twin Peaks' easily out-dazzles all the new network shows...this you gotta see." —TOM SHALES, THE WASHINGTON POST

"**Intelligent, gorgeously filmed** and highly stylized. TV has never seen a small town like 'Twin Peaks'." —NEWSDAY

" 'Twin Peaks'...**like nothing else** on television." —LOS ANGELES TIMES

New Series

▲ T W I N   P E A K S ▲

Special Preview Tonight
9/8:00 Central ⊙

political activists both recognize the fragmentary nature of "the public" and realize that effective mobilization of "public opinion" is possible only through strategies of amalgamation.

The media blitz that surrounded the premiere of *Twin Peaks* is quite literally a textbook example of the skillful manipulation of the discourses of cultural legitimation that have hitherto been used to attribute value to media other than television. The full-page ad that appeared in the *New York Times* the day the pilot premiered (6 April 1990) is a case in point. In bold, oversized letters we are told: "Twin Peaks—the series that will change TV," according to *Connoisseur* magazine. Two evaluative criteria are reiterated throughout the glowing reviews quoted in the ad—a romantic-modernist glorification of originality and the shock of the new it produces, and an all-purpose notion of connoisseurship (see fig. 9-1). Throughout this initial wave of reviews in the popular press, *Twin Peaks* is valorized in cinematic terms, a medium that, judging by these reviews, enjoys a far higher degree of cultural status than television, especially when it involves David Lynch, already promoted as a genius director.

Many reviews bestowed automatic status on the program because it was the product of an *auteur*—a filmmaker with a recognizable signature. Richard Zoglin's review in *Time* (9 April 1990), entitled "Like Nothing Else on Earth: David Lynch's *Twin Peaks* may be the most original show on TV," describes the "Lynchian touches" and the director's art school training. The notion that great television might be made only by a great filmmaker also pervades Terence Rafferty's review in *The New Yorker* (9 April 1990). After referring to Lynch as an "all-American surrealist," Rafferty states that "within five minutes of the opening of *Twin Peaks* we know we're in David Lynch's world—unmistakable even on a small screen." The reliance on this evaluative criteria appears in its most bald-faced form in *Newsweek*'s cover story (1 October 1990) on Lynch, in which an "avant-garde" portrait of the director is accompanied by the graphic, "David Lynch—The Wild at Art Genius Behind *Twin Peaks*."

The discrete filmlike nature of the pilot was emphasized explicitly in an ad quoted in the television spot that ran during the week of the premiere: "It's must-see, must-tape television," a statement that stresses the singularity of the program. After the first few episodes had appeared, however, the avant-garde *auteur* mode of evaluation began to dissipate as *Twin Peaks* came to be conceived no longer as a discrete cinematic pilot, but rather as a television serial. The next major article in *Time* (7 May 1990) concerns the *Twin Peaks* "mania," how it has become a topic of "coffee wagon" conversation around offices. The article refers to the show's "trendiness" and includes a chart detailing the character configuration, complete with cutesy hearts and coffee cups, all of which emphasize its soap opera dimensions. The article features, interestingly, this quote from a regular viewer: "It's only a TV show, but you feel like a cultural idiot if you can't quote it on Fridays." At this point, when *Twin Peaks* is no longer being described as "hauntingly original," it returns to being just TV.

The issue of "cultural literacy," raised indirectly by the viewer's statement, involves this very shift in evaluative criteria. What does it mean to be "culturally literate" about *Twin Peaks*? Should one regard it as an unprecedented *auteurist*/avant-gardist incursion into the vast wasteland of mere TV? Or should one adopt a sense of knowing detachment that asserts, "I know it's just all TV trash, but I enjoy it ironically"?[28] The answer is not a matter of either/or but *both*, because a postmodern cultural literacy recognizes exactly this kind of variability. *Twin Peaks* is a polysemic phenomenon alternately valorized as would-be cinema and would-be soap opera. The cover stories on *Twin Peaks* that appeared in *Newsweek, Rolling Stone,* and *Soap Opera Weekly* (16 October 1990) reflect the polysemic nature of signs that constitute this program. The *Newsweek* "Wild at Art" cover features only Lynch as mad genius, whereas the *Rolling Stone* cover shows three of the program's stars vamping it up. *Soap Opera Weekly* features a large photo of Lynch with smaller inset photos of the stars, but surrounds both with other soap stories and photos—"Behind the scenes at *The Bold and the Beautiful*," "It's not all Romance at *Lovings* Dual Wedding"—in addition to the "Curious Revelations" from *Peaks* cast members. In each case, the significance or cultural resonance of the series changes fundamentally in accordance with the evaluative criteria employed by each magazine as it frames the phenomenon according to its own discursive agenda.

Although the press coverage of the *Twin Peaks* phenomenon accentuates its polysemic, multiaccentual nature, the semiotic variability of the program is not restricted to the diverse ways it is given significance at the point of reception. The style of *Twin Peaks* is aggressively eclectic, utilizing a number of visual, narrative, and thematic conventions from Gothic horror, science fiction, and the police procedural as well as the soap opera. This eclecticism is further intensified by the variable treatment each genre receives in particular scenes. At one moment, the conventions of a genre are taken "seriously"; in another scene, they might be subjected to the sort of ambivalent parody that Linda Hutcheon associates with postmodern textuality. These generic and tonal variations occur within scenes as well as across scenes, sometimes oscillating on a line-by-line basis, or across episodes when scenes set in paradigmatic relationship to one another (through the use of the same character, setting, or soundtrack music) are given virtually antithetical treatments. The movement in and out of parodic discourse is common in all of the episodes. For example, in the pilot, when Dale Cooper and Harry Truman are going through Laura Palmer's diary and personal effects, the dialogue, delivery, and soundtrack music all operate according to the conventions of the Jack Webb police procedural. But the "just the facts, ma'am" tone of Cooper's discourse about cocaine, safety deposit boxes, and court orders is shattered by the concluding line of the scene, which is delivered in exactly the same manner: "Diane, I'm holding in my hand a box of chocolate bunnies."

This sort of tonal variation has led a number of critics to conclude that *Twin Peaks* is mere camp, an ironic frolic among the rustic bumpkins and the TV trash they devour along with their doughnuts. But the series is never just camp; the parodic perspective alternates with more straightforward presentation, encouraging an empathetic response rather than the ironic distance of the explicitly parodic. In the third episode, for example, when Dale Cooper explains his "deductive technique involving mind-body coordination"—complete with a blackboard, a map of Tibet, and rock throwing (fig. 9-2)—the scene becomes a thoroughgoing burlesque of the traditional final scene of detective novels, films, or television programs when the detective explains how he/she solved the crime, usually through a hyperrational deduction process. The introduction of the Dalai Lama, dream states, and rocks transports ratiocination (crime solving by rational deduction) into the realm of irrational spirituality, thereby parodying one of the fundamental "givens" of detective fiction. The absurd misuse of conventions defies the viewer to take the scene seriously. However, the scene at the end of episode fifteen in which Leland, possessed by Bob, brutally murders Maddie is one of the most horrifying murder scenes ever to appear on prime-time television; it defies the viewer *not* to empathize with the innocent victim, not to be deeply disturbed by the insanity and violence, which are intensified by the editing and sound distortions.

The death of Leland at the end of episode seventeen exemplifies not just this scene-to-scene variation but also the paradigmatic variation mentioned above, in which the same textual elements from earlier episodes are repeated but given completely different inflections. As Leland dies in Cooper's arms, he realizes that he has killed three young women, including his daughter Laura, and in the moments when he is dying, the framing, dialogue, acting style, reaction shots, and nondiegetic music all contribute to the pathetic nature of the scene, encouraging the viewer to

9-2

empathize wholeheartedly with the horrified father (fig. 9-3). Particularly interesting here is that two key elements contributing to this pathos were used parodically in earlier episodes: Cooper's Tibetan spiritualism, previously used as a signifier of his goofiness, is here given integrity as something that comforts the dying man, describing what he apparently sees at the point of death; and "Laura Palmer's Theme," previously used parodically to accompany any number of "soap opera" love scenes, here accompanies a scene of tragic paternal love.

It could be argued that this tonal oscillation and generic amalgamation, in which viewers are encouraged to activate ever-shifting sets of expectations and decoding strategies, is simply one of those "Lynchian tricks" —that in *Twin Peaks*, as in *Blue Velvet*, Lynch labors to catch his viewers *between* sets of expectations, producing the shock of the newly juxtaposed. Although this oscillation in tonality is undeniably a characteristic of Lynch's more recent projects, it is also reflective of changes in television entertainment and of viewer involvement in that entertainment. That viewers would take a great deal of pleasure in this oscillation and juxtaposition is symptomatic of the "suspended" nature of viewer involvement in television that developed well before the arrival of *Twin Peaks*. The ongoing oscillation in discursive register and generic conventions describes not

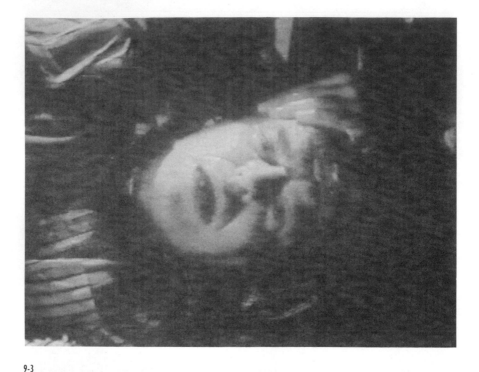

9-3

just *Twin Peaks* but the very act of moving up and down the televisual scale of the cable box. While watching *Twin Peaks*, viewers may be overtly encouraged to move in and out of an ironic position, but watching other television soap operas (nighttime or daytime) involves for many viewers a similar process of oscillation in which emotional involvement alternates with ironic detachment. Viewing perspectives are no longer mutually exclusive, but set in perpetual alternation.[29]

What distinguishes *Twin Peaks* from, say, *Dallas* or *Knots Landing* is not that it encourages this alternation in viewing positions but that it explicitly acknowledges this oscillation and the suspended nature of television viewing. In other words, *Twin Peaks* doesn't just acknowledge the multiple subject positions that television generates; it recognizes that one of the great pleasures of the televisual text is that very suspension and exploits it for its own ends.

If the postmodern condition is one in which we as individual subjects are constantly engaged in the process of negotiating the array of signs and subject positions that surround us, *Twin Peaks* and other forms of hyperconscious popular culture address themselves directly to this condition, situating themselves exactly in the arcs and gaps that result when these positions don't coalesce. By taking the array as their "setting" and redefining "narrative action" in terms of the exploitation of the array, these texts redefine the nature of entertainment in contemporary cultures. The concerns of postmodern television and postmodern theory, then, are thoroughly intertwined, because both are responses to the contingent, conflicted set of circumstances that constitute cultural life at the end of the twentieth century.

NOTES

I would like to thank Ava Preacher Collins and Hilary Radner for their contributions to the completion of this manuscript.

1. Jonathan Arac, *Critical Genealogies* (New York: Columbia University Press, 1987), p. 284.

2. John Barth, "The Literature of Replenishment," in *The Friday Book* (New York: Putnam, 1984), pp. 193–206.

3. Charles Jencks, *The Language of Post-Modern Architecture*, 5th ed. (New York: Rizzoli, 1987).

4. Robert Venturi, Denise Scott Brown, and Steven Izenour, *Learning from Las Vegas* (Cambridge, Mass.: MIT Press, 1972).

5. Allan Bloom, *The Closing of the American Mind* (New York: Simon and Schuster, 1987); Jean-Louis Baudrillard, "The Implosion of Meaning in the Media and the Information of the Social in the Masses," in *Myths of Information: Technology and Post-Industrial Culture*, ed. Kathleen Woodward (Madison, Wis.: Coda Press, 1980), pp. 137–48.

6. Umberto Eco, postscript to *The Name of the Rose* (New York: Harcourt Brace Jovanovich, 1984).

7. Linda Hutcheon, "The Politics of Postmodernism, Parody, and History," *Cultural Critique* 5 (Winter 1986–87): 179–207.

8. Jane Feuer, "The MTM Style," in *MTM: "Quality Television,"* ed. Jane Feuer, Paul Kerr, and Tise Vahimagi (London: British Film Institute, 1984), pp. 32–60.

9. Jim Collins, "Appropriating Like *Krazy*: From Pop Art to Meta-Pop," in *Modernity and Mass Culture*, ed. James Naremore and Patrick Brantlinger (Bloomington: Indiana University Press, 1991), pp. 203–23.

10. John Caughie, "Playing at Being American: Game and Tactics," in *Logics of Television: Essays in Cultural Criticism*, ed. Patricia Mellencamp (Bloomington: Indiana University Press, 1990), pp. 54–55.

11. For a detailed analysis of the changes in theories of the subject, see Paul Smith, *Discerning the Subject* (Minneapolis: University of Minnesota Press, 1988).

12. Chantal Mouffe, "Radical Democracy: Modern or Postmodern?," in *Universal Abandon?*, ed. Andrew Ross (Minneapolis: University of Minnesota Press, 1988), p. 44.

13. Linda Nicholson and Nancy Fraser, "Social Criticism without Philosophy: An Encounter between Feminism and Postmodernism," in *Feminism and Postmodernism*, ed. Linda Nicholson (New York: Routledge, 1990), pp. 34–35.

14. John Fiske, "Popular Discrimination," in *Modernity and Mass Culture*,

ed. James Naremore and Patrick Brantlinger (Bloomington: Indiana University Press, 1991), pp. 103–16; Ien Ang, *Watching "Dallas": Soap Opera and the Melodramatic Imagination*, trans. Della Couling (London: Methuen, 1985).

15. Michel de Certeau, *The Practice of Everyday Life* (Berkeley: University of California Press, 1984).

16. Jencks, *Language of Post-Modern Architecture*.

17. George Lipsitz, "Cruising around the Historical Bloc: Postmodernism and Popular Music in East Los Angeles," *Cultural Critique*, no. 5 (Winter 1986–87): 161.

18. See Fredric Jameson, "Postmodernism, or the Cultural Logic of Late Capitalism," *New Left Review* 146 (July/August 1984), and "Postmodernism and Consumer Society," in *The Anti-Aesthetic: Essays on Postmodern Culture*, ed. Hal Foster (Port Townsend, Wash.: Bay Press, 1983), pp. 111–25.

19. Jameson, "Cognitive Mapping," in *Marxism and the Interpretation of Culture*, ed. Cary Nelson and Lawrence Grossberg (Urbana: University of Illinois Press, 1988), pp. 347–57.

20. Raymond Williams, *Culture and Society, 1780–1950* (New York: Columbia University Press, 1983).

21. See especially Hilary Radner, *Shopping Around: Feminine Culture and the Will to Pleasure* (New York: Routledge, 1992).

22. See Jean-François Lyotard, *The Postmodern Condition: A Report on Knowledge* (Minneapolis: University of Minnesota Press, 1984); Richard Rorty, *Contingency, Irony and Solidarity* (Cambridge: Cambridge University Press, 1989); Barbara Herrnstein Smith, *Contingencies of Value* (Cambridge, Mass.: Harvard University Press, 1988).

23. Christopher Norris, *What's Wrong with Postmodernism?* (Baltimore, Md.: Johns Hopkins University Press, 1990), p. 182.

24. Dick Hebdige, "After the Masses," *Marxism Today*, January 1989, pp. 51–52.

25. Barbara Herrnstein Smith, "Value without Truth Value," in *Life after Postmodernism*, ed. John Fekete (New York: St. Martin's Press, 1987), p. 1.

26. *Entertainment Weekly*, 4 March 1990.

27. *Time*, 9 April 1990, p. 97.

28. Ang, *Watching "Dallas."*

29. Jane Feuer, "Reading *Dynasty*: Television and Reception Theory," *South Atlantic Quarterly* 88, no. 2 (Spring 1989): 443–60.

FOR FURTHER READING

The most useful introductions to postmodernism as it first developed in architecture are Charles Jencks, *The Language of Post-Modern Architecture*, 5th ed. (New York: Rizzoli, 1987); Paolo Portoghesi, *After Modern Architecture* (New York: Rizzoli, 1980); and Jencks's more recent *Postmodernism: The New Classicism in Art and Architecture* (New York: Rizzoli, 1987), which makes many of the same arguments as his earlier work but adds substantial analysis of painting in its delineation of the various forms of "free-style classicism." Although Robert Venturi, Denise Scott Brown, and Steven Izenour, *Learning from Las Vegas* (Cambridge, Mass.: MIT Press, 1972), doesn't present a detailed account of postmodernism per se, it has been massively influential in providing a theoretical framework for the shift from the International Style to more vernacular styles. Venturi's *Complexity and Contradiction in Architecture* (New York: Museum of Modern Art, 1966) was also a landmark work in redefining the aesthetic and ideological criteria for determining the value of different architectural styles. The journal *Architectural Design* is a useful reference point for following the development of postmodernism. See especially the issue entitled *Postmodernism on Trial*, no. 88 (1991).

Outside of architecture, seminal works that defined postmodernism in other media and disciplines include Jean-François Lyotard, *The Postmodern Condition: A Report on Knowledge* (Minneapolis: University of Minnesota Press, 1984); John Barth, *The Friday Book* (New York: Putnam, 1984); Umberto Eco, postscript to *The Name of the Rose* (New York: Harcourt Brace Jovanovich, 1984) and *Travels in Hyperreality* (New York: Harcourt Brace Jovanovich, 1986); Ihab Hassan, *The Postmodern Turn: Essays in Postmodern Theory and Culture* (Columbus: Ohio State University Press, 1987); and Jean-Louis Baudrillard, *Simulations* (New York: Semiotexte, 1983) and *The Ecstasy of Communication* (New York: Semiotexte, 1988). More recently, Linda Hutcheon's *A Poetics of Postmodernism* (New York: Methuen, 1987) and *The Politics of Postmodernism* (New York: Routledge, 1990) develop the importance of parody and intertextuality in contemporary literature, photography, and architecture.

The ideological aspects of postmodernism, as a style and as a condition, are explored in Fredric Jameson's seminal essay, "Postmodernism, or the Cultural Logic of Late Capitalism," *New Left Review* 146 (July/August 1984); and more recently by David Harvey, *The Condition of Postmodernity* (Cambridge: Basil Blackwell, 1989), and Henry Giroux, *Postmodernism, Feminism, and Cultural Politics* (Albany: State University of New York Press, 1991). There are also a number of useful anthologies that give a good overview of the development of the "politics" of postmodernism: Hal Foster, ed., *The*

Anti-Aesthetic: Essays on Postmodern Culture (Port Townsend, Wash.: Bay Press, 1983); Linda Nicholson, ed., *Feminism and Postmodernism* (New York: Routledge, 1990); and Andrew Ross, ed., *Universal Abandon?* (Minneapolis: University of Minnesota Press, 1988). For a discussion of the philosophical as well as the political dimensions of postmodern debate, see John MacGowan, *Postmodernism and Its Critics* (Ithaca, N.Y.: Cornell University Press, 1991); Christopher Norris, *What's Wrong with Postmodernism?* (Baltimore, Md.: John Hopkins University Press, 1990); and Ingeborg Hoesterey, *Zeitgeist in Babel* (Bloomington: Indiana University Press, 1991).

For more specific discussions of the relationship between postmodernism and popular culture, see Dick Hebdige, *Hiding in the Light* (New York: Routledge, 1988); Andreas Huyssen, *After the Great Divide: Modernism, Mass Culture, Postmodernism* (Bloomington: Indiana University Press, 1986); and Jim Collins, *Uncommon Cultures: Postmodernism and Popular Culture* (New York: Routledge, 1990). Studies of postmodern television have begun to appear only recently, and the number of titles is still limited. For useful, if somewhat preliminary, investigations of the relationship between postmodernism and television, see E. Ann Kaplan, *Rocking around the Clock: Music Television, Postmodernism and Consumer Culture* (London: Methuen, 1987); *Journal of Communication Inquiry* 10, no. 1 (1986), special issue on music videos; and Jim Collins, "Watching Ourselves Watch Television, or Who's Your Agent?," *Cultural Studies* 3, no. 3 (October 1989): 261–81. See also Lynne Joyrich, "Critical and Textual Hypermasculininty," and John Caughie, "Playing at Being American: Game and Tactics," both in *Logics of Television: Essays in Cultural Criticism*, ed. Patricia Mellencamp (Bloomington: Indiana University Press, 1990), pp. 156–72, 44–58.

Questions Rather Than Answers

After reading the preceding chapters, each presenting a different critical approach to television, you may wonder what exactly one television critic is to do with all these different strategies. Should you become a particular kind of critic (that is, a semiotician or a feminist critic)? When is it necessary to do "readings" of TV as "text," and when is it important to conduct ethnographies about the everyday lives of audiences? Can't you do both? Does each chapter offer a different "tool" to be used in performing critical operations on television, or particular kinds of television? Does being a television critic entail drawing equally from all of the critical theories and concepts outlined here? Do they collectively add up to "the way" to do television criticism? And, perhaps most importantly, is there some kind of recipe for combining them that the author of the Afterword will finally reveal?

These are some of the questions I will address in this essay, but you should be warned that this afterword will not offer a comprehensive perspective—an "overview"—of the essays that precede it and of the field in general, nor will it pretend that there are final solutions and unequivocal answers. And although it is important to recognize the *strategic* nature of television criticism in calling attention to a set of practices so embedded in everyday life that we seldom see them as such, we must also recognize that there are still (frankly, there always will be) issues regarding television that get marginalized by television criticism.

One way to begin thinking about the preceding chapters' relation to one another is to recognize that the question "how should one conduct television criticism?" is connected to the question "what exactly is one studying when one does TV criticism?" These chapters collectively demonstrate that there is no essential definition of television, that whatever the expression *television* means, it is understood through a variety of agencies, settings, discourses, and audiences. They also affirm that "television" re-fers to a variety of interrelated processes—signifying, narrative, read-ing, economic, industrial, technological, political, ideological, and cultural processes. Television, then, is a historical and socially situated *site* where these processes converge, as well as a set of historical and socially situ-ated *practices*, habits, and conventions for reproducing these processes. Thus two primary objectives of television criticism should be to under-stand how these multiple practices constitute "television" and to consider their relation to broader processes in which television is historically and socially caught up.

As should be apparent to the reader who has made it this far, each of the preceding chapters shares certain basic assumptions while at the same time each constructs television in a different way. Most of these shared assumptions have been touched on by Robert Allen in the introduction. All the chapters reflect a deep suspicion of traditional social science's ability to account for either the distinctiveness or the complexities of tele-vision using research methods developed for the natural sciences. This suspicion grows out of the various ways that structuralist and post-structuralist theories have called into question the existence of a "real world" that can be known apart from language, culture, and ideology. It is not, therefore, that mass communication research methods are more "ob-jective" or "scientific" than the kinds of analysis proposed here, but rather that the discourses of both critics and scientists are always enabled and constrained by language and culture, and the objects of their analyses are always mediated by languages and cultures. The criticism described here attempts to understand the implications of television's being at the center of multiple processes in the late twentieth century. Particularly in its postmodernist variances, TV criticism continually plays on the ambigu-ities and contradictions surrounding the fact that television both is and is not the "real world" that one is analyzing.

The emergence of television criticism out of semiotic and structuralist theories about culture and society has also encouraged a rethinking of mass communication research's predilection to understand all media in terms of a linear model of communication (sender-message-receiver) wherein the sender maintains relative control of the communication pro-cess. All of these chapters, in one fashion or another, continually qualify the independence of encoders or decoders, preferring to see them as bound to (and in some theories, constituted by) the language-like systems or processes through which sense, identity, and reality are produced. Collec-tively, these essays encourage us to consider: (a) how television signifies;

(b) how television narratives are related to earlier and competing narratives and semiotic systems; (c) how those producing television must always work within—how they are constrained and enabled by—this historical field of narratives and sign systems; and (d) how narratives produce their own model readers and how audiences "read" television through a narrative "literacy" or competence.

The chapters on genre, ideological, psychoanalytic, feminist, and cultural studies of television all suggest a relation between television's narrative or signifying practices and the formation of ideologies and culture. As I will elaborate below, television criticism, like contemporary cultural studies, has reconceptualized ideology and culture within the metaphor of language and signification while underscoring how all forms of signification are inextricable from the ideologies and cultures of social groups. On the one hand, therefore, the form that television takes (its ways of organizing itself into narratives, its generic distinctions and conventions, and so on) and the various ways of "reading" TV are all seen as bound by the broader systems for making sense and assigning values that sustain social relations. New ways of televisual storytelling emerge, and audiences watch new programs. However, the reception of television always occurs within value systems that are not confined to television itself but that are produced through other sites, discourses, cultural forms, and commodities or groups of consumers. On the other hand, television's narrative and signifying systems are also frequently seen as *generating* ideologies, tastes, and cultures. And particularly since the 1950s, television has become the most "central" form of culture and has produced some of the most dominant ways of seeing and understanding one's world (or the world as one's own) and of organizing the temporal and spatial features of everyday life.

Beyond these shared assumptions, however, lie a number of crucial points of debate. Because the purpose of this book is to introduce key concepts in critical theories of television and to demonstrate how they might be implemented, these chapters have not dwelt upon the debates over or among these theories. The degree to which the critical approaches begin to diverge and even conflict has much to do with the various ways in which they share certain key concepts while explaining or inflecting them differently. Psychoanalytic theories, for example, offer a different explanation of how "subjects" are formed and about the TV-viewer relation than do ideological or reader-response theories. In the remaining paragraphs of this section, therefore, I will foreground some of the contested areas of television criticism. I want to consider how certain concepts get reformulated within and across these critical theories of television. But in order to avoid suggesting that these concepts (for example, the television production process, the textuality of television, the audience, culture) have some kind of essential meaning outside of these various formulations, I will review each of the critical theories discussed here and organize this review around clusters of issues pertaining to those concepts.

Because much of contemporary television criticism builds upon semiotic and structuralist theories of society and culture, debates frequently arise over the degree to which one *ever* gets outside of signification. In other words, to what degree is the material world always already defined by language and culture? Certainly semiotics addresses the relation between signs and their referents, between language-art-culture and the "real" world or Nature. Pre-television modernist paintings frequently played upon these distinctions, as in René Magritte's realist painting of a pipe, under which is written, "This is not a pipe." (Why? Because it is an *image* of a pipe.) But one of the consequences of doing semiotic analysis in the age of television is that the relation between the sign and the referent seems, as theories of postmodernism are quick to point out, to have collapsed. It's not just that TV increasingly refers to itself but that there is little difference between the "world" that it has constructed and the material world where it is ubiquitous. (In this sense, television can be said to signify differently in some important ways from a pipe or a painting.)

Thus there may indeed be a difference between a video image of basketball player Michael Jordan and the Michael Jordan one sees when one attends a Chicago Bulls game, between the Bulls game on television and the perception of the game in a basketball arena. But Jordan's identity —indeed his very "reality"—is produced in part through his appearance in multiple television settings (such that he seems to be everywhere). TV blurs and plays upon his being "on stage" versus "backstage," in the arena versus out in the world, playing ball versus promoting a product—or doing both versus being himself, being himself versus being Spike Lee. The ritual introduction of the Bulls for each home game is (as much if not more than for any other professional sports event) produced for television as a kind of program "signature," and in the age of superstations like WGN, this production weds the arena itself to a network image and to a mythology of a new "media city," Chicago.

Semiotic theories of television and semiotic analyses in the age of television find it as difficult to ignore the relation between textual and extratextual processes as to come to easy, unequivocal terms with their differences. One of the challenges for television criticism has been to reconcile semiotic theory's generalization that all of culture is comprised of signifying forms with its interest in identifying the specific signifying features of these multiple forms. Television signifies through different practices than film or theater or dance or music, but it also is a form that reproduces and *recodes* all of these and other practices.

Like theories of signification, narrative theory offers a way to understand television as both conventional and complex. There are several aspects of the way that narrative theory examines television that are particularly problematic, however, when considered in relation to some of the other theories. Although narrative theory may help identify the distinctive features of television, as contrasted with literature or film, it also risks essentializing television as a medium that can be conveniently explained as series or serialized narrative. For instance, is there nothing significant (even in understanding TV as a distinctive narrative form) about how the use of voice-over narration in *Magnum, P.I.* emerges out of and reworks the same strategy as it is found in detective films, or how the "mature" Kevin Arnold's voice-over narration in *The Wonder Years* reworks a strategy from detective fiction—or how the kind of "cumulative narrative" of *Magnum, P.I.* is not exactly an example of series or serialized narrative but becomes a form of exploring and recovering a televised past that is reworked in *The Wonder Years*?[1] Likewise, narrative theory's emergence out of literary studies often increases its tendency to analyze television in critical terms better suited to the kind of *discrete* narrative text that is commonly associated with literature, film, or even oral folktales as they are discussed by Vladimir Propp. For this reason, the most convenient objects of study for narratological criticism of television have often been episodic series or serials (a broadcast of *Murphy Brown* or *Designing Women*) rather than the "flow" qualities that critics after Raymond Williams have associated with television and radio.

Where, after all, does a television narrative begin or end? Does it end only when it is canceled? In that case, what should we do with such series as *The Andy Griffith Show*, which has been in continuous syndication since its network run was canceled decades ago? Moreover, many viewers today don't watch just one program at a time, and they may not even see one program in its entirety. Consider the particular challenges of analyzing the Monday night programming on CBS (where *Murphy Brown* and *Designing Women* appear) as a narrative.[2] Why couldn't audience "zapping" be understood as a form of producing and reading a narrative? Is such viewing behavior only accountable in the kind of reader-response criticism that Allen discusses? How would one have to rethink narrative and narrative theory to incorporate this kind of analysis? It is also worth mentioning, in this regard, that issues concerning the limits of a text have become part of a reorientation of narrative criticism of literature and film in the age of television and alongside television criticism's attempt to come to terms with flow.[3]

Sarah Kozloff's notion of the network as a kind of "supernarrator" and Nick Browne's concept of television as "super-text" offer some ways of thinking about television narrative in terms of broadcasting media's flow qualities.[4] The notion of the supernarrator poses some particularly important challenges to narrative criticism if one recognizes television's increasing penchant for recycling films and broadcasts. Does, for instance, a series like *The Donna Reed Show* become a different narrative when it is rebroadcast on such cable channels as Nick-at-Nite, where it is, in a sense, recoded and renarrated? There are, of course, some important tradeoffs in adopting the terminology of narrative criticism to discuss networks and producers. The emergence of narrative theory in literary studies enabled critics to think about film and television as texts, not just as economic products. But the very textuality of narrative theory means that it offers little way of accounting for things outside the text; it is more interested, for instance, in "implied authors" as narrators than in production companies, producers, or networks as agents of particular narrative styles.

Narrative theory's attempt to explain how narrative meaning is produced and by whom (what we might call narrative agency) is particularly problematic when considered through some of the other kinds of television criticism discussed here. When television criticism moves closer to ideological and cultural analysis, it tends to see narrative agency in broader terms of culture, ideology, and narrative itself (that is, a social group's narrative logic and structure enables and constrains future narratives, authors, and audiences). And in the wake of audience-oriented criticism, narrative agency is also tied to the audience's activity as "readers," decoders, and producers of meaning, ideology, and culture—not to mention their own video narratives.

In short, narrative theory raises questions about the "viewer" and the "audience" that have become the point of debate for much of the current critical study of television audiences. As is evident from the explanations of the various strands of television criticism in this book, there are some significant differences concerning formulations of the viewer, the audience, and watching television. The "audience-oriented" criticism discussed by Allen offers a useful starting point for focusing on these differences. By directing attention to the rhetorical strategies of television, some forms of viewer criticism extend narrative theory's interest in how viewers are situated—offered a place within—the narrative world of television's address. They consider how television's various forms of address, whether or not they involve direct appeals to the viewer, construct an implied or model viewer—a place and perspective for the viewer—within the narrative world. In this sense, they attempt to explain how the viewer's perception and "reading" is shaped *by* the text itself.

"Reader-response" criticism also works within the assumption that the process of watching television can be explained through the viewer's engagement with television as a text. This kind of audience criticism, however, focuses more squarely upon the viewer's role in performing "gap filling" operations on particular texts by weaving together multiple strands of signification. Reader-response criticism implies that viewers are guided by the formal structure of the text they are "reading," but beyond that they may read the text in any number of ways.

As Allen notes, a common objection to critical approaches derived from reader-response theory—particularly by those who see television as bound up with broader social and cultural processes—is that they discuss the viewer in ideal terms, that is, as a generalized Everyman, ignoring or minimizing the viewer's race, gender, age, nationality, and so forth, as well as the social context of viewing. This is a particularly dangerous oversight in applying reception theory to television, given TV's attempt to "target" viewers and to produce a kind of television that delivers audiences (as consumers) to sponsors and networks.

Furthermore, if (as some semiotic theory reminds us) viewers read a text in terms of their "literacy" or competence to follow televisions "languages" and to decipher its codes, then a critic must also recognize that audience readings are bound not only by the text and their place in social relations, but also by their narrative competence to read.[5] Indeed, some forms of audience study, particularly those that examine television through cultural studies, have begun formulating the interplay of these factors. From this perspective, audiences in Italy may read *Miami Vice* differently than audiences in the United States, not because Italian audiences are better or worse at following U.S. television than are U.S. audiences, but because their popular culture is comprised of its own (though perhaps shared in some respects) ways of sense making, its own narrative practices and logics. In fact, Italian television may attempt to recode U.S. programs for the "literacies" of Italian audiences. Before Madonna's concert in Torino in 1987, Italian television produced an introduction about the legacy of Madonna in Italy and her "roots" in a provincial Italian community. Or one could say that *Miami Vice*'s use of Italian *style* (Versaci clothes, Ferrari cars, Memphis furniture) offers Italian audiences familiar codes, even though their appearance in a U.S. television series may call into question Italians' sense of the expression "made in Italy."

Beyond the potential variations and overlaps between readings by different national audiences, one might also consider the relation of audience readings among different cultures in one nation. Eric Michaels, for instance, has written a number of provocative essays about the way the Walpiris (an Australian aboriginal community) read U.S. television and how their readings of television have encouraged their production of television and transformed their culture in relation to both their previous oral traditions and the surrounding white Australian culture.[6]

Thus one of the pivotal questions in television studies is the degree to which meaning is determined by the text, by viewers' competencies, and by their positions in the social formation. Almost fifteen years ago, David Morley asked how a critic might best come to terms with the fit between a television text's positioning of a viewer (its attempt to construct a model reader) and the viewer's status as "subject" to broader social, cultural, and discursive *formations*.[7] Morley believes that viewers are not entirely free to read television as they want, but neither can those forces or conditions that enable and constrain readings be understood as singular and uniform. In some respects, the issue that Morley posed has never been quite resolved (and some critics still refuse to address it at all). Not only is it difficult to come to easy critical terms with the limits of audience readings, but the multiplicity of determinations to which he points makes the study of television audiences a task requiring a recognition of the many kinds of television criticism discussed here.

The view that "reader-response" criticism fails to explain television viewing in contextual terms may lead a critic to more sociological and ethnographic modes of analysis. But ethnography still must analyze an audience through its production of *discourses* about television. Viewers produce yet more "texts" as they talk about television. Furthermore, if one agrees that audiences cannot be generalized through a single viewer or even a single family, then is one forever open to complaints about the sufficiency of numbers of viewers analyzed? Ethnographic analysis and cultural studies of television viewing have, in particular, raised another important issue along these lines: To what degree is a television viewer only a viewer of television? And isn't it possible that, despite television's centrality in everyday life, it has a different status among different cultures? MTV may, for example, be one way in which young audiences make sense of the world, and it may help them form a sense of themselves (form identities within social relations); but music videos may not necessarily have the same status in their everyday life as do other television genres, and television may not have the same status as other media discourses and cultural forms such as radio, magazines, and compact discs.

Genre Criticism: TV Criticism as Historical Process

One way of organizing the variety of issues these essays raise is to focus on one approach for a moment and to examine how these issues enter into its discussion of television. Of all the forms of criticism discussed in this book, genre criticism is most often concerned with the historical features of television narrative and of narrative's ideological and cultural implications.[8] Particularly given the numerous critical revaluations of the ahistoricism of structuralist and semiotic criticism, and in the wake of attempts to rethink the relation between texts and contexts, genre criticism has increasingly attempted to explain genres as dynamic *process*.

Through film studies in the 1970s, genre criticism increasingly took up structuralism's interest in identifying the structural similarities between stories to explain how those similarities (as a kind of narrative logic) formed the basis for a cultural logic of the society telling the stories. In film criticism, theories of genre as *ritual* often elaborated this thesis from structuralism to explain how *narrative conventions* became the basis for implicit "contracts" between those who made films and those who watched them and how narrative conventions mediated or reconciled a society's most fundamental conflicts and contradictions. It was argued that because genres were the site for building consensus, they were also the basis for forming ideology (or, to retain the anthropological terminology, a society's "mythology"). Most important, perhaps, "ritual" and cultural studies of film genres introduced issues of narrative's relation to historical contexts and of narrative convention, contravention, and transformation as a way of thinking about cultural continuity and discontinuity. Such film genre critics as Will Wright, John Cawelti, and Tom Schatz asked how transformations in the Hollywood Western from the 1940s through the 1960s restructured and rearticulated cultural myths about manifest destiny and the nation.[9]

But how did these "myths" get into genre films? And how are generic conventions related to the economic and institutional forces that drive the production of films and television programs? For example, to this point there has been almost no work on how the differences between film and television genres might be accounted for, in part, through structural differences between the pre–World War II film industry and the postwar television industry, or how there have also been important historical convergences between filmmaking and television production and genre in Hollywood. Prime-time TV Westerns—one of the first television genres to be produced by Hollywood studios during the late 1950s and early 1960s—reformulated Western narratives through the emerging TV conventions of domestic comedy and drama (for example, the Cartwright home was the central setting for *Bonanza*) and through the narrative framework of series television (for example, the narratives of *Rawhide* and *Wagon Train* were organized as "treks" from one week to the next).

Robert Allen's work on soap operas does explore the historical relation between television and radio both as industries and as narrative forms.[10] Work by David Marc, Horace Newcomb, and Robert Alley discusses genre and authorship in terms of particular television producers, and their work attempts to identify similarities and differences between authorship, narrative, and genre in television criticism and literary or film criticism.[11] Jane Feuer's comparison of MTM Productions and Norman Lear's Tandem Productions in the 1970s is a useful example of what production "styles" have to do with different organizations of the production process, with the historic reformulation of a television genre (comedy), and with the transformation of cultural myths and ideologies (about family, gender, and race).[12]

But little work in television genre has attempted to address the relation between television programming strategies and genre. Unlike the film production and distribution system, television genres have much to do with programming practices—how individual programs are organized within daily or weekly schedules. One might examine how television in a specific country is temporally organized through programming particular genres at certain times (in the United States, game shows air during the morning and sports on the weekend). Particular networks may have encouraged and been shaped by particular genres and specific formulations of that genre. Consider the popularity of "rural sitcoms" on CBS during the 1960s. And in the age of cable television, entire networks may construct an image and a model reader around particular genres, as have ESPN ("the sports channel") and Nickleodeon's Nick-at-Nite ("TV for the TV generation"). Some cable networks have produced variations on traditional genres that contribute to their network image. The Nashville Network and MTV, for instance, produce their own game shows—*Top Card* on TNN and *Remote Control* on MTV—that test participants' familiarity with the "lore" of their specific music cultures.

Although critical treatments, which I have mentioned above, of the relation between genre and the production system obliquely consider genre in terms of programming practices, only Allen's study of American soap operas has attempted to tie all these concerns to a consideration of the audience. Significantly, studies of women audiences and ways that women watch television have devoted considerable attention to particular television genres such as the soap opera and to the place of "women's television" in programming practices and the everyday life of female viewers.[13] They have also raised important issues about specific genres as "masculine" or "feminine" narrative forms.[14] These studies not only consider that commercial television "targets" consumers of particular products and particular television genres, but that television genre offers a way of thinking about the narrative/cultural production of gendered identities and gendered ways of watching television or of seeing the world through television. From this perspective, one might also consider how the viewer's generic "literacy" is not restricted to television—how, for instance, audiences of soaps, music video, or sports television may also read certain fanzines and prefer certain musical or movie genres. In the age of proliferating cable channels, it becomes particularly important for genre criticism to take up issues raised by audience and cultural studies; thus, in addition to genre criticism's interest in historical processes—the emergence of continual reformulations—of television narrative, it may increasingly need to consider how television networks and audiences have attempted to construct identities through genre-specific programming.

Rethinking Ideology through TV Criticism

As we move toward a consideration of ideological criticism of television, it is worth noting that in genre studies (as in semiotic and narrative criticism) there will always be considerable argument concerning the degree to which genres—as codes and conventions—regulate or are regulated by the production and reading of genre texts and the degree to which that regulation is an enabling condition or merely a constraint for the way television tells stories. I say "always" because these issues are not confined to genre theory and cannot readily be explained away by any of the other critical approaches discussed here. They are, nevertheless, issues that come sharply into focus when we look at theories of television as ideological form or practice.

By emphasizing the historical features of genre and criticism, Feuer's chapter directs attention to an area of significant development in ideological criticism. Increasingly, scholars have questioned the degree to which ideology refers to a stable and unified "way of seeing" and have debated the possibility of ideological change and resistance—particularly within popular culture and through popular forms such as television. And as the chapters by Mimi White, Ann Kaplan, and John Fiske affirm, Marxist criticism (out of which theories of ideology emerged) has itself been divided over these issues.

In television criticism, the first issue (concerning the agency of ideology) becomes complicated as one begins to consider ideological criticism's relation to the other critical modes discussed here. White, Kaplan, Flitterman-Lewis, and Fiske all reject the notion that ideology simply and automatically reproduces itself in its subjects (as Louis Althusser's conceptualization of the term implied) as well as the view that ideology is only a "false consciousness" perpetuated by and for those who control the means of economic production (as more classical Marxist theory would have it). They share, with other critical theories based on structuralism, a strong regard for the ways that ideology is *produced* and *reproduced* through narrative and language or (in semiotic terms) through "language-like" processes.[15] But this assumption itself begs a number of questions, particularly regarding the degree to which the viewer or audience (rather than the text) can be seen as the site where meanings, pleasures, and ideologies are produced. As I suggested above about audience criticism, there are some important ambiguities about whether television produces itself and its meanings through all viewers in the same way, whether it "targets" audiences (modifies its discourses) to maintain its centrality for and "dominance" over multiple audiences, whether its meanings are produced by viewers with "already constructed" ways of seeing, and whether its engagement by viewers with multiple "literacies" suggests only that the meanings and ideology *of television* (rather than of the society at large) are never guaranteed.

Even if one were, however, to see the television text as that which produces and regulates ideology, what text should criticism use to "read" ideology? Can ideology be read from or through a single episode? or one advertisement? or the programs of a particular genre? How should ideological criticism account for television's "flow" qualities? Should one attend, in this sense, only to TV programmers' attempts to maintain narrative continuity through "tie-ins" across several programs on their network? Or to what extent, as Newcomb and Hirsch have argued, is one evening's programming comprised of multiple ideological discourses (some privileged more than others in different programs and some conflicting with other ones), so that it becomes difficult to discuss television as offering unequivocal ideological conclusions?[16] To what extent does audience "zapping" or channel switching make problematic the notion that television maintains ideological continuity, and to what extent does channel switching simply move viewers more quickly and effortlessly into "viewing zones" more conducive to their way of seeing as ideological subjects? Finally, how should one come to terms with the ethnographers' claim that TV criticism should devote less attention to the television broadcast as a site of ideological production and instead examine what is said around the set in the home? To what extent do these discourses around the set engage or resonate with the ideologies "of television"?

Certainly the second two issues in ideological criticism (the degree to which ideology refers to a stable and unified "way of seeing" and the possibility of ideological transformation and resistance) are embedded in the questions that I have just posed. In one sense, questions concerning TV flow, the limits of the television text, and the audience are all tied to rethinking theories of ideology as *structure*—theories most common in literary or film criticism, in which a film or literary work is more often examined as a discrete object. As Raymond Williams has noted, when one understands ideology and hegemony as processes rather than as stable, unified systems or structures, it may become more useful to speak of "the hegemonic" rather than "hegemony," of "the dominant" rather than "domination."[17] In this sense, ideological "resistance" must either be seen as part of the process or as an opposition to something that is more fixed. The increased interest in Antonio Gramsci's writings about culture and hegemony shown by contemporary ideological criticism and cultural studies of television could be seen as an attempt to rethink earlier notions of ideology through the kind of endlessly "recombinant" culture identified in postmodernist theory, and more specifically through the kinds of problems for ideological criticism posed by television and by living in a "television culture."

In the 1970s, some film theorists turned to the avant-garde cinema as a potential way out of what they saw as the ideological straitjacket of Hollywood cinema. The practices of cinematic modernism seemed to represent a "counteraesthetic" with great "counterhegemonic" potential. However, the very practices that historically had distinguished a modernist aesthetic were rapidly co-opted by commercial television, advertising, and other popular forms, so that television itself seemed to fulfill both the dream and the nightmare of many modernist discourses about art and culture (for example, that whole societies would someday learn to think of the world through montage and juxtaposition, that frames between the museum/art and life would be eroded or blurred in a new practice). In most cases, efforts to invoke television as the central metaphor for the cultural logic of postmodernism and late capitalism foreclosed the possi bility of seeing television or television culture as site for social struggle and a "politics of resistance." In the 1980s, some critics saw one genre of television—the music video—as representing a "counteraesthetic" to traditional television style and form. However, as Ann Kaplan and others have discussed, MTV came to represent not the creation of a *modernist* TV avant-garde but the *postmodern* form *par excellence*.[18]

Politics, Postmodernism, and Psychoanalysis

I will return below to this related but significantly different issue of what "cultural politics" might mean or look like in a postmodern culture. Certainly John Fiske's call to recognize the ways in which television is a site for cultural politics warrants this kind of consideration. But an Althusserian conception of ideology carries with it the danger of freezing our understanding of television at a particular historical moment (television *is* what it *was* in the 1970s and 1980s). And the more we see television as an unchanging "thing," the more we are likely to regard it as maintaining a stable, monolithic ideology. Whether one agrees with Horace Newcomb's claim that there are no *purely* dominant ideologies in television, and whether one agrees with Fiske that one need look to audiences to find instances of "resistance," the issue in television criticism of what we mean by ideology must be considered through the changing and multiple *practices* of the industries, narratives, and audiences associated with "television." Particularly since the 1980s, one of the challenges for ideological TV criticism has been to address the significance of the proliferation of broadcasting, cable, and satellite networks (in the United States, for instance, such services now include the Christian Broadcasting Network and Black Entertainment Television) and of audiences watching television through devices that can accelerate channel switching or refract the screen into multiple programs. How, specifically, are social relations and identity produced in the new television age?

Psychoanalytic criticism, in particular, examines how identity is formed through the subject's relationship to the narrative world on the screen. Not only, therefore, does this form of TV criticism wed psychoanalytic theory to narrative theory, but its concern with the imaginary-real relation between the narrative and the viewer also ties it to ideological criticism. During the 1970s, psychoanalytic and ideological film criticism most often sought to identify the *dominant* signifying practices that enabled cinema (as an "apparatus") to produce a way of looking that coincided with and perpetuated the *dominant* ideology. Thus cinema was said to produce its own spectators whose identity, subjectivity, or place in familial-social relations was, in turn, produced through their watching of films. Viewers were, in this sense, seen as subjects *in* film's narrative address and subject *to* the dominant ideology that that address produced.

Psychoanalytic criticism's explanation of how films *positioned* viewers (as narrative and ideological subjects) came under attack, however, by British cultural studies adherents because it seemed to suggest that texts "produced" subjects in a fairly mechanical and predictable way.[19] They also questioned psychoanalytic criticism's assumption that a given film interpellated all viewers in the same way and that all Hollywood films went about their ideological work in the same way. This particular point of contestation becomes significant when one begins to compare the ways in which identity and subjects are produced through television as opposed to film. An attempt to identify the specific mechanisms through which television produces identity may well involve comparisons of film and television, but film and TV must be understood less as fundamentally or essentially different processes of subject formation than as a wide range of practices that historically gain definition through numerous agents—of which criticism itself is one.

One of the challenges for psychoanalytic criticism of television is that psychoanalytic film criticism (particularly criticism rooted in Freudian as opposed to Lacanian theory) has found that movie watching offers some provocative analogies with the consideration of narrative as dream, or vice versa, and with the theorization of the spectator as voyeur or as an "infant before the mirror." As Flitterman-Lewis points out, one of the reasons that psychoanalytic film criticism has not gained the same hold on television is that these analogies are more difficult to sustain. I would add that many of them were predicated on metaphors of "looking" that tended to privilege the film image over sound. If Rick Altman and others are correct in arguing that, in television, *sound* functions to "hail" viewers, to maintain continuity within TV flow, and to the audience that "the TV image is manufactured and broadcast just for me [the viewer]," then can psychoanalytic television criticism modify those metaphors and analogies and still maintain the explanatory power of its theory?[20] We might also ask how psychoanalytic criticism would address the *rapidity* with which the viewer may (either through "zapping" among channels or through one channel's flow of multiple narrative fragments) continually re-form identifications through fantasy. Can psychoanalytic film or literary criticism ever come to terms with the fact that, as Flitterman Lewis notes, television doesn't demand the audience's "gaze" but rather may be "watched" (or even listened to) in a state of distraction?

The most conspicuous legacy of psychoanalytic film criticism for television criticism is its tendency to privilege the importance of the *screen* and to define the TV screen in terms of its larger cinematic cousin. Can psychoanalytic criticism account for the rapt attention of the video game player or the use of the screen for computer work in the same way as it would the "tele-spectator"? Psychoanalytic television criticism may also run the risk of attempting to perpetuate psychoanalytic literary and film criticism's formulation of the text as a discrete object of study, thus examining how a viewer is caught up in a relation of fantasy with one episode or even one series. Or conversely, psychoanalytic television criticism may, as did film criticism, generalize all of television as a larger, unified operation of fantasy, arguing (with Heath and Skirrow) that various televisual narratives matter less than the overall "communicating situation." If the latter is the case, is there one form of narrative that best illustrates that situation —and is soap opera, for example, the best illustration or the essential form of television narrative? Would sports on ESPN or music videos on Black Entertainment Television be better examples or even significantly different modes of forming imaginary identifications?

Psychoanalytic criticism offers us a very important way of rethinking social and cognitive researchers' longstanding preoccupation with "real" viewers. But it has also generalized the mass audience through idealized notions of the spectator and has typically tended to downplay the variety of ways in which individual viewers or groups of viewers form imaginary-real bonds with narratives. Thus, although psychoanalytic criticism draws upon a theory of subject "formation" (as passage from a preadult world, where distinctions are first drawn, to an adult world of language and social relations), psychoanalytic film or television criticism has not been enthusiastic about analyzing differences in the ways that very young children and adults form identifications through television. Thus far they have left that arena to social and cognitive media research.

Like some narrative theory and some reader-response and reception criticism, psychoanalytic criticism tends to see television viewers as caught up in and "formed" as subjects through their relation with the text. But unlike reader-response criticism, it does not want to see viewers either as "real" individuals who read television or as differently constituted sets of "narrative competencies." Contemporary psychoanalytic theory draws upon semiotics and structuralism because it recognizes that the components of the unconscious (desire, repressions, anxieties) manifest themselves in a world organized through language and narrative. But psychoanalytic criticism adds to narrative and semiotic criticism a recognition that more is going on when one watches television than simply the production of *meanings* or *readings*, that TV criticism also needs to explain how the audience's *pleasures* have just as much to do with fantasy and the unconscious. Psychoanalytic criticism may well be right to underscore the difference between the scientific study of how "real" people watch television and psychoanalytic readings of how television constructs viewers as subjects. But if psychoanalytic criticism's only point is that television produces a relation with the viewer that blurs the distinction between the real and the imaginary, then it leaves little room to understand how viewers, as subjects of multiple and competing discourses in everyday life, are sites of *struggles* over constructing, defining, and claiming identity and determining what is Real.

Television, Gender, and Identity

Psychoanalytic criticism's concern with how identity is formed through different media has been a particularly powerful current in feminist criticism and in efforts to understand television's role in the production of gendered identities or subjects. As Ann Kaplan indicates, however, the multiplicity of feminisms and the often conflicted nature of feminist criticism are related to some of the debates surrounding psychoanalysis that I have outlined and to feminist criticism's engagement with other forms of criticism presented here. Feminist criticism builds upon semiotic theory to argue that sexual identity and gender differences are marked through both signs and language—that is, not only through word choices such as "gal" or "queer" but also through fashion and a culturally specific lexicon of images. Feminist criticism has tapped narrative theory to consider how "masculine" and "feminine" are categories constructed through stories and conversation and are culturally constituted "modes" of address.

Genre theory offers a framework for conceptualizing how the industry may have promoted certain kinds of literature, film, or television as "woman's" narratives (thus the tendency to refer to melodramas as the "woman's film" or "female weepy"). In addition, genre theory helps explain how cultural distinctions between "masculine" and "feminine" may be produced or reformulated differently through different genres. The related issue of whether there *are* masculine and feminine narratives or genres is implicated in audience studies of how women read television. There have already been numerous audience studies of how women read soap opera or MTV and of the place television (and "women's" genres that circulate through television and other media) occupies in the everyday lives of female audiences. One of the central issues in feminist studies of the audience has been, as Annette Kuhn explains, coming to terms with how film or television produces gendered subjectivity in distinct ways and how male and female audiences, as variegated social groups, engage film and/or television.[21]

Ideological theory has offered a means of considering how the conventionalization of televisual signs and narratives produce stereotypes, myths, and ideologies of male/female differences. Ideological criticism of television has also explored how men and women find their places in social relations, or rather how women find their place in a patriarchal ideology. Cultural studies of male and female audiences have attempted to understand how certain media practices and ways of reading become a focal point for the formation of male and female aesthetics, ideologies, and cultures. With this approach, one must forego the notion of a single, monolithic ideology and recognize that culture is as much a terrain of shared ways of seeing as it is one of competing and conflicting ideologies. Feminist cultural studies (and we need to acknowledge that feminism has entered into, challenged, and reformulated all of these modes of criticism) has been particularly interested in forging ways of understanding the psychic and social implications surrounding the production and reception of meaning and gendered identities.

More than feminist criticism of any other media or cultural form, feminist television criticism faces a particular challenge in coming to terms with whether television is capable of accommodating a feminist discourse or, for that matter, any form of counterhegemonic narrative. This issue has everything to do with whether one believes that ideological "resistance" occurs against a fairly stable ideology or whether one sees resistance as part of a cultural politics through which ideologies are formed and transformed, compete and conflict. This issue also pertains to whether women are generalized as viewer-subject (as tended to be the case in psychoanalytic criticism) or are considered as a complex and variegated audience, and whether "femininity" means the same thing to all women.

In another sense, however, the study of television raises larger questions about the very aims of both criticism and feminism. Feminist critics of film during the 1970s and the early 1980s frequently argued that commercial films reproduced a patriarchal ideology and thus saw film criticism as a process of deconstructing the relation between film's mode of narrative address and its affirmation of patriarchy. Besides equating film criticism with deconstruction, feminist film critics also attempted to locate in independent filmmaking the potential for a feminist intervention and counteraesthetic.

By the 1970s and 1980s, however, television had assumed a much different status than film in everyday life. Thus, although some veins of feminist criticism have not entirely abandoned the potential of film or video for producing a feminist counteraesthetic, feminist television criticism has attempted to come to terms (particularly in the wake of audience-oriented criticism) with how television has pervaded the everyday lives of women. Feminist analysis of particular television texts, such as Kaplan's reading of the Madonna videos, underscores the ambiguities of television as either patriarchal or feminist. Kaplan's analysis particularly demonstrates the ambivalences of feminist criticism toward contemporary television's (and particularly MTV's) ability to produce or accommodate a counteraesthetic. As Kaplan and Fiske both seem to ask, is one to read Madonna as the product of a network given to fetishizing female sexuality for a young male audience or as a deconstruction of the ideological codes of sexuality in music video and music culture that perpetuate this fetishization?

Inadvertently, the case of Madonna's music videos also hints at the ambiguities, for feminist television criticism, surrounding the role of contemporary cable and satellite television (ranging from networks "for women," such as Lifetime, to politically "alternative" channels such as Channel 4 in Britain and RAI 3 in Italy). If Madonna's videos amplify contradictions of female sexual identity and of male/female difference, do they operate though a single mode of address—that is, are these contradictions restricted or most compelling to viewers of MTV (both male and female)? Do music videos on the Black Entertainment Television network or on The Nashville Network operate within the same narrative conventions as those on MTV? What ideological significance should be attached to their similarities and differences? Do they, in other words, produce a fairly coherent ideological discourse on gender? And what might their construction of male and female roles and identity have to do with their distinctive ways of representing race, ethnicity, and class differences? For instance, is Reba McIntyre's country video, "Fancy," any more or less resistant to patriarchal ideology than Madonna's videos? "Fancy" interlaces two narrative rites of passage. One follows the clandestine return of a famous/successful female country performer—portrayed by McIntyre—to the rural homestead of her childhood and the grave of her mother; the other relates the "fall" of the adolescent Fancy from a country life to—because of her family's poverty—a life of prostitution and exploitation by male promoters in a nearby city. Like the Madonna videos, this one's narrative dwells on the contradictions of a musical style (the commercialization of country ballads and female performers), of the star's mythic status and meanings (particularly those produced in the age of country music videos' imaging of star), and of gendered myths and stereotypes within "country culture" (the "fallen" woman, the "beatific," lacy female singers of country ballads, and the "legitimate" professional woman).

Addressing these questions about the production of gendered identities in the age of cable and satellite television would involve analysis of music videos and other "texts" as well as examination of programming practices and network efforts to construct distinctive identities. It would also be necessary to study how viewers relate to these texts and practices and how audiences for the multiplicity of channels differ and overlap. But if this broad a research agenda is necessary to capture the complexities of, in this case, TV and gender, are we still conducting television criticism? Does an understanding of television necessitate the location of television within a larger cultural context? Or, to turn the question around, has television become so pervasive—so central to our understanding of culture—that one cannot do cultural studies without studying television? Or must cultural studies recognize that television texts and audiences are implicated in a much broader, more complex field of intertextual relations, allegiances, and alliances?

Ethnographic and cultural studies of female fan groups have recently offered some very provocative ways of considering how gendered identity is formed by redrawing the boundaries and "networking" of "television culture." I am thinking about Constance Penley's study of female fans of *Star Trek* who re-produce, through newsletters and videos, *Star Trek* episodes and other "masculine" television narratives, often by producing their own music videos from clips of episodes and "rescripting," through this music, narratives of male bonding.[22] The circulation of these videos and newsletters become the basis for forming the identity of the club and of those who consider themselves its members. In this way, their activities both expand and redirect the social and cultural flow of television narrative.

Television Studies/Cultural Studies

The questions that I have posed above about the relation between television criticism and cultural studies also call attention to their historic convergence. Over the 1970s and 1980s, both television criticism and cultural studies emerged within and have attempted to mediate studies in mass communication and the humanities. Television criticism and cultural studies have also, for this reason, frequently been cited as either the cause or the result of "crises" in these two areas of study. At U.S. universities, both are often considered marginal in English or language departments, as indeed they are in mass communication departments; yet in those fields they are central features of debates over the curriculum and over what constitutes a proper object of study. Should one study television alongside William Shakespeare or Virginia Woolf, and if television and literature are both "cultural forms," what place does either have in a curriculum given traditionally to training media professionals or communication researchers? Interestingly enough, many of those academic programs that have attempted to accommodate cultural studies have also attempted to accommodate television criticism.

Having said this, however, we need to recognize that cultural studies is as variegated and conflicted a field as television criticism. The debates within and over cultural studies certainly have something to do with its appropriation of a variety of critical theories and with its interest in tackling a broad range of cultural forms (from oral narrative, to literature, to television, to dance and fashion). What, for example, is Fiske analyzing in his Madonna example? Is he interested in Madonna as a star? In stars as signs, stereotypes, or myths? Does his analysis of multiple Madonna videos and her film suggest that he wants to analyze Madonna as a narrative—as a figure reproduced through a story/history? Is he interested in Madonna or Madonna's videos? In distinguishing between video and film as signifying or narrative practices? Does he see Madonna or her videos the site where ideologies of gender are produced? Or is he analyzing Madonna audiences? Are they viewers or fans (and does the difference matter for his analysis)? Is the audience analyzed as "readers" of Madonna or consumers of Madonna? And if they are consumers, why doesn't Fiske devote more attention to Madonna as industry? Is that implied by his definition of "television culture"? Or does his emphasis on the *activity* of viewers, as readers or consumers, make discussions of the businesses that promote Madonna and Madonna consumption less relevant?

As the above list of questions suggests, such diverse attentions and such interdisciplinarity risk losing the specificity of any one of these questions. Thus, although cultural studies may seem to be the most all-encompassing of the kinds of television criticism presented here, its worst manifestations (and I see Fiske's essay as one of the better) have great difficulty juggling all the aspects of culture they set out to explain. Some cultural studies, for instance, have been attacked for weakening the critical bite of such terms as *ideology* and *culture* by making them *too* all-encompassing and by collapsing their differences. (What, one argument goes, is ideology if culture is the site of "politics"?)

Cultural studies' attempt to situate television and television audiences within the broader terrain of (media) culture and cultural politics also poses the threat of losing the specificity of "television" or of "television culture." In particular I am thinking of work that might equate television with other forms of culture, in the way that some political economy work on TV seems to see television as just another commodity, and of work that might ignore how television is a more or less significant form for producing the culture of a particular audience. But I am also referring to the importance of acknowledging the historical and geographic complexity of television—that is, recognizing that "television culture" always has a historical and geographic specificity. Although explanations of television as cultural process or as the site of cultural formation may therefore draw examples to demonstrate and analyze these processes, we cannot easily ignore the way in which the selection of examples will constitute what one means by "television." How coherent has "television culture" ever been in any nation? When did it emerge? What have been its historical continuities and transformations? What is its geography? What, in other words, is the relation between local, national, and global television cultures?

If, for example, it was important during the 1970s for Fiske and Hartley to discuss how television had become the "central" cultural form that produced dominant ways of processing the world and its changes, it is in the 1990s just as crucial to consider how television culture in many countries is comprised by multiple channels, all of which strive to become the arbiters of cultural identity for different audiences.[23] In other words, what happens to television's function as cultural arbiter and unifier when "television" itself is no longer a unified, limited set of services and programs? Television may continue to be a central, even dominant cultural force, but increasingly, in the United States and elsewhere, it is without a "center" itself.

Along with the observation that cultural studies needs to acknowledge the historical and geographic features of television, it is worth stating one more time that both cultural studies and television criticism have emerged within certain nationally specific intellectual traditions and in relation to nationally specific television practices. Even though cultural studies may be seen as "interdisciplinary" and as having borrowed from a wide range of critical theories, it has also been co-opted and defined in relation to certain intellectual traditions, pedagogies, and cultures. Its curious relationship to other (and frequently more established) disciplines have made it seem, as John Hartley wryly notes, as though "it has no unified theory, textual canon, disciplinary truths, agreed methodology, common syllabus, examinable content, or professional body, no bodily integrity at all."[24] There is a tendency, of course, to try to legitimate any new field of study by giving it an intellectual pedigree and set of traditions. As Hartley, Meaghan Morris, and others have noted with some uneasiness and suspicion, this has already begun to occur as cultural studies has found its way, as a "discipline," into university curricula.[25]

What seems crucial for cultural studies *and* television criticism is the need to maintain a historical and geographic flexibility through interdisciplinarity. The *edge* of cultural studies (and, I hope, of television criticism) is its ability to adjust to the rapidity with which media culture changes and makes itself an invisible and taken-for-granted part of everyday life. This requires the continual development of strategies for amplifying and addressing these changes and this taken-for-grantedness and the continual rethinking of accepted critical terminology. Hence it is one thing to say that television programming changes so quickly that examples may be out of date within six months, or that so much airs on cable television in just one evening that it would take a battery of VCRs to record it all. It is quite another thing to say that television criticism should be content to explain television through examples that are some years old—particularly if little effort is made to acknowledge the historical specificity of the examples analyzed. One of the challenges for contemporary television criticism is, therefore, to recognize its roots in literary and film criticism and to avoid being content to analyze series television because it is the closest TV equivalent to a literary or cinematic story. If, as Fiske contends, the danger for cultural studies of television is that neither "culture" nor "television" are understood as sites for a kind of politics (that is, a cultural politics), then a keen awareness of television's transformations, changing meanings, "new" technologies, and so forth becomes tantamount to developing the critical strategies for understanding and engaging that politics.

Postmodernism and the "Networked" Society

In some respects, theories of postmodernism have been particularly quick to consider the economic, ideological, and cultural implications of a society "networked" through post–World War II media technologies. According to some of these theories, television is a metaphor for the postmodern condition (confirming the adage that there is nothing outside of television), though one could also explain postmodernist theory as a consequence of doing cultural theory and analysis in the age of television. What is, therefore, "new" or "post-" about the cultural environment that theories of postmodernism describe is the extent to which television—more than pre–World War II cultural forms such as literature, theater, or cinema—has become the central metaphor and the central site for defining cultural rupture and continuity.

Postmodernist criticism (particularly analysis that builds on theories by Jean Baudrillard) has tended to dwell on the rapid proliferation of media technologies to argue that these media have produced a *totalizing effect*, meaning that there is nothing "outside" the simulations they produce—no difference between the real and nature, between the sign and its referent, only the endless circle of media reproducing themselves. From this perspective, Max Headroom may provide an even more compelling example than Madonna. Not only was Max both the most authentic *and* the most digitally synthesized "talking head" on the television monitor, but he was endlessly serialized (along with other television personalities) as a spokes*person* in TV ads, as "host" of his own talk show on Cinemax, and as a character in an ABC television series that itself reworked a British television drama broadcast in the United States.

It is not that theories of postmodernism see the media as producing meanings, ideology, or subjects; these theories emphasize that media reproduce themselves as "networkings." In this regard, there is no clear sense of differences among media or between media and their "subjects," only endless recombinations and mutations. Thus the economy and technology of television are, in this sense, the same as those of video recorders, and those who operate computers are merely extensions—themselves terminals in the expansion of boundless circuitry. This totalizing effect is not so much an *explosion* from some central source as it is an *implosion* of differences that only give rise to "surfaces" (a metaphor replacing the notion of "screens") that are at once immediate and global. The "new" media are also frequently seen by theories of postmodernism as having radically called into question more traditional (and somehow more "authentic") forms of narrative and culture and as having radically destabilized or deflated the canons by which narratives and culture were defined. There is nothing to be "read" in the semiotic sense because there is no specific text, no "code," no ideology—only networkings, "surfaces," and simulations.

In some ways, theories of postmodernism are the outcome—the radical consequence—of earlier critical efforts to argue that film and other media *produce* subjects and the world through ideology. They push to an extreme the structuralist thesis (particularly as articulated by Barthes) that the difference between nature and culture had collapsed through forms of signification in the postwar West. There is, however, an important difference between suggesting (as Baudrillard does) that the totalizing effect of media has produced a world beyond meaning, language, or reading and suggesting (as Stuart Hall does) that "there is no *one, final, absolute* meaning—no *ultimate* signified, only the endlessly sliding chain of signification . . . and infinite multiplicity of codings."[26] For this reason, there is considerable debate over whether one can somehow understand the "postmodern subject" (discussed by Jim Collins) as somehow outside of hegemonic process or ideological interpellation or the formation of cultures. In other words, does being a postmodern subject mean that identity is impossible simply because we are caught up in a recombinant world or because we are constructed across multiple discourses and cultures? The importance of this issue, particularly for cultural studies, lies in deciding whether contemporary media culture is a site for struggles over identity or struggles to form allegiances and alliances (not just self-replicating "networks"). To give up on the issue is to foreclose media culture and television as an important site for thinking about and envisioning cultural politics.

One of the challenges now faced by television criticism is how to rethink the meaning and appearance of politics in the "new times" suggested by theories of postmodern culture and how allegiances and alliances are formed through the complex and multiple processes that constitute television as a cultural form. To say that television has become our most central cultural form does not mean that it is totalizing; to suggest as much would be to grant to television and to its various networks the privilege they would most like to grant themselves as arbiters of culture and taste. Television criticism also needs to understand how television has attempted to accommodate and co-opt emerging media technologies and consumers and how connections between the two have gradually transformed the meaning and status of television in everyday life.

(Post-)Postscriptum: Television Criticism
beyond "TV Culture"

The recognition that "television" is a variety of changing practices, tech niques, and technologies also helps underscore how, in the 1990s, the very notion of "TV culture" must also change. No longer are television monitors located only in the home. Over the course of the 1980s, they became not only large enough for video projection in larger spaces and before larger audiences (the "sports bar," "simulcasting" at musical and sports events, in-flight movies and instructions) but small enough to transport outside the home and into a variety of "nondomestic" activities. The video monitor is now used to receive images transmitted from beneath the ocean, under the ground, outer space, and inside the human body.

The home itself has become a complex network of domestic technologies. Just as television reorganized domestic time and space, domestic leisure, and domestic roles during the 1950s, it now brings together and is co-opted by a variety of other technologies (both in the home and linking the home to broader networks). The television monitor is connected to a VCR in over half of U.S. homes; in some countries where there is almost no broadcast television, the TV monitor is used almost exclusively for watching home videos. Both the VCR and the television monitor have become indispensable to the use and sales of home video cameras. Home computers have become increasingly bound up—through modems and fax copiers—with telecommunications, and because computers can be linked to television monitors, they have opened television sets to telecommunication uses and to the variety of other uses to which one can put a computer. Video game technology has transformed the television set into a display monitor for computer games that previously could be found only in a video arcade.

The new technologies of 1990s television culture not only challenge our assumptions about narrative, genre, and "viewing" television, they have also influenced "older" forms of television. In 1990 ABC broadcast a made-for-TV movie entitled *Extreme Close-up*, which dealt with a young man's attempts to come to terms with his mother's suicide by reconstructing, out of home videotapes, the events that led up to her death. The narrative is entirely organized around and through the teenager's point of view, depicting his "secret" vision of family and school life through the lens of "his" video camera. As in such films as *Sherman's March* and *sex, lies, and videotape*, the boy's identity—particularly his sexuality and his adolescence—is mediated through the replaying and narrating of his clandestinely made videos (of school and a girl) and other "home-movie videos" that he has kept (of his mother and family).

Within the narrative codes of television, this movie is a much different text and a much different treatment of video than those that characterize the aforementioned feature films, which were first run in theaters. All three movies, however, affirm the degree to which the home video camera has replaced the literary diary, the photographic family album, and the Super-8 home movie as a mode of recording a personal or family past as story/history. And *Extreme Close-up* attests to the extent that broadcast television has attempted to direct, through narrative, the changing relation of viewers to a new media environment. One of the ironies of using this TV film as an example of contemporary TV narrative is that, a year later, a U.S. student's clandestine video of his high school classroom was picked up by broadcast television "news magazines" to document the troubled state of public education in the United States.

America's Funniest Home Videos, which broadcasts videos sent in by viewers, also serves as an example of how the differences between public and private narratives and between national broadcasts and family or personal narratives have been blurred. MTV has occasionally conducted similar contests by soliciting their viewers' own music videos, some of which may "star" the amateur video producer. As these examples indicate, the form of home videos not only can share the same screen as national broadcast videos, but amateur videos also may be constructed within the conventions of broadcast video (an amateur video artist might make a video that mimics Madonna), and their co-optation by broadcast television modifies the narrative conventions of broadcast TV. As a site for cultural politics, the television set becomes an interface for articulating "family" and personal identity through national broadcasting and for constructing "the nation" around images and narratives of/from family and individual life.

The "interactive" features of these examples raise another set of issues for television criticism in the 1990s. The "narrowcasting" strategies of cable television throughout the 1980s were, in part, an attempt to deliver specific audiences to advertisers (or at least to convince sponsors that they were reaching the right demographic audience). As cable channels multiplied, it became increasingly important for each network to advertise its own programs and itself, to the point that advertisements framed and linked programs through a network "style." (Consider, for instance, the similarities and differences between the ways that Nick-at-Nite's and the Christian Broadcast Network's advertising codes their various televi-sion reruns.) And because VCRs and remote controls emerged alongside cable broadcasting, such network strategies became even more promi-nent. With the new technologies, audiences could not only "zap" through, fast-forward, or edit out ads, but from the various TV offerings, they could construct personal texts that were "in synch with" their everyday routines.

Domestic video game packages for the television set also established a kind of "interactive" relation between viewers and what appeared on the screen. Because video games can be described as narratives (with begin-nings and endings, but also with a serialization of the contest), they estab-lished a different discursive relation between viewer and text than that associated with traditional broadcast forms of narrative. With a video game, the viewer becomes implicated in the story/contest through charac-ters, but he/she can direct the characters—"narrate" their actions—with a "joy stick." Not only, therefore, have video games contributed to a blur-ring of the differences between television narrative and gaming, but they also have made it necessary to rethink the relation between television and the viewer.

Current "interactive" forms of television link the TV monitor with other domestic technologies, both old and new. Most current forms of interac-tive television, such as home shopping networks or televised contests, still rely on telephones. Similarly, "1-900" telephone services (lonely hearts lines, "sex talk," fan news, contests, and so on) depend on television ad-vertising for their success. Already, however, there have been experimen-tal attempts in some metropolitan areas to implement the technology for more direct interchanges between television and telecommunication sys-tems in the home and even for viewer manipulation of what appears on the screen during live and taped broadcasts. As some critics have pointed out, this kind of interactive television serves as a way for networks to "measure" the numbers of viewers. It also draws a finer distinction be-tween television and telecommunication at the same time that it redirects the traffic of signs and narratives across a changing media geography (of new networkings on top of older ones) that will potentially link viewers with one another by establishing new allegiances and alliances.

Through television, computer, and telecommunication technologies, the home becomes reconnected to new networkings that comprise "the out-side world." "Dating" programs, for example, have become increasingly tied in with telephone dating services and computer dating networks. Services that offer home shopping through "computer-link" networks like

Prodigy share and compete for the same viewers and consumers as the Home Shopping Network or J.C. Penney's "television catalog." As Constance Penley and Henry Jenkins have separately noted, fans of *Star Trek* and *Twin Peaks* have created computer networks to trade narratives about (and thus to expand and rearticulate) the two series. Traders in old television episodes use computer networking to conduct acquisitions and to disseminate information about television's past. Some of these computer networkings affirm how new technologies can be used to organize new alliances around or through commercially sanctioned networks. Other interactive systems, such as Prodigy, have already demonstrated the extent to which the question of network "ownership" is very much alive: Prodigy, for instance, attempted to censor users of its "interactive" system when users began to create "bulletin boards" to complain about the system itself.

Certainly the degree to which these new technologies find their way into everyday life has something to do with issues of "economic and cultural capital" (see Fiske). Not only can some people better afford certain domestic technologies, but their use (and intimidation factor) has just as much to do with the cultural capital of users. I'm thinking of the ongoing David Letterman joke about his mother's repeated telephone calls because she is unable to operate her VCR. Both economic capital and cultural capital, therefore, become important factors in understanding how new allegiances and alliances are formed amid changing domestic technologies.[27]

Although traditional broadcast television's relation to telecommunications and computer networking make it increasingly necessary for television criticism to recognize the changing nature of "television culture," these changing relations do not make the kinds of criticism presented herein obsolete. Some of the central issues in this book—particularly those regarding the degree to which viewers control or are produced by television —are still (and will be) very much at stake in the future of media and cultural studies. These changing relations will, however, require that television criticism continually rethink its own key concepts and how they define and constitute their object of study, and they will require that television critics continually keep in mind how their own cultural capital (their own technological "literacy" and competence) enables and constrains their access to certain kinds of media cultures.

NOTES

1. For more on *Magnum, P.I.* as "cumulative narrative," see Christopher Anderson, "Reflections on *Magnum, P.I.*," in *Television: The Critical View*, ed. Horace Newcomb, 4th ed. (New York: Oxford University Press, 1987), pp. 112–25.

2. See a similar analysis by Horace Newcomb, "One Night of Prime-Time," in *Media, Myths, and Narratives*, ed. James Carey (Newbury Park, Calif.: Sage, 1988).

3. Here I am thinking of literary studies that build upon Roland Barthes' distinction between "work" and "text." See Barthes, "From Work to Text," in *Image, Music, Text*, trans. Stephen Heath (New York: Hill and Wang, 1977), pp. 155–64.

4. Nick Browne, "The Political Economy of the Television (Super) Text," *Quarterly Review of Film Studies* 9, no. 3 (Summer 1984): 174–82.

5. See Umberto Eco's discussion of "discursive competence" in *A Theory of Semiotics* (Bloomington: Indiana University Press, 1976). Also see Francesco Casetti, "Looking for the Spectator," *Iris* 1, no. 2 (1983): 15–29.

6. Eric Michaels, *For a Cultural Future: Frances Jupurrurla Makes TV at Yuendumu*, Art and Criticism Series, vol. 3 (Sydney: Artspace, 1987). For an overview of Michaels's work, see *Continuum* 3, no. 2 (1990).

7. David Morley, "Texts, Readers, Subjects," in *Culture, Media, Language*, ed. Stuart Hall et al. (London: Hutchinson, 1980).

8. This is not to say, as Feuer indicates, that genre criticism can be ahistorical (given to discussing similarities between television comedy in the 1950s and the 1980s) or that television histories always acknowledge genre criticism's interest in how a "new" narrative formulation (e.g., Garry Shandling's "backstage" narratives in the late 1980s) occur within the historical continuities and discontinuities of narrative codes and conventions (e.g., the "backstage" features of the early *Jack Benny Show* or *The Burns and Allen Show*).

9. Thomas Schatz, *Hollywood Genres: Formula, Filmmaking, and the Studio System* (New York: Random House, 1981); Will Wright, *Six Guns and Society: A Structural Study of the Western* (Berkeley: University of California Press, 1975); John Cawelti, *Adventure, Mystery, and Romance* (Chicago: University of Chicago Press, 1976).

10. Robert C. Allen, *Speaking of Soap Operas* (Chapel Hill: University of North Carolina Press, 1985).

11. Horace Newcomb and Robert Alley, *The Producer's Medium: Conversations with Creators of American TV* (New York: Oxford University Press, 1983); David Marc, *Demographic Vistas: Television in American*

Culture (Philadelphia: University of Pennsylvania Press, 1984).

12. Jane Feuer, Paul Kerr, and Tise Vahimagi, *MTM: "Quality Television"* (London: British Film Institute, 1984).

13. See, for example, Charlotte Brunsdon, *"Crossroads"*: Notes on Soap Opera," and Tania Modleski, "The Rhythms of Reception: Daytime Television and Women's Work," in *Regarding Television—Critical Approaches: An Anthology*, ed. E. Ann Kaplan, American Film Institute Monograph Series, vol. 2 (Frederick, Md.: University Publications of America, 1983), pp. 76–83, 67–75; Dorothy Hobson, *"Crossroads": The Drama of a Soap Opera* (London: Methuen, 1982).

14. See, for example, Lisa Lewis, *Gender Politics and MTV: Voicing the Difference* (Philadelphia: Temple University Press, 1990). Also see John Fiske, "Gendered Television: Femininity" and "Gendered Television: Masculinity," in *Television Culture* (London: Methuen, 1987).

15. See, in particular, early attempts to theorize ideology through semiotics and structuralism in Valentin N. Volosinov, *Marxism and the Philosophy of Language*, trans. Ladislav Matejka and I. R. Titunik (Cambridge, Mass.: Harvard University Press, 1986); and Roland Barthes, *Mythologies*, trans. Annette Lavers (New York: Hill and Wang, 1972).

16. Horace Newcomb and Paul M. Hirsch, "Television as a Cultural Forum: Implications for Research," *Quarterly Review of Film Studies* 8, no. 3 (1983): 45–55.

17. Raymond Williams, *Marxism and Literature* (New York: Oxford University Press, 1977), pp. 112–13.

18. On the aesthetic potential of video art, see Judith Barry, "This Is Not a Paradox," in *Illuminating Video: An Essential Guide to Video Art*, ed. Doug Hall and Sally Jo Fifer (San Francisco, Calif.: Bay Area Video Coalition, 1991), pp. 249–58.

19. See Rosalind Coward, "Class, 'Culture,' and the Social Formation," *Screen* 18, no. 1 (1977): 75–106; and the response to that essay, Iain Chambers et al., "Debate: Marxism and Culture," *Screen* 18, no. 4 (Winter 1977/78): 109–19.

20. Rick Altman, "Television/Sound," in *Studies in Entertainment: Critical Approaches to Mass Culture*, ed. Tania Modleski (Bloomington: Indiana University Press, 1986), pp. 39–54.

21. Annette Kuhn, "Women's Genres: Melodrama, Soap Opera, and Theory," *Screen* 25, no. 1 (1984): 18–28.

22. Constance Penley, "Feminism, Psychoanalysis, and the Study of Popular Culture," in *Cultural Studies*, ed. Lawrence Grossberg, Cary Nelson, and Paula Treichler (New York: Routledge, 1991).

23. John Fiske and John Hartley, *Reading Television* (London: Methuen, 1978).

24. John Hartley, "Popular Reality: A (Hair)Brush with Cultural Studies," *Continuum* 4, no. 2 (1991): 5–18.

25. Meaghan Morris, "The Banality of Cultural Studies," in *Logics of Television: Essays in Cultural Criticism*, ed. Patricia Mellencamp (Bloomington: Indiana University Press, 1990), pp. 14–43.

26. Lawrence Grossberg, ed., "On Postmodernism and Articulation: An Interview with Stuart Hall," *Journal of Communication Inquiry* 10, no. 2 (Summer 1986): 49–50.

27. See Roger Silverstone, E. Hirsch, and David Morley, "Information and Communication Technologies and the Moral Economy of the Household," in *Consuming Technologies: Media and Information in Domestic Space*, ed. Roger Silverstone and E. Hirsch (London: Routledge, 1992).

TELEVISION

CRITICISM

A SELECTIVE BIBLIOGRAPHY

diane negra

This updated bibliography of television criticism is based on the one prepared for the first edition by Robert C. Allen, Jane Desmond, and Ginger Walsh.

Articles

Altman, Karen E. "Television as Gendered Technology: Advertising the American Television Set." *Journal of Popular Film and Television* 17 (1989): 46–56.

Alvarado, Manuel. "Teaching Television." *Screen Education* 31 (1979): 25–28.

Aufderheide, Pat. "Music Videos: The Look of the Sound." *Journal of Communication* 36 (1986): 57–78.

Babrow, Austin S. "Audience Motivation, Viewing Context, Media Content, and Form: The Interactional Emergence of Soap Opera Entertainment." *Communication Studies* 41 (1990): 343–61.

Banks, Jane, and Jonathan David Tankel. "Science as Fiction: Technology in Prime-Time Television." *Critical Studies in Mass Communication* 7 (1990): 24–36.

Barker, David. "'It's Been Real': Forms of Television Representation." *Critical Studies in Mass Communication* 5 (1988): 42–56.

———. "*St. Elsewhere*: The Power of History." *Wide Angle* 11 (1989): 32–47.

———. "Television Production Techniques as Communication." *Critical Studies in Mass Communication* 2 (1985): 234–46.

Baron, Dennis E. "Against Interpretation: The Linguistic Structure of American Drama." *Journal of Popular Culture* 7 (1974): 946–54.

Bazalgette, Cary, and Richard Paterson. "Real Entertainment: The Iranian Embassy Siege." *Screen Education* 37 (1980/81): 55–67.

Ben-Horin, Daniel. "Television without Tears: An Outline of the Socialist Approach to Popular Television." *Socialist Revolution* 7 (1977): 7–35.

Berger, Arthur Asa. "The Hidden Compulsion in Television." *Journal of the University Film Association* 30 (1978): 41–46.

Berko, Lili. "Simulation and High Concept Imagery: The Case of Max Headroom." *Wide Angle* 10 (1988): 50–61.

Black, Peter. "Can One Person Criticise the Full Range of Television?" *Journal of the Society of Film and Television Arts* 2 (1973): 4–5.

Blair, Karin. "The Garden in the Machine: The Why of *Star Trek.*" *Journal of Popular Culture* 13 (1979): 310–20.

Boddy, William. "Entering *The Twilight Zone.*" *Screen* 25 (1984): 98–108.

Boyd, Douglas A. "The Janus Effect? Imported Television Entertainment Programming in Developing Countries." *Critical Studies in Mass Communication* 1 (1984): 379–91.

Boyd-Bowman, Susan. "*The Day After*: Representations of the Nuclear Holocaust." *Screen* 25 (1984): 71–97.

———. "The MTM Phenomenon." *Screen* 26 (1985): 75–87.

Branston, Gill. "TV as Institution." *Screen* 25 (1984): 85–94.

Breen, Myles, and Farrel Corcoran. "Myth in the Television Discourse." *Communications Monographs* 49 (1982): 127–36.

Brown, Jane D., and Kenneth Campbell. "Race and Gender in Music Videos: The Same Beat but a Different Drummer." *Journal of Communication* 36 (1986): 94–106.

Brown, Mary Ellen. "The Dialectic of the Feminine: Melodrama and Commodity in the Ferraro Pepsi Commercial." *Communication-Information* 9 (1987): 335–54.

Browne, Nick. "The Political Economy of the Television (Super)Text." *Quarterly Review of Film Studies* 9 (1984): 174–82.

Bruck, Peter. "The Social Production of Texts: On the Relation Production/Product in the News Media." *Communication-Information* 4 (1982): 92–124.

Brunsdon, Charlotte. "*Crossroads*: Notes on Soap Opera." *Screen* 22 (1981): 32–37.

Bryant, John. "Emma, Lucy, and the American Situation Comedy of Manners." *Journal of Popular Culture* 13 (1979): 248–55.

Budd, Mike, Robert M. Entman, and Clay Steinman. "The Affirmative Character of U.S. Cultural Studies." *Critical Studies in Mass Communication* 7 (1990): 169–84.

Burns, Gary. "Dreams and Mediation in Music Video." *Wide Angle* 10 (1988): 41–61.

Burton, Humphrey. "Criticism at the Receiving End." *Journal of the Society of Film and Television Arts* 2 (1973): 12–14.

Buscombe, Edward. "British Broadcasting and International Communications —an Introduction." *Screen* 24 (1983): 4–5.

———. "Creativity in Television." *Screen Education* 35 (1980): 5–18.

———. "*The Sweeny*—Better than Nothing?" *Screen Education* 20 (1976): 66–69.

Butler, Jeremy. "Notes on the Soap Opera Apparatus: Televisual Style and *As the World Turns*." *Cinema Journal* 25 (1986): 53–70.

Byars, Jackie. "Reading Feminine Discourse: Prime-Time Television in the U.S." *Communication* 9 (1987): 289–303.

Campbell, Richard. "Securing the Middle Ground: Reporter Formulas in *60 Minutes*." *Critical Studies in Mass Communication* 4 (1987): 325–50.

Campbell, Richard, and Jimmie L. Reeves. "TV News Narration and Common Sense: Updating the Soviet Threat." *Journal of Film and Video* 41 (1989): 58–74.

Cantor, Muriel G. "Prime-Time Fathers: A Study in Continuity and Change." *Critical Studies in Mass Communication* 7 (1990): 275–85.

Carey, John. "A Primer on Interactive Television." *Journal of the University Film Association* 30 (1978): 35–40.

Carpenter, Richard. "*I Spy* and *Mission: Impossible*: Gimmicks and a Fairy Tale." *Journal of Popular Culture* 1 (1967): 286–90.

———. "Ritual, Aesthetics, and TV." *Journal of Popular Culture* 3 (1969): 251–59.

Carragee, Kevin M. "Interpretive Media Study and Interpretive Social Science." *Critical Studies in Mass Communication* 7 (1990): 81–96.

Caughie, John. "Progressive Television and Documentary Drama." *Screen* 21 (1980): 9–35.

———. "Rhetoric, Pleasure, and 'Art Television'—*Dreams of Leaving*." *Screen* 22 (1981): 9–31.

———. "Television Criticism." *Screen* 25 (1984): 109–21.

Cawelti, John. "Beatles, Batman, and the New Aesthetic." *Midway* 9 (1968): 49–70.

Charland, Maurice. "The Private Eye: From Print to Television." *Journal of Popular Culture* 12 (1979): 210–15.

Cohn, William H. "History for the Masses: Television Portrays the Past." *Journal of Popular Culture* 10 (1976): 280–89.

Collet, Jean. "A Good Use of TV: *6×2*." *Jump Cut* 27 (1982): 61–63.

Collins, Jim. "Watching Ourselves Watch Television, or Who's Your Agent?" *Cultural Studies* 3 (1989): 261–81.

Connell, Ian. "Commercial Broadcasting and the British Left." *Screen* 24 (1983): 70–80.

———. "Televising Terrorism." *Screen* 25 (1984): 76–79.

Corcoran, Farrel. "Television as Ideological Apparatus: The Power and the Pleasure." *Critical Studies in Mass Communication* 1 (1984): 131–45.

Cosgrave, Stuart. "Refusing Consent—the *Oi for England* Project." *Screen* 24 (1983): 92–96.

Dahlgren, Peter. "TV News as a Social Relation." *Media, Culture, and Society* 3 (1981): 291–302.

Davitian, Lauren-Glenn. "Building the Empire: Access as Community Animation." *Journal of Film and Video* 39, no. 3 (1987): 35–39.

Day-Lewis, Sean. "The Specialization Issue and Other Problems for the Critic." *Journal of the Society of Film and Television Arts* 2 (1973): 6–8.

Deming, Caren J. "*Hill Street Blues* as Narrative." *Critical Studies in Mass Communication* 2 (1985): 1–22.

Deming, Robert H. "Discourse/Talk/Television." *Screen* 26 (1985): 88–92.

———. "The Television Spectator-Subject." *Journal of Film and Video* 37 (1985): 49–63.

Dennington, John, and John Tulloch. "Cops, Consensus, and Ideology." *Screen Education* 20 (1976): 37–46.

Derry, Charles. "Television Soap Operas: Incest, Bigamy, and Fatal Disease." *Journal of the University Film and Video Association* 35 (1983): 4–16.

Doane, Mary Ann. "Misrecognition and Identity." *Cine-Tracts* 3 (1980): 25–32.

Dow, Bonnie J. "Hegemony, Feminist Criticism, and *The Mary Tyler Moore Show.*" *Critical Studies in Mass Communication* 7 (1990): 216–27.

Drummond, Phillip. "Structural and Narrative Constraints and Strategies in *The Sweeny.*" *Screen Education* 20 (1976): 15–35.

Dyer, Richard. "Victim: Hermeneutic Project." *Film Forum* 1 (1975): 6–18.

Easley, Greg, and Lauren Rabinowitz. "'No Controles': Music Video and Cultural Difference." *Wide Angle* 10 (1988): 62–69.

Eaton, Mick, and Steve Neale. "On the Air." *Screen* 24 (1983): 62–70.

Eco, Umberto. "Can Television Teach?" *Screen Education* 31 (1979): 15–24.

Elliot, Philip, Graham Murdock, and Philip Schlesinger. "'Terrorism' and the State: A Case Study of the Discourses of Television." *Media, Culture, and Society* 5 (1983): 155–77.

Ellison, Mary. "The Manipulating Eye: Black Images in Non-Documentary TV." *Journal of Popular Culture* 18 (1985): 73–80.

Ettema, James S., and Theodore L. Glasser. "Narrative Form and Moral Force: The Realization of Innocence and Guilt through Investigative Journalism." *Journal of Communication* 38 (1988): 8–26.

Evans, William A. "The Interpretive Turn in Media Research: Innovation, Iteration, or Illusion?" *Critical Studies in Mass Communication* 7 (1990): 147–68.

Feuer, Jane. "Melodrama, Serial Form, and Television Today." *Screen* 25 (1984): 4–16.

———. "Narrative Form in Television." In *High Theory/Low Culture*, edited by Colin MacCabe, pp. 101–14. Manchester, Eng.: Manchester University Press, 1986.

Finch, Mark. "Sex and Address in *Dynasty*." *Screen* 27 (1986): 24–42.

Fiske, John. "*Cagney and Lacey*: Reading Characters Structurally and Politically." *Communication* 9 (1987): 399–426.

———. "Ethnosemiotics: Some Personal and Theoretical Reflections." *Cultural Studies* 4 (1990): 85–99.

———. "The Semiotics of Television." *Critical Studies in Mass Communication* 2 (1985): 176–83.

———. "Television: The Flow and the Text." *Madog* 1 (1978): 7–14.

———. "Television: Polysemy and Popularity." *Critical Studies in Mass Communication* 3 (1986): 391–408.

———. "Television and Popular Culture: Reflections on British and Australian Critical Practice." *Critical Studies in Mass Communication* 3 (1986): 200–216.

Flitterman, Sandy. "Thighs and Whiskers: The Fascination of *Magnum, P.I.*" *Screen* 26 (1985) 42–58.

Forbes, Jill. "Everyone Needs Standards — French Television." *Screen* 24 (1983): 28–39.

Forbes, Jill, and Richard Nice. "Pandora's Box: Television and the 1978 French General Elections." *Media, Culture, and Society* 1 (1979): 35–50.

Foss, Karen A., and Stephen W. Littlejohn. "*The Day After*: Rhetorical Vision in an Ironic Frame." *Critical Studies in Mass Communication* 3 (1986): 317–36.

Gardner, Carl, and Margaret Henry. "Racism, Anti-racism and Access Television: The Making of *Open Door*." *Screen Education* 31 (1979): 69–81.

Gardner, Carl, and Julie Sheppard. "Transforming Television—Part One, the Limits of Left Policy." *Screen* 25 (1984): 26–40.

Garnham, Nicholas. "Public Service versus the Market." *Screen* 24 (1983): 6–27.

———. "Television Documentary and Ideology." *Screen* 13 (1972): 109–15.

Gibson, William. "Network News: Elements of a Theory." *Social Text* 3 (1980): 88–111.

Gilbert, W. Stephen. "The TV Play: Outside the Consensus." *Screen Education* 35 (1980): 35–44.

Gitlin, Todd. "Media Sociology: The Dominant Paradigm." *Theory and Society* 6 (1978): 205–53.

———. "Spotlight and Shadows: Television and the Culture of Politics." *College English* 38 (1977): 789–801.

Glynn, Kevin. "Tabloid Television's Transgressive Aesthetic: *A Current Affair* and the 'Shows That Taste Forgot.'" *Wide Angle* 12 (1990): 22–44.

Goodwin, Andrew. "Music Video in the (Post)Modern World." *Screen* 28 (1987): 36–55.

Gray, Herman. "Television and the New Black Man: Black Male Images in Prime-Time Situation Comedy." *Media, Culture, and Society* 8 (1986): 223–42.

——. "Television, Black Americans, and the American Dream." *Critical Studies in Mass Communication* 6 (1989): 376–86.

Grealy, Jim. "Notes on Popular Culture." *Screen Education* 22 (1977): 5–11.

Greenberg, Bradley S., Kimberly Neuendorf, Nancy Buerkel-Rothfuss, and Laura Henderson. "The Soaps: What's On and Who Cares?" *Journal of Broadcasting* 26 (1982): 519–35.

Greenberg, Harvey R. "In Search of Spock: A Psychoanalytic Inquiry." *Journal of Popular Film and Television* 12 (1984): 52–65.

Gripsrud, Jostein. "Toward a Flexible Methodology in Studying Media Meaning: *Dynasty* in Norway." *Critical Studies in Mass Communication* 7 (1990): 117–28.

Grossberg, Lawrence. "The In-Difference of Television." *Screen* 28 (1987): 28–45.

——. "Postmodernity and Affect: All Dressed Up with No Place to Go." *Communication* 10 (1988): 271–93.

Grossberg, Lawrence, and Paula A. Treichler. "Intersection of Power: Criticism-Television-Gender." *Communication* 9 (1987): 273–87.

Gutch, Robin. "Whose Telly Anyway?" *Screen* 25 (1984): 122–27.

Hall, Stuart. "Deviancy, Politics and the Media." In *Deviance and Social Control*, edited by P. Rock and M. McIntosh, pp. 261–305. London: Tavistock, 1974.

Halloran, James D. "Understanding Television." *Screen Education* 14 (1975): 4–13.

Hanke, Robert. "Hegemonic Masculinity in *thirtysomething*." *Critical Studies in Mass Communication* 7 (1990): 231–48.

Hartley, John. "Television and the Power of Dirt." *Australian Journal of Cultural Studies* 1 (1983): 68–82.

Hartley, John, and John Fiske. "Myth—Representation: A Cultural Reading of *News at Ten*." *Communications Studies Bulletin* 4 (1977): 12–33.

Harvey, Lisa St. Clair. "Temporary Insanity: Fun, Games, and Transformational Ritual in American Music Video." *Journal of Popular Culture* 24 (1990): 39–64.

Hay, James. "Rereading Early Television Advertising: When Wasn't the Ad the Story?" *Journal of Film and Video* 41 (1989): 4–20.

Heath, Stephen, and Gillian Skirrow. "Television: A World in Action." *Screen* 18 (1977): 7–59.

Herridge, Peter. "Television, the 'Riots,' and Research." *Screen* 24 (1983): 86–91.

Hilmes, Michele. "The Television Apparatus: Direct Address." *Journal of Film and Video* 37 (1985): 27–36.

———. "Where Everybody Knows Your Name: *Cheers* and the Mediation of Cultures." *Wide Angle* 12 (1990): 64–73.

Himmelstein, Hal. "Kodak's 'America': Images from the American Eden." *Journal of Film and Video* 41 (1989): 75–94.

Hoffer, Tom W., and Richard Alan Nelson. "Docudrama on American Television." *Journal of the University Film Association* 30 (1978): 21–28.

Homans, Peter. "Psychology and Popular Culture: Ideological Reflections on *M*A*S*H*." *Journal of Popular Culture* 17 (1983): 3–21.

Honeyford, Susan. "Women and Television." *Screen* 21 (1980): 49–52.

Houston, Beverle. "Viewing Television: The Metapsychology of Endless Consumption." *Quarterly Review of Film Studies* 9 (1984): 183–95.

Hurd, Geoff. "*The Sweeny*—Contradiction and Coherence." *Screen Education* 20 (1976): 47–53.

Janes, Barry T. "History and Structure of Public Access Television." *Journal of Film and Video* 39 (1987): 14–23.

Jenkins, Henry. "*Star Trek* Rerun, Reread, Rewritten: Fan Writing as Textual Poaching." *Critical Studies in Mass Communication* 5 (1988): 85–107.

Jhally, Sut, and Bill Livant. "Watching as Working: The Valorization of Audience Consciousness." *Journal of Communication* 36 (1986): 124–43.

Joyrich, Lynne. "All That Television Allows: TV Melodrama, Postmodernism, and Consumer Culture." *Camera Obscura* 16 (1988): 129–53.

Kagan, Norman. "Amos 'n' Andy: Twenty Years Late, or Two Decades Early?" *Journal of Popular Culture* 9 (1975): 71–76.

Kaplan, E. Ann. "History, Spectatorship, and Gender Address in Music Television." *Journal of Communication Inquiry* 10 (1986): 3–14.

———. "A Post-Modern Play of the Signifier? Advertising, Pastiche and Schizophrenia in Music Television." In *Television in Transition*, edited by Phillip Drummond and Richard Paterson, pp. 146–63. London: British Film Institute, 1985.

———. "Sexual Difference, Pleasure and the Construction of the Spectator in Music Television." *Oxford Literary Review* 8 (1986): 113–23.

Kaplan, Frederick I. "Intimacy and Conformity in American Soap Opera." *Journal of Popular Culture* 9 (1975): 622–25.

Kellner, Douglas. "TV, Ideology, and Emancipatory Popular Culture." *Socialist Review* 9 (1979): 13–53.

Kepley, Vance. "The Weaver Years at NBC." *Wide Angle* 12 (1990): 46–63.

Kerr, Paul. "Situation Comedies." *Screen* 24 (1983): 71–74.

Kervin, Denise. "Ambivalent Pleasure from *Married . . . With Children*." *Journal of Film and Video* 42 (1990): 42–52.

———. "Reality According to Television News: Pictures from El Salvador." *Wide Angle* 7 (1985): 61–71.

Kinder, Marsha. "Music Video and the Spectator: Television, Ideology, and Dream." *Film Quarterly* 38 (1984): 3–15.

King, Scott Benjamin. "Sonny's Virtues: The Gender Negotiations of *Miami Vice.*" *Screen* 31 (1988): 281–95.

Kreizenbeck, Alan. "Soaps: Promiscuity, Adultery, and 'New Improved Cheer.'" *Journal of Popular Culture* 17 (1983): 175–81.

Laing, Dave. "Music Video—Industrial Product, Cultural Form." *Screen* 26 (1985): 78–83.

Langer, John. "Television's 'Personality System.'" *Media, Culture, and Society* 3 (1981): 351–66.

Larson, James F., Emile G. McAnany, and J. Douglas Storey. "News of Latin America on Network Television, 1972–1981: A Northern Perspective on the Southern Hemisphere." *Critical Studies in Mass Communication* 3 (1986): 169–83.

Lawrence, Amy. "The Aesthetics of the Image: The Hanging of Colonel Higgins: A CBS Newsbreak." *Wide Angle* 12 (1990): 7–11.

Leibman, Nina C. "Leave Mother Out: The Fifties Family in American Film and Television." *Wide Angle* 10 (1988): 24–41.

———. "Mini-Series/Maxi-Messages: Ideology and the Interaction between Peter the Great, AETNA, AT&T, and Ford." *Journal of Film and Video* 39 (1987): 5–18.

Lembo, Ronald, and Kenneth H. Tucker. "Culture, Television, and Opposition: Rethinking Cultural Studies." *Critical Studies in Mass Communication* 7 (1990): 97–116.

Lemish, Dafna. "The Rules of Viewing Television in Public Places." *Journal of Broadcasting* 26 (1982): 757–81.

Levinson, Richard M. "From Olive Oyl to Sweet Polly Purebred: Sex Role Stereotypes and Televised Cartoons." *Journal of Popular Culture* 9 (1975): 561–72.

Lewis, Lisa A. "Form and Female Authorship in Music Video." *Communication* 9 (1987): 355–77.

Liebes, Tamar. "Cultural Differences in the Retelling of Television Fiction." *Critical Studies in Mass Communication* 5 (1988): 277–92.

Linick, Anthony. "Britannia Rules the Air Waves: Television Programming in Transatlantic Perspective." *Journal of Popular Culture* 7 (1974): 918–27.

———. "Magic and Identity in Television Programming." *Journal of Popular Culture* 3 (1970): 644–55.

Lopate, Carol. "Daytime Television: You'll Never Want to Leave Home." *Radical America* 2 (1977): 33–51.

Lowry, Dennis T., and David E. Towles. "Soap Opera Portrayals of Sex, Contraception, and Sexually Transmitted Diseases." *Journal of Communication* 39 (1989): 76–83.

Lusted, David. "Feeding the Panic and Breaking the Cycle—Popular TV and Schoolchildren." *Screen* 24 (1983): 81–93.

McAdow, Ron. "Experience of Soap Opera." *Journal of Popular Culture* 7 (1974): 955–65.

MacDonald, J. Fred. "Black Perimeters—Paul Robeson, Nat King Cole, and the Role of Blacks in American TV." *Journal of Popular Film and Television* 7 (1979): 246–64.

———. "The Cold War as Entertainment in 'Fifties Television." *Journal of Popular Film and Television* 7 (1978): 3–31.

McGrath, John. "TV Drama: The Case Against Naturalism." *Sight and Sound* 46 (1977): 100–105.

McKinley, Robert. "Culture Meets Nature on the Six O'Clock News." *Journal of Popular Culture* 17 (1983): 109–14.

Mander, Mary. "*Dallas*: The Mythology of Crime and Moral Occult." *Journal of Popular Culture* 17 (1983): 44–50.

Manvell, Roger. "Why Television Criticism Differs from Other Forms of Criticism." *Journal of the Society of Film and Television Arts* 2 (1973): 1–3.

Marchetti, Gina. "Class, Ideology, and Commercial Television: An Analysis of *The A-Team*." *Journal of Film and Video* 39 (1987): 19–28.

Mayne, Judith. "*L.A. Law* and Prime-Time Feminism." *Discourse: Journal for Theoretical Studies in Media and Culture* 2 (1988): 30–47.

Meehan, Eileen R. "Conceptualizing Culture as Commodity: The Problem of Television." *Critical Studies in Mass Communication* 3 (1986): 448–57.

Mellencamp, Patricia. "Situation and Simulation: An Introduction to *I Love Lucy*." *Screen* 26 (1985): 35–40.

Merlman, Richard. "Power and Community in Television." *Journal of Popular Culture* 2 (1968): 63–80.

Modleski, Tania. "The Search for Tomorrow in Today's Soap Operas: Notes on a Feminine Narrative Form." *Film Quarterly* 33 (1979): 12–21.

Mohr, Howard. "TV Weather Programs." *Journal of Popular Culture* 4 (1971): 628–33.

Montgomery, Kathryn. "Writing about Television in the Popular Press." *Critical Studies in Mass Communication* 2 (1985): 74–89.

Morse, Margaret. "Talk, Talk, Talk—the Space of Discourse in Television." *Screen* 26 (1985): 2–15.

Mould, David H. "Historical Trends in the Criticism of the Newsreel and Television News, 1930–1955." *Journal of Popular Film and Television* 12 (1984): 118–26.

Murdock, Graham. "Authorship and Organization." *Screen Education* 35 (1980): 19–34.

Naficy, Hamid. "Television Intertextuality and the Discourse of the Nuclear Family." *Journal of Film and Video* 41 (1989): 42–59.

Newcomb, Horace. "American Television Criticism, 1970–1985." *Critical Studies in Mass Communication* 3 (1986): 217–28.

———. "On the Dialogic Aspects of Mass Communication." *Critical Studies in Mass Communication* 1 (1984): 34–50.

Newcomb, Horace, and Paul M. Hirsch. "Television as a Cultural Forum: Implications for Research." *Quarterly Review of Film Studies* 8 (1983): 45–56.

Norton, Suzanne Frentz. "Tea Time on the 'Telly': British and Australian Soap Opera." *Journal of Popular Culture* 19 (1985): 3–19.

Nowell-Smith, Geoffrey. "Television—Football—the World." *Screen* 19 (25): 45–59.

Oakley, Giles. "Cinematic Comparisons." *Screen* 24 (1983): 81–85.

Olson, Scott R. "Meta-Television: Popular Postmodernism." *Critical Studies in Mass Communication* 4 (1987): 284–300.

Page, Malcolm. "The British Television Play: A Review Article." *Journal of Popular Culture* 5 (1972): 806–20.

Paterson, Richard. "Planning the Family: The Art of the Television Schedule." *Screen Education* 35 (1980): 79–86.

———"The Sweeny." *Screen Education* 20 (1976): 5–14.

Pearson, Tony. "Teaching Television." *Screen* 24 (1983): 35–43.

Petro, Patrice. "Mass Culture and the Feminine: The 'Place' of Television in Film Studies." *Cinema Journal* 25 (1986): 5–21.

Piccirillo, M. S. "On the Authenticity of Televisual Experience: A Critical Exploration of Para-Social Closure." *Critical Studies in Mass Communication* 3 (1986): 337–55.

Poole, Michael. "The Cult of the Generalist: British Television Criticism, 1936–83." *Screen* 25 (1984): 41–62.

Porter, Dennis. "Soap Time: Thoughts on a Commodity Art Form." *College English* 38 (1977): 782–88.

Porter, Vincent. "Video Recording and the Teacher." *Screen Education* 35 (1980): 87–90.

Pringle, Ashley. "A Methodology for Television Analysis with Reference to the Drama Series." *Screen* 13 (1972): 117–28.

Probyn, Elspeth. "New Traditionalism and Post-Feminism: TV Does the Home." *Screen* 31 (1988): 147–59.

Rakow, Lana F., and Kimberlie Kralich. "Woman as Sign in Television News." *Journal of Communication* 41 (1991): 8–23.

Rentschler, Eric. "Musical Cinema, Music Video, Music Television." *Film Quarterly* 43 (1990): 2–14.

Requena, Jesus G. "Narrativity/Discursivity in the American Television Film." *Screen* 22 (1981): 38–42.

Roberts, John. "Postmodern Television and the Visual Arts." *Screen* 28 (1987): 118–27.

Ross, Andrew. "*Miami Vice*: Selling In." *Communication* 9 (1987): 305–34.

———. "Postmodernism and Universal Abandon." *Communication* 10 (1988): 247–58.

Rothenbuhler, Eric W. "The Living Room Celebration of the Olympic Games." *Journal of Communication* 38 (1988): 61–81.

Sahin, Haluk. "Ideology of Television: Theoretical Framework and a Case Study." *Media, Culture, and Society* 1 (1979): 161–70.

Sahin, Haluk, and J. P. Robinson. "Beyond the Realm of Necessity: Television and the Colonization of Leisure." *Media, Culture, and Society* 3 (1981): 85–96.

Scannell, Paddy. "The Social Eye of Television, 1946–1955." *Media, Culture, and Society* 1 (1979): 97–106.

Schulze, Laurie Jane. "*Getting Physical*: Text/Context/Reading and the Made-for-Television Movie." *Cinema Journal* 25 (1986): 35–50.

Schwichtenberg, Cathy. "Articulating the People's Politics: Manhood and Right-Wing Populism in *The A-Team*." *Communication* 9 (1987): 379–98.

———. "*Charlie's Angels* (ABC-TV)." *Jump Cut* 24/25 (1981): 13–15.

———. "*The Love Boat*: The Packaging and Selling of Love, Heterosexual Romance, and Family." *Media, Culture, and Society* 6 (1984): 301–11.

Seiter, Ellen. "Eco's TV Guide: The Soaps." *Tabloid* 6 (1981): 36–43.

———. "Making Distinctions in TV Audience Research: Case Study of a Troubling Interview." *Cultural Studies* 4 (1990): 61–84.

———. "Men, Sex, and Money in Recent Family Melodrama." *Journal of the University Film and Video Association* 35 (1983): 17–27.

———. "Promise and Contradiction: The Daytime Television Serials." *Screen* 23 (1982): 150–63.

———. "'To Teach and to Sell': Irna Phillips and Her Sponsors, 1930–1954." *Journal of Film and Video* 41 (1989): 21–35.

Selnow, Gary W. "Solving Problems on Prime-Time Television." *Journal of Communication* 36 (1986): 63–72.

Shatzkin, Roger. "*Shogun* (NBC-TV)." *Jump Cut* 24/25 (1981): 16.

Silverstone, Roger. "An Approach to the Structural Analysis of the Television Message." *Screen* 17 (1976): 9–40.

———. "Narrative Strategies in Television Science—a Case Study." *Media, Culture, and Society* 6 (1984): 377–410.

———. "The Right to Speak: On a Poetic for Television Documentary." *Media, Culture, and Society* 5 (1983): 137–54.

Simpson, Philip. "Talking Heads." *Screen* 25 (1984): 80–84.

Smith, Keith. "Viewings: Which, to Whom and for What?" *Journal of the*

Society of Film and Television Arts 2 (1973): 10–12.

Spence, Jo. "An *Omnibus* Dossier." *Screen* 24 (1983): 40–52.

Spence, Louise. "Life's Little Problems . . . and Pleasures: An Investigation into the Narrative Structures of *The Young and the Restless.*" *Quarterly Review of Film Studies* 9 (1984): 301–8.

Spigel, Lynn. "The Domestic Economy of Television Viewing in Postwar America." *Critical Studies in Mass Communication* 6 (1989): 337–54.

———. "Installing the Television Set: Popular Discourses on Television and Domestic Space, 1948–1955." *Camera Obscura* 16 (1988): 12–49.

Stein, Howard F. "In Search of *Roots*: An Epic of Origins and Destiny." *Journal of Popular Culture* 11 (1977): 11–17.

Steinman, Clay. "Reception of Theory: Film/Television Studies and the Frankfurt School." *Journal of Film and Video* 40 (1988): 4–19.

Stone, Douglas. "TV Movies and How They Get That Way." *Journal of Popular Film and Television* 7 (1979): 147–49.

Surlin, Stuart. "Television Criticism in Canada." *Critical Studies in Mass Communications* 2 (1985): 80–83.

Sun, Se-Wen, and James Lull. "The Adolescent Audience for Music Videos and Why They Watch." *Journal of Communication* 36 (1986): 115–25.

Thomas, Sari. "Reality, Fiction, and Television." *Journal of the University Film Association* 30 (1978): 29–34.

Thompson, John O. "Tragic Flow." *Screen Education* 35 (1980): 45–58.

Thomson, David. "TV Weather." *Sight and Sound* 49 (1980): 87–90.

Thorburn, David. "Television as an Aesthetic Medium." *Critical Studies in Mass Communication* 4 (1987): 161–73.

Timberg, Bernard, and Hal Himmelstein. "Television Commercials and the Contradictions of Everyday Life: A Follow-Up to Himmelstein's Production Study of the Kodak 'America' Commercial." *Journal of Film and Video* 41 (1989): 67–79.

Tolson, Andrew. "Anecdotal Television." *Screen* 26 (1985): 18–27.

Tomasulo, Frank P. "The Spectator-in-the-Tube: The Rhetoric of Donahue." *Journal of the University Film and Video Association* 36 (1984): 5–12.

Trevino, Jesus Salvador. "Latino Portrayals in Film and Television." *Jump Cut* 30 (1985): 14–16.

Tuchman, Gaye. "Television News and the Metaphor of Myth." *Studies in the Anthropology of Visual Culture* 5 (1978): 56–62.

Tulloch, John. "Gradgrind's Heirs: The Quiz and the Presentation of Knowledge by British Television." *Screen Education* 19 (1976): 3–13.

Tyrell, William Blake. "*Star Trek* as Myth and Television as Mythmaker." *Journal of Popular Culture* 10 (1977): 711–19.

Verschuure, Eric P. "Stumble, Bumble, Mumble: TV's Image of the South." *Jour-*

nal of Popular Culture 16 (1982): 92–96.

Vianello, Robert. "The Power Politics of 'Live' Television." *Journal of Film and Video* 37 (1985): 26–40.

Viera, John David. "Terrorism at the BBC: The IRA on British Television." *Journal of Film and Video* 40 (1988): 28–36.

Watson, Mary Ann. "Television Criticism in the Popular Press." *Critical Studies in Mass Communication* 2 (1985): 66–74.

Wexman, Virginia Wright. "Returning From The Moon: Jackie Gleason, the Carnivalesque, and Television Comedy." *Journal of Film and Video* 42 (1990): 20–32.

White, Duffield. "Television Non-Fiction as Historical Narrative." *Journal of Popular Culture* 7 (1974): 928–33.

White, Mimi. "Crossing Wavelengths: The Diegetic and Referential Imaginary of American Commercial Television." *Cinema Journal* 25 (1986): 51–64.

———. "Television Genres: Intertextuality." *Journal of Film and Video* 37 (1985): 41–47.

Williams, Brien R., and Cheryl Fulton. "A Study of Visual Style and Creativity in Television." *Journal of the University Film and Video Association* 36 (1984): 23–35.

Williams, Carol Traynor. "It's Not So Much 'You've Come a Long Way Baby'—as 'You're Gonna Make It After All.'" *Journal of Popular Culture* 7 (1974): 981–89.

Williams, Martin. "TV: Tell Me a Story." *Journal of Popular Culture* 7 (1974): 895–99.

Williams, Raymond. "Television and Teaching." *Screen Education* 31 (1979): 5–14.

Woal, Michael B. "Defamiliariziation in Television Viewing: Aesthetic and Rhetorical Modes of Experiencing Television." *Journal of the University Film and Video Association* 34 (1982): 25–32.

Wren-Lewis, Justin. "The Encoding/Decoding Model: Criticisms and Redevelopments for Research on Decoding." *Media, Culture, and Society* 5 (1983): 179–97.

———. "TV Coverage of the Riots." *Screen Education* 40 (1981–82): 15–33.

Wright, John L. "TUNE-IN: The Focus of Television Criticism." *Journal of Popular Culture* 7 (1974): 887–94.

Wyver, John. "Screening Television." *Screen* 24 (1983): 75–80.

Zelizer, Barbie. "What's Rather Public about Dan Rather: TV Journalism and the Emergence of Celebrity." *Journal of Popular Film and Television* 17 (1989): 74–80.

Zettl, Herbert. "The Rare Case of Television Aesthetics." *Journal of the University Film Association* 30 (1978): 3–8.

Zimmerman, Patricia R. "Good Girls, Bad Women: The Role of Older Women on *Dynasty.*" *Journal of Film and Video* 37 (1985): 89–92.

Zynda, Thomas H. "The Metaphoric Vision of *Hill Street Blues.*" *Journal of Popular Film and Television* 14 (1986): 100–113.

Books

Allen, Robert C. *Speaking of Soap Operas.* Chapel Hill: University of North Carolina Press, 1985.

Ang, Ien. *Desperately Seeking the Audience.* London: Routledge, 1990.

———. *Watching "Dallas": Soap Opera and the Melodramatic Imagination.* Translated by Della Couling. London: Methuen, 1985.

Arlen, Michael J. *The Camera Age: Essays on Television.* New York: Farrar, Straus and Giroux, 1981.

———. *The Living Room War.* Middlesex, Eng.: Harmondsworth, 1982.

———. *The View from Highway 1: Essays on Television.* New York: Farrar, Straus and Giroux, 1976.

Berger, Arthur Asa. *Television as an Instrument of Terror: Essays on Media, Popular Culture, and Everyday Life.* New Brunswick, N.J.: Transaction Books, 1980.

———. *The TV-Guided American.* New York: Walker Publishing Company, 1976.

Berman, Ronald. *How Television Sees Its Audience: A Look at the Looking Glass.* Newbury Park, Calif.: Sage Publications, 1987.

Brunsdon, Charlotte, and David Morley. *Everyday Television: "Nationwide."* London: British Film Institute, 1978.

Buckingham, David. *Public Secrets: "EastEnders" and Its Audience.* London: British Film Institute, 1987.

Bussell, Jan. *The Art of Television.* London: Faber and Faber, 1952.

Buxton, David. *From "The Avengers" to "Miami Vice": Form and Ideology in Television Series.* New York: Manchester University Press, 1990.

Cantor, Muriel G., and, Suzanne Pingree. *The Soap Opera.* Beverly Hills, Calif.: Sage, 1983.

Cassata, Mary, and Thomas Skill. *Life on Daytime Television: Tuning in American Serial Drama.* Norwood, N.J.: Ablex, 1983.

Conrad, Peter. *Television: The Medium and Its Manners.* Boston: Routledge and Kegan Paul, 1982.

Denisoff, L. Serge. *Inside MTV.* London: Transaction Publishers, 1989.

Dyer, Richard. *Light Entertainment.* London: British Film Institute, 1973.

Dyer, Richard, Christine Geraghty, Marion Jordan, Terry Lovell, Richard

Paterson, and John Stewart. *Coronation Street*. London: British Film Institute, 1981.

Edmonds, Robert. *The Sights and Sounds of Television; How the Aesthetic Experience Influences Our Feelings*. New York: Teachers College Press, 1982.

Elliott, Philip. *The Making of a Television Series*. London: Constable, 1972.

Ellis, John. *Visible Fictions: Cinema, Television, Video*. London: Routledge and Kegan Paul, 1982.

Ellison, Harlan. *The Glass Teat: Essays of Opinion on the Subject of Television*. New York: Ace Books, 1970.

———. *The Other Glass Teat*. New York: Pyramid Books, 1975.

Epstein, Edward J. *News from Nowhere*. New York: Random House, 1974.

Esslin, Martin. *The Age of Television*. San Francisco: W. H. Freeman and Company, 1982.

Feuer, Jane, Paul Kerr, and, Tise Vahimagi. *MTM: "Quality Television."* London: British Film Institute, 1984.

Fiske, John. *Introduction to Communication Studies*. London: Methuen, 1982.

———. *Reading the Popular*. Boston: Unwin and Hyman, 1987.

———. *Television Culture*. London: Methuen, 1987.

———. *Understanding Popular Culture*. Boston: Unwin and Hyman, 1989.

Fiske, John, and John Hartley. *Reading Television*. London: Methuen, 1978.

Foster, Harold M. *The New Literacy: The Language of Film and Television*. Urbana, Ill.: National Council of Teachers of English, 1979.

Fowles, Jib. *Television Viewers vs. Media Snobs: What TV Does for People*. New York: Stein and Day, 1982.

Freeman, Don. *Eyes as Big as Cantaloupes: An Irreverant Look at TV*. San Diego, Calif.: Joyce Press, 1978.

———. *In a Flea's Navel: A Critic's Love Affair with Television*. New York: A. S. Barnes and Company, 1980.

Garnham, Nicholas. *Structures of Television*. London: British Film Institute, 1978.

Gitlin, Todd. *Inside Prime Time*. New York: Pantheon, 1985.

Glasgow University Media Group. *Bad News*. London: Routledge and Kegan Paul, 1976.

———. *More Bad News*. London: Routledge and Kegan Paul, 1980.

Goethals, Gregor T. *The TV Ritual: Worship at the Video Altar*. Boston: Beacon Press, 1981.

Goldlust, John. *Playing for Keeps: Sport, Media and Society*. Melbourne: Longman Cheshire, 1987.

Gunter, Barrie. *Behind and in Front of the Screen: Television's Involvement with Family Life*. London: Libbey, 1987.

———. *Poor Reception: Misunderstanding and Forgetting Broadcast News*.

Hillsdale, N.J.: L. Erlbaum Associates, 1987.

———. *Violence on Television: What the Viewers Think*. London: John Libbey, 1988.

Hall, Stuart, and Paddy Whannel. *The Popular Arts*. London: Pantheon Books, 1964.

Hall, Stuart, Dorothy Hobson, Andrew Lowe, and Paul Willis. *Culture, Media, Language*. London: Hutchinson, 1980.

Hanson, Jarice. *Understanding Video: Applications, Impact, and Theory*. Newbury Park, Calif.: Sage Publications, 1987.

Hartley, John. *Understanding News*. London: Methuen, 1983.

Heeter, Carrie. *Cableviewing*. Norwood, N.J.: Ablex, 1988.

Higgins, Anthony Paul. *Talking about Television*. London: British Film Institute, 1966.

Himmelstein, Hal. *On the Small Screen: New Approaches in Television and Video Criticism*. New York: Praeger, 1981.

———. *Television Myth and the American Mind*. New York: Praeger, 1984.

Hobson, Dorothy. *"Crossroads": The Drama of a Soap Opera*. London: Methuen, 1982.

Hodge, Bob. *Children and Television: A Semiotic Approach*. Stanford, Calif.: Stanford University Press, 1986.

Intintoli, M. *Taking Soaps Seriously*. New York: Praeger, 1985.

Jensen, Joli. *Redeeming Modernity: American Media Criticism as Social Criticism*. Newbury Park, Calif.: Sage Publications, 1990.

Kaminsky, Stuart M., and Jeffrey H. Mahan. *American Television Genres*. Chicago: Nelson-Hall, 1985.

Kaplan, E. Ann. *Rocking around the Clock: Music Television, Postmodernism, and Consumer Culture*. New York: Methuen, 1987.

———. *Postmodernism and Its Discontents: Theories, Practices*. New York: Verso, 1988.

Kottak, Conrad Phillip. *Prime-Time Society: An Anthropological Analysis of Television and Culture*. Belmont, Calif.: Wadsworth, 1990.

Levy, Mark R. *Home Video and the Changing Nature of the Television Audience*. London: John Libbey, 1988.

Lewis, Lisa. *Gender, Politics, and MTV: Voicing the Difference*. Philadelphia: Temple University Press, 1990.

Lindheim, Richard D. *Primetime: Network Television Programming*. Boston: Focal Press, 1987.

Livingstone, Sonia M. *Making Sense of Television: The Pyschology of Audience Interpretation*. New York: Pergamon Press, 1990.

MacDonald, J. Fred. *Blacks and White TV: Afro-Americans in Television and Video Criticism*. Chicago: Nelson-Hall, 1983.

Marc, David. *Demographic Vistas: Television in American Culture*. Philadelphia: University of Pennsylvania Press, 1984.

Mayer, Martin. *About Television*. New York: Harper and Row, 1972.

Meehan, Diane M. *Ladies of the Evening: Women Characters of Prime-Time
Television*. Metuchen, N.J.: Scarecrow Press, 1983.

Mellencamp, Patricia. *Logics of Television*. Bloomington: Indiana University
Press, 1990.

Miller, Mark Crispin. *Boxed In: The Culture of TV*. Evanston, Ill.: Northwestern University Press, 1988.

Modleski, Tania. *Loving with a Vengeance: Mass-Produced Fantasies for
Women*. London: Methuen, 1982.

Morley, David. *Family Television: Cultural Power and Domestic Leisure*.
London: Comedia, 1986.

———. *The "Nationwide" Audience: Structure and Decoding*. London: British
Film Institute, 1980.

Neal, Steve. *Genre*. London: British Film Institute, 1980.

Newcomb, Horace. *TV: The Most Popular Art*. New York: Anchor, 1974.

Newcomb, Horace, and Dick Adler. *The Producer's Medium: Conversations
with Creators of American TV*. New York: Oxford University Press, 1983.

Orlik, Peter B. *Critiquing Radio and Television Content*. Needham, Mass.:
Allyn and Bacon, 1988.

Palmer, Edward L. *Children in the Cradle of Television*. Lexington, Mass.: Lexington Books, 1987.

Palmer, Patricia. *The Lively Audience: A Study of Children around the TV Set*.
Boston: Allen and Unwin, 1986.

Philo, Greg. *Seeing and Believing: The Influence of Television*. New York:
Routledge, 1990.

Poole, Michael, and John Wyver. *Powerplays: Trevor Griffiths in Television*.
London: British Film Institute, 1984.

Rosmarin, Adena. *The Power of Genre*. Minneapolis: University of Minnesota
Press, 1985.

Silverstone, Roger. *The Message of Television: Myth and Narrative in Contemporary Culture*. London: Heinemann, 1981.

Sklar, Robert. *Prime-Time America*. New York: Oxford University Press, 1980.

Sopkin, Charles. *Seven Glorious Days, Seven Fun-Filled Nights*. New York:
Simon and Schuster, 1968.

Taylor, Ella. *Prime-Time Families: Television Culture in Postwar America*.
Berkeley: University of California Press, 1989.

Thompson, John O. *Monty Python: Complete and Utter Theory of the Gro-
tesque*. London: British Film Institute, 1982.

Tulloch, John. *Television Drama: Agency, Audience, and Myth*. New York:

Routledge, 1990.

Tulloch, John, and Alvardo, Manuel. *"Doctor Who": The Unfolding Text.* London: Macmillan, 1983.

Tulloch, John, and Albert Moran. *A Country Practice: "Quality Soap."* Sydney: Currency Press, 1986.

Watson, James. *Television in Transition: A Report on the New Electonics Media.* Chicago: Crain Books, 1983.

Wicking, Christopher, and Tise Vahimagi. *The American Vein: Directors and Direction in Television.* New York: E. P. Dutton, 1979.

Williams, Raymond. *Television: Technology and Cultural Form.* New York: Schocken Books, 1975.

Williamson, Judith. *Decoding Advertisements: Ideology and Meaning in Advertising.* London: Marion Boyars, 1978.

Zettl, Herbert. *Sight, Sound, Motion: Applied Media Aesthetics.* Belmont, Calif.: Wadsworth, 1973.

Anthologies

Adler, Richard, and Douglas Cater, eds. *Television as a Cultural Force.* New York: Praeger, 1975.

Baehr, Helen, and Gillian Dyer, eds. *Boxed In: Women and Television.* New York: Pandora, 1987.

Batra, Narayan Dass, ed. *The Hour of Television: Critical Approaches.* Metuchen, N.J.: Scarecrow Press, 1987.

Bennett, Tony, Susan Boyd-Bowman, Colin Mercer, and Janet Woollacott, eds. *Popular Television and Film: A Reader.* London: British Film Institute/Open University Press, 1981.

Brandt, George W., ed. *British Television Drama.* Cambridge: Cambridge University Press, 1981.

Brown, Les, and Savannah Waring Walker, eds. *Fast Forward: The New Television and American Society Essays from Channels of Comunications.* Kansas City: Andrews and McMeel, 1983.

Caughie, John, ed. *Television, Ideology and Exchange.* London: British Film Insitute, 1978.

D'Agostino, Peter, ed. *Transmission: Theory and Practice for a New Television Aesthetics.* New York: Tanham Press, 1985.

Davis, Douglas, and Allison Simmons, eds. *The New Television: A Public/Private Art.* Cambridge, Mass.: MIT Press, 1977.

Drummond, Philip, and Richard Paterson, eds. *Television and Its Audience.* London: British Film Institute, 1988.

———. *Television in Transition*. London: British Film Institute, 1985.

Fiske, John, ed. *Myths of Oz: Reading Australian Popular Culture*. Boston: Allen and Unwin, 1987.

Hazard, Patrick D., ed. *TV as an Art: Some Essays on Criticism*. Champaign, Ill.: National Council of Teachers of English, 1966.

Henderson, Katherine Usher, and Joseph Anthony Mazzeo, eds. *The Meanings of the Medium: Perspectives on the Art of Television*. New York: Praeger. 1990.

Kaplan, E. Ann, ed. *Regarding Television—Critical Approaches: An Anthology*. American Film Institute Monograph Series, vol. 2. Frederick, Md.: University Publications of America, 1983.

Lowe, Carl, ed. *Television and American Culture*. New York: W. H. Wilson Company, 1981.

MacCabe, Colin, ed. *High Theory/Low Culture: Analyzing Popular Television and Film*. Manchester, Eng.: Manchester University Press, 1986.

Masterman, Len, ed. *Television Mythologies: Stars, Shows and Signs*. London: Comedia/UK Media Press, 1984.

Newcomb, Horace, ed. *Television: The Critical View*. 4th ed. Oxford: Oxford University Press, 1987.

O'Connor, J. E., ed. *American History/American Television: Interpreting the Video Past*. New York: Frederick Ungar, 1983.

Pribram, E. Deidre, ed. *Female Spectators: Looking at Film and Television*. New York: Verso, 1988.

Rowland, Willard D., Jr., and Bruce Watkins, eds. *Interpreting Television: Current Research Perspectives*. Beverly Hills, Calif.: Sage, 1984.

Seiter, Ellen, Borchers Hans, Gabriele Kreutzner, and Eva-Marie Warth, eds. *Remote Control: Television, Audiences, and Cultural Power*. New York: Routledge, 1989.

Robert C. Allen is Smith Professor of Radio, Television, and Motion Pictures and associate dean of the College of Arts and Sciences at the University of North Carolina at Chapel Hill. He is author of *Speaking of Soap Operas* and *Horrible Prettiness: Burlesque and American Culture* and coauthor of *Film History: Theory and Practice.*

Jim Collins is associate professor of communication and English and director of film and television studies at the University of Notre Dame. He is author of *Uncommon Cultures: Popular Culture and Postmodernism* and co-editor of the forthcoming *Film Theory Goes to the Movies.*

Jane Feuer is associate professor of English at the University of Pittsburgh. She is author of *The Hollywood Musical* and coauthor of *MTM: "Quality Television."*

John Fiske is professor of communication arts at the University of Wisconsin-Madison. He is coauthor of *Reading Television* and *Myths of Oz: Reading Australian Popular Culture* and author of *Television Culture, Understanding Popular Culture,* and *Reading the Popular.*

Sandy Flitterman-Lewis is associate professor of English and cinema studies at Rutgers University. She is author of *To Desire Differently: Feminism and the French Cinema* and

coauthor of *New Vocabularies in Film Semiotics.* She originally suggested the title *Channels of Discourse.*

James Hay is associate professor of media and cultural studies at the University of Illinois. He is the author of *Popular Culture in Fascist Italy* and a forthcoming book on historical narrative and the social production of memory in the age of television.

E. Ann Kaplan directs the Humanities Institute at the State University of New York at Stony Brook and is professor of English and comparative literature. She is the author of *Women and Film: Both Sides of the Camera, Rocking around the Clock: Music Television, Postmodernism, and Consumer Culture,* and the forthcoming *Motherhood and Representation: Maternity Discourse in Popular Culture.* She has edited *Regarding Television —Critical Approaches: An Anthology, Postmodernism and Its Discontents: Theories and Practices,* and *Psychoanalysis and Cinema.*

Sarah Kozloff is visiting assistant professor and director of the Luce Program on Cinema, Literacy, and Culture at Vassar College. She is author of *Invisible Storytellers: Voice-Over Narration in American Fiction Film.*

Ellen Seiter is associate professor of English at the University of Oregon. She is coeditor of *Remote Control:*

Television Audiences and Cultural Power and author of a forthcoming book on children's consumer culture.

Mimi White is associate professor and chair of the Department of Radio, Television, and Film at Northwestern University. She is coauthor of *Media Knowledge: Readings in Popular Culture, Pedagogy, and Critical Citizenship* and author of the forthcoming *Tele-Advising: Therapeutic Discourse in American Television*.

Diane Negra recently completed her M.A. in Radio, Television, and Motion Pictures at the University of North Carolina at Chapel Hill.

INDEX